DICTIONARY OF
SPANISH SLANG
AND COLLOQUIAL
EXPRESSIONS

Michael Mahler, M.A., M.A.T.

D0958635

BARRON'S

All inquiries should be addressed to:
Barron's Educational Series, Inc.
250 Wireless Boulevard
Hauppauge, NY 11788
http://www.barronseduc.com

International Standard Book Number 0-7641-0619-8

Library of Congress Catalog Card Number 99-72143

Printed in the United States of America
9 8 7 6

Contents

ACKNOWLEDGMENTS

No dictionary comes into existence without the contribution of many people, and this one is no different. Maríangela Litwin gave invaluable editorial assistance in general and also assisted with Colombian and Venezuelan words and expressions. Miguel Pineda and Derek Sully provided insight and examples of Mexican slang. Carlos Miranda, Pablo Donatti, and Diana Iannariello helped out on slang from the Southern Cone. Roxanna González Olaechea and Luis Comas assisted with Peruvian terms. Yvette Cruz and Myrsa Landrón provided slang from Cuba and Puerto Rico, respectively. Nely and Salvador Baires covered Central America, and Jaime Gómez Trabadela Roldan helped with Spain. Luisa Ruiz assisted with the typing of the manuscript. I was also helped by many others too numerous to include here. To all I am indebted for their knowledge, assistance, and friendship.

I owe special thanks to my wife, Soledad, for sharing her language and her life with me. To her I dedicate this book.

Michael Mahler
Dallas, Texas

What Is Slang?

In the preface of *Dictionary of American Slang, Second Supplemented Edition,* Stuart Berg Flexner says that American slang, ". . . is the body of words and expressions frequently used by or intelligible to a rather large portion of the American public, but not accepted as good, formal usage by the majority." He adds that, "American slang tries for a quick, easy, personal mode of speech. It comes mostly from cant, jargon, and argot words. . . ." Most of us know what slang is and we recognize where, when, and how we can use it. We know the formal or "correct" word for things, we know some of the alternative words for them, and most of us even know the taboo words that we usually don't employ in mixed company. When in doubt, we consult a dictionary. Flexner says, "Slang is best defined by a dictionary that points out who uses slang and what 'flavor' it conveys." This dictionary has many flavors.

What Kind of Slang Do You Have Here?

North Americans tend to think of Spanish as being divided into many dialects, even though it is the official language of 21 countries and the second language of the United States. In the preparation of this dictionary, correspondents and informants from all the countries where Spanish is spoken were asked to list terms and expressions that were uniquely native to their lands. As expected, the majority of terms listed were shared with other Spanish-speaking countries and many had their origin in Spain. Spanish is a rich paella of a language, seasoned with the flavors and spices of slangs from all the countries that speak it. That is what *Dictionary of Spanish Slang* provides: an alphabetically arranged collection of national and supranational slang terms and colloquial expressions.

Why a dictionary of Spanish slang or any slang for that matter? The writer, the artist, the dramatist, the cinematographer and anyone who strives for reality in human communication will use slang because slang is what we all use. Slang is everywhere, in books, magazines, film, video, at home, in school, in the courtroom, even in church. Therefore, a dictionary of Spanish slang will be useful to the learner who wishes to more thoroughly understand the language used in daily life.

Where Did We Get All These Words and Expressions?

Over the thirty years that I have been a student of Spanish (and English) I have been jotting down words. As an interpreter and translator I have been looking up words and expressions as part of my work. My sources have been students, housewives, businessmen, murderers, drug addicts, drug pushers, artists, bankers, accountants, colleagues, teachers, professors, interpreters, and translators.

Spanish-language media is a rich source of material. Spanish-language films readily available in the U.S. thanks to many video outlets are another source. The internet is a cornucopia of information for the lexicographer. One can connect to *www.mundohispano.net* and from there to all the major Spanish-language periodicals. Through the internet came the most recent entries in the Dictionary, *"Emilio"* and *"Ismael,"* both being used for the ubiquitous "E-mail."

Interest in slang in general increased with the publication of the *Dictionary of American Slang* mentioned earlier. In Spain, Camilo José Cela became a "slangologist" when he published his *Diccionario Secreto.* Victor León advanced our knowledge of peninsular Spanish slang in 1980 with the publication of his landmark *Diccionario del Argot Español* (Alianza Editorial, Madrid). Other works consulted in the preparation of this work are *Diccionario de Voces Coloquiales de Puerto Rico* by Gabriel Vicente Maura (Editorial Zemi, 1984) and *Diccionario del Argot y Jerga Limeño o Jerga Criolla del Perú* by Guillermo E. Bendezú Neyra (Editora e Importadora Lima). No investigator of Mexican slang can avoid the rich reference provided in *Picardía Mexicana* by A. Jimenez (Editores Mexicanos Unidos), Bernard H. Hamel's *Bilingual Dictionary of Mexican Spanish* (Bilingual Book Press, 1996), and *The Dictionary of Chicano Spanish* by Roberto A. Galván and Richard V. Teschner (National Textbook Company, 1989).

How Is the Information Organized?

Our information is organized in the following way:

1. **THE SPANISH WORD OR IDIOM IS LISTED IN CAPS AND BOLD.**
2. *The region, part of speech, tone, and category are listed in lower-case italics.*
3. A definition is given in standard English, followed when possible by one or more English slang equivalents.
4. *A Spanish-language example follows. The entry word or phrase appears in lowercase italics.*
5. "An English-language translation of the Spanish example, set off with quotation marks, appears at the end." English slang is used when possible.

These translations are quite liberal. Rather than attempting to match metaphor for metaphor we have opted to convey the meaning using metaphors that would be more understandable to American English readers. For example, the Spanish *"Es más campo que las amapolas"* (lit. He is more country than the poppies) is translated as "He's more country than the Grand Ole Opry," since the Spanish allusion to the poppy flower would not convey the same feeling of country as the image of the Grand Ole Opry conveys in English.

Verbs are presented in the infinitive form.
DESCOJONARSE, *Spain, prnl. v.* To break up laughing. *Nos descojonamos viendo las películas antiguas de Cantinflas.* "We cracked up laughing, watching the old Cantinflas movies."

Nouns are listed in the masculine form except when the entry is only for the feminine. **ARAÑA,** *Spain, n.* Opportunist. (Lit. Spider.) *Ese es una araña.* "That guy is a hustler."

Adjectives are listed with both the masculine and feminine endings. When the entry could be an adjective or a noun it is so indicated. **COLADO, DA,** *L.Am./S, adj. or n.* Party crasher. *Ese tipo que está parado junto al sofá es un colado, nadie lo llamó.* "That guy standing next to the sofa is a party crasher; no one invited him."

Idiomatic expressions are simply listed by the first word of the expression, i.e. **ALMA EN UN HILO,** *L.Am./S, idiom.* Nervous. If there is a key word, it is listed independently with a cross-reference to the idiom: **ALA See ESTAR TOCADO DEL ALA.**

Interjections are listed with the appropriate punctuation. **¡DALE!, 1.** *L.Am./S, interj.* O.K., affirmative, let's do it. *¿Les parece bien si vamos al boliche? ¡Dale!* "How about if we go to the bar? Let's do it!" **2.** *Spain, interj.* Hit it!, Go, go! *¡Dale Rodríguez! Necesitamos un gol.* "Hit it Rodriguez! We need a goal."

Categories

If the expression belongs to what one may consider the common bank of slang expression, no category is given. Most entries fall within this non-category, and most of what we English speakers refer to as "off color" are included here. It is not the role of the lexicographer to provide a social or moral judgement, and for this reason entries are not set apart by such classifications as "sexual," "vulgar," or "marginal." The reader may make his or her own judgment. However, when the expression belongs to a very narrow category, such as criminal slang, it is listed as such. There are four categories:

  1. Criminal slang. This category includes terms, expressions, and idioms used by police officers, persons accused of crimes, and persons convicted of crimes. Some of this slang comes from the prison environment (*chabolo,* prison cell), some from the police station (*braceletes,* handcuffs), and some from the street (*dar pájara,* to deceive).

2. **Military slang.** Terms are drawn from the relatively closed society of the military service. Some of these terms do filter into everyday speech as military men and women rejoin civilian society (*milico,* G.I., *abuelo,* short-timer).

3. **Youth slang.** This is the most volatile slang, changing almost as fast as the styles of music or clothing. This slang relates also to changes in technology and many internet terms could be considered youth slang since young people are the drivers of this technology. Many of the terms used by the young become mainstream standard slang. Consider how we are still using "cool" to express a positive opinion about something. Young Spanish speakers use *fenómeno* to communicate essentially the same idea.

4. **Sports slang.** This is a field in itself and there is current research in progress on the changes in sports terminology. Many of the soccer terms used in Spanish for years were essentially English words, such as *fútbol, gol, penalty.* While these core words are not changing, many other terms used by sportscasters are being created, e.g., *concretar* (to score).

ABBREVIATIONS

adj. = adjective
Car. = Caribbean
crim. = criminal
interj. = interjection
hum. = humorous
L.Am. = Latin America
L.Am./C = Latin America/Central
L.Am./N = Latin America/North
L.Am./S = Latin America/South
Lit. = literally
n. = noun
neg. = negative
pl. = plural
prnl. v. = pronominal verb
v. = verb

A CHALECO, *L.Am./N, idiom.* Obligatorily, having to do something. *A chaleco lo pusieron en la cana.* "They had to put him in the klink."

A CUARENTA Y SE ACABÓ LA CUENTA, *L.Am./N, idiom, vulg.* Retort to someone who says "A veinte" responding to an insult to his/her mother. *"¡Tu madre!" "¡A veinte!" "¡A cuarenta y se acabó la cuenta!"* " 'Your mother!' 'And twenty of yours!' 'And forty of yours and that's it!' "

A ESTE PASO, *L.Am., idiom.* At this rate. *A este paso nunca vamos a terminar de pelear.* "At this rate we are never going to stop fighting."

A GOLPE DE ALPARGATA, *Spain, idiom.* To walk, to go on foot. *Va a golpe de alpargata.* "He is going on foot."

A GOLPE DE CALCETÍN, *L.Am./N, idiom, hum.* Walking. *Como no servía el elevador, tuvimos que subir cinco pisos a golpe de calcetín.* "Since the elevator wasn't working we had to walk five flights hoofing it."

A GRITO PELADO, *L.Am./S, idiom.* With raised voice, yelling, screaming. *Alberto lamentó a grito pelado la muerte de su madre.* "Alberto lamented his mother's death with a screaming bout."

A HUEVO, *Spain, idiom.* Easy, without difficulty. *Le dieron el trabajo a huevo. No tuvo que examinarse ni entrevis-*

1

tarse. "They gave him the job on a silver platter. He didn't have to take a test or an interview."

A LA BESTIA, *Spain, idiom.* Using force rather than intelligence or skill. *El boxeador ganó el asalto a la bestia.* "The boxer won the round by brute force."

A LA BRAVA, *L.Am./N, idiom.* Without care or concern. *Como el niño nuevo está muy grandote, me quitó mi lugar a la brava.* "Since the new kid is very big he took my place just like that."

A LA BRIGADINA, *Car., idiom.* Poorly done. Inferior manufacture. *Esos nuevos edificios los hicieron a la brigadina.* "These new buildings were made half-assed."

A LA CAÑONA, *Car., adv.* Obligatorily. *Tengo que terminar el trabajo a la cañona para mañana.* "I'm under the gun to finish this job for tomorrow."

A LA CHINGADA, *L.Am./N, idiom.* Expression equivalent to "to hell" as in "go to hell." *Como estaba dando mucha lata el borrachito, lo mandé a la chingada.* "Since the little drunk was bothering so much I told him to go to hell."

A LA MARCHANTA, *L.Am./S, idiom.* Carelessly, hurried. *Pintaron esa casa a la marchanta.* "They painted that house fast and shoddy."

A LAS QUINIENTAS, *L.Am./S, idiom.* Very late at night. *Cada vez que José sale con sus amigos vuelve a las quinientas.* "Every time that Jose goes out with his friends he returns in the wee hours of the morning."

A LO LOCO, *L.Am., idiom.* Crazily, on a lark. *Decidimos hacer el viaje a lo loco.* "We decided to take the trip on a lark."

A LOS PEDOS, *L.Am./S, idiom.* Fast, speeding, like a bat out of hell. *El carro que atropelló a Mari corría a los pedos.* "The car that hit Mari was going like a bat out of hell."

A MEDIOS, *L.Am., idiom, hum.* Half drunk. *Mi tío Roberto anda a medios todos los días.* "My Uncle Roberto is half lit every day."

A MORIR, *L.Am./N, idiom.* Much. *Hoy cuando venía a la oficina por la mañana, había gente a morir en el metro.* "Going to the office this morning, there were a lot of people on the subway."

A PALO SECO, *Spain, idiom.* To drink something straight. *No sé cómo puedes tomar la ginebra a palo seco.* "I don't know how you can drink gin straight."

A PATÍN, *L.Am./N, idiom, hum.* On foot, walking. *Como no traíamos dinero después del cine, nos venimos a patín.* "Since we didn't have change after the movie, we came back on foot."

A PATIVILCA, *L.Am./S, idiom.* To walk. *Se nos reventó la llanta, iremos a pativilca.* "We got a flat tire, so we will walk."

A PINCEL, *Spain, idiom, hum.* On foot, walking. *Es tan pobre que todos los días se va a la escuela a pincel.* "He is so poor that everyday he goes to school on foot."

A POCO, *L.Am./N, idiom.* Don't tell me. *A poco no lo pasaste bien en mi fiesta.* "Don't tell me you didn't have a good time at my party."

A PURO HUEVO, *Spain, idiom.* With a lot of effort. *Jorge terminó sus estudios a puro huevo.* "Jorge finished his studies on balls alone."

A RAÍZ, *L.Am./N, idiom.* Barefoot. *Como eran muy pobres, andaban a raíz con todos sus hijos.* "Since they were very poor, they walked with all their kids barefoot."

A TODA, *L.Am./S, adv.* Fast. *Me tocó manejar a toda para llegar a tiempo.* "I had to drive full out to get here on time."

A TODA MADRE, *L.Am./N, idiom.* Maximum cool, the most. *Yo llego a casa, me tomo unas chelas, veo tele y me siento a toda madre.* "I get home, have a few cool ones, watch TV, and feel awesome."

A TODO DAR, *Spain, idiom.* Flat out, to the limit. *Ese muchacho nuevo con quien andas, se ve que es a todo dar.* "You can tell that the new fella you're going out with is the most."

A TODO METER, *Spain, idiom.* All-out, top speed. *Cuando le dieron las noticias, Pedro salió de aquí a todo meter.* "When they gave him the news, Pedro left here like a bat out of hell."

A TODO TRAPO, *L.Am./S, idiom.* Fast, at full speed, at full tilt. *La moto me adelantó a todo trapo.* "The motocycle passed me at full tilt."

¡A TOMAR POR CULO!, *Spain, idiom.* Stick it up your ass! *Echaron a Pepe del trabajo por mandar al jefe a tomar por culo.* "They fired Pepe from the job for telling the boss to stick it up his ass."

A TRANCAS Y BARRANCAS, *Spain, idiom.* With difficulty. *No quería decírmelo, lo tuve que sacar a trancas y barrancas.* "He didn't want to tell me; I had to pull it and yank it out of him."

¡A VEINTE!, *L.Am./N, idiom.* Response to an insult to one's mother. *"¡Chinga tu madre!" me dijo. "¡A veinte!" le contesté yo.* " 'Fuck your mother,' he said to me. 'Fuck yours,' I answered back."

¡A VOLAR CON ALAS!, *U.S., idiom.* Get out of here! Scram! Beat it! *Oye, ¡vete a volar con alas!* "Listen, get out of here!"

ABACORAO, RA, 1. *Car., adj.* Very busy. *Estoy muy abacorao, tengo que tener este trabajo para mañana.* "I'm really busy, I have to have this job for tomorrow." **2.** *Car., adj.* Very much in debt. *Los López están bien abacoraos.* "The Lopezes are over their head in debt."

ABANDERADO, *L.Am./N, n., sports.* Line judge. *El abanderado le echó un penalty a Rodríguez.* "The line judge gave a penalty to Rodriguez."

ABANICAR EL AIRE, *U.S., idiom, sports.* To strike out. *López abanicó el aire y perdió el partido.* "Lopez hit the air and lost the game."

ABANICO, *U.S., n., sports.* Easy strike. (Lit. Fan.) *El lanzador sabía que tenía un abanico por delante.* "The pitcher knew he had an easy strike in front of him."

ABATATARSE, *L.Am./S, prnl. v.* To get confused. *Cuando la poli le estaba haciendo preguntas se abatató.* "When the police were asking him questions, he got confused."

ABEJÓN, *Car., n.* Persistent suitor. *Ese muchacho no deja a Mari in paz, es un verdadero abejón.* "That boy doesn't leave Mari alone, he is a regular bumblebee."

ABOFARSE, *L.Am./N, prnl. v.* To stuff oneself. *Yo me abofé el Día de Acción de Gracias.* "I stuffed myself on Thanksgiving."

ABOGADO, DA DE TROMPITO, *Car., idiom.* An ignorant lawyer. *Perdió el caso porque tenía un abogado de trompito.* "He lost the case because he had a lawyer who only knows how to blow his own horn."

ABOGÁNSTER, *L.Am./N, n., hum.* Shyster. *El abogánster me bajó mil pesos, disque para gastos.* "The shyster squeezed me for a thousand pesos saying it was for expenses."

ABOLILLADO, DA, *U.S., adj.* White-like, behaving like a white person. *El hermano de Lupe era un abolillado.* "Lupe's brother plays being white."

ABOLILLAR, *U.S., v.* To act like an Anglo. *No le querían a René porque siempre estaba abolillando.* "They didn't like Rene because he was always acting like a white dude."

ABOLLAR, 1. *L.Am./N, v.* To oppress, to keep down. *Julio tiene muy abollado a su hijo.* "Julio has a tight reign on his son." **2.** *L.Am./S, v.* To steal, to rip off. *Le abollaron su radiocasetera* "They stole his boombox."

ABOMBADO, *L.Am./S, adj.* Stupid, foolish, dopey. *Me sentí abombado después del examen.* "I felt dopey after the test."

ABORREGARSE, *Spain, prnl. v.* To blindly follow another's lead, to go along like a sheep. *Se aborregó Julio con la política derechista.* "Julio let right-wing politics cloud his mind."

ABORTO, *Spain, n.* (Lit. Abortion.) A very ugly person. *Ese hombre es un verdadero aborto.* "That man has a bad case of the uglies."

ABRAZADO, *Spain, adj., crim.* Detained by the police. (Lit. Embraced.) *Lorenzo quedó abrazado por la poli.* "Lorenzo was grabbed by the cops."

ABRIGO, *Spain, idiom, crim.* Dangerous, to be watched. *Preso número 20 es de abrigo.* "Heads up with prisoner number 20."

ABRIR CANCHA, *L.Am./N, idiom.* To make room. *"¡Abran cancha que me cago!" gritó corriendo al baño.* " 'Make room, I'm about to shit in my pants!' he yelled, as he ran to the bathroom."

ABRIR EL COCO, *Car., idiom.* Ready to learn. *Esteban es un niño que se abre el coco.* "Esteban is a boy who is open to learning."

ABRIR EL PARAGUAS, *Car., idiom.* To defend oneself against veiled verbal attacks. *Daniel se defiende abriendo el paraguas en contra de sus enemigos.* "Daniel defends himself by putting up a shield against his enemies."

ABRIR VALLA, *Car., idiom.* To take off, to hit the road. *Cuando vio la bronca que se iba a formar, abrió valla.* "When she saw all hell was going to break loose, she hit the road."

ABRIRSE, *Spain, prnl. v.* To take off, to go away, to leave suddenly, to flee. (Lit. To open up.) *En cuanto oyeron las sirenas se abrieron.* "As soon as they heard the sirens, they took off."

ABROCHAR, *L.Am./N, v., crim.* To catch, to capture. (Lit. To button up.) *Los azules abrocharon a mi cuñado.* "The cops grabbed my brother-in-law."

ABUCHARAR, *Spain, v.* To intimidate, to cow. *Las pandillas abucharararon a Pepe.* "The gangs put the fear into Pepe."

ABUELO, *Spain, n., mil.* Short-timer, soldier with less than six months left. (Lit. Grandfather.) *El sargento López es el abuelo de la sección.* "Sergeant Lopez is the platoon's short-timer."

ABUNDIO See SER MÁS TONTO QUE ABUNDIO

ABURRIRSE COMO UNA OSTRA, *L.Am., Spain, idiom.* To be very bored. *La charla de Roberto me aburrió como una ostra.* "Roberto's talk bored me stiff."

ABUSADO, 1. *L.Am./N, adj., youth.* Intelligent, sharp. (Lit. Abused.) *El hijo de Juan es un chico bien abusado.* "Juan's boy is a real sharp kid." **2.** *L.Am./N, adj. youth.* On guard, alert. *De noche, uno tiene que estar abusado en ese barrio.* "You have to be on guard at night at that neighborhood."

¡ABUSADO!, *L.Am./N, interj.* Look out! *¡Abusado! ¡Que se cae la escalera!* "Look out! The ladder is going to fall!"

ACABADERO, *L.Am./N, n.* The last straw. *Julia le dijo a Álvaro que su última borrachera era el acabadero.* "Julia told Alvaro that his last drunk was the last straw."

ACABARSE COMO LA FIESTA DE EL GUATAO, *Car., idiom.* To end up in a ruckus. *Juan y Álvaro empezaron a discutir y la cosa acabó como la fiesta de El Guatao.* "Juan and Alvaro started to argue and it ended up in a ruckus."

ACADÉMICO, *Car., adj.* Said of something that doesn't work. Theoretical. (Lit. Academic.) *Antonio, tu idea es puramente académica, no creo que funcione en la realidad.* "Antonio, your idea is purely academic; I don't believe it will work in reality."

ACAIS, *Spain, pl. n., crim.* Eyes. *Me duelen los acais.* "My peepers ache."

ACAMALADO, DA, *L.Am./S, adj.* Shacked up. *Arturo está acamalado con Delfina.* "Arturo is shacked up with Delfina."

ACANTINFLADO, *L.Am./N, adj.* Derivative from *Cantinflas,* the Mexican comedian. *Pepe es muy gracioso, tiene* *un humor acantinflado.* "Pepe is very funny; he's got a Chaplinesque wit."

ACARREAR, *L.Am./N, v.* To mobilize. (Lit. To carry.) *Tenemos que acarrear a nuestros amigos para que nos ayuden.* "We have to get our friends mobilized so that they will help us."

ACATUS, *Spain, n.* Money. *Estoy frito, no me queda acatus.* "I'm broke, I'm out of dough."

ACEITE, *Spain, n., drugs.* (Lit. Oil.) High quality hashish of an oily consistency. *Raul compró tres kilos de aceite.* "Raul bought three kilos of oily hashish."

ACEITUNAS See CAMBIAR EL AGUA DE LAS ACEITUNAS

ACEITUNO, NA, *Spain, n., crim.* Spanish civil guard, a national police force. *¡Agua! Aquí vienen unos aceitunos.* "Watch out, here comes the heat."

ACELERADO, *L.Am./N, adj.* Hyper, frantic. (Lit. Accelerated.) *No me gusta andar con Chuy. Se toma tres cervezas y se pone muy acelerado.* "I don't like to hang out with Chuy. He takes three beers and gets hyper."

ACELERARSE, *L.Am./N, prnl. v.* To get agitated, excited. *"No te aceleres" me dijo Paco, cuando el otro me mentó la madre.* " 'Don't get so uptight,' Paco said, when the other guy said something about my mother."

ACELERE, *L.Am./N, n.* Agitation. *"¿Qué acelere traes?" le pregunté a mi hermano cuando tiró la mochila.* " 'What are you so upset about?' I asked my brother when he threw his backpack."

ACERA See SER DE LA ACERA DE ENFRENTE, SER DE LA OTRA ACERA

ACHACADO, DA, *L.Am./S, adj.* In bad shape. *Voy a botar este pantalón, ya está muy achacado.* "I am going to pitch these pants; they are all worn out already."

ACHACARSE, *L.Am./S, prnl. v.* To get sad. *Juan se achacó cuando supo que María salía conmigo.* "Juan got down in the dumps when he found out that Maria was going out with me."

ACHANTADO, DA, 1. *L.Am./S, adj.* Embarrassed. *Se cayó delante de todos y quedó súper achantada.* "She fell down in front of everybody and was super embarrassed." **2.** *L.Am./C, adj.* To feel lazy. *Juan anda muy achantado, ni siquiera tiene ganas de salir de la casa.* "Juan is feeling real lazy; he doesn't even feel like going out of the house."

ACHANTAO, TÁ, *Car., adj.* Person lacking in spirit, unambitious, withdrawn, lazy. *Tomás es un achantao, no se anima para nada.* "Thomas is a sad sack; he doesn't get excited over anything."

ACHANTAR, *Spain, v.* To shut up, to shut one's mouth. *Achanta la boca antes de que te dé una bofetada.* "Shut up before I sock it to you."

ACHANTAR EL BISTEC, *Spain, idiom.* To shut up. *¡Achanta el bistec, por favor!* "Shut your mouth, please!"

ACHAPLINARSE, *L.Am./S, prnl. v.* To hesitate and to run away in the manner of Charlie Chaplin. *Se achaplinó Rodolfo al darse cuenta que tenía que pagar.* "Rodolfo did a Charlie Chaplin when he found out he had to pay."

ACHARÁ, *L.Am./C, idiom.* What a shame, what a pity. *Achará que Guillermo no haya ganado la beca.* "What a shame that Guillermo didn't win."

ACHARES, *Spain, pl. n.* Jealousy. *Pablo está abrumado de sus achares.* "Pablo is overwhelmed by jealousy."

ACHARITA, *L.Am./C, n.* What a shame, what a pity. *Qué acharita que no me puedas acompañar a la reunión.* "What a shame that you can't come with me to the meeting."

ACHATARSE, *L.Am./N, prnl. v.* To become embarrassed. *No te achates Pedro, esta gente es de confianza.* "Don't be embarrassed Pedro; these are people you can trust."

ACHECHAR, *L.Am./N, v.* To pamper. *Ay, Antonio, a tu*

9

mujer le gusta achecharte. "Hey, Antonio, your wife likes to pamper you."

ACHICHARRAR, *Spain, v., crim.* To riddle with bullets. *Achicharraron a los dos bandidos cuando salieron del banco.* "They burned the two hoods when they came out of the bank."

ACHICHINCLE, 1. *L.Am./N, n.* Errand boy, gofer. *No pude hablar con el secretario, cada día me pasaban a su achichincle.* "I couldn't talk to the clerk; every day they sent me to his gofer." **2.** *Car., n., adj.* Sycophant, bootlicker, brownnoser, kiss ass. *Armando es un achichincle, siempre está haciendo favores para el jefe.* "Armando is a brownnoser; he is always doing favors for the boss."

ACHICOPALAR, *L.Am./N, v.* To be depressed. *"No te achicopales", me dijo el maestro, "el mes que entra vas a sacar puros cienes".* " 'Don't put yourself down,' the teacher told me, 'next month you are just going to get hundreds.' "

ACHINAO, NÁ, *Car., adj.* Said of an oriental-looking person, one with slanted eyes. *La novia de Pablo es una chica achiná, tiene los ojos almendrados.* "Pablo's girlfriend is an oriental-looking girl; she has almond eyes."

ACHINARSE, *L.Am./N, prnl. v.* To get goose bumps. *Me achina la piel cada vez que oigo el himno nacional.* "I get goose bumps every time I hear the national anthem."

ACHOCADOR, RA, *Car., adj.* Seller of adulterated drugs. *Ese desgraciado es un achocador, la droga que vende está muy cortada.* "That bum is a stepper; the drugs he sells are cut a lot."

ACHOCAÍTO, TA, *Car., adj.* Black coffee with very little sugar. *Me gusta tomar mi achocaíto por la mañana.* "I like the jolt of black coffee with little sugar in the morning."

ACHOCAO, CÁ, 1. *Car., adj.* Person with terrible headache. *Mi hija está achocá, parece que tiene jaqueca.* "My daughter is suffering from headaches; I think she has migraines." **2.** *Car., adj.* Person who received a terrible blow to the head and is unconscious. *Vi que el muchacho fue achocao y todavía no se ha recuperado.* "I saw that the kid was knocked out and he still has not recovered." **3.** *Car., adj.* Person drugged with adulterated drugs. *El jovencito está achocao a causa de una droga mala.* "The young fellow got sick as a result of a bad drug."

ACHOCAR, 1. *Car., v.* To sell adulterated drugs. *En esa esquina se ponen unos maleantes a achocar drogas.* "Some thugs set up on that corner to push cut drugs." **2.** *Car., v.* To strike a blow to the head of a person or animal leaving it unconscious or dead. *Se quedó sin conocimiento cuando le achocaron.* "He was knocked out when they bashed him on the head."

ACHOLINAO, NÁ, *Car., adj.* Person or animal who has no will to do things. *No entiendo por qué estoy tan acholinao, ¿será a causa de la depresión?* "I don't understand why I am so down in the dumps; could it be due to depression?"

ACHONGAR, *Car., v.* To shame. *Elizabeth se quedó achongada cuando se dio cuenta que no llevaba dinero.* "Elizabeth was mortified when she realized that she didn't have money with her."

ACHONGARSE, *Car., v.* To be ashamed. *Mi hijo se achongó cuando se dio cuenta de lo que había hecho.* "My son had egg on his face when he had realized what he had done."

ACHORADO, DA, *L.Am./S, adj.* Vulgar, brazen. *Sería mejor no caminar por esa calle, está llena de achorados.* "It would be best not to walk down that street. It's full of lowlifes."

ACHUCHADO, DA, *Spain, adj.* In a tight, difficult situation. *Ahora no tengo trabajo y las cosas están un poco achuchadas.* "Right now I don't have work and things are a little tight."

ACHUCHAR, *Spain, v.* To push, to hug or to squeeze tightly. *¡Chiquillo, no me achuches tanto!* "Boy, don't squeeze me so much!"

ACHUCHÓN, *Spain, n.* Tight hug or squeeze. *Su novio le dio un achuchón al despedirse.* "Her boyfriend gave her a squeeze when he said goodbye."

ÁCIDO, 1. *Spain, n., drugs.* LSD. (Lit. Acid.) *En los sesenta el ácido estaba de moda en California.* "In the sixties acid was the rage in California." **2.** *Car., n.* Unpleasant or disagreeable person. *El dependiente en esa tienda es un ácido, no sé cómo puede vender.* "The clerk in that store is a jerk. I don't know how he can sell anything."

ACIGUATAR, *Spain, v., crim.* To detain. *Aciguataron a los hermanos Gómez en Marbella.* "They rounded up the Gomez brothers in Marbella."

ACLAYOS, *L.Am./N, pl. n., crim.* Eyes, peepers. *Oye mano, ¿viste los aclayos tan azules que tiene esa muchacha?* "Hey bro, did you see the blue eyes that girl has?"

ACOJONADO, DA, *Spain, adj.* Frightened. *El tío tenía a su mujer tan acojonada que la pobre no sabía qué hacer.* "The guy had his wife so frightened that the poor thing didn't know what to do."

ACOJONADOR, RA, *Spain, adj.* Terrifying, amazing, surprising. *¡Luisa es acojonadora!* "Luisa's incredible!"

ACOJONAMIENTO, *Spain, n.* Fear. *Él estaba paralizado de acojonamiento.* "He was paralyzed by terror."

ACOJONANTE, *Spain, adj.* Terrifying, amazing, surprising. *Esteban es un tío acojonante.* "Esteban is an amazing guy."

ACOJONAR, *Spain, v.* To terrify, to intimidate, to amaze. *Esa película te va a acojonar.* "That movie is going to scare you."

ACOJONARSE, *Spain, prnl. v.* To get frightened. *Se acojona con cualquier cosa.* "Anything scares him."

ACOJONO, *Spain, n.* Fear, scare. *Tengo acojono de entrar en esa barriada.* "I'm afraid to go into that neighborhood."

ACOMPAÑAR A LA FLACA, *L.Am./N, idiom.* To die, to kick the bucket. *Yo como todavía no quiero acompañar a la flaca, no como tacos en esa fonda.* "Since I am not ready to go with the Grim Reaper, I don't eat tacos at that restaurant."

ACOMPLETADORES, *L.Am./N, pl. n., hum.* Beans (meaning basic sustenance). *No gano mucho, pero sí saco para los acompletadores.* "I don't make much, but I get enough for my beans."

ACOQUI, *Spain, adv., crim.* Here. *Te lo tendré acoqui mañana.* "I'll have it here for you tomorrow."

ACORDARSE, *Spain, prnl. v.* Used in insults generally directed toward members of one's family. *Me acuerdo de tu madre.* "I'm reminded of your mama."

ACORDEÓN, *L.Am./N, n.* Cheat sheet, crib sheet. (Lit. Accordion.) *El maestro agarró a mi hijo con un acordeón en el examen.* "The teacher caught my son with a cheat sheet at the test."

ACOSTARSE, *Spain, prnl. v.* To have sex with someone. *Guillermo se acostó anoche con la esposa de su jefe.* "Guillermo went to bed last night with his boss's wife."

ACUCHARAR, *Spain, v.* To intimidate, to frighten. *Oye, el profe te tiene achucharado.* "Hey, the prof's got you intimidated."

ACUÑARSE, *Car., v.* To crash a party, to be an uninvited guest. *Tres jovencitos se acuñaron a la fiesta de mi hija.* "Three young guys crashed my daughter's party."

¡ADIÓ!, *L.Am./C, interj.* Expression of incredulity. Unbelievable! *¡Adió! No puedo creer que seas tú.* "Oh my God! I can't believe it's you."

ADMINISTRADOR, DORA, *Car., adj.* Person who prospers by taking advantage of others. (Lit. Administrator.) *Esa muchacha es bien administradora, siempre aprovecha de los amigos.* "That girl is slick, she always takes advantage of her friends."

ADMINISTRAR, *Car., v.* To obtain money by deceit or praise. (Lit. To administer.) *El tipo quiere administrar a todo viejo que pueda.* "That character wants to rip off every old person he can."

ADOQUÍN, *Spain, n.* Dim-witted and ignorant. (Lit. Cobblestone.) *¡Vaya adoquín!* "What a dimwit!"

ADORMIDERA, *Car., n.* Deceitful and demagogic language, smooth talk. *Con la adormidera que tiene ese, puede engañar a cualquiera.* "With his smooth talk he could fool anybody."

ADRENALÍTICO, CA, *L.Am., adj.* Flashy. *Luisa venía muy adrenalítica a la fiesta.* "Luisa was real flashy when she came to the party."

ADVENEDIZO, ZA, *Car., adj.* Novice, beginner, wet behind the ears. *Yo no voy a ese dentista advenedizo. Querrá aprender conmigo.* "I am not going to that greenhorn dentist. He'll want to learn on me."

AEROPIRATA, *Car., n.* Skyjacker. *D.B. Cooper fue un famosísimo aeropirata.* "D.B. Cooper was a famous skyjacker."

AEROPIRATERÍA, *Car., n.* Skyjacking. *Parece que se han reducido los casos de aeropiratería en los últimos años.* "It seems that the cases of skyjacking have decreased in recent years."

AFANAR, *L.Am./S, v.* To rob, to rip off. *Le afanaron todos los ahorros a mi abuela.* "They ripped off all of my grandmother's savings."

AFANE, *L.Am./N, n., crim.* Thief, crook. *A ese afane nunca lo agarrarán.* "They'll never catch that crook."

AFANO, 1. *L.Am./S, n.* Rip-off. *Querían cobrarme el doble, ¡vaya afano!* "They wanted to charge me double, what a rip-off." **2.** *L.Am./S, n.* Robbery. *Dicen que hubo un afano en la tienda anoche.* "They say that there was a robbery at the store last night."

AFEITAR, *Spain, v.* To throw a pitch or pass that brushes someone's face. (Lit. To shave.) *El jugador de Barcelona* *afeitó al jugador de Sevilla.* "The Barcelona player gave the Seville player a shave."

AFEITAR EN SECO, *Spain, idiom.* To kill. *Afeitaron al sinvergüenza en seco.* "They took care of the bastard."

AFGANO, *Spain, n., drugs.* (Lit. Afghan.) Variety of dark hashish from Afghanistan. *Carlos me habló de gran cantidad de afgano.* "Carlos told me about a large quantity of Afghan stuff."

AFISIADO, DA, 1. *Car., adj.* Heavily into work or debt. *Julián está afisiado de trabajo y deudas.* "Julian is smothered in work and debt." **2.** *Car., adj.* Person who suffers chronic eroticism. *Tengo un amigo que está afisiado por sus pasiones y no puede controlarse.* "I have a friend who is overwhelmed by his passions; he can't control himself."

AFLÚS, *L.Am./N, adj.* Without money, broke, busted. *No puedo ir contigo, ando algo aflús.* "I can't go with you; I am kind of broke."

AFORAR, *Spain, v.* To chip in, to fork over. *Aforemos ahora para no tener líos más tarde.* "Let's fork over now so we don't have problems later."

AFRENTAO, TÁ, *Car., adj.* Glutton, avaricious person, piggish, tightwad. *Ese afrentao quiere todo para sí mismo.* "That glutton wants everything for himself."

AFRO, *n.* Afro hairdo. *En los años sesenta a los jóvenes les gustaba llevar el cabello al estilo afro.* "In the 1960s young people liked to wear Afro hairstyles."

AGACHAR, 1. *Car., v.* To hide something in a secure place. (Lit. To crouch, to squat.) *Los ladrones agacharon el dinero donde nadie lo encontraría.* "The thieves stashed the money where nobody would find it." **2.** *L.Am./N, v.* To hold back something worthwhile. *La policía agachó lo que sabía en mi favor.* "The police held back what they knew in my favor."

AGACHARSE, 1. *Car., prnl. v.* To hide. (Lit. To crouch, to squat oneself.) *Los tres tipos se fugaron y se agacharon* *en una casa en el campo.* "The three guys fled and hid in a country house." **2.** *L.Am./N, prnl. v.* To give in. *No tenía más remedio, tuve que agacharme y pagar la multa.* "I had no alternative, I had to give in and pay the fine."

AGACHÓN, NA, 1. *Car., adj.* Lazy, irresponsible, unproductive. *El hijo de la jueza es bien agachón, ni trabaja ni estudia.* "The judge's son is a real bum; he neither works nor studies." **2.** *L.Am./N, n.* Coward, weakling. *No seas agachón manito, ponte valiente.* "Don't be a weakling little bro, be brave."

AGALLADO, DA, *Car., adj.* Angry. *Mi mujer estaba bien agallada conmigo por llegar tan tarde.* "My wife was real upset with me for arriving so late."

AGALLAR, *Car., v.* To bother, to annoy. *Hay jóvenes que no hacen más que agallar a sus padres.* "There are young people who don't do anything but annoy their parents."

AGALLARSE, *Car., prnl. v.* To get angry, to get upset. *Ese tipo se agalla por cualquier cosa.* "That guy gets his feathers up over anything."

AGALLUDO, DA, *L.Am./N, adj.* Gutsy. *El nuevo boxeador es bien agalludo.* "The new boxer is real gutsy."

AGANDALLARSE, *L.Am./N, prnl. v.* To eat. *Mi cuñado está en mi casa agandallándose.* "My brother-in-law is chowing down at my house."

AGARRADA, *L.Am./N, n.* Argument. *Lupita tuvo una agarrada con el novio anoche.* "Lupita had a down and out with her boyfriend last night."

AGARRADO, DA, 1. *L.Am./S, adj.* In love. (Lit. Caught.) *Julián está bien agarrado de Maruja.* "Julian is really flipped over Maruja." **2.** *L.Am./S, adj. or n.* Stingy, tight, tightwad, skinflint. *Mi abuelo es un agarrado, no suelta la guita para nada.* "My grandfather is a skinflint; he doesn't let loose of his cash for anything."

AGARRAR AIRE, *U.S., idiom.* To catch a cold. *No sé dónde agarré el aire, pero me siento muy mal.* "I don't know where I caught a cold, but I feel real bad."

AGARRAR BOLETO, *L.Am./N, idiom.* To get in trouble. *¿Agarraste boleto por llegar tarde?* "Did you get in trouble for arriving late?"

AGARRAR EL SUEÑO, *U.S., idiom.* To fall asleep. *Juan no agarró el sueño hasta muy tarde.* "Juan didn't fall asleep until real late."

AGARRAR EN CURVA, *L.Am./N, idiom.* To catch by surprise. *Estudié bien la lección pero el profe, como que me quiso agarrar en curva.* "I did study the lesson well, but the prof, well, he wanted to catch me by surprise."

AGARRAR LA BOTELLA, *U.S., idiom.* To drink excessively, to hit the bottle. *El padre de Mateo estaba agarrando la botella mucho.* "Mateo's father was hitting the bottle a lot."

AGARRAR LA ONDA, *L.Am./N, idiom, youth.* To understand, to get it. *Yo al principio no le agarraba bien la onda, hasta que él me lo explicó mejor después.* "I didn't catch it at first, until he explained it to me better later."

AGARRAR PA'L LESEO, *L.Am./S, idiom.* To deceive, to fool. *Miguel me agarró pa'l leseo diciéndome que se iba a casar con Isabel.* "Miguel fooled me when he said he was going to get married to Isabel."

AGARRAR PARA, *U.S., idiom.* To take off toward some destination, to head for. *Yo me fui para San Francisco y ellos se agarraron para San Diego.* "I went to San Francisco and they took off for San Diego."

AGARRARLA, *Spain, idiom.* To get drunk. (Lit. To grab it.) *Pedro la agarró pero bien.* "Pedro really got soused."

AGARRARSE, *Spain, idiom.* Woman with a voluptuous body. *Tiene donde agarrarse.* "She's got something to hold onto."

AGARRE, *Car., n.* Penis. (Lit. Handle.) *Ese viejo verde quiere mostrar su agarre a cada muchacha que pasa.* "That dirty old man wants to show his prick to every girl that goes by."

AGARRÓN, *L.Am./N, n.* Fight, argument. *¡Vaya agarrón*

17

que tuvieron mis padres ayer! "What a brouhaha my parents had yesterday!"

AGASAJO, *L.Am./N, n.* Petting session. (Lit. Banquet.) *Anoche estuve con Lupita y nos dimos unos agasajos de aquellos.* "Last night I was with Lupita and we had some awesome petting session."

AGAYÚ, YÚA, *Car., adj.* Bold, brazen, audacious. *¡Qué agayúa es esa chica! No es ni corta ni mohína.* "That girl is really bold! She is neither shy nor bashful."

AGENCIAR, *Spain, v.* To rob. *Los ladrones agenciaron un coche y se abrieron por la carretera de Valencia.* "The thieves swiped a car and took off down the Valencia highway."

AGENTAO, TÁ, *Car., adj.* Presumptuous and fastidious person, somebody puffed up with self-importance. *No tolero gente tan agentá. Se creen mejor que nadie.* "I can't stand such snobbish people. They think they are better than anybody."

AGILIPOLLADO, DA, *Spain, adj.* Stupefied, dumbstruck. *Se quedó agilipollada.* "She was dumbstruck."

AGILIPOLLARSE, *Spain, v.* To get dopey or stupid. *Siempre se está agilipollando.* "He's always getting dopey."

AGREGAO, GÁ, *Car., n.* Sharecropper. *Ese es un agregao en la finca de mi abuelo.* "That one is a sharecropper on my grandfather's farm."

AGREGARSE, *Car., prnl. v.* To cuddle up with another person. *A los recién casados les gusta agregarse con su pareja y a los viejos también.* "Newlyweds like to cuddle up with their partner—and old people too."

AGRINGARSE, *Car., prnl. v.* To follow Anglo customs, to act like a "gringo." *Se está agringando mucho la hija de los González.* "The Gonzalez daughter is getting gringofied."

AGUA, 1. *Spain, n.* Warning that the police are coming, or of some other danger. (Lit. Water.) *Pablo dio el agua y todos se fueron corriendo.* "Pablo gave the alarm and everybody took off." **2.** *interj.* Exclamation to warn of danger. *¡Agua!* "Look out!" **See also MEAR AGUA BENDITA**

AGUA DE RIÑÓN, *Spain, n.* Urine. *Cuidado, cuando lleves serenata que no te vayan a tirar agua de riñón desde el balcón.* "Be careful when you are serenading that they don't throw piss on you from the balcony."

AGUA Y AJO, *L.Am./S, idiom.* Admonition to be patient. (Lit. Water and garlic, euphemism for *Aguanta y jódete,* "Put up with it and fuck yourself.") *"Oye, ¿cuándo vamos a comer?" "Pronto, ¡Agua y ajo!"* " 'Hey, when are we going to eat?' 'Soon, so cool it!' "

AGUACATAO, TÁ, *Car., adj.* Stupid. *Ese muchacho es muy guapo pero aguacatao también.* "That boy is real handsome but he is also not too bright."

AGUACATE, 1. *L.Am./N, n., mil.* Mexican Army G.I. *Alfredo es un aguacate del ejército.* "Alfredo is a Mexican G.I." **2.** *L.Am./N, n.* Testicle. (Lit. Avocado.) *Ese cabrón no tiene los aguacates para decirme eso.* "That bastard doesn't have the balls to tell me that."

AGUACATÓN, NA, *Car., adj.* Party pooper. *Lorenzo, no seas aguacatón, ven, te voy a presentar a unas chicas.* "Lorenzo, don't be a party pooper. Come, I will introduce you to some girls."

AGUACHAO, CHÁ, *Car., adj.* Watered-down drink. *No me gusta ese bar, todas las bebidas son aguachás.* "I don't like that bar, all the drinks are watered down."

AGUADOR, *L.Am./N, n.* Lookout. *Pepe se quedó atrás como aguador.* "Pepe stayed behind as a lookout."

AGUAJERO, RA, 1. *Car., n.* Boogeyman or boogeywoman. *Mi hermano se pone muy aguajero con los niños y luego lloran de susto.* "My brother acts like a real boogeyman with the kids and later they cry out of fear." **2.** *Car., adj.* A fibber. *No se puede creer nada de lo que dice Mario, es muy aguajero.* "You can't believe anything that Mario says; he is a real fibber."

AGUANTÓN, TONA, *Car., adj.* Person who puts up with

more than is normal. *La Sra. Jiménez es muy aguantona, su marido es muy mujeriego.* "Mrs. Jimenez has the patience of a real saint. Her husband is a real ladies' man."

AGUAPARSE, *Car., prnl. v.* To become bold or brazen. *Mira Lupe, no te aguapes conmigo, así no vas a adelantar nada.* "Look Lupe, don't get smart with me. You are not going to get anywhere that way."

AGUAPIRINGA, *Car., n.* Poorly prepared drink. *¡Barman! Por favor, cámbieme esta aguapiringa por un martini de verdad.* "Bartender! Please change this dirty water for a real martini."

AGUARSE LA FIESTA, *L.Am./S, idiom.* To ruin the party or plans. *Se nos aguó la fiesta porque cancelaron el concierto.* "Our plans got ruined because they canceled the concert."

AGUAS, *L.Am./N, pl. n.* Tip. (Lit. Waters.) *Después de lavar el coche del patrón, nos dio para nuestras aguas.* "After washing the boss's car, he gave us a tip."

¡AGUAS!, *L.Am./N, interj.* Look out! (Lit. Waters.) *¡Aguas! gritó el ciclista justo antes de atropellarnos.* " 'Look out!' yelled the guy with the bicycle before he ran over us."

AGÜEVARSE, *L.Am., prnl. v.* To get sad, to get down in the dumps. *Se agüevó Julio mucho cuando le dije que me iba.* "Julio got down in the dumps when I told him I was leaving."

ÁGUILA See PONERSE ÁGUILA, *U.S., idiom.* To be heads up, to get on guard. *Hay que ponerse águila cuando se anda con esa gente.* "You've got to be sharp when you are with those people."

¡ÁGUILA!, *U.S., interj.* Look out! Watch out! *¡Águila! ¡Que vienen los azules!* "Look out! Here come the cops!"

AGÜITA, *U.S., n.* Drizzle. *Todo el día caía agüita.* "It drizzled all day."

AGÜITARSE, *L.Am./C, prnl. v.* To get sad. *Está para agüitarse eso de que te atropellen a tu perro.* "To have your dog run over is reason enough to get sad."

AGÜITAS, *Car., n.* Urine. *Arrestaron a los soldados por hacer agüitas en la calle.* "They arrested the soldiers for peeing in the street."

AGUJA, *Spain, idiom.* To drive a vehicle or motorcycle at full tilt. (Lit. Needle.) *A Rolando le gusta tumbar la aguja cuando conduce.* "Roland likes to peg the speedometer needle when he drives."

AGUJERO, 1. *Spain, n.* Vagina. (Lit. Hole.) *El imbécil estaba tan borracho que no encontraba el agujero.* "The jerk was so drunk that he couldn't find the hole." **2.** *Spain, n., Business.* A firm's missing money. Hidden losses. *Parte del presupuesto se fue por el agujero, quién sabe dónde.* "Part of the budget went down the hole. Who knows where." **3.** *U.S., n.* Anus, asshole. *Pepe le dijo que se lo metiera por el agujero.* "Pepe told him to stick it up his ass."

AGUSAO, SÁ, *Car., adj.* Quick, sharp person. *El director de esa empresa es un tipo muy agusao.* "The director of that firm is a real sharp guy."

AGUSARSE, *Car., prnl. v.* To become bright, quick, sharp. *La nueva secretaria se está agusando en el trabajo, entiende de inmediato.* "The new secretary is getting sharp on the job; she understands things immediately."

AGUZADILLO, LLA, *U.S., n.* Little rascal. *El aguzadillo de Joselito es bien fregón.* "The little rascal Joselito is very annoying."

AHÍ ESTÁ PINTADO, DA, *L.Am./S, idiom.* To do something typical or expected. *Llegó tarde otra vez, ahí está pintado.* "He arrived late again, as expected."

AHÍ MUERE, *L.Am./N, idiom.* Expression to bring something to an end. That's it! *"Ahí muere!" dijo Tomás a Beto después de ponerle el ojo moro.* " 'That's it!' said Thomas to Beto after giving him a black eye."

AHÍ NOMÁS, *L.Am., idiom.* That's just the way it is. *"¿Cómo hiciste para conseguirte una vieja tan* *buenota?" "Ahí nomás".* " 'What did you do to get yourself such a nice babe?' 'I just did.' "

AHÍ SE VA, *L.Am./N, idiom.* Whatever. *"¿Qué vamos a hacer ahora que nos quitaron el carro?" "Ahí se va".* " 'What are we going to do now that they took away the car?' 'Whatever.' "

AHOGADO, DA, *L.Am./N, adj.* Drunk. (Lit. Drowned.) *Pedro está ahogado otra vez.* "Pedro is plastered again."

AHORCADORA, *L.Am./N, n.* Necktie. (Lit. Hangman's noose.) *Tengo ganas de quitarme esta ahorcadora.* "I feel like taking this noose off."

AHORCARSE, *Spain, prnl. v.* To get married. (Lit. To hang oneself.) *Juan va a ahorcarse el sábado.* "Juan is getting hitched on Saturday."

AHUCHAR, *L.Am./N, v.* To urge on, to egg on. *Vamos al partido a ahucharle a nuestro equipo.* "Let's go to the game, to root for our team."

AHUECAR EL ALA, *Spain, idiom.* To take off, to flee, to leave. *Ahuequemos el ala, la película empieza en diez minutos.* "Let's get flying, the movie starts in ten minutes."

AHUEVADO, DA, *L.Am./S, adj.* Stupid, slow. *Andrés anda como ahuevado desde que se ennovió con Julia.* "Andres has been kind of dopey since he became Julia's boyfriend."

AHUEVONADO, DA, *L.Am., adj.* Stunned, dazed, downhearted, depressed. *Arturo se quedó ahuevonado cuando le dieron las malas noticias.* "Arturo was stunned when they gave him the bad news."

AHUICHOTE, *U.S., n.* Pimp. *El ahuichote azotaba mucho a sus mujeres.* "The pimp beat his women a lot."

AHUMADO, DA, *L.Am./N, adj.* Drunk. (Lit. Smoked.) *Pablo llegó a la fiesta bien ahumado.* "Pablo showed up at the party really smashed."

¡AIRE!, *U.S., interj.* Get out of here! Scram! (Lit. Air.)

¡Aire! No quiero verte más aquí. "Get out! I don't want to see you here anymore."

AIRE, 1. *Car., n.* Air conditioner. (Lit. Air.) *Pusieron un aire en la casa de la señora Mora ayer. La pobre se asfixiaba antes.* "They put an air conditioner in Mrs. Mora's house yesterday. The poor thing had been suffocating." **2.** *U.S., n.* Gas. *¡Ay! Tengo la tripa llena de aire.* "Oh! My gut's full of gas."

AJÍ, *Car., adj.* Cantankerous or grumpy person. (Lit. Pepper.) *Su abuelo es un viejo ají. Nunca lo veo sonreír.* "His grandfather is an old reprobate. I never see him smile."

AJIBARARSE, *Car., prnl. v.* To become a country bumpkin or hillbilly. *Hijo, con esa ropa te estás ajibarando.* "Son, with those clothes you are turning into a hick."

AJIGOLONES, *L.Am./N, pl. n.* Troubles. *Con tantos ajigolones Julia está muy deprimida.* "With so many troubles Julia is very depressed."

AJILAO, LÁ, *Car., adj.* Skinny, skin and bones. *Mi amigo, estás ajilao, ¿tu mujer no te da de comer?* "My friend, you are skin and bones; doesn't your wife feed you?"

AJILAR, 1. *Car., v.* To lose weight. *Todo el mundo quiere ajilar.* "Everybody wants to slim down." **2.** *Car., v.* To walk fast. *¡Ajílate Rosario! Así te vas a poner en condición.* "Get those feet moving, Rosario! That's how you are going to get in shape."

AJILIMOJILI, *L.Am./N, n.* Involvement, mess. *¿Y quién causó este ajilimojili?* "And who caused this mess?"

AJO, *Spain, n., drugs,* Piece of cardboard impregnated with LSD. (Lit. Garlic.) *Le pillaron con un ajo en el bolsillo.* "They caught him with an acid square in his pocket."

AJOS Y CEBOLLAS, *L.Am./N, idiom.* Curse words, dirty words, vulgar language. *Ese viejo es tan mal diciente que todo lo que le sale son ajos y cebollas.* "That old guy has got such a bad mouth that all he says are four-letter words."

AJOTADO, *L.Am./N, adj.* Effeminate. *El nuevo empleado tiene un aspecto un poco ajotado.* "The new employee looks kind of feminine."

AJUMADO, DA, *L.Am./N, adj.* Drunk. *Ya está ajumado Álvaro, empezó a tomar muy temprano.* "Alvaro is already smashed; he started drinking very early."

¡AL CARAJO!, *interj.* To hell with it!, To hell with you! *¡Al carajo contigo! No te puedo hablar de nada.* "To hell with you, I can't tell you anything!"

AL CHAS CHAS, *L.Am./N, idiom.* Cash. *Compré el carro al chas chas.* "I bought the car in cash."

AL LOTE, *L.Am./S, idiom.* Carelessly. *Hicieron el trabajo al lote, lo más seguro es que hay defectos.* "They did a shoddy job. Surely there are going to be defects."

AL MANGO, 1. *L.Am./S, idiom.* Dedicatedly, seriously. *Voy a prepararme al mango para el examen.* "I'm going to seriously prepare for the test." **2.** *L.Am./S, idiom.* Full volume, full speed, full tilt, full blast. *Mi hijo siempre pone la tele al mango.* "My son always puts the TV at full blast."

AL PEDO, *L.Am./S, idiom.* Uselessly, to no avail, for nothing. *Fui corriendo para comprar la lotería al pedo, porque no gané.* "I ran to buy the lottery for nothing, because I didn't win."

AL PELO, *L.Am./S, adj.* Very well, just right. *El arreglo que le hiciste al carro quedó al pelo.* "The repair you did on the car was just right."

AL PURO CHINGADAZO, *L.Am./N, idiom.* Perfect, exactly, precisely. *Mi hijo hizo la maniobra al puro chingadazo y ganó el concurso.* "My son aced the maneuver and won the contest."

AL RECLE, *U.S., idiom.* In a while, in a little bit. *Ahorita te veo al recle.* "Now I'll see you in a little while."

AL TIRO, *L.Am./S, idiom.* Fast, immediately. *Después de la llamada el Sr. López salió al tiro.* "After the phone call, Mr. Lopez took off like a flash."

ALA See **ESTAR TOCADO DEL ALA**

ALA DE MOSCA, *Spain, n., drugs.* Bad quality cocaine. (Lit. Fly's wing.) *Se enfermó el muchacho porque le dieron ala de mosca.* "The kid got sick because they gave him bad coke."

ALABIAR, *Car., v.* To flatter with honeyed words. *Diego tiene facilidad para alabiar a las mujeres.* "Diego is good at smooth talking to women."

ALACRÁN, *Car., n.* Needle marks left by drug injections. (Lit. Scorpion.) *Cuando se arremangó la camisa se le veía la marca del alacrán.* "When he rolled up his sleeve you could see the needle tracks."

ALACRANERA, *Car., n.* Hangout for hoodlums and drug addicts. *Ten cuidado con esa casa, es una alacranera.* "Be careful with that house, it's a den of scorpions."

ALARES, *Spain, pl. n., crim.* Pants. *Ella es la que lleva los alares.* "She's the one who wears the pants."

ALAS, *L.Am./S, n.* Armpits. (Lit. Wings.) *No te le acerques mucho porque tiene unas alas poderosas.* "Don't get so close; he has very powerful armpits."

ALAZÁN, *Car., adj.* Albino with red hair. (Lit. White horse.) *Nuestro vecino era alazán. Dicen que los alazanes padecen de la vista.* "They say that albinos with red hair have vision problems."

ALAZANA, *Car., n.* Cocaine. *¡Qué pena me da ver a Gonzalo! Está consumido por la alazana.* "It hurts me to see Gonzalo! He is consumed by coke."

ALBAZO, *L.Am./N, n.* Dawn raid or operation. *Los azules montaron un albazo para arrestar a los traficantes.* "The cops set up a dawn raid to arrest the traffickers."

ALBONDIGUILLA, *Spain, n.* A ball of nasal mucus. (Lit. Little hamburgers.) *El imbécil estaba liándose en la nariz, haciendo albondiguillas.* "The idiot was messing around with his nose, making booger balls."

¡ALBORNOZ!, *L.Am./S, interj.* And not you? "*Josefa es* *bien miedosa". "¡Albornoz!"* " 'Josefa is a real scaredy cat.' 'And you're not?' "

ALBOROTARSE, *Car., v.* To become angry, to yell, to scream. *Todos las mañanas nos alborotamos sobre quien entra el baño primero.* "Every morning we get into a yelling match over who gets into the bathroom first."

ALBUR, 1. *Car., n.* Lie, rumor. *Esa historia que me contaste tiene que ser un albur.* "That story you told me has to be bull." **2.** *L.Am./N, n.* Double meaning, play on words, pun. *Mis primos siempre andan con sus albures. Les dices algo y te lo reviven.* "My cousins are always making puns. If you tell them something, they turn it into a joke."

ALCAGÜETE, TA, *Car., adj. or n.* Parent or grandparent who spoils his/her children or grandchildren. *Tu padre es bien alcagüete con sus nietos.* "Your father is a person who really spoils his grandchildren."

ALCAGÜETERÍA, *Car., n.* Action of spoiling children. *Los abuelos se dedican a la alcagüetería.* "Grandparents are involved in spoiling kids."

ALCAHUETE, *L.Am./S,* Informer, snitch. *El preso no quiso decir nada por temor de ser considerado alcahuete.* "The prisoner didn't want to say anything for fear of being considered a snitch."

ALCANCÍA, 1. *Spain, n.* Vagina. (Lit. Money box, piggy bank.) *Mujer, tengo ganas de meter el rollo en tu alcancía.* "Woman, I feel like putting this wad in your money box." **2.** *L.Am./N, n., crim.* Jail, prison, penitentiary, klink. *Mi jefe pasó tres años en la alcancía.* "My boss spent three years in the pen."

ALCOHOLISTA, *U.S., n.* Alcoholic, drunk. *A Julio le botaron por ser alcoholista.* "They fired Julio because he is an alcoholic."

ALDABAS, *Spain, pl. n.* Breasts. (Lit. Door knocker.) *¡Qué buenas aldabas!* "What a pair of knockers!"

ALEBRESTARSE, *L.Am./N, prnl. v.* To get annoyed, angry, pissed off. *Se alebrestó cuando no le quisieron devolver* *su dinero.* "He got bent out of shape when they didn't want to return his money."

ALEGRÍAS, *Spain, pl. n.* Testicles. (Lit. Happiness.) *Armando siempre está rascando sus alegrías.* "Armando is always scratching the family jewels."

ALEGRÓN, NA, *L.Am./N, adj.* Flirtatious. *El marido de Susana es bien alegrón.* "Susana's husband is very flirtatious."

ALEMÁN See CHISTE ALEMÁN

ALEMANITA See HACERSE UNA ALEMANITA

ALERÓN, *Spain, n.* Armpit. (Lit. Aileron.) *Escondió la coca en el alerón.* "He hid the coke in his armpit."

ALETEO, *Car., n.* Last words in a lost argument. (Lit. Flapping of wings.) *Daniel ya no tenía razón, sólo le quedaba el aleteo del derrotado.* "Daniel no longer was right, all he had left was the wing flapping of the loser."

ALGODONERO, ERA, *U.S., adj. or n.* Freeloader. *Cierra la puerta, que aquí viene ese algodonero Pedro.* "Close the door, here comes Pedro the freeloader."

ALIGERAR, 1. *Spain, prnl. v., crim.* To run off, to take off, to clear out, to skip out, to split. *Se aligeraron los maleantes cuando vieron la poli.* "The robbers split when they saw the fuzz." **2.** *Spain, prnl. v., crim.* To rob, to steal. *Yo sé que aligeraste ese reloj.* "I know that you ripped off that watch."

ALINEADO, DA, *U.S., adj. or n.* Straight. *Ese muchacho es bien alineado, puedes contar con él.* "That fellow is real straight. You can count on him."

ALINEAR, *U.S., v.* To go straight. *Cuando salió Alvaro de la cárcel, alineó su vida y no tuvo más problemas.* "When Alvaro left the pen, he straightened out his life and he didn't have more problems."

ALIPUZ, *L.Am./N, n.* Drink. *Él no sabe comer sin echarse su alipuz.* "He doesn't know how to eat without having his drink."

ALIVIANADO, DA, *U.S., adj.* Turned on, high. *Cuando llegó Luisa a casa estaba bien alivianada.* "When Luisa got home she was really high."

ALIVIANAR, 1. *L.Am./N, v.* To make it easier. *Yo le pedí a Lalo que me alivianara con cincuenta pesos para la entrada del cine.* "I asked Lalo if he could calm me down with fifty pesos for the admission to the movie." **2.** *U.S., v.* To go straight. *Me prometió mi hermano que iba a alivianarse.* "My brother promised me that he would go straight." **3.** *U.S., v.* To straighten someone out. *Voy a alivianar a ese chismoso.* "I am going to straighten out that tattletale."

ALIVIAR, *Spain, v., crim.* To rob, to steal. (Lit. To relieve.) *El chorizo me alivió el reloj.* "The crook relieved me of my watch."

ALIVIARSE, *L.Am./N, prnl. v.* To give birth. (Lit. To relieve oneself.) *Laura se alivia para el mes de septiembre.* "Laura gives birth in September."

ALMA EN UN HILO, *L.Am./S, idiom.* Nervous. *Habla de una vez por todas, me tienes con el alma en un hilo.* "Speak once and for all; you've got my heart in my throat."

ALMEJA, 1. *Spain, n.* Vagina. (Lit. Clam.) *¡Bájate la falda, se te ve la almeja!* "Lower your skirt; one can see your pussy." **2.** *Spain, idiom.* To sing out of tune. *Pobre muchacho, canta como una almeja.* "Poor fella, he sings way out of tune."

¡ALOHA!, *L.Am./S, interj.* Hi! (Lit. Hawaiian greeting.) *¡Aloha! Cuánto tiempo sin verte!* "Aloha! It's been a long time."

¡ALOJA!, *U.S., interj.* Hi! (Variation of *aloha*.) *¡Aloja amigos! ¿Cómo andan?* "Hi pals! How's it going?"

ALONDRA, *Spain, n.* Bricklayer. (Lit. Lark.) *Las alondras dejaron de trabajar y se pusieron de huelga.* "The bricklayers quit working and went on strike."

ALPARGATA See A GOLPE DE ALPARGATA, TENER CARA DE ALPARGATA VIEJA

ALPISTE, *Spain, n.* Alcoholic drink, wine, booze. (Lit. Birdseed.) *¡Oye! Vamos a tomarnos el alpiste.* "Hey, let's go and have some booze."

ALUCINADO, DA, *Spain, adj.* (Lit. Hallucinated.) Astounded, astonished, amazed, fascinated. *No me mires así, con esa cara de alucinada.* "Don't give me that astounded look."

ALUCINANTE, 1. *Spain, adj.* Astonishing, amazing, fascinating. (Lit. Hallucinatory.) *Esas noticias son realmente alucinantes.* "That news is really amazing." **2.** *L.Am./S, adj.* Impressive. *El concierto de anoche estuvo alucinante.* "Last night's concert was a dream."

ALUCINAR, 1. *Spain. v.* To astound, to astonish, to amaze, to fascinate. (Lit. To hallucinate.) *Siempre quieres alucinarme con tus cuentos.* "You always want to astound me with your stories." **2.** *Spain, v., drugs.* To hallucinate. *Está alucinando por los efectos del ácido.* "He's hallucinating from the effects of the acid."

ALUCINAR EN COLORES, *Spain, idiom.* To get surprised. *Cuando me dijeron que había ganado, aluciné en colores.* "When they told me I had won I thought I was dreaming."

ALUCINAR PESAO, *L.Am./S, idiom.* To imagine the impossible. *"Sé que mi padre me va a regalar un auto". "¡Estás alucinando pesao!"* " 'I know my father is going to give me a car.' 'You are hallucinating!' "

ALUMBRADO, DA, *U.S., adj.* High or drunk, lit. *Su marido llegó a casa muy alumbrado.* "Her husband arrived home very lit."

ALZADO, DA, *L.Am./N, adj.* Conceited, stuck-up. *Es muy alzado con su riqueza.* "He's real stuck-up with his wealth."

AMA, *Spain, n.* Dominatrix. *La mujer alta es la ama que te va a castigar.* "The tall woman is the pain mistress who'll punish you."

AMACHADO, DA, *U.S., adj.* Stubborn. *No coopera*

Ricardo. Es bien amachado. "Ricardo doesn't cooperate; he is real stubborn."

AMAÑARSE, *L.Am./S, prnl. v.* To be attached to something, to hold affection for. *Está la pobre amañada en su pueblo y no quiere venirse con nosotros.* "The poor thing is attached to her village and she doesn't want to come with us."

AMANERADO, *L.Am./N, adj.* Effeminate. *Siempre me molesta platicar con Toño porque es muy amanerado.* "It always bothers me to chat with Tonio because he is very faggy."

AMANILLADO, DA, *Spain, adj., crim.* Handcuffed. *Traían a los muchachos amanillados como delincuentes.* "They had the boys handcuffed like criminals."

AMANSADOR, RA, *Car., n.* Good-looking neighborhood man or woman. (Lit. Tamer.) *Rodrigo es el amansador del barrio. Todas las chicas están locas por él.* "Rodrigo is the hunk of the neighborhood. All the girls are crazy about him."

AMAPOLA, *Spain, n.* Vagina. (Lit. Poppy.) *Oye mi amor, dame un poquito de tu lindísima amapola.* "Listen my love, give me a little of your pretty little flower."

AMARICONADO, *Spain, adj.* Effeminate. *El camarero tiene us aspecto amariconado.* "The waiter looks a bit fairyish."

AMARICONARSE, 1. *Car., prnl. v.* To get scared. *Cuando vio a tanta gente persiguiéndolo, se amariconó y se entregó.* "When he saw so many people chasing him, he chickened out and turned himself in." **2.** *L. Am./S, Car., prnl. v.* To adopt certain effeminate mannerisms. *¿Te diste cuenta de que el director se está amariconando?* "Did you notice that the director is getting a little light on his feet?"

AMARIPOSADO, *Spain, adj.* Effeminate. *Esa oficina está llena de amariposados.* "That office is full of fairies."

AMARRADO, DA, *U.S., adj.* Married, hitched. (Lit. Tied up.) *Esa calota está amarrada.* "That babe is hitched."

AMARRAO, Á, 1. *Car., adj.* Skinflint, tight, cheap. *No vamos a tener un carro nuevo porque mi padre es un amarrao.* "We are not going to get a new car, because my father is a skinflint." **2.** *L.Am., adj.* Married. *Él no llevaba anillo pero me dijeron que está amarrao.* "He wasn't wearing a ring but they told me he was hitched."

AMARRAR, *U.S., v.* To get married, to get hitched. (Lit. To tie up.) *Tu ex se va a amarrar el sábado.* "Your ex is going to get hitched on Saturday."

AMARRARSE, 1. *Car., prnl. v.* To get married, to get hitched. (Lit. To tie oneself.) *Mi hijo Jaime se amarró en marzo y estamos muy contentos.* "My son Jaime got hitched in March and we are very happy." **2.** *Car., prnl. v.* To act cheap or stingy. *Siempre que estoy en un restaurante con Jorge se amarra delante de la gente.* "Every time I am in a restaurant with Jorge he acts stingy in front of the people."

AMARRARSE UNA PERRA, *L.Am./S, idiom.* To get drunk. *Nos amarramos una perra anoche, que hasta se nos olvidó donde vivíamos.* "We got so drunk last night, we even forgot where we lived."

AMASADOR, *Car., n.* Man who likes to paw women while he speaks with them. (Lit. Kneader.) *El profe viejo es un amasador, siempre está echando mano a las estudiantes.* "The old prof is a feeler. He is always putting his hands on the students."

AMBIA, *Car., n.* Buddy. *Pepe y Julio son ambias fuertes, se conocen de toda la vida.* "Pepe and Julio are close buddies; they've known each other all their lives."

AMELCOCHAO, CHÁ, *Car., adj.* Confusing illegal or immoral matter. *El cuñado de Juan siempre se mete en cosas amelcochás.* "Juan's brother is always getting into funny businesses."

AMELONADO, DA, *Spain, adj.* Enamoured, in love. *Antonio está amelonado con la hija de César.* "Antonio is nuts about Cesar's daughter."

AMERICUCHO, CHA, *Car., adj.* Non-Puerto Rican Americans or those who act like them. *Ciertos sectores tienen resentimientos en contra de los americuchos.* "Certain sectors have resentments against the 'Americuchos.' "

AMIGO, GA, *Spain, n.* Girlfriend, lover. (Lit. Friend.) *Pío tiene una amiga nueva. ¿Cuánto durará ésta?* "Pio has a new girlfriend. How long will this one last?"

AMIGO FALSO, *Spain, idiom.* False cognate. *Los amigos falsos son palabras similares que significan cosas distintas.* "False cognates are similar words that mean different things."

AMIGUETE, *n.* Friend, especially one with influence. *Tú me puedes ayudar porque tienes un amiguete en el ayuntamiento.* "You can help me because you have a little friend at city hall."

AMOLADO, DA, *U.S., adj.* Broke, down and out. *Después de perder su trabajo, Ignacio se quedó amolado.* "After losing his job, Ignacio was left down and out."

AMPLI, *L. Am./N, n.* Amplifier. *Para el concierto vamos a necesitar un ampli nuevo.* "For the concert we are going to need a new amplifier."

AMUERMADO, DA, 1. *Spain, adj.* Bored, depressed. *Está Mercedes amuermada de tanto hablar.* "Mercedes is bored from so much talk." **2.** *Spain, adj.* Drug-induced stupor. *Se quedó la muchacha amuermada, no sé lo que ha tomado.* "The girl got dopey; I don't know what she took."

ANALFABESTIA, *Spain, n., hum.* Illiterate. *Pepe, cuando te escucho leer en voz alta me suenas analfabestia.* "Pepe, when I listen to you read out loud, you sound like an illiterate brute."

ANARCO, CA, *Spain, adj. or n.* Anarchist. *Alfonso se da de anarco.* "Alfonso acts like he's an anarchist."

ANCA, *U.S., prep.* At someone's house. *Tu mujer está anca Antonia.* "Your wife is at Antonia's house."

ANCAS, *L.Am./N, pl. n.* Hips. *Cargaba a su hermanito en ancas.* "She carried her little brother on her hip."

¡ANDA!, *Spain, interj.* Expression of anger, disgust, or disbelief. *¡Anda ya!* "Get out of here already!"

¡ÁNDALE!, *L.Am./N, interj.* That's it! Right on! *"Entonces no es su esposa sino su amante." "¡Ándale!"* " 'So it's not your wife but rather your mistress.' 'That's it!' "

¡ÁNDALE PUES!, *L.Am./N, interj.* Ok, then! Alright! *Nos vemos mañana. ¡Ándale pues!* "We will see each other tomorrow. All right then!"

ANDALUZA, *Spain, n.* Orangeade with white wine. (Lit. Andalusian.) *Lo que refresca en estos días de calor es una andaluza con hielo.* "What is refreshing on these hot days is an *andaluza* with ice."

ANDAR ABRAZANDO POSTES, *L.Am./S, idiom.* To be drunk. *Para las doce Pepe ya andaba abrazando postes.* "By twelve Pepe was already smashed."

ANDAR AL ALBA, *U.S., idiom.* To be on guard, to be heads up. *Hay que andar al alba en ese barrio.* "You have to be heads up in that neighborhood."

ANDAR BRUJO, JA, *U.S., idiom.* To be broke. *No puedo ir contigo, ando brujo hoy.* "I can't go with you; I am broke today."

ANDAR CARGADO, *U.S., idiom, drugs.* To be carrying drugs or weapons. *Esos batos andan cargados.* "Those dudes are carrying."

ANDAR CON EL CUTIS FLOJO, *L.Am./N, idiom.* To have diarrhea, to have the runs. *No sé lo que me hizo daño, pero todo el día he andado con el cutis flojo.* "I don't know what made me sick, but I've had the runs all day long."

ANDAR CON EL RABO CAÍDO, *U.S., idiom.* To be depressed, to be down in the dumps. *¿Qué te pasa? Andas con el rabo caído.* "What is the matter with you? You look depressed."

ANDAR CON MAL TAPÓN, *L.Am./N, idiom.* To be constipated. *No es bueno comer fruta verde, después andas con mal tapón.* "It's not good to eat green fruit; later, you're all blocked up."

ANDAR CON PELOTA, *U.S., idiom.* To be in love, to be carrying the torch for someone. *Me parece que ella anda con pelota para Julio.* "I think she is carrying a torch for Julio."

ANDAR DE MOJADO, *U.S., idiom.* To be an illegal immigrant. *Dicen que Jorge anda de mojado.* "They say that Jorge is illegal."

ANDAR ELÉCTRICO, *U.S., idiom.* To be drunk or stoned. *¿Viste que Lorenzo andaba eléctrico?* "Did you see that Lorenzo was stoned?"

ANDAR EN LA MOVIDA, *U.S., idiom.* To be promiscuous, to be sowing one's wild oats, to be in the action. *Los padres de Isabel tienen problemas con ella porque anda en la movida.* "Isabel's parents have problems with her because she's sleeping around."

ANDAR EN PEDO CON, *U.S., idiom.* To be in trouble with someone. *Metiste la pata y ya andas en pedo con el jefe.* "You stuck your foot in it and now you are in trouble with the boss."

ANDAR EN PELOTAS, *Spain, L.Am., idiom.* To walk naked. *María andaba en pelotas en la playa.* "Maria walked naked on the beach."

ANDAR ENTRE DOS VELAS, *Spain, idiom.* To be tipsy. *Mira a Javier, está andando entre dos velas ya.* "Look at Javier, he's tipsy already."

ANDAR JINETEANDO ALAZÁN, *L.Am./N, idiom.* To menstruate. *Esa muchacha anda de mal humor. Debe andar jineteando alazán.* "That girl is in a bad mood. She must have the rag on."

ANDAR PEDO, *L.Am./N, idiom.* To be drunk. *Jaime anda pedo a diario. No sale de las cantinas.* "Jaime is drunk everyday. He doesn't leave the bars."

ANDAR PUNTO, *Spain, idiom.* To be drunk. *Anoche andaba yo punto y ahora tengo la resaca.* "Last night I was plastered and now I have a hangover."

ANDAR SOCADO, DA, *U.S., idiom.* To have lost everything, to be wiped out. *Lalo fue a Las Vegas y ahora anda socado.* "Lalo went to Las Vegas and now he is wiped out."

ANDAR TINIADO, DA, *U.S., idiom, drugs.* To be high on inhalants. *No te metas con ese, anda tiniado.* "Don't bother with him, he is high on sniffers."

¡ÁNDELE PUES! *L.Am. N, interj.* Alright! OK! *"¿Vamos a Chihuahua?" "¡Ándele pues!"* " 'Shall we go to Chihuahua?' 'OK!' "

ANDOBA, *Spain, n.* Guy, character, so and so. *Este andoba viene y me dice "Deme algo, no he comido".* "This so and so comes up to me and says, 'Give me something, I haven't eaten.' "

ANFETA, *Spain, n., drugs.* Amphetamine. *Le metieron en la cárcel por vender anfeta.* "They sent him up the river for selling uppers."

ANGARRIO, RIA, *L.Am./S, adj.* Very thin. *Tienes que comer más porque estás como un angarrio.* "You have to eat more because you are like a pole."

ANGARRO, *Spain, n., crim.* Cigarette. *Amigo, échame un angarro, se me acabaron los míos.* "Friend, toss me a coffin nail; I ran out of mine."

ÁNGEL CUSTODIO, *L.Am./N, n.* Condom. (Lit. Guardian angel.) *No me quiso hacer caso aquélla porque no traía mi ángel custodio.* "That one didn't want to get it on with me because I wasn't carrying my protection."

ANGELITO, TA, 1. *L.Am./S, n.* Gullible person, sucker, innocent. (Lit. Little angel.) *¡Qué angelito es mi hermano! Se cree todo lo que le dicen.* "What an innocent my brother is! He believes everthing he is told." **2.** *Car., adj.* Unreliable, untrustworthy. (Lit. Angel-like.) *No se puede* *confiar nada a ese angelito.* "You can't trust anything to that little angel." **3.** *Spain, n., crim.* Dangerous individual, nasty customer. *Ten cuidado con ese angelito. Dicen que apuñaló a un hombre.* "Be careful of that little angel. They say he stabbed a man."

ANGINAS, *L.Am./N, pl. n.* Women's breasts, tits, boobs. *¡Qué buenas anginas tiene la Juana!* "What nice tits Juana has!"

ANGLÉS, *Spain, n., pl.* Testicles, balls, nuts. *No tienes los anglés para pelear con él.* "You don't have the balls to fight him."

ANGLICÓN, NA, *Spain, n., adj.* Englishman or English-woman. *El bar estaba lleno de anglicones.* "The bar was full of Brits."

ÁNGULO, *Car., n.* Common fund among several addicts for the purchase of drugs. *Los drogadictos hicieron un ángulo para comprar más nieve.* "The drug addicts put their bread together to buy more snow."

ANILLO, *Spain, idiom.* Asshole. *¡Métalo por el anillo de cuero!* "Stick it where the sun doesn't shine."

ANIMAL DE BELLOTA, *Spain, idiom.* Pig, jerk, stupid. *Daniel, no seas animal de bellota.* "Daniel, don't be a jerk."

AÑO See SER DEL AÑO LA PERA

AÑO CATAPLÚN, *Spain, idiom.* Many years ago. *Tu padre hizo el servicio en el año cataplún.* "Your father did his military service back during the crash."

AÑOÑI, *L.Am./S, interj.* Expression of affirmation. *Este verano vamos a visitar Miami. ¡Añoñi!* "This summer we are going to visit Miami. Whoopee!"

ANSI, *U.S., adv.* Like this, this way. *Le agarré ansi.* "I grabbed him like this."

ANTENAS, *Spain, n., pl.* Ears. (Lit. Antennae.) *Cuidado con lo que dices, Juanita tiene las antenas paradas.* "Be careful with what you say, Juanita has her antennas up."

ANTIER, *L.Am./N, adv.* Day before yesterday. *A aquél no lo veo desde antier.* "I haven't seen that guy since the day before yesterday."

ANTIPARABÓLICO, *L.Am./S, adj.* Indifferent. *Jaime es antiparabólico en cuanto a quién gana el partido.* "It's all the same to Jaime as to who wins the game."

ANTIPARRAS, *Spain, pl. n., crim.* Eyeglasses. *Vamos a pegarle al tipo de las antiparras.* "Let's hit the guy with the blinkers."

ANTOJITOS, *L.Am./N, n., pl.* Hors d'ouvres, appetizers. *No hay quién resista los antojitos mexicanos.* "Nobody can resist Mexican appetizers."

¿A'ONDE LA VISTE?, *L.Am./S, idiom.* Expression of disbelief. *"¿Te dijeron que me dieron la beca?" "¿A'onde la viste?"* " 'They told you they gave me the scholarship?' 'Where'd you hear that?' "

APACHURRAR, *L.Am./S, v.* To put down, to oppress, to bruise. *Oye, no debes apachurrar a tu hijo así.* "Hey, you shouldn't put down your son like that."

APAGAR LOS OJOS, *U.S., idiom.* To give a black eye, to give a shiner. *Rodríguez le apagó los ojos a Jiménez.* "Rodriguez gave Jimenez a black eye."

APAGAVELAS, *Car., n.* The last person to leave a party. *Anoche, Ramiro fue el apagavelas de la fiesta.* "Last night Ramiro closed up the party."

APALANCADO, DA, 1. *Spain, adj.* Hidden, put away. *Tienen el botín apalancado en un sitio seguro.* "They have the loot in a safe place." **2.** *Spain, adj.* Temporarily housed with a friend or acquaintance. *Julio está apalancado en el piso de Antonio.* "Julio is crashing at Antonio's apartment."

APALANCAR, 1. *Spain, v.* To store, to hide. *Vamos a apalancar la nieve en el taller de Rodrigo.* "Let's stash the snow in Rodrigo's yard." **2.** *Spain, v.* To stay with someone temporarily. *Te vamos a apalancar en casa de Isabel.* "We are going to put you up at Isabel's."

APALANCARSE, *Spain, prnl. v.* To set oneself up at a place. *El viejito se apalancó en la esquina para vender globos.* "The old guy set himself up on the corner to sell balloons."

APALANQUE, *Spain, n.* Temporary lodging with a friend or acquaintance. *Tengo apalanque en casa de Gustavo.* "I've got temporary digs at Gustavo's."

APALASTRAO, TRÁ, *Car., adj.* Very drunk. *Antonio, no puedo más, siempre tienes que venir a casa apalastrao.* "Antonio, I can't take it anymore; you always have to come home plastered."

APAÑADO, DA, *Spain, adj.* To be useful, to be handy. *Sara es una muchacha muy apañada, sabe hacer de todo.* "Sara is a very handy girl. She knows how to do everything."

APAÑAR, *Car., v.* To save money. *Apañé lo que pude para las vacaciones, pero no era suficiente.* "I saved all I could for the vacation, but it was not enough."

APAÑAR AIRE, *U.S., idiom.* To escape or to get away from someone. *Cuando Pedro vio venir al cobrador, apañó el aire.* "When Pedro saw the collector coming, he took off."

APAÑO, *Spain, n.* Living together, continuing an irregular love relationship. *Jaime tiene apaño con su amiguita Jimena.* "Jaime has an arrangement with his girlfriend Jimena."

APANTALLAR, *L.Am./N, v.* To show off. *Nos quiso apantallar con su coche nuevo.* "He wanted to show off his new car to us."

APAPACHAR, *L.Am./N, v.* To feel up, to grope, to paw, to spoil. *No me gusta ir con Miguel, siempre me esta apapachando.* "I don't like to go with Miguel, he's always pawing me."

APAPACHE, *L.Am./N, n.* Caress. *Anoche nos estábamos dando de apapaches con mi novio.* "Last night my boyfriend and I were petting."

APAPUJAO, JÁ, *Car., adj.* Dazed, stunned. *Cuando vio que* *le habían arrestado, su padre se quedó apapujá.* "When he saw that they had arrested him, his father was shocked."

APARADOR, *Spain, n.* Tits. (Lit. Sideboard, dresser.) *¡Qué buen aparador tiene la gachí!* "What a nice pair she has got!"

APARATO, 1. *L.Am., n.* Penis, vagina. (Lit. apparatus.) *El aparato de los viejitos tiene poco uso.* "The old folks' gadgets don't have a lot of use." **2.** *n., drugs.* Syringe. *Se enfermó con el SIDA por usar un aparato sucio.* "He got sick with AIDS from using a dirty needle."

APEAR, *Car., v.* To overcharge for something. *Perdone Ud., pero me apeó diez pesos en la compra.* "Excuse me, but you ripped me off ten pesos on the purchase."

APEARSE, *Spain, prnl. v.* Premature penis withdrawal. (Lit. To get off, to dismount.) *Se apeó en marcha.* "He pulled out just before he came."

APEARSE DEL BURRO, *Spain, idiom.* To give in. *Tuvimos una discusión y por fin Pepe se apeó del burro.* "We had an argument and finally Pepe gave in."

APEARSE DEL CARRO, *Spain, idiom.* Stop, cease, desist. *Apéate del carro ya. No quiero más discusión.* "Get off it already! I don't want more argument."

APECHAR, *Car., v.* To stand up in a fight, to attack. *A Héctor le gusta apechar a la oposición.* "Hector likes to stand up to the opposition."

APECHUGAR, *L.Am./S, v.* To deal with a difficult situation, to keep going in spite of adversity. *Ricardo apechugó el problema en el trabajo y salió ganando.* "Ricardo faced the problem at work and came out ahead."

APEDREAR, *L.Am./N, v.* To stink. *A Chuy le apedrean los pies.* "Chuy's feet stink."

APENDEJARSE, *Car., prnl. v.* To be afraid, to chicken out. *Pepe iba a tirarse del trampolín más alto, pero a última hora se apendejó.* "Pepe was going to dive from the highest board, but at the last moment he chickened out."

APESTAR, *U.S., v.* To be out of style or fashion, to be out of it, passé. (Lit. To stink.) *Oye, apaga esa música. ¡Ya apesta!* "Listen, turn off that music. It is so old it stinks!"

APICHONADO, DA, *L.Am./S, adj.* Sick, ill, under the weather. *Ud. tiene cara de apichonado, ¿se siente mal?* "You're looking a little under the weather; aren't you feeling well?"

APICHONARSE, *L.Am./S, prnl. v.* To get sick, to catch a cold. *Cuando fui a esquiar me apichoné. Ahora no puedo salir.* "When I went skiing I caught a cold. Now I can't go out."

APIMPLARSE, *Spain, prnl. v.* To get drunk, to be lightly inebriated. *Anoche Mari Paz se apimpló en la feria.* "Last night Mari Paz got a little tipsy at the fair."

APIO, 1. *Spain, n.* Homosexual, effeminate. (Lit. Celery.) *Es un apio.* "He's a fag." **2.** *Spain, n.* Penis. *Le arrimó el apio.* "He put it up against her."

APIOLAR, *Spain, v.* To kill. *La apioló.* "He bumped her off."

APITUTADO, DA, *L.Am./S, adj.* Person who receives something undeservedly by way of influence or connections. *El hijo del alcade es un apitutado.* "The mayor's son is a favored boy."

APLASTADO COMO UN SAPO, *L.Am./S, idiom.* Dead tired, wrung out. *Después del partido me quedé aplastado como un sapo.* "After the game I was wrung out like a wet rag."

APLATANADO, *L.Am./N, adj.* Tired, worn out. *Omar es tan aplatanado que nunca quiere jugar fútbol.* "Omar is so worn out that he never wants to play soccer."

APLAUDIR EL BELFO, *Spain, idiom.* To slap. *Cuando le dijo eso, la muchacha le aplaudió el belfo.* "When he said that, the girl popped him."

APLAUDIR LA CARA, *Spain, idiom.* To slap. *La muchacha le aplaudió la cara por haberla insultado.* "The girl slapped his face for insulting her."

APOLILLADO, DA, *L.Am./S, adj.* Asleep. *No hagan ruido niños, que su papá está apolillado.* "Don't make noise, kids; your daddy is cutting z's."

APOLTRONARSE, 1. *Car., prnl. v.* To get set up with a good government job. *María Luisa se apoltronó en correos.* "Maria Luisa got herself a cushy job at the post office." **2.** *L. Am./S, prnl. v.* To remain at one place for lack of initiative. *Se apoltronó en el mismo trabajo por 20 años.* "He glued himself to that job for 20 years."

APRETADO, DA, *L.Am./N, adj.* **1.** Arrogant, presumptuous. (Lit. Tight.) *A mí no me gusta salir con las muchachas con dinero porque son unas apretadas.* "I don't like to go out with girls that have money because they are snobbish." **2.** *L.Am./N, n.* Virgin. *Rosa es jovencita y seguro que apretada.* "Rosa is very young, and I bet she's a virgin." **3.** *L.Am., adj.* Stingy, tight. *Mis tíos no compran nada, son más apretados que zapatos nuevos.* "My aunt and uncle don't buy anything; they are tighter than new shoes."

APRETADOR, *U.S., n.* Brassiere. (Lit. Squeezer.) *Esa niña no lleva apretador.* "That babe isn't wearing a bra."

APRETAO, TÁ, *L.Am., adj.* Short on cash. *No puedo ir ahora porque estoy un poco apretao.* "I can't go now because I am a little bit tight on money."

APRETARSE, 1. *L.Am./S, prnl. v.* To do some heavy petting. (Lit. To tighten up.) *Los novios se apretaban en el cine.* "The couple was doing some heavy petting at the movies." **2.** *L.Am./N, prnl. v.* To refuse, to turn down. *Cuando le pedí prestado a Oscar, se apretó y no me quiso dar nada.* "When I asked Oscar for a loan he refused and he didn't want to give me anything."

APRIMORARSE, *Car., prnl. v.* To fall in love at first sight. *Rodrigo y Julia se aprimoraron en la boda de mi her-*

mana. "Rodrigo and Julia fell in love at first sight at my sister's wedding."

APRONTAO, TÁ, 1. *Car., adj.* Busybody. *Lolita es una aprontá que quiere saber los asuntos de todo el mundo.* "Lolita is a busybody who wants to know everybody's business." **2.** *Car., adj.* An impulsive individual. *Juan es un aprontao que no piensa antes de hacer algo.* "Juan is too quick on the draw and he doesn't think before doing something."

APROVECHARSE, *Spain, prnl. v.* To grope, to cop a feel, to feel up. (Lit. To take advantage of someone.) *En el metro siempre hay una oportunidad de aprovecharse.* "There is always a chance to cop a feel in the subway."

¡APÚNTAME UNA!, *Car., idiom.* Give me some credit! *¡Oye Marisa, apúntame una! Es la quinta vez que te he sacado de apuros.* "Hey Marisa, give me some credit! It's the fifth time I've gotten you out of trouble."

APUNTAR, 1. *L.Am., v.* To jot down. (Lit. To aim.) *Déjame apuntar tu número de teléfono.* "Let me jot down your telephone number." **2.** *L.Am., v.* To sign up. *Apúntame para la excursión al parque.* "Sign me up for the park excursion."

APUNTARSE, *L.Am./S, prnl. v.* To go along with, to do what everybody else does. *¿Por qué quieres apuntarte siempre con los demás?* "Why do you always want to go along with everybody else?"

APURÓN, *Car., n.* Economic difficulty. *Ahora mismo esa familia está pasando por un apurón. Necesitan ayuda.* "Right now that family is going through hard times. They need help."

¡ARACA!, *L.Am./S, interj.* Look out! *¡Araca! ¡Te vas a caer en ese hueco!* "Look out! You're going to fall in that hole!"

ARAJAI, *Spain, n., crim.* Priest, minister, chaplain. (Equivalent to American penal or military "padre.") *Voy a hablar con el arajai.* "I'm going to talk to the padre."

ARALES, *Spain, pl. n.* Pants. *Ya sabemos quien lleva los arales en esa familia.* "We already know who wears the pants in that family."

ARAMEO See JURAR EN ARAMEO

ARAÑA, *Spain, n.* Opportunist. (Lit. Spider.) *Ese es una araña.* "That guy is a hustler."

ARAO, RÁ, *Car., adj.* Stupid, slow. *El dependiente nuevo es tan arao que no creo que dure mucho allí.* "The new clerk is so slow that I don't believe he will last there very long."

¡ARASTA!, *L.Am./C, interj.* Interjection expressing surprise, admiration, disgust. *¡Carasta! Me hubiera gustado ir al partido con ellos.* "Damn! I would have liked to go to the game with them."

ARATE, *Spain, n.* Temper. *¡Qué mal arate tiene!* "What a short fuse he has!"

ARDILLA, *Spain, n.* Quick, sharp, bright. (Lit. Squirrel.) *Es más listo que una ardilla.* "He's sharp as a tack."

ÁREA DE LOS SUSTOS, *Spain, idiom, sports.* The penalty zone. *Ahí va, está en el área de los sustos.* "There he goes; he's in the penalty zone."

ARENCA, *Car., n.* Very skinny person. *La hermana de Miguel es la arenca a la izquierda.* "Miguel's sister is the beanpole on the left."

ARGOLLA, 1. *Car., n.* In baseball, a zero inning. *Y así termina la entrada, en una argolla.* "And that's how the first inning ends—in a big round zero." **2.** *U.S., n.* Wedding ring. *¿Viste que Beto lleva argolla?* "Did you see that Beto is wearing a wedding ring?"

ARGÜENDE, *L.Am./N, n.* Scandal, fuss. *Cuando pasó el accidente, se asomó mi papá por la puerta para ver el argüende.* "When the accident happened, my father looked out the door to see the commotion."

ARGUILA, *Spain, n. drugs.* Bong. *Estaban probando la marihuana con una arguila.* "They were sampling the pot with a bong."

ARIETE, *Spain, n., sports.* Team's center forward. (Lit. Battering ram.) *Jorge es el ariete del Sevilla.* "Jorge is Seville's center forward."

ARMA, *n.* Penis, dick. (Lit. Weapon.) *Cuando vio a la muchacha, se le puso el arma en alza.* "When he saw the broad, his weapon stood to attention."

ARMADO See ESTAR ARMADO

ARMAR, *Spain, v., drugs.* To roll a joint. (Lit. To assemble.) *Armé un porro.* "I rolled a joint."

ARMAR UN ESCÁNDALO, *Car., idiom.* To cause a ruckus. *María se enteró de que el marido la engañaba y le armó un tremendo escándalo en el medio de la calle.* "Maria found out that her husband cheated on her and she raised holy hell in the middle of the street."

ARMARIO, *Spain, n., sports.* Awkward, unskilled player. (Lit. Wardrobe.) *Leonardo es un armario cuando se trata de fútbol.* "Leonardo is all left feet when it comes to soccer."

ARMARLA, *L.Am./N, idiom.* To cause trouble, to start a ruckus. *Gustavo sabe que va a armarla con sus cuñados si sigue pegándole a la esposa.* "Gustavo knows that there is going to be hell with his brothers-in-law if he continues to hurt his wife."

ARMARSE, 1. *L.Am./N, prnl. v.* To get an erection. (Lit. To get armed.) *En cuanto la vio, se armó.* "As soon as he saw her he got stiff." **2.** *L.Am./S, prnl. v.* To get rich. *Con sólo un viaje se armó.* "With just one trip he made a killing."

ARPÓN, *Spain, n., drugs.* Syringe. (Lit. Harpoon.) *Murió de un arpón sucio.* "He died of a dirty needle."

ARQUITONTO, *L.Am./N, n., hum.* Stupid architect. *Los arquitontos disfrazan sus errores con puras plantitas.* "The dumb-ass architects cover up their mistakes with plants."

ARRANAR(SE), *L.Am./N, v.* To sleep, to lie down. *En lugar de correr tras la pelota, el perro se arranó.* "Instead of running after the ball, the dog just laid down."

ARRANQUE, *Spain, n.* Last drink with friends. *Vamos a tomar el arranque.* "Let's have one for the road."

ARRASAO, SÁ, *Car., adj.* Broke. *No puedo ir contigo porque estoy totalmente arrasao.* "I can't go with you because I am completely broke."

ARRASTRADO, DA, *L.Am./S, adj. or n.* Bootlicker, apple polisher, ass kisser. (Lit. Dragged.) *Daniel es un arrastrado.* "Daniel is an ass kisser."

ARRASTRAR EL ALA, *L.Am./S, v.* To court, to carry a candle for. *Juan le está arrastrando el ala a Marcela y ella ni le mira.* "Juan is carrying the torch for Marcela and she doesn't even give him a glance."

ARRASTRAR LA COBIJA, *L.Am./N, idiom.* To be depressed or very sad. *Después de que la novia terminó con él, andaba arrastrando la cobija.* "After his girlfriend broke up with him he was really sulking."

ARRATONAO, NÁ, *Car., adj.* Ratface. *El hombre arratonao es el que robó la bici.* "The rat-faced man is the one who stole the bike."

ARREADOR, DORA, *U.S., n.* Driver. *Mi padre es arreador de camión.* "My father is a truck driver."

ARREAR, *U.S., v.* To drive. *Daniel estuvo arreando toda la noche.* "Daniel was driving all night long."

ARREBATABOLSAS, *L.Am./N, n., crim.* Purse snatcher. *El ladrón fue detenido por arrebatabolsas.* "The thief was arrested for being a purse snatcher."

ARRECHARSE, *L.Am./S, prnl. v.* To get angry. *Tú Pepa te arrechas por nada.* "Pepa, you get pissed off over nothing."

ARRECHO, CHA, *L.Am./S, adj.* Difficult, ill-humored, angry. *El jefe siempre está arrecho.* "The boss is always pissed off."

ARREGLAR, *Car., v.* To castrate an animal. (Lit. To fix.) *Para adoptar un perro lo tienen que arreglar primero.* "In order to adopt a dog they have to fix it first."

ARREGLATODO, *L.Am./S, adj.* Handyman. *Mi papá siempre ha sido un arreglatodo.* "My dad has always been a handyman."

ARREJUNTARSE, *Spain, prnl. v.* To live together without being married. *Se arrejuntaron.* "They shacked up."

ARREMOLINARSE, *L.Am., prnl. v.* To rubberneck. *Cuando ocurrió el accidente se arremolinó la gente.* "When the accident occurred, the people milled around."

ARRIMARSE, *Spain, prnl. v.* To move in together, to live together without being married. *Juan y Petra se arrimaron el año pasado.* "Juan and Petra moved in together last year."

ARRIMO, 1. *Spain, n.* Living together, continuing an irregular love relationship. *El arrimo es muy conveniente, además se duerme calentito.* "Getting together is real convenient; besides, you sleep warm." **2.** *Spain, n.* Lover. *¿Sabes quién es el arrimo de ella?* "Do you know who her squeeze is?"

ARROCERO, RA, *L.Am./S, n.* Party or gate-crasher. *Se metió un arrocero en la fiesta.* "A party crasher got into the party."

ARROLEAR, *U.S., v.* To go for a ride. *Vamos a arrolear por el barrio de Lupio.* "We are going for a ride through Lupio's neighborhood."

ARROZ CON CULO, *Car., idiom.* Ruckus, confusion. *La reunión empezó bien pero luego se formó un arroz con culo.* "The meeting started all right, but later all hell broke out."

ARRUGARSE, 1. *L.Am., prnl. v.* To change one's mind, to renege. (Lit. To get wrinkled.) *No quiero que después te arrugues al encontrar algo mejor.* "I don't want you going back on me because you found something better." **2.** *Spain, prnl. v.* To go back on a deal or agreement. *Él iba a comprarme la moto, luego se arrugó.* "He was going to buy the cycle from me but then he welched on the deal."

ARTILLERÍA, *L.Am./N, n., sports.* Team's forward

players. (Lit. Artillery.) *Lo que falta en el equipo es una buena artillería.* "What the team is lacking is a good forward section."

ARTILLERO, *L.Am./N, n., sports.* (Lit. Gunner.) Forward player of a team or any hard-hitting and scoring player. *Tienen el mejor artillero de la liga.* "They have the best scorer in the league."

ASADURA, *Spain, n.* Sluggish and slow person. *¡Vaya asadura estás hecho!* "You're just a lazy hunk of liver!"

ASALTACUNAS, *Spain, n.* Cradle robber. *Julio es asaltacunas, su amiguita sólo tiene diecisiete años.* "Julio is a cradle robber; his girlfriend is only seventeen."

ASAR, *Spain, v., crim.* To kill with a firearm, to riddle with bullets. (Lit. To roast.) *Fue asado por la policía.* "He was stitched by the police."

ASCO, *L.Am., n.* Disgusting person. (Lit. Nausea, disgust.) *¡Qué asco de hombre!* "What a sleazeball!"

ASERE, *Car., n.* Friend, pal, buddy. *Asere, ¿quieres ir a tomarte unas cervezas conmigo?* "Hey, buddy, do you want to have a couple of beers with me?"

ASFIXIADO, DA, 1. *Spain, adj.* Person excessively worried about his/her own problems. (Lit. Asphyxiated.) *María es una asfixiada de preocupación.* "Maria is a woman smothered with worry." **2.** *L.Am./N, idiom.* To be broke. *No puedo ir de vacaciones porque estoy asfixiado.* "I can't go on vacation because I'm broke."

ASINAR, *Spain, v., crim.* To get. *Asina cinco años arriba.* "He's got five years up the river."

ASISTONTO, *L.Am./N, n., hum.* Dumb-ass assistant. (Play on *asistente* [assistant] and *tonto* [dumb or stupid].) *Cuando fui a hablar con el gerente, me pasaron con el asistonto.* "When I went to talk to the manager, they sent me to the fool under him."

¡ASMA!, *Spain, interj., crim.* Listen! *¡Asma! ¡Que viene el guardia!* "Listen, the guard is coming!"

47

ASOLEADO, DA, *U.S., adj.* Silly, crazy, dippy. (Lit. Sunny.) *La novia de Oscar está bien asoleada.* "Oscar's girlfriend is real goofy."

ASPIRADORA, *Spain, n., drugs.* (Lit. Vacuum cleaner.) A joint prepared by using the paper of a cigarette once the tabacco is emptied out. *Llevaba cinco aspiradoras encima.* "She was carrying five joints looking like ordinary cigarettes."

ASPIRINO, NA, *U.S., n.* Person who gets high on aspirin. *Tu hermano es un aspirino.* "Your brother is an aspirin freak."

ASTILLA, 1. *Spain, n., crim.* (Lit. Splinter.) A bribe, usually given to court personnel to move or stall a case. *El secretario aceptó una astilla del presidente de la comisión.* "The clerk accepted a little something from the president of the commission." **2.** *Spain, n., drugs.* Hashish left over after dividing it into portions. *Después de repartir la marihuana Manolo se quedó con la astilla.* "After distributing the grass Manolo kept the splinter." **3.** *Spain, n., crim.* Share of the proceeds obtained from a robbery or swindle. *Dividieron la astilla en partes iguales.* "They divided the booty in equal shares."

ASUNTILLO, 1. *Spain, n.* Passing sexual relationship, affair. *Pablo tiene un asuntillo con la mujer del boticario.* "Pablo is having an affair with the pharmacist's wife." **2.** *Spain, n.* Small business, usually rather illegal. *Teníamos un asuntillo aparte.* "We had a little thing going on the side."

ASUNTO, *Spain, n.* Euphemisms for vagina, penis, menstruation, copulation, shacking up. (Lit. Subject.) *Teníamos un asunto entre los dos.* "We had a thing between us."

ATAO, *L.Am./S, n.* Problem. *Alonso siempre se hace ataos, cuando la cosa es muy sencilla.* "Alonso always creates difficulties, when the thing is very simple."

ATAOSO, SA, *L.Am./S, adj.* Person who sees problems with everything. *Julia es muy ataosa, no se puede contar con ella para nada.* "Julia is a real wet blanket, you can't count on her for anything."

ATAQUE DE CUERNOS, *Spain, idiom.* Violent reaction caused by jealousy. *Le dio un ataque de cuernos.* "He flew into a jealous rage."

ATASABAO, Á, *Spain, adj., crim.* Dead. *¿Qué hiciste con él? Está atasabao.* "What did you do with him? He's dead."

ATASABAR, *Spain, v., crim.* To kill. *Lo atasabaron a puñaladas.* "They stabbed him to death."

ATENEÍSTA, *Car., n.* Person who talks a lot and does little. *El comité decidió no darle el puesto a Álvaro porque es un ateneísta.* "The committee decided not to give the position to Alvaro because he is full of hot air."

ATENIDO, DA, *L.Am./S, adj.* Person who takes advantage of others. *Ayúdame a limpiar la casa, no seas atenido.* "Help me to clean the house; don't be a bum."

¡ATÍZALE!, *U.S., interj.* Hurry up! Get a move on! *¡Atízale! Tenemos que terminar pronto.* "Get a move on! We have to finish soon."

ATIZAR MOTA, *L.Am./N, idiom, drugs.* To smoke grass. *Fui con mi amigo Benja para atizar mota.* "I went with my friend Benja to smoke grass."

ATOLIGAR, *Spain, v., crim.* To detain. *Le atoligaron en el metro.* "They nabbed him in the subway."

ATOLLAR, *L.Am./C, v.* To hit, to strike, to strike a blow. *Le atollaron porque no quería darles su gorro.* "They hit him because he didn't want to give them his cap."

ATOLLARSE, *L.Am./C, prnl. v.* To smear or spread on something. *El doctor me dijo que me atollara crema para bloquear los efectos del sol.* "The doctor told me to smear a cream on myself to block the effects of the sun."

ATÓMICO, CA, 1. *Car., n., drugs.* Drug addict. (Lit. Atomic.) *Ese muchacho no va a ser nada. Es un atómico.*

"That boy isn't going to be anything. He is a drug head."
2. *Car., n.* Alcoholic. *Despidieron al padre de Ramón por ser un atómico.* "They fired Ramon's father for being a lush."

ATORNILLARSE, *Car., prnl. v.* To be determined to keep a position of command or supervision. (Lit. To screw oneself in.) *Luisa se atornilló bien como presidenta de la comisión. No hay quien la saque.* "Luisa got herself in tight as president of the committee. There's no one to get her out."

ATORRANTE, *L.Am./S, adj.* **1.** Lazy, indolent. *Voy a dejar a Gustavo por ser tan atorrante.* "I am going to leave Gustavo because he is such a loafer." **2.** *L.Am., n.* Vagrant, tramp. *Mira al atorrante durmiendo en la calle.* "Look at the bum sleeping on the street." **3.** *L.Am., n.* Uncouth, uncultivated person. *¿Ese atorrante pretende ser profesor?* "That redneck pretends to be a professor?"

ATRACAR, 1. *L.Am./S, v.* To pet, to neck. (Lit. To dock.) *Carlos estaba atracando con Lorena cuando entró su madre.* "Carlos was petting with Lorena when his mother came in." **2.** *Car., v.* To hit, to smack. *El hombre estaba atracándole fuerte a José cuando llegó la policía.* "The man was smacking Jose hard when the police arrived."

ATRACARLE A UNO LAS PAPAS, *Car., idiom.* To tell the unadorned truth, to tell it straight. *Adolfo le atracó las papas a Carmen y le dijo que olía mal.* "Adolfo let Carmen have it straight; he told her that she smelled bad."

ATROCHAR, *Car., v.* In baseball, to catch the ball in the catcher's mitt. *Y Rodríguez atrocha la pelota y Jiménez la poncha.* "And Rodriguez catches the ball and Jimenez strikes out."

AÚPA, 1. *Spain, interj.* Expression of warning. *¡Aúpa!* "Look out!" **2.** *Spain, interj.* Enormous. *Esa historia fue de aúpa.* "That story was a whopper."

AUREOLA See ESTAR MÁS ARRIBA DE LA AUREOLA

AVENTADO, *L.Am./N, adj.* Daring, brave, gutsy. *Esteban es muy aventado, no le da miedo nada.* "Esteban is real gutsy; he is not afraid of anything."

AVENTÓN, 1. *L.Am./N, n.* Push. *Le dieron un aventón y se cayó por la barranca.* "They gave him a shove and he fell over the cliff." **2.** *L.Am./N, n.* Ride. *Juan, ¿me puedes dar un aventón para casa?* "Juan, can you give me a ride home?"

AVERÍA, *Spain, idiom.* Problem, difficulty. (Lit. Damage.) *Me causa toda clase de avería.* "He causes me all kinds of problems."

AVIADOR, *L.Am./N, n.* Government employee who only shows up on payday. (Lit. Flier.) *Fui a pedir trabajo de aviador a mi compadre, el diputado.* "I went to ask for a cushy government job from my pal, the representative."

AVÍO, *Spain, n.* Lover. (Lit. Provisioning, equipment.) *Ella es su avío.* "She's his thing."

AVIÓN, *L.Am./S, adj.* Smart, sharp, quick. (Lit. Airplane.) *Tu hermano es bien avión, va a tener buen futuro.* "Your brother is real sharp, he's going to have a good future."

AVIONA, *L.Am./S, adj.* Easy woman. *Manolo siempre anda con avionas, nunca le va a salir una buena pareja.* "Manolo is always running around with easy women; he'll never find a good match."

AVISPADO, DA, *L.Am., adj.* Alert, sharp. *Desde que nació, Daniel ha sido muy avispado.* "Ever since he was born Daniel has been very quick."

AVIVARSE, *L.Am./S, prnl. v.* To liven up, to wake up, to look alive. *¡Avívense amigos, aquí viene el jefe!* "Look alive pals, here comes the boss."

¡AY CHUPAYA!, *L.Am./S, idiom.* Expression of amazement. *¡Ay, chupaya! Sin querer solté la lengua.* "Wow! Without meaning to, I let it out."

AY NOS VIDRIOS, *U.S., idiom, youth.* See you later. *Ay nos vidrios compadre.* "See you later, buddy."

¡AY QUE COÑO!, *Spain, idiom.* Expression of dejection, disappointment. *¡Ay que coño! Me jodieron la paga otra vez.* "Shit! They fucked up my pay again."

AZAGATA, *L.Am./N, n., hum.* Flight attendant. *No me gusta volar con esa línea, las azagatas están muy feas.* "I don't like to fly with that airline, the flight attendants are very ugly."

AZORRILLADO, DA, *L.Am./N, adj.* Scared, stunned. *Le presiona tanto el profesor a Miguel que ya lo trae azorrillado.* "The prof is pressing Miguel so much that he has him scared to death."

AZOTARSE, *L.Am./N, prnl. v.* To exaggerate. *Se azota mucho Luis cuando habla del dinero de su papá.* "Luis exaggerates a lot when he talks about his father's money."

AZOTE DE BARRIO, *L.Am./S, idiom.* Criminal who concentrates on a particular neighborhood. *Parece que los robos fueron hechos por un azote de barrio.* "It looks like the robberies were done by a specialist on that neighborhood."

AZOTEA, *Spain, n.* Head. (Lit. Roof.) *Ese no está bien en la azotea.* "He's not all right upstairs."

AZUL, *L.Am./N, n., crim.* Uniformed police officer. (Lit. Blue.) *No pudimos colarnos al estadio porque había muchos azules afuera.* "We couldn't sneak into the stadium because there was a lot of fuzz outside."

BABALAO, *Car., n.* Santero priest. *Si sigues con esa racha de mala suerte vas a tener que ir a ver a un babalao.* "If you continue to have that streak of bad luck you're going to have to see a Santero priest."

BABEARSE, *Car., prnl. v.* To drool over a woman or anything desired. *Estaban babeándose todos los hombres cuando pasó la nueva secretaria.* "All the men were drooling when the new secretary passed by."

BABILLA, *L.Am./S, n.* Ugly girl. *¿Saliste con esa babilla?* "You went out with that dog?"

BABOSADA, *L.Am./N, n.* Silly comment. *¿Oiste la babosada que dijo Isabel?* "Did you hear the silly comment that Isabel made?"

BABOSO, SA, 1. *L.Am./S, n.* Annoying person. *Ese tipo es un baboso.* "That guy is a jerk." **2.** *L.Am./S, adj.* In love, gaga, nuts about. *Lili se pone babosa cuando le hablas de Carlos.* "Lili gets gaga when you talk to her about Carlos." **3.** *L.Am./N, adj.* Fool, stupid, dummy. *Raúl es tan baboso que se la creyó cuando le dijimos que se había sacado la lotería.* "Raul is such a jerk that he believed it when we told him that he had won the lottery." **4.** *Spain, n.* Lecher. *Y este baboso se acerca queriendo aprovecharse de la muchacha.* "And this leech comes over, trying to cop a feel."

BACALADA, *Spain, n., crim.* Bribe. *Le echó una bacalada*

53

a la mano del oficial. "He greased the officer's palm."

BACALAO, 1. *Spain, n.* Vagina, cunt, pussy. (Lit. Codfish.) *¡Tiene un bacalao enorme!* "She's got a huge pussy!" **2.** *Spain, n., drugs.* Heroin. *Este está buscando bacalao.* "This guy is looking for some horse." **3.** *Car., n.* Excessively skinny person. *¡Alfonso, estás hecho un bacalao! Parece que ya no comes.* "Alfonso, you are as skinny as a rail! Could it be that you are not eating?"

BACÁN, 1. *L.Am./S, adj.* Great, fantastic, fabulous. *El nuevo disco de los Hanson está bacán.* "The new Hanson CD is cool." **2.** *L.Am./S, adj.* Conceited. *Desde que le compraron una moto se cree un bacancito.* "Since they bought him a motorcycle, he thinks he is the greatest."

BACANO, NA, *L.Am./S, adj., youth.* Someone or something good or excellent. *Qué casa tan bacana se compró Olga.* "What a cool house Olga bought."

BACHA, 1. *L.Am./N, n., drugs.* Marijuana butt, roach. *"¡Pasa la bacha que se apaga!"* "Give me the roach, it's about to go out!" **2.** *U.S., n.* Cigarette butt. *No tires las bachas al suelo, Ramón.* "Don't throw the butts on the floor, Ramon."

BACHATA, 1. *Car., n.* Fuss, ruckus, disorder. *¿De qué era esa bachata en tu casa anoche?* "What was all the fuss about last night?" **2.** *Car., n.* A drink made with beer, water, and sugar. *Tengo ganas de tomarme una bachata.* "I feel like having a bachata."

BACHATERO, RA, *Car., adj.* Hell-raiser, joker. *Me gusta salir con Álvaro, es muy bachatero.* "I like to go out with Alvaro, he is a real hell-raiser."

BACHICHA, 1. *L. Am./S, adj.* Italian. *Ese bachicha llegó de Bari.* "That wop arrived from Bari." **2.** *L.Am./N, n., drugs.* Marijuana butt, roach. *Los borrachitos fumaban puras bachichas.* "The drunks just smoked roaches."

BADULAQUE, *Car., adj.* Lazy person, bum. *La hija de Isabel es muy badulaque. No ayuda en nada.* "Isabel's daughter is a real lazy bones. She doesn't help out in anything."

BADULAQUERÍA, *Car., n.* Mean thing. *Pepita me hizo una badulaquería. Me dejó todos los platos sucios en la mesa.* "Pepita pulled a fast one on me. She left all the dirty plates on the table."

BAGRE, 1. *L.Am., adj.* Ugly person. (Lit. Catfish.) *Yo no quiero ser novia de Beto, es un bagre.* "I don't want to be Beto's girlfriend. He is very ugly." **2.** *L.Am./N, n.* Jerk. *Tu primo es un bagre.* "Your cousin is a jerk."

BAILAR, 1. *L.Am./N, v.* To beat. (Lit. To dance.) *Los americanos nos bailaron en béisbol.* "The Americans beat us at baseball." **2.** *L.Am./N, v.* To defraud, to cheat. *A mi abuela le bailaron sus ahorros.* "They cheated my grandmother out of her savings." **3.** *Spain, v., crim.* To rob, to steal. *Esos ladrones bailaron el auto de Pepe.* "Those hoods stole Pepe's car."

BAILE, 1. *Spain, n., sports.* Two players on the same team passing the ball back and forth to kill time. (Lit. Dance.) *Rodríguez y López hicieron el baile hasta el final y ganaron 1 a 0.* "Rodriguez and Lopez stalled the ball for the remaining time and won 1 to 0." **2.** *Car., n.* Subject of conversation, gossip. *El baile es que Manolo está acostándose con la mujer de su amigo.* "The news is that Manolo is going to bed with his friend's wife."

BAILONGO, *Spain, n.* Low-down dance. *Una pareja estaba bailando un bailongo en una pequeña pista de baile.* "A couple was doing a dirty little dance on a small dance floor."

BAISO, SA, *U.S., n., youth.* Young person. *Ese baiso es del norte.* "That kid is from the north."

BAJADA, 1. *Spain, n., drugs.* Downer. *Uno de los efectos de la anfeta es la bajada después.* "One of the effects of uppers is the downer afterwards." **2.** *Car., n.* Fellatio and/or cunnilingus. *Hay quién tiene preferencia por la bajada.* "There are those who prefer muff diving."

BAJADA AL PILÓN, *Spain, idiom.* Fellatio. *Esa piba me hizo una bajada al pilón de muerte.* "That babe gave me a fantastic blow job."

BAJADO DE LA SIERRA A TAMBORAZOS, *L.Am./N, idiom, hum.* Country bumpkin, hick. *Era tan ignorante que parecía bajado de la sierra a tamborazos.* "He was so ignorant that it seemed he had just come down from the hills."

BAJADOR, *Car., n.* Cunnilinguist. *¡Qué bajador es ese cabrón!* "What a pussy-eater that bastard is!"

BAJANTE, *Car., n.* After-dinner drink. *A mi me gusta tomar una copa de anís dulce como bajante.* "I like to have a glass of anisette as an after-dinner drink."

BAJAR, *L.Am./N, v., crim.* To rob, to steal. (Lit. To go down.) *Me bajaron el billetero cuando venía en el autobús.* "They stole my wallet when I was on the bus."

BAJAR DE CUADRO, *Car., idiom.* To drop in standing. *El equipo de los Tiburones ya bajó de cuadro.* "The Tiburones team has dropped in standing."

BAJARSE, *Spain, v.* To perform oral sex. *Aquella pareja no hacía más que bajarse.* "That couple did nothing but go down on each other."

BAJARSE AL PILÓN, *Spain, idiom.* Fellatio. *Es hora de bajarse al pilón.* "It's time to get down to the meat of the matter."

BAJARSE LOS PANTALONES, *Spain, idiom, rude.* To give in, to give up. (Lit. To lower one's pants.) *José no tuvo más remedio que bajarse los pantalones y firmar el contrato.* "Jose had no alternative but to give in and sign the contract."

BAJETE, TA, *Car., adj.* Short person. *Alvarito es un muchacho bajete.* "Alvarito is a short fellow."

BAJÓN, *L.Am./S, n.* Depression. *Me dio un bajón cuando supe que te ibas.* "I had a real downer when I found out you were leaving."

BAJONEAO, NEÁ, *L.Am./S, adj.* Depressed. *Pepita anda bajoneá porque no la invitaron a la fiesta.* "Pepita is feeling blue because they didn't invite her to the party."

BAJONEARSE, *L.Am./S, prnl. v.* To get depressed, to get down in the dumps. *Mi madre se bajonea con cualquier cosa.* "My mother gets down in the dumps over anything."

BALA FRÍA, *L.Am./S, idiom.* Fast food. *En el aeropuerto sólo venden balas frías.* "They only sell fast food at the airport."

BALAJÚ, *Car., n.* Very thin person. *Tomás es un balajú. Casi se le ve el esqueleto.* "Tomas is like a rail. You can almost see his skeleton."

BALDEAR, *Spain, v.* To cut someone with a knife. *El muchacho fue baldeado por un maleante.* "The boy was cut by a hoodlum."

BALDEO, 1. *Spain, n., crim.* Knife, switchblade. *Estaban peleando cuando éste le pega un baldeo.* "They were fighting when this guy sticks him with a knife." **2.** *L. Am./N, n.* Cleanup. *Llegamos a la casa nueva y antes de nada le dimos un baldeo.* "We arrived at the new house and before anything else we gave it a cleanup."

BALÍN, *L.Am./N, adj.* Useless, worthless. *Decían que ese era bueno para jugar, pero salió bien balín.* "They said that he was a good player, but he turned out to be worthless."

BALLENA, *Spain, n.* Obese person. (Lit. Whale.) *El hombre era una ballena, los policías no lo podían levantar.* "The man was a whale; the cops could not lift him up."

BALONA, *L.Am./N, n.* Favor. *Házme la balona y díle a la maestra que sí les ayudé con el proyecto.* "Do me a favor, tell the teacher that I helped you out on the project."

BALONES, *Spain, pl. n.* Big breasts. (Lit. Balloons.) *A la chica le gustaba lucir sus balones con un suéter apretado.* "The girl liked to show off her boobs with a tight sweater."

BALSA/BARSA, *L.Am./S, adj. or n.* Freeloader. *¡No seas balsa! No puedo pagar siempre yo.* "Don't be a free-loader! I can't always be paying."

BALURDO, DA, *L.Am./S, adj. or n.* Absurd, ridiculous, strange, weird. *El hermano de Pedro es bien balurdo.* "Pedro's brother is a real weirdo."

BAMBA, *L.Am./N, n.* Stroke of luck. *Carlos ganó el juego de pura bamba.* "Carlos won the game by pure luck."

BAMBALÁN, NA, *Car., n.* Fool, bum. *Esos chicos son unos bambalanes. Van perjudicando sus futuros.* "Those kids are bums. They are ruining their futures."

BAÑÁRSELA, *L.Am./N, prnl. v.* To go too far. *Jorge se la bañó cuando le dijo al profe que teníamos permiso.* "Jorge went too far when he told the prof that we had per-mission."

BANCA, *Car., n., sports.* In cock fighting, the fighting cocks belonging to one owner. (Lit. Bank.) *La banca de Pepe González ganó la noche.* "Pepe Gonzalez' roost of birds won the night."

BANCAR, *L.Am./S, v.* To pay, to handle expenses. *¿Pero tú qué crees, que voy a bancarte la cerveza?* "But do you think I'm going to bankroll your beer?"

BANCARSE, 1. *L.Am./S, prnl. v.* To tolerate, to be patient. *No me banco a los idiotas.* "I can't put up with idiots." **2.** *L.Am./S, prnl. v.* To wait. *Te banco quince minutos y no más.* "I'll wait for you fifteen minutes and no more."

BANDERA, 1. *Spain, n., drugs.* A large marijuana joint. (Lit. Flag.) *Los maleantes estaban compartiendo una bandera.* "The hoodlums were sharing a big joint." **2.** *Spain, adj. or n., rude.* Woman with a great figure. *Esa bandera trabaja en la farmacia.* "That awesome chick works at the pharmacy." **3.** *L.Am./S, n.* Indiscreet, careless person. *Matilde es una bandera, no le puedes decir nada.* "Matilde is a big mouth; you can't tell her anything."

BANDERILLA, *Spain, n.* A shish kebab on a toothpick. *Me* *encantan la banderillas que ponen en la feria.* "I love the little shish kebabs they serve at the fair."

BANDERITA See BANDERA

BANDO See SER DEL OTRO BANDO

BANDOLERO, RA, *U.S., adj. or n.* Lazy person, lazy bum. (Lit. Highwayman.) *No le des trabajo a ese bandolero.* "Don't give work to that lazy bum."

BANQUEAR, 1. *Car., v.* To be the banker in a card game. *Cuando juego al póquer me gusta banquear.* "When I play poker, I like to bank." **2.** *Car., v., sports.* In billards, to do a bank shot. *Pablo banquea muy bien y por eso tiene éxito en el billar.* "Pablo does bank shots very well and that's why he's successful at billards."

BANQUEARSE, *Car., prnl. v.* To defraud someone of their money. *Siempre hay alguien que se banquea el dinero de los viejos.* "There is always someone to relieve the elderly of their money."

BANQUETA, *L.Am./N, n.* Sidewalk. *Hay que barrer la banqueta todos los días.* "The sidewalk has to be swept every day."

BANQUETE, *L.Am., idiom.* Enthusiastic groping and feeling up. (Lit. Banquet.) *Los amantes se dieron un banquete.* "The lovers went crazy feeling each other up."

BANQUILLO, 1. *Spain, L.Am., n., sports.* The bench where the reserve players and coach sit. *El entrenador se levantó del banquillo con mal genio.* "The coach got up from the bench with a bad temper."

BARAJERO, RA, *U.S., adj. or n.* Card player, card nut. *Eduardo perdió todo por ser barajero.* "Eduardo lost everything for being a card nut."

BARANDA, 1. *L.Am./S, n.* Bad odor. *En esta casa siempre hay baranda a tabaco.* "In this house there is always a stink of tobacco." **2.** *Spain, n., crim.* The boss, the director. *El baranda nos tenía trabajando como bestias toda la mañana.* "The boss had us working like dogs all morning."

BARATO, TA, *U.S., adj. or n.* Deadbeat. (Lit. Cheap.) *No le presto más a ese porque es un barato.* "I don't lend to that guy anymore because he's a deadbeat."

BARATÓN, ONA, *U.S., adj. or n.* Low-class, vulgar, common. *No me gusta la nueva novia de mi hijo, se ve muy baratona.* "I don't like my son's new girlfriend; she's too common-looking."

BÁRBARO, RA, 1. *Spain, adj.* Great, colossal, fantastic, sensational. (Lit. Barbaric.) *¡Vaya gol! ¡Qué bárbaro!* "What a goal! Fantastic!" **2.** *L.Am., adj.* A lot of fun, a blast. *La celebración de año nuevo fué bárbara.* "The New Year's celebration was a blast!"

BARBAS, *Spain, n.* Bearded man. (Lit. Beards.) *El barbas en la esquina hablando con Pedro es mi padre.* "The bearded guy on the corner talking with Pedro is my father."

BARBERO, *L.Am./N, n.* Kissass, brownnoser, apple polisher. (Lit. Barber.) *Juan es tan barbero que el profe le subió la nota.* "Juan is such a brownnoser that the prof raised his grade."

BARBI, *Spain, adj.* Self-assured, fine-looking. (From "Barbie," the doll.) *Hola guapa, estás muy barbi.* "Hi beautiful, you're looking fine."

BARCO, *Car., n.* Good student. (Lit. Ship.) *José Manuel es el barco de la vecindad.* "Jose Manuel is the brain of the neighborhood."

BARDAJE, *Spain, n.* Passive homosexual. *El bardaje ese es demasiado delicado.* "That girlie boy is too delicate."

BARÉ, *Spain, n.* Five-peseta coin. *Le presté veinte barés a Fernando.* "I lent Fernando one hundred pesetas."

BARETO, *Spain, n.* Bar. *Dicen que van a cerrar el bareto de Daniel por falta de clientes.* "They say that they are going to close Daniel's bar for lack of customers."

BARO, 1. *Car., n.* Any unit of money. *Esta camisa me costó treinta baros.* "This shirt cost me thirty bucks." **2.** *Car., n.* Dominican peso. *Préstame 500 baros para comprarme el* *vestido, sí?* "Lend me five hundred pesos so I can buy a dress, okay?" **3.** *Spain, n., crim.* Five-peseta coin (un duro). *De veras no me queda ni un baro. ¿Puedes prestarme 20 duros?* "Really I don't have a coin left. Can you lend me 100 pesetas?"

BARRECHA, *Spain, n.* Drink made of anisette from Cazalla de la Sierra and muscatel wine. *Goza Juan, esta es una barrecha hecha con anís El Clavel.* "Juan, this is a barrecha made with El Clavel anisette."

BARRER, *L.Am./N, v.* To look someone up and down, to give a once over. (Lit. To sweep.) *El hombre barrió a la mujer de pie a cabeza.* "The man swept the woman from head to toe."

BARRERA DEL SONIDO, *L.Am./N, idiom.* Anus, ass. *El traje de baño de la muchacha apenas le tapaba la barrera del sonido.* "That girl's bathing suit hardly covered her ass."

BARRIGA See CARGAR LA BARRIGA, HACER LA BARRIGA, RASCARSE LA BARRIGA, TENER BARRIGA

BARRILA, *Spain, n.* Fight, commotion, trouble. *Hubo barrila en el casino anoche y tuvo que intervenir la poli.* "There was a ruckus at the casino last night and the police had to get involved." **See also DAR LA BARRILA**

BARRIO See IRSE AL OTRO BARRIO, MANDAR AL OTRO BARRIO

BARRIO CHINO, *Spain, idiom.* Red-light district. (Lit. Chinatown.) *El lugar más divertido de la ciudad es el barrio chino.* "The most fun place in the city is the red-light district."

BARRIO DE LOS CALVOS, *Spain, idiom.* Cemetery. *Le dijeron que si no pagaba las drogas le iban a mandar al barrio de los calvos.* "They told him that if he didn't pay for the drugs, they'd send him to the quiet place."

BARRITA, *Spain, n., drugs.* A bar of hashish. (Lit. Little bar.) *Le pillaron vendiendo una barrita a unos adoles-*

centes. "They caught him selling a bar of hashish to some teenagers."

BARTOLO, *L.Am./N, adj.* Stupid, slow. *Rubén es tan bartolo que nunca termina la tarea.* "Ruben is so slow that he never finishes the task."

BÁRTULOS See LIAR LOS BÁRTULOS

BARULLO, *Spain, adv.* A lot, galore. *Había gente a barullo en la feria.* "There were a bunch of people at the fair."

BASCA, 1. *Spain, n.* People, crowd, group of friends. *Fuimos con la basca al concierto.* "We went with the group to the concert." **2.** *Spain, n., crim.* Gang. *Pepe está con esa basca de ladrones de autos.* "Pepe is with that gang of car thieves."

BASCULEAR, *L.Am./N, v.* To search, to frisk. *En esa disco no hay problemas porque te basculean a la entrada.* "There have never been problems at that disco because they frisk you at the entrance."

BASES, *L.Am./C, pl. n.* Feet. (Lit. Bases.) *Tengo las bases hinchadas de tanto andar.* "My dogs are swollen from so much walking."

BASILÓN, LONA, *Car., adj.* A little tipsy. *Anoche la madre de Adelfa estaba un poquito basilona.* "Last night Adelfa's mother was a little tipsy."

BASTES, *Spain, pl. n., crim.* Fingers. *Los carteristas tienen que cuidarse los bastes.* "Pickpockets have to take care of their fingers."

BASTO, TA, *Spain, adj.* Tough, ordinary, vulgar, crude, coarse. *Esa mujer es más basta que sostén de hojalata.* "That woman is cruder than a tin bra."

BASURAS, *Spain, n.* Trash collector. (Lit. Garbage.) *El basuras llega aquí a las cinco y media de la madrugada.* "The trash guy gets here at five-thirty in the morning."

BASUREAR, *L.Am./S, v.* To treat like trash. *Néstor le basurea a todo el mundo. No quiere a nadie.* "Nestor trashes everybody. He doesn't like anyone."

BATACLÁN, *Car., n.* Agitation, commotion. *Hubo un bataclán en el trabajo ayer.* "There was a big ruckus at work yesterday."

BATACLANA, *L.Am., n.* Cabaret girl. *Esta noche quiero conquistar a la bataclana que me gusta.* "Tonight I want to win over that cabaret girl I like."

BATALLITAS, *Spain, pl. n.* War stories. (Lit. Little wars.) *El viejo siempre estaba contando batallitas.* "The old man was always telling war stories."

BATATA, 1. *Car., n.* Heavy, lethargic person. (Lit. Potato.) *Ildefonso es una batata, no va a ninguna parte.* "Ildefonso is a couch potato; he doesn't go anywhere." **2.** *Car., n.* Fist. *Nunca le levantes la batata a un policía.* "Never lift your fist to a police officer." **3.** *Car., n.* Cushy government job. *Por fin el señor Molino encontró una batata para su hijo con los tribunales.* "Finally Mr. Molino found a cushy job for his son with the courts."

BATEAR POR LA IZQUIERDA, BATEAR DE ZURDA, *L.Am./N, idiom.* Homosexual. *Como se viste el amigo de Pancho, se nota que batea por la izquierda.* "By the way Pancho's friend dresses, you can tell that he is batting on the left."

BATEO, *Car., n.* Batting. *Trujillo es el tercero en la orden de bateo.* "Trujillo is third in the batting order."

BATERÍA, *Car., n.* Battery (baseball). *Ese equipo tiene que cambiar de batería si quieren mejorar sus puntajes.* "That team is going to have to change the battery if they want to improve their scores."

BATIDA, 1. *Car., n.* Police roundup. *El asesino fue cogido en una batida que había montado la policía.* "The murderer was caught in a roundup the police had set up." **2.** *Car., n.* Milk shake. *A mi madre le encantan las batidas de chocolate.* "My mother loves chocolate milk shakes."

BATIDO, *Spain, n.* Milk shake. *Un batido de fresa es lo que me apetece ahora.* "What I feel like having now is a strawberry milk shake."

BATIDOR, *L.Am./S, n., crim.* Informer, stool pigeon, squealer. *Dicen que fue un batidor quién entregó a los líderes de la huelga.* "They saw that it was a stool pigeon who turned in the strike leaders."

BATO, TA, *U.S., n.* Guy or gal, dude, chick. *Ese bato es mi compadre.* "That dude is my buddy."

BATO CALOTE, *U.S., idiom.* Big guy. *Ese bato calote es buena gente.* "That big guy is a good person."

BATO DE COLEGIO, *U.S., idiom, youth.* Educated person. *Lupita sale con un bato de colegio.* "Lupita is going out with a Joe College."

BATO RELAJE, *U.S., idiom.* Punk. *Oye, bato relaje, déjame tranquilo.* "Listen punk, leave me alone."

BATO TIRILONGO, *U.S., idiom.* Gang member. *Cuidado con ese, es un bato tirilongo.* "Be careful with that guy, he's in a gang."

BATUTA, *Spain, n., crim.* Jimmy. (Lit. Baton.) *Abrió la puerta con una batuta.* "He jimmied the door open."

BAULERO, *Car., adj.* Henpecked husband who cannot go out alone. *César va a todas partes con su mujer. El tipo es muy baulero.* "Cesar goes everywhere with his wife. The guy is very henpecked."

BAUTISTA, *Spain, n.* Majordomo, chief butler. *Diego es el bautista de la casa de la duquesa.* "Diego is the chief butler of the Duchess's house."

BAUTIZAR, *L.Am./N, v.* To water down a drink. (Lit. To baptize.) *No me gustan los jaiboles de esa cantina porque los bautizan mucho.* "I don't like the highballs at that bar because they water them down a lot."

BAYÚ, *Car., n.* Party, blast. *Anoche fuimos a un bayú de miedo. No terminó hasta las cinco de la mañana.* "Last night we went to a wild blast. It wasn't over until five in the morning."

BAYUSCO, CA, *Car., adj.* Blusher, person who gets flushed when angry. *Manolo es muy bayusco, se nota en* *seguida cuando está enojado.* "Manolo is a blusher; you can tell right away when he is angry."

BEATA, *Spain, n.* Peseta. *Ud. nunca quiere soltar la beata.* "You never want to spend a dime."

BEBEAGUA, 1. *Car., adj.* Person who pilfers at work. *Matilde, no seas bebeagua, si necesitas algo pídemelo y te lo daré.* "Matilde, don't be a scrounger; if you need something let me know and I will give it to you." **2.** *Car., n.* Person who accepts bribes. *Hay un funcionario bebeagua en la corte que te puede arreglar el asunto.* "There is an official on the take at the court who can fix the matter for you."

BEBERCIO, *Spain, n.* Any type of drink. *Vamos a echar un bebercio.* "Let's toss one down."

BEIBI, *n.* Girl, girlfriend. (From English "baby.") *Ven conmigo beibi.* "Come with me, baby."

BEJUCO, 1. *Car., n.* Telephone earpiece. *Cuando Nenita agarra el bejuco no sabe cuando acabar.* "When Nenita gets hold of the earpiece she doesn't know when to stop." **2.** *Car., n.* Vein where drugs are injected, main line. *El adicto tenía el bejuco muy señalado.* "The addict had a very pronounced main line." **3.** *L.Am./S, adj. or n.* Angry, anger. *Se puso bejuco y no me quiere hablar.* "She got pissed and doesn't want to talk to me."

BEJUQUERÍA, *Car., n.* Disheveled hair. *Pero chica, ¿dónde vas tú con esa bejuquería?* "But girl, where are you going with that bad hair?"

BELDUQUE, *U.S., n., crim.* Knife. *Le agarraron en el aeropuerto por llevar un belduque.* "They grabbed him at the airport for carrying a knife."

BELLOTA, *Spain, n., crim.* Bullet. (Lit. Acorn.) *Era una pistola de seis bellotas.* "It was a six-shooter."

BEMBÉ, *Car., n.* Family party. *El domingo tuvimos un bembé en casa por el bautizo de mi sobrino.* "Sunday we had a get-together at home for my nephew's baptism."

BEMBO, *L.Am./N, adj.* Stupid. *No aguanto a ese bembo.* "I can't stand that idiot."

BEMOLES, *Spain, n.* Fortitude, strength. *A ver si tienes los bemoles para decirle eso al jefe en su cara.* "Let's see if you have the balls to tell that to the boss's face."

BENEFICIARSE, *Spain, v.* To possess sexually, to screw. *Héctor quería beneficiarse de la novia.* "Hector wanted to screw his girlfriend."

BEO, *Spain, n.* Vagina, cunt. *¿A qué beo miras?* "What cunt are you looking at?"

BERBECÍ, *L.Am./N, n.* Short-tempered individual. *El marido de Isabel es un berbecí. No sé cómo lo aguanta.* "Isabel's husband is a short-fused guy. I don't know how she puts up with him."

BERENJENA, *Spain, n.* Penis, prick. (Lit. Eggplant.) *Lo que busca esa buscona es la berenjena esta.* "What that broad is looking for is this dick."

BERREAR, *Spain, v.* To inform on, to talk. *Cuidado con ese, berrea mucho.* "Be careful with that guy; he squeals a lot."

BERREARSE, *Spain, v., crim.* To squeal, to rat on. *Su mejor amigo se le berreó.* "His best friend squealed on him."

BERRENCHINA, 1. *Car., n.* Yelling and screaming match. *Mis padres armaron una berrenchina anoche.* "My parents got into a big fight last night." **2.** *Car., n.* Feud. *Los profes Jiménez y López ya no se hablan debido a una berrenchina que tenían.* "The profs Jimenez and Lopez no longer talk because of a bitter argument they had."

BERRETÍN, *L.Am./S, n.* Fancy, whim, caprice, a weakness for. *Mi madre tiene el berretín de ir a la peluquería todos los sábados.* "My mother has a weakness for going to the beauty salon on Saturdays."

BERRINCHE, *L.Am./N, n.* Tantrum, fit. *No me gusta cuando viene el hijo de Sara porque siempre echa berrinches.* "I don't like it when Sara's boy comes; he is always throwing tantrums."

BERZOTAS, *Spain, n.* Stupid person, idiot. *Pedro es un berzotas.* "Pedro is a jerk."

BESAR LA LONA, *Spain, idiom, sports.* To be knocked down in boxing. *En el quinto asalto García besó la lona.* "In the fifth round Garcia hit the canvas."

BESO BLANCO, *Spain, idiom.* Kiss on the mouth. (Lit. White kiss.) *Estaban en la etapa de besos blancos.* "They were in the kissing stage."

BESO FRANCÉS, *Spain, idiom.* French kiss. *Los novios avanzaron a los besos franceses.* "The sweethearts advanced to French kisses."

BESO NEGRO, *Spain, idiom.* Kiss on the anus. (Lit. Black kiss.) *El extraño quería arrendar un vídeo de besos negros.* "The weirdo wanted to rent a video on anal kisses."

BESTIAL, *L.Am./S, adj.* The most, the coolest, hot, very hot, the hottest. (Lit. Bestial.) *La casa que te compraste es bestial.* "The house you bought is the coolest."

BESUGO, *Spain, n., adj.* Stupid. (Lit. Red snapper.) *David es un besugo.* "David is an idiot."

BI, *Spain, adj.* Bisexual. *El dueño del restaurante es un bi.* "The owner of the restaurant is a switch-hitter."

BIBERÓN, *Spain, n.* Breast of a nursing woman. (Lit. Baby bottle.) *Julia está dándole el biberón al bebé.* "Julia is nursing the baby."

BIBLIA, *Spain, n., drugs.* Booklet of papers to roll a joint. (Lit. Bible.) *Cuando lo registraron no encontraron más que la biblia en su bolsillo.* "When they searched him, all they found was his book of papers."

BICA, *U.S., n.* Money. *No puedo pagar porque no tengo bica.* "I can't pay because I don't have any cash."

BICHE, 1. *L.Am./N, adj.* Blonde. *Samuel tiene una novia biche.* "Samuel has a blonde girlfriend." **2.** *L.Am./N, adj.* Scatterbrained, stupid. *Dicen que las biches son biches.* "They say that blondes are scatterbrained."

BICHI, *L.Am./N, adj.* Naked. *Cuando llegué a casa el niño*

estaba bichi y tuve que buscar su ropa para ponérsela.
"When I got home, the boy was naked and I had to find
his clothes to dress him."

BICHICOME, *L.Am./S, n.* Homeless person. (From English "Beachcomber.") *Estamos organizando un grupo
para ayudar a los bichicomes de nuestra ciudad.* "We are
organizing a group to help the homeless of our city."

BICHICORI, *L.Am./N, adj.* Skinny. *¡Qué bichicori te
quedaste Juan!* "You got real thin Juan!"

BICHO, 1. *Car., n.* Strange person or animal. (Lit. Bug, in-
sect.) *El novio de Lucinda es un bicho raro.* "Lucinda's
boyfriend is a weirdo." **2.** *Car., n.* Criminal, hoodlum.
Tenga Ud. cuidado en esa barriada, está llena de bichos.
"You be careful in that neighborhood; it's full of hoodlums." **3.** *Spain, n., drugs.* Dose of LSD. *Sólo quedaba un
bicho.* "There was only one hit left." **4.** *Spain, n., mil.* Recruit. *El cabo regañó al bicho.* "The corporal chewed
out the grunt." **5.** *L.Am., n.* Penis. *¡Uy! ¡Qué bicho tan
grande tienes!* "Wow! What a huge prick you got!"

BICI, *L.Am./S, n.* Bicycle. *Para mi cumpleaños quiero que
me regales una bici bien linda.* "For my birthday I want
you to give me a pretty bike."

BICICLETA, *Car., n.* Easy woman. (Lit. Bicycle.) *Antonio
está saliendo con la bicicleta del barrio.* "Antonio is
going out with the neighborhood easy rider."

BICLA, *L.Am./S, n.* Bicycle. *Se robaron su bicla de la
puerta de su casa.* "They ripped off his bike right outside
the front door of his house."

BICOCA, *Car., n.* Something easy to do. *Te puedo ayudar
siempre que sea una bicoca. No estoy para complica-
ciones.* "I can help you as long as it's a cinch. I am not
ready for complications."

BIELA, *Spain, n.* Leg. (Lit. Connecting rod.) *Me duelen las
bielas.* "My sticks hurt."

BIEN CON COJONES, *Car., idiom.* Very well, fucking
good. *Ese tipo es buena persona, me cae bien con co-*

jones. "That guy is a good person. I like him fucking good."

BIGOTE, 1. *Spain, idiom.* Great, extraordinary, tremendous. (Lit. Mustache.) *Ese disco es de bigote.* "That CD is super cool." **2.** *Car., n.* Useless vehicle, wreck, jalopy. *El auto de mi yerno es un bigote, pero no quiere deshacerse de él.* "My son-in-law's car is a wreck, but he doesn't want to get rid of it."

BIGOTES, 1. *Spain, n.* Mustachioed person. (Lit. Mustaches.) *¿Qué te dijo bigotes?* "What did the mustachioed guy say to you?" **2.** *Car., pl. n.* Leftovers. *Echaremos los bigotes a los animales.* "We'll throw the leftovers to the animals."

BIKINI, *Spain, n.* Grilled ham and cheese sandwich. (Lit. Bikini.) *Comí un bikini en la cafetería.* "I had a grilled ham and cheese at the cafeteria."

BILLAR DE BOLSILLO, *L.Am./N, n.* Pocket pool. *A la hora del recreo todos los muchachos estaban jugando billar de bolsillo.* "At recess all the boys were playing pocket pool."

BILLETE, *Spain, n.* One-thousand-peseta note. (Lit. Bill.) *Gasté mi último billete.* "I spent my last thousand pesetas."

BILMA, *Car., n.* Mustard plaster or home remedy. *Mi abuela es muy creyente en las bilmas para los resfriados.* "My grandmother is a believer in home remedies for colds."

BILORDO, DA, *Car., adj.* Absent-minded elderly person. *El juez ya está muy bilordo para el puesto que tiene.* "The judge is real flaky for the position he has."

BIMBA, 1. *Car., n.* Big belly. *Sigue comiendo y la bimba te va a llegar al suelo.* "Keep eating and the gut is going to reach the floor." **2.** *L.Am./N, n.* Drunken binge, drinking bout. *Anoche agarré una bimba y ahora tengo que aguantar la cruda.* "Last night I got stoned and now I have to put up with the hangover."

BIMBO, 1. *Car., n.* Police car. *Pasó el bimbo por aquí hace* *quince minutos.* "The fuzzmobile passed by 15 minutes ago." **2. BIMBO, BA,** *Car., adj.* Full, after a meal. *"Come más hijo". "No, gracias mamá, ya estoy bimbo de tanto comer".* " 'Eat some more, son.' 'No thanks, mom. I'm full from eating so much.' "

BIRLAR, *Spain, v.* To steal, to swipe. *Birlaron la tele de Fernandito.* "They swiped little Fernando's TV."

BIRMANO, *Spain, n.* Erotic massage followed by intercourse. (Lit. Burmese.) *En el puticlub le ofrecieron un birmano.* "At the hooker joint he was offered a burmese."

BIRRA, *Spain, L.Am./S, n.* Beer. (From Italian "beer.") *Quiero una birra para calmar la sed.* "I want a beer to quench my thirst."

BIRRIONGA, *U.S., n.* Beer. *Vamos a echarnos unas birriongas.* "Let's have a couple of beers."

BIRUJI, *Spain, n.* Intense cold, freezing wind. *Soplaba un biruji que pelaba.* "A cold wind was blowing that could peel your skin off."

BISA See BISABUELO

BISABUELO, *Spain, n., mil.* Soldier with less than three months of active service remaining. (Lit. Great-grandfather.) *El cabo Rodríguez es el bisabuelo de la sección.* "Corporal Rodriguez is the short-timer of the platoon."

BISAGRA See BISABUELO

BISNES, *Spain, n.* Shady business. (From English "business.") *Me parece que están metidos en algún bisnes.* "I think they are involved in some shady business."

BISNI See BISNES

BISTEC, *Spain, n.* Tongue. (Lit. Beefsteak.) *La tía no dejaba de mover el bistec.* "The broad wouldn't stop talking."

BISUTA, *Spain, n.* Costume jewelry. *El trinquetero estaba vendiendo bisuta.* "The trinket man was selling costume jewelery."

BISUTERO, RA, *Spain, n.* Seller of costume jewelry.

Compré el anillo a un bisutero. "I bought the ring from a costume jewelry seller."

BITUTE, *L.Am./S, n.* Food. *El bitute estuvo buenísimo, señorita.* "The meal was great, Miss."

BIZCOCHO, *L.Am./S, n.* Pretty woman. *La hermana de Roberto es un bizcocho.* "Roberto's sister is a cream puff." **See also MOJAR EL BIZCOCHO**

BLANCA, 1. *Spain, n., drugs.* Cocaine. (Lit. White.) *A ese desgraciado lo controla la blanca.* "That poor wretch is controlled by the white stuff." **2.** *Spain, n., mil.* A soldier's military papers. *El sargento tenía toda la blanca en su carpeta.* "The sergeant had all his papers in his briefcase."

BLANCA NIEVES, *Car., idiom.* White-powdered drugs such as heroin, cocaine, or snow. (Lit. Snow White.) *Los jóvenes están experimentando con la Blanca Nieves.* "The young people are experimenting with snow."

BLANCO, CA, *Spain, adj., crim.* Clean. (Lit. White.) *Mis antecedentes son bien blancos.* "My record is real clean."

BLANDENGUE, *L.Am./S, Car., adj.* Soft, weak person. *No seas blandengue Ramón, reclama tus derechos.* "Don't be a wimp Ramon, claim your rights."

BLANQUEADA, *Car., n.* In baseball, a game where one team is scoreless. (Lit. Whiteout.) *El equipo nuestro tuvo una blanqueada ayer, diez a cero.* "Our team had a white-out yesterday: ten to nothing."

BLANQUEAR DINERO, *Spain, L.Am., v., crim.* To launder money. *Condenaron a los acusados por blanquear dinero de drogas.* "They convicted the defendants for laundering drug money."

BLANQUEO, *Spain, L.Am., n.* Action of laundering money. *El blanqueo de dinero es un delito.* "Laundering money is a crime."

BLOQUEAR, *Spain, L.Am., v., sports.* To block hits, shots, or blows, depending on the sport. *El portero bloqueaba cada ataque a la portería.* "The goalie blocked each attack on the goal."

BOBALES, *Spain, n.* Fool, stupid person. *Esos bobales no sabían quitarse del medio.* "Those fools didn't know how to get out of the way."

BOBO, *Car., n.* Baby's pacifier. (Lit. Fool.) *Nos volvimos locos buscando el bobo de Miguelito.* "We went crazy looking for little Michael's pacifier."

BOCA, 1. *L.Am./C, n.* Snack, munchies. (Lit. Mouth.) *Vamos al bar del hotel, allí sirven bocas con las bebidas.* "Let's go to the hotel bar; there they serve munchies with the drinks." **2.** *Spain, n., crim.* Prison official. *Venían las bocas a inspeccionar la celda.* "The guards were coming to inspect the cell."

BOCANA, *Car., n.* Vulgarity said in a loud voice. *Todos se callaron cuando oyeron la bocana de Alberto.* "Everybody shut up when they heard Alberto's loud obscenity."

BOCATA, *Spain, n.* Sandwich. *¿Quieres una bocata?* "Do you want a sandwich?"

BOCHAR, *L.Am./S, v.* To fail. (From Italian "bocciare.") *Si no estudias, seguro que volverás a bochar en inglés.* "If you don't study you're surely going to flunk English."

BOCHINCHE, *n.* Disorder, fight, brawl. *Los viernes siempre hay bochinche en ese bar.* "On Fridays there is always a brawl in that bar."

BOCÓN, NA, 1. *L.Am./S, n., adj.* Talker. *Por bocón la mafia le arrancó la lengua.* "For being a big mouth, the Mafia ripped out his tongue." **2.** *Car., n., adj.* Know-it-all, smart-ass. *Ese niño es bocón hasta con la maestra. Siempre tiene que decir la última palabra.* "That boy is a smart aleck even with the teacher. He always has to have the last word." **3.** *L.Am./S, n., adj.* Gossip. *No confío en ti pues sé que eres un bocón.* "I can't trust you because you're a big mouth." **4.** *U.S., n.* Loudmouth. *En todas las fiestas tenemos que escuchar a ese bocón.* "At all the parties we have to listen to that loudmouth."

BOCOY, *Car., n., youth.* Short, potbellied person. *El padre de Jaime es un bocoy. Me parece que le gusta la cerveza.*

"Jaime's father is a potbellied guy. I think he likes beer."

BODEGA, *U.S., Car., n.* Small grocery store. (Lit. Wine cellar.) *Voy a la bodega a comprar café y azúcar.* "I am going to the grocery store to buy coffee and sugar."

BODEGAS, *Spain, n.* One who is given to drink. (Lit. Wine cellars.) *Ese bodegas siempre está en el bar.* "That lush is always at the bar."

BODI, *Spain, n., rude.* Body. (From English "body.") *¡Vaya bodi!* "What a bod!"

BODRIO, *Spain, n.* Literary work of poor quality. *Ese bodrio fue un desastre, tuve que dejarlo después de 20 páginas.* "That literary trash was a disaster; I had to put it down after 20 pages."

BOFEADO, *L.Am./N, adj.* Out of breath. *Después de subir las escaleras, ya echaba el bofe.* "After coming up the steps, I was already out of breath."

BOFEARSE, *L.Am./N, prnl. v.* To get out of breath. *Corrí tanto que quedé bofeado.* "I ran so much that I got out of breath."

BOFETADA, *Spain, n.* To run into something. (Lit. Slap.) *"¿Qué te pasó?" "Me di una bofetada con la puerta".* " 'What happened to you?' 'I hit myself with the door.' "

BOFIA, *Spain, n., crim.* Police. *¡Agua! Viene la bofia.* "Look out! Here come the police."

BOLA, 1. *L.Am./S, adj.* Stupid, slow. (Lit. Ball.) *Ese tipo es una bola, no deberías aceptarle la invitación.* "That guy is a jerk; you shouldn't accept his invitation." **2.** *Spain, n., crim.* Release granted a prisoner. *Le dieron bola al preso.* "They released the prisoner." **3.** *n.* Testicle, ball. *Ese tío no tiene bolas para pelear.* "That guy doesn't have the balls to fight." **4.** *Car., n., youth.* Rumor. *Oí la bola de que José Luis no fue aprobado en inglés.* "I heard the rumor that Jose Luis failed English." **5.** *Car., n., sports.* In baseball, a ball, a bad pitch. *Ya Martínez tiene dos bolas y dos estraics.* "Martinez already has two balls and two strikes."

BOLAMEN, *Spain, n.* Testicles. *No tienes bolamen para decirle eso.* "You don't have the balls to say that to him."

BOLAS, *L.Am./N, pl. n.* Testicles. (Lit. Balls.) *No usaba calzones porque le gustaba traer las bolas sueltas.* "He didn't wear underwear because he liked his balls hanging loose."

BOLAZO, *L.Am./S, n.* Lie, tall tale, exaggeration. *Pepe le contó un bolazo a su padre cuando le preguntó dónde estaba.* "Pepe told his father a big one when he asked him where he was."

BOLEARSE, *L.Am./S, prnl. v.* To get rich quick without effort. *Adrián se boleó con el negocio de la internet.* "Adrian made a killing with the internet business."

BOLETA, *L.Am./S, n.* Party pooper. *Isabel es una boleta. No quería bailar con los muchachos.* "Isabel is a party pooper. She didn't want to dance with the fellas."

BOLICHE, *L.Am./S, n.* **1.** Bar, tavern. *Siempre vamos al boliche después del trabajo.* "We always go to the bar after work." **2.** *L.Am./S, n.* Small grocery store. *José se acuesta con la dueña del boliche.* "Jose goes to bed with the store owner."

BOLILLO, LLA, *U.S., n.* White, non-Hispanic, Anglo. *Angela está saliendo con un bolillo.* "Angela is going out with a honky."

BOLIN See TENER LA LENGUA MONTADA SOBRE BOLINES

BOLINGA, 1. *Spain, n.* Drunk person. *Mira al bolinga que acaba de salir del bar.* "Look at the drunk who just left the bar." **2.** *Spain, n.* State of drunkeness. *Anoche tenía una bolinga que no veía.* "Last night I had one hell of a jag on."

BOLLERA, *Spain, n.* Lesbian. *Esa chica es bollera.* "That girl is a dyke."

BOLLO, 1. *L.Am./S, n.* Good-looking man or woman. (Lit. Bun.) *La prima de Héctor es un bollo y va a salir conmigo.* "Hector's cousin is awesome and she's going out with me." **2.** *Spain, n.* Vagina. *Las chicas que bailan en esa revista tienen el bollito afeitado.* "The girls that dance in that review have their pussies shaved." **3.** *Car., n.* A mess. *¡Vaya bollo lo del divorcio de Carmen y Pedro! Hay mucha amargura en eso.* "What a mess about Carmen and Pedro's divorce! There is a lot of bitterness in that."

BOLO, 1. *Spain, n.* Penis. *Deja de jugar con el bolo.* "Stop playing around with your dick." **2.** *U.S., n.* Dollar. *Luis está ganando muchos bolos en esa chamba.* "Luis is making a lot of bucks with that job."

BOLSA, *Spain, n.* Scrotum, balls. (Lit. Bag.) *¡Uy! Le dieron una patada en la bolsa. Hasta a mí me duele.* "Ouch! They kicked him in the nuts. It even hurts me."

BOLSEAR, *L.Am./N, v., crim.* To pick pockets. *Se subía a los buses sólo para bolsear a los pasajeros.* "He got on buses just to pick the passengers' pockets."

BOLSERO, *L.Am./S, adj.* Always asking for or borrowing things. *Guillermo es bien bolsero, no le da pena andar pidiendo prestado.* "Guillermo is a real pest; he's not ashamed of borrowing all the time."

BOLULÚ, *Spain, n.* Commotion, fuss. *¿De qué es este bolulú?* "What's all this fuss about?"

BOMBA, 1. *Spain, adj. or adv.* Fabulous, great. (Lit. Bomb.) *¡Qué bomba estás!* "You're so fine!" **2.** *L.Am./S, adj.* Drunk. *¡Todos en la fiesta terminaron bomba!* "Everybody at the party ended up sloshed!"

BOMBACHAS, *L.Am./S, pl. n.* Panties. *Me compré unas bombachas muy sexis.* "I bought some real sexy panties."

BOMBEAR, *Spain, v., drugs.* To inject heroin. *Ellos estaban bombeando caballo.* "They were pumping horse."

BOMBETA, *L.Am./C, n.* Showoff, conceited person. *Matilde es muy bombeta. Se cree que es la más guapa.* "Matilde is all puffed up with herself. She thinks she is the prettiest."

BOMBO, 1. *Spain, n.* Swelling from pregnancy. (Lit. Bass drum.) *Luisa no podía disimular su embarazo porque ya llevaba bombo.* "Luisa couldn't hide her pregnancy because she was already carrying a drum." **2. BOMBO, BA,** *L.Am./N, adj.* Tired, whipped. *Después de salir de la escuela quedé bombo.* "After getting out of school, I was whipped." **3. BOMBO, BA,** *U.S., adj.* Wealthy, rich. *Dicen que el padre de Pepita es muy bombo.* "They say that the Pepita's father is really rich."

BOMBÓN, *Spain, n.* Beautiful woman. (Lit. Bonbon.) *Mejor un bombón para dos que una mierda para uno.* "Better a candy for two than a piece of shit for one."

BOMBONA, *Spain, n., crim.* Police car. *Vi una bombona a la vuelta de la esquina.* "I saw a cop car around the corner."

BONCHE, 1. *Car., n.* Bunch of friends. *Todos en bonche nos fuimos a celebrar el triunfo del equipo.* "We all went in a bunch to celebrate the teams' victory." **2.** *L.Am./S, n.* Party, blowout. *Para celebrar su cumpleaños tuvimos un bonche fabuloso.* "To celebrate his birthday we had a fabulous blowout."

BONDI, *L.Am./S, n.* Bus or van pool. *Tomo el bondi en la esquina de mi calle.* "I catch the bus at the corner of my street."

¡BONETE!, *L.Am./N, interj.* No way! *¡Bonete! Tu estás loca si crees que voy contigo a la fiesta.* "No way! You are crazy if you think I am going to the party with you."

BONIATO, *Spain, n.* Thousand-peseta note. *¿Cuántos boniatos tienes tú allí?* "How many greenbacks do you have there?"

BOQUERAS, *Spain, n., crim.* Prison officer. *¡Cuidado, que te va a oír el boqueras!* "Be careful, the guard is going to hear you!"

BOQUI, *Spain, n., crim.* Prison officer. *Su cuñado es boqui en la trena.* "His brother-in-law is a guard at the pen."

BOQUINA, *Spain, n.* Mouth. *Le pegaron un guantazo en la* *boquina.* "They slapped him in the mouth."

BORDE, 1. *Spain, adj.* Mean. (Lit. Edge.) *¡No seas borde Julio!* "Don't be mean, Julio!" **2.** *Spain, adj.* Vulgar, impolite. *Se nota que es borde por su manera de hablar.* "You can tell he's a brute by his way of talking."

BORICUA, *Car., n.* Puerto Rican. *Hay muchos boricuas en Detroit.* "There are a lot of Puerto Ricans in Detroit."

BORINCANO, NA, *Car., adj.* Puerto Rican. *En Dallas hay una pequeña comunidad borincana.* "In Dallas there is a small Puerto Rican community."

BORLAS, *Spain, pl. n.* Testicles. *Ese torero sí tiene borlas.* "That bullfighter really has balls."

BORONA, *L.Am./C, n.* What is left. (Lit. Crumbs.) *Tú coges lo mejor para ti y a mí me dejas las boronas.* "You take the best for yourself and leave me with the crumbs."

BORRAR DEL MAPA, *Spain, idiom.* To eliminate, to kill. *Al hermano de Félix lo borraron del mapa.* "They got rid of Felix's brother."

BORRARSE, *L.Am./S, prnl. v.* To disappear. *Oye, Juan, ¿dónde estuviste? Te borraste de aquí hace más de un año.* "Hey, Juan, where were you? You disappeared from here more than a year ago."

BOS, *Spain, U.S., n.* Boss. (From English "boss.") *Aquí viene el bos.* "Here comes the boss."

BOSQUE, *Car., n., sports.* In baseball, outfield. *Pegó uno fuerte para el bosque pero lo agarró Jiménez.* "He hit a hard one to the outfield but Jimenez caught it."

BOSTA, *L.Am./S, n.* Mean person, bastard, fucker. *El padrastro de Juana es una bosta y le hace la vida imposible.* "Juana's stepfather is a dick and he makes her life impossible."

BOSTEZO, *L.Am./C, adj.* Boring person. (Lit. Yawn.) *No puedo estar mucho tiempo con Lázaro, es un bostezo.* "I can't be with Lazaro for very long; he's such a drag."

BOTADO, DA, *L.Am./S, adj.* Easy. *Tomar esas medidas es* *botado, no me demoraré nada.* "To take these steps is a cinch. It won't take long at all."

BOTAFUEGO, *Car., n.* Person with radical, rigid ideas. (Lit. Spitfire.) *El hermano mayor de Marcos es un botafuego. No acepta otras ideas.* "Marcos's older brother is a firebrand. He doesn't accept other ideas."

BOTANA, *L.Am./N, n.* Snack, appetizer. *Nos sirvieron taquitos de botana.* "They served us taquitos as a snack."

BOTAPEDOS, *L.Am./N, n.* Anus, ass. *Recuerda siempre de limpiarte el botapedos después de ir al baño.* "Remember always to wipe your butt after going to the bathroom."

BOTAR, 1. *L.Am./S, v.* To throw out. *Mi mujer siempre me bota los papeles importantes.* "My wife always throws my important papers out." **2.** *L.Am./S, v.* To end a relationship. *Mi novio me botó ayer.* "My boyfriend kicked me out yesterday."

BOTAR CORRIENTE, *L.Am./S, idiom.* To have a deep conversation, to solve the world's problems. *Nuestros padres están botando corriente en el estudio.* "Our fathers are solving the world's problems in the study."

BOTAR LA BABA, *L.Am./S, idiom.* To be drooling for someone. *Luís está botando la baba por Angela y ella no lo sabe.* "Luis is drooling for Angela and she doesn't even know it."

BOTAR LA BOLA, *Car., idiom.* To do something outstanding. *La hija de Manolo y Graciela botó la bola cuando dio su presentación.* "Manolo and Graciela's daughter hit one out of the park when she made her presentation."

BOTARATE, *Car., adj.* Spendthrift. *Mi cuñado nunca tendrá nada, es un botarate.* "My brother-in-law will never have anything; he is a spendthrift."

BOTARSE, *Car., prnl. v.* To entertain sumptuously. *El señor Roldán se botó en el bautizo de su nieto.* "Mr. Roldan went all out for his grandson's baptism."

BOTE, 1. *L.Am./N, Car., n., crim.* Jail. (Lit. Boat.) *Lo* *metieron en el bote anoche por andar borracho en la calle.* "They put him in the clink last night for being drunk on the street." **2.** *Spain, n.* Tip jar. *Aquí tienes pa'l bote.* "Here's something for the tip jar." **See also CHUPAR BOTE, DAR EL BOTE, DARSE EL BOTE**

BOTE PRONTO, *Spain, idiom.* All of a sudden, off the top of one's head. *El entrevistador quería que contestara yo de bote pronto.* "The interviewer wanted me to answer off the top of my head."

BOTELLÍN, *Spain, n.* Small bottle of beer. *Deme un botellín, por favor.* "Give me a pony of beer, please."

BOTICA See TENER LA BOTICA ABIERTA

BOTIJA, 1. *Car., n.* Awkward, fat person. *Se ven muchas botijas en los supermercados.* "You see a lot of rolly pollies in the supermarket." **2.** *L.Am./S, n.* Child. *Luisa no puede venir con nosotros, tiene que cuidar la botija.* "Luisa can't come with us; she has to take care of her child."

BOTIJO, 1. *Spain, n.* Short, fat person. *Jorge es el botijo que ves allí.* "Jorge is the dumpy little guy you see there." **2.** *Spain, n.* Big breasts. *¡Qué botijos tiene la gachí!* "What a pair that chick has!"

BOTO, TA, *U.S., n.* Alcoholic, drunk, lush. *Ese desgraciado es un boto y hay que ayudarle.* "That poor guy is a lush and must be helped."

BOTON, *L.Am./S, n., crim.* Police officer, cop, fuzz. (Lit. Button.) *Había botones por todas partes buscando al ladrón.* "There was fuzz all over the place looking for the thief."

BOTONES, 1. *Spain, pl. n.* Testicles. *Ese cobarde no tiene botones.* "That coward doesn't have any balls." **2.** *Spain, pl. n.* Nipples. *Con esa blusa se te ven los botones.* "With that blouse one can see your nipples."

BOX, *U.S., n.* Boxing. *A mí me gusta mucho mirar el box en la tele.* "I really like to watch boxing on TV."

BOYA See ESTAR DE BOYA

BOYANTE, *Car., adj.* Flush, as in having cash. *Te quedaste boyante con el cheque de la lotería, ¿verdad?* "You got flush with the lottery check, right?"

BOYER, *Spain, n.* Sexual voyeur. (From French "voyeur.") *Le arrestaron por ser boyer.* "They arrested him for being a Peeping Tom."

BOYERA, *Car., n.* Lesbian. *"¿Cómo se llama ese programa de boyeras en la tele?" "No sé, no miro esas cosas"* " 'What do you call that program about dykes on TV?' 'I don't know, I don't watch those things.' "

BRAGA See ESTAR HECHO UNA BRAGA

BRAGA(S), *Spain, n.* Snob. *El Sr. López es un bragas.* "Mr. Lopez is a snob."

BRAGAZAS, *Spain, n.* Real snob. *¡Qué bragazas está hecha Julia!* "What a snob Julia has become!"

BRAGUETAZO See DAR EL BRAGUETAZO

BRAGUETA See ENTERARSE POR LA BRAGUETA

BRASAS, *Spain, n.* Nasty, boring person. *Ese brasas no nos dejaba en paz, siempre tenía otra pregunta.* "That jerk wouldn't leave us alone; he always had another question."

BRAVA, *Spain, n., crim.* Jimmy. Tool to open doors or windows. *El ladrón dejó su brava en el lugar del robo.* "The thief left his jimmy at the robbery site." **See also DAR BRAVA**

BREJES, *Spain, n., crim.* Years of sentence. *Lo condenaron a seis brejes.* "They sentenced him to six years."

BRETE, *L.Am., n.* Work. *No puedo salir ahora, todavía tengo mucho brete.* "I can't go out with you now; I still have a lot of work."

BRETEAR, *L.Am./C, v.* To work. *Roberto bretea en el taller de los López.* "Robert works at the Lopez shop."

BRINCACHARCO, *Car., n.* Pants with a high hem, high-waters. *Beto parece un campesino con esos brincacharcos.* "Beto looks like a hick with those high-waters."

BRINCAPOZO, *Car., n.* Pants with a high hem, high-waters. *Julio siempre compra los pantalones muy chicos y parecen brincapozos.* "Julio always buys pants that are too small and they look like high-waters."

BRINCOTEO, *Car., n., youth.* Informal dance or party. *Organizamos de pronto un brincoteo y bailamos toda la noche.* "We got a party going and danced all night long."

BROCHA See ¡VOY CON LA BROCHA!, DAR BROCHA

BROCHA GORDA, *L.Am./N, n.* House painter. *Mi tío Manuel es artista de brocha gorda.* "My Uncle Manuel is a house painter."

BRÓDER, *Spain, n., youth.* Friend, companion. (From English "brother.") *Oye bróder, vamos a tomar unos chatos.* "Hey bro, let's have a few drinks."

BRONCA, *L.Am./S, n.* Fight. *Anoche en la fiesta se armó una bronca de padre y señor mío.* "The fight last night at the party was the end of the world." **See also ECHAR UNA BRONCA, DAR LA BRONCA, MONTARSE LA BRONCA**

BRONCAS, *Spain, n.* Person who gets into everybody's business. *El director es un broncas, discute con todo el mundo.* "The director is a pain in the ass; he argues with everybody."

BRONCO, CA, *L.Am./N, adj.* Aggressive. *El amigo de Ticha es muy bronco, a diario busca pleito.* "Tito's friend is very aggressive; he is always looking for trouble."

BROWN SUGAR, *Spain, n., drugs.* Heroin. *La poli encontró tres kilos de brown sugar.* "The police found three kilos of brown horse."

BRUJA, 1. *L.Am./S, idiom.* Mother-in-law. (Lit. Witch.) *Este fin de semana viene la bruja a visitarnos.* "This weekend my mother-in-law is coming to visit us." **2.** *Car., n.* Girlfriend of a married man. *La bruja del director es una rubia de Miami.* "The director's girl is a blonde from Miami." **See also ESTAR BRUJA**

BRUTAL, *L.Am., adj., youth.* (Lit. Brutal.) Fantastic, great, extraordinary, enormous, gigantic. *El concierto fue brutal.* "The concert was the most."

BRUTÁLICO, *U.S., adj., youth.* Fantastic, cool, out of sight. *El carro de Roberto es brutálico.* "Roberto's car is out of sight."

BUBARRON, *Car., n.* Homosexual. *El Zodíaco es un club de bubarrones.* "The Zodiac is a gay club."

BUCA, *U.S., n., youth.* Girl. *Esa buca es muy bonita.* "That chick is very pretty."

BUCHANTE, *Spain, n.* Shot. *Lo primero que voy a hacer cuando salga es trincarme un buchante de coñac.* "The first thing I'm going to do when I get out is to throw down a shot of cognac."

BUCHE, *L.Am./N, n.* Mouth. (Lit. Beak.) *¡Cierra el buche y no hagas ruido!* "Shut your trap and don't make any noise."

BUCHE Y PLUMA, *Car., idiom.* All talk, hot air. (Lit. Beak and feather.) *En realidad no tiene tanto dinero, es puro buche y pluma.* "In reality he doesn't have so much money; he is pure mouth and feathers."

BUCHIPLUMA, *Car., n.* Person who promises but doesn't deliver. *Yo no le daría el contrato a ese, es un buchipluma, habla mucho pero no cumple.* "I wouldn't give the contract to that guy; he is all mouth— he talks a lot but doesn't deliver."

BUCHÓN, *L.Am./S, n., crim.* Informer, stool pidgeon, squealer. *Los presos sospecharon que era un buchón el responsable por su arresto.* "The prisoners suspected that the one responsible for their arrest was a squealer."

BUCO, *Spain, n., drugs.* Injection of any drug into a vein. *El adicto necesitaba un buco de heroína.* "The addict needed a hit of heroin."

BUCOSEXUAL, *Car., adj.* Oral sex. *Ese viejo sólo alquila videos bucosexuales.* "That old fella rents only oral sex videos."

BUDÚ, *Car., n.* Voodoo. *En esa casa creo que practican el budú.* "At that house I think they practice voodoo."

¡BUENA!, *L.Am./S, interj.* Expression of approval. (Lit. Good.) *¡Buena, cumpa! La hiciste verídica.* "Great, pal! You did it right on."

BUENA EDUCACIÓN, *L.Am./N, n.* Nice breasts, tits, boobs. *A la vecina del nueve, se le nota la buena educación.* "Our neighbor in number nine has some nice boobs, as you can tell."

BUENA PAPA, *L.Am./S, idiom.* Good person. *Me gusta tu amigo, es buena papa.* "I like your friend; he's a good man."

BUENA PERCHA, *L.Am./N, n.* Shapely woman. *Tiene muy buena percha la amiga de Claudia.* "Claudia's friend is well-stacked."

BUENA/MALA ONDA, *L.Am., adj.* Good or bad. *Mi mamá es muy buena onda, ella sí me deja tener novio.* "My mom is real good people; she'll let me have a boyfriend."

BUENASA, *L.Am., adj.* Attractive young woman. *Supiste escoger muy bien, la niña está buenasa.* "You knew how to choose real well. That babe is the coolest."

BUENO See ESTAR BUENO, NA

BUEY, *L.Am./N, adj.* Stupid. (Lit. Ox.) *Carlos es tan buey que se alegra cuando se saca un 0 de calificación.* "Carlos is so stupid that he is happy when he gets a 0."

BÚFALO, 1. *Car., n.* American nickel. (Lit. Buffalo.) *Ahora el teléfono público requiere más búfalos.* "Now the public phone requires more nickels." **2.** *Car., n.* Ugly man. *El nuevo marido de Isabel es un búfalo.* "Isabel's new husband is an ugly dude."

BUFANDA, *Spain, n.* Tip to a public official. (Lit. Scarf.) *Le dieron la bufanda al funcionario del registro.* "They gave a little something extra to the registry official."

BUFARLE LOS RIELES A ALGUIEN, *L.Am./N, idiom.*

To smell bad, to stink. *No me gusta jugar básquet con Pedro porque le bufan los rieles.* "I don't like to play basketball with Pedro because his armpits stink."

BUFE, *L.Am./N, n.* Stink, bad smell. *Yolanda nunca se baña, me llega su bufe hasta mi lugar.* "Yolanda never bathes, and I can smell her stink even in my place."

BUFO See BUFOSO

BUFOSO, *L.Am./S, n.* Pistol, gun. *El hombre traía el bufoso metido en su bolsillo.* "The man had the rod in his pocket."

BUGA, *Spain, n.* Car. *¿Viste la buga nueva de Miguel?* "Did you see Miguel's new wheels?"

BUGARRÓN, *Car., n.* Homosexual. *Pedro no quiere que nadie sepa que es bugarrón pero no lo puede disimular.* "Pedro doesn't want anybody to know he is gay, but he can't hide it."

BUGATI See BUGA

BUGUI See BUGA

BUGUI-BUGUI, *Car., n., youth,* Boogie-woogie. *Los jóvenes de hoy están resucitando el bugui-bugui.* "Today's youth are reviving the boogie-woogie."

BUITRE, 1. *Spain, n.* Moocher, scrounger. (Lit. Vulture.) *¡Cierra la puerta! Allí viene ese buitre Lalo.* "Close the door! Here comes that moocher, Lalo." **2.** *Spain, n.* Tow truck driver. *El buitre me llevó el coche y ahora tengo que pagar para recuperarlo.* "The tow buzzard took my car and now I have to pay to get it back." **3.** *L.Am./S, n.* Vomit. *Se mandó un buitre en medio de la tienda.* "He threw up right in the middle of the store."

BUITREAR, 1. *Spain, v.* To mooch, to scrounge, to bum. *Ese hombre viene por aquí buitreando todos los días.* "That man comes scrounging around here every day." **2.** *L.Am./S, v.* To vomit. *¡Me buitreé los pantalones!* "I vomited on my pants!"

BUJA, *Spain, n.* Active homosexual. *En ese bar se ligan los bujas.* "In that bar the gays get together."

BUJARRA, *Spain, adj.* Effeminate, homosexual. *Ese hombre es bien bujarra.* "That man is very limp-wristed."

BUJARRON See BUJA

BUJIO, *Spain, n., crim.* Hiding place, stash. *La poli quiere saber dónde tiene su bujio.* "The cops want to know where he has his stash."

BULE, *L.Am./N, n.* Whorehouse. *No me gusta ir a la calle Orompello, hay puros bules.* "I don't like to go to Orompello Street; there's a lot of whorehouses there."

BULICO, CA, *Car., adj.* Cowardly. *El nuevo gallo de pelea que tiene Álvaro es muy bulico.* "The new fighting cock Alvaro has is very chicken."

BULLA, *Car., n.* Argument, fight, disagreement, row. *Los amigos tuvieron una bulla en la taberna anoche, pero ya hicieron las paces.* "The friends had a fight at the tavern last night but they made up."

BULLARENQUE, *Spain, n.* Woman's behind, fat ass. *¡Vaya bullarenque de esa!* "What a fat ass she's got!"

BULLATE, *Spain, n.* Ass. *En la trena te va a doler el bullate.* "In the joint your ass is going to hurt."

BULTO, *Spain, n., mil.* Recruit. (Lit. Bundle.) *Tenemos siete bultos en la sección.* "We have seven grunts in our platoon."

BULULÚ, *Spain, n.* Uproar. *¿De qué era el bululú en la taberna anoche?* "What was the ruckus in the tavern last night?"

BÚNKER, *Spain, n.* The far right. (Lit. Bunker.) *El búnker no va a aceptar un candidato tan liberal.* "The far right is not going to accept such a liberal candidate."

BUNKERICANO, *Spain, adj.* Reactionary, of the far right. *Fernando es bunkericano.* "Fernando is a right-winger."

BUQUI, *L.Am./N, n.* Child. *Al buqui lo consienten en todo.* "They spoil the kid in everything."

BUQUI, QUIA, *U.S., n., youth.* Child, kid, rugrat. *Vamos a llevar los buquis al cine.* "We are going to take the

85

rugrats to the movies."

BURDA, 1. *Spain, n., crim.* Door. *Trincaron la burda anoche y robaron todo.* "They jimmied the door last night and stole everything." **2.** *L.Am./S, adv.* Very, much. *Vida mía te quiero burda.* "Sweetheart, I love you lots."

BUREO, *Car., n.* Ruckus, commotion, argument. *Hubo un bureo en el trabajo hoy. Despidieron a veinte personas.* "There was a ruckus at work today. They fired twenty people." **See also IR DE BUREO**

BURRA, 1. *Spain, n.* Bicycle. (Lit. Donkey.) *¡Niño! ¿Dónde dejaste la burra?* "Boy! Where did you leave your bike?" **2.** *Spain, n.* Motorcycle. *Le quitaron la burra al poli.* "They took the cop's motorcycle." **3.** *L.Am./N, n.* Bus. *Todas las mañanas hay unas colas terribles esperando a que pase la burra.* "Every morning there are terrible lines waiting for the bus to pass." **4.** *L.Am./S, n.* Very old car. *Esta burra tiene muchos años y todavía anda.* "This wreck is very old, but it still runs."

BURRACA, *Spain, n.* Low-class whore. *La burraca lo dejó con gonorrea.* "That cheap whore left him with gonorrhea."

BURRADA, *L.Am./S, Spain, n.* A stupid thing, a dumb trick. *Acabo de cometer una burrada. Mandé al jefe al infierno.* "I just did a stupid thing. I told the boss to go to hell."

BURREAR, *Spain, v.* To deceive, to swindle, to rob. *Me burreó mi amor y mi dinero.* "She betrayed my love and stole my money."

BURRICIEGO, GA, *L.Am./N, n.* Person with poor eyesight. *Desde que conozco a Nacho, siempre ha usado lentes de burriciego.* "Since I've known Nacho he has always used thick glasses."

BURRO, 1. *L.Am./N, n.* Drunk. (Lit. Donkey.) *De pura rabia decidí ponerme burro.* "Out of anger I decided to get plastered." **2.** *Car., n.* Homosexual. *Ese burro quiere abrir un bar de bugarrones en nuestro barrio.* "That fag wants to open a gay bar in our neighborhood." **3.** *Spain,* *adj.* Stupid, ignorant. *¡Qué burro eres!* "How stupid you are!" **4.** *Spain, n., drugs.* Heroin. *Estamos viendo mucho burro por España.* "We are seeing a lot of horse around Spain." **See also APEARSE DEL BURRO**

BURROCRACIA, *Spain, n.* Bureaucracy. (Play on words Burro and Burocracia.) *Álvaro es parte de la burrocracia.* "Alvaro belongs to the burrocracy."

BURRÓCRATA, *Spain, n.* Bureaucrat. (Play on words Burro and Burócrata.) *Estos burrócratas no entienden nada.* "Those burrocrats don't understand a thing."

BUSARDA, 1. *L.Am./S, n.* Stomach, gut, belly. *Le pegaron dos tiros en la busarda.* "They put two rounds into his gut." **2.** *L.Am./S, n.* Love handles. *No me pongo vestido de baño porque se me ve la busarda.* "I don't put on a bathing suit because you can see my love handles."

BUSCABULLA, *L.Am./N, n.* Troublemaker. *Cuidado con Tomás, es un buscabulla.* "Be careful with Thomas; he is a troublemaker."

BUSCAPLEITOS, *Car., n.* Person who looks for clients for a lawyer. *Siempre que hay un accidente de aviación se llenan los hoteles de buscapleitos.* "Whenever there is a plane accident, the hotels fill up with ambulance chasers."

BUSCAR LAS PULGAS A ALGUIEN, *Spain, idiom.* To provoke, to incite. *Lorenzo siempre le está buscando las pulgas a Josefa.* "Lorenzo is always trying to get Josefa's goat."

BUSCAS, *L.Am./N, n.* Perks, extra income. *Lo bueno de ese trabajo es que tiene muchas buscas.* "The good thing about this job is that it has a lot of perks."

BUSCATOQUES, *U.S., n., drugs.* Addict looking for a fix. *Ese buscatoques está desesperado, cuidado con él.* "That addict is desperate for a fix; be careful with him."

BUSCAVIDAS, *L.Am./N, n.* Gossiper. *Cuidado con lo que dices a Carlota, es una buscavidas.* "Be careful what you say to Carlota; she is a gossip."

BUSCONA, *L.Am./N, Spain, n.* Whore. *Hay muchas buscónas por esa barriada.* "There are a lot of hookers around that neighborhood."

BUSNO, *Spain, n.* What gypsies call non-gypsies. *Muchos busnos piensan que somos ladrones.* "Many non-gypsies think we're thieves."

BUSO, SA, *U.S., adj.* Intelligent, clever. *El hijo de Rodrigo es bien buso.* "Rodrigo's son is very clever."

BUTEN, *Spain, adj.* Excellent, fantastic, great. *La comida fue de buten.* "The meal was out of this world."

BUTIFARRA, 1. *Spain, n.* Penis, cock, dick. (Lit. Sausage.) *Lo que quiere esa es que le meta la butifarra en el bollo.* "What that one wants is to have my sausage up her roll." **2.** *Car., n.* Long, boring speech. *No sé cómo puedes aguantar las butifarras del profesor de sociología.* "I don't know how you can stand the long-winded speeches of the sociology professor."

BUTRÓN, *Spain, n., crim.* Type of jacket with inner pockets worn by shoplifters. *El mechero llevaba un montón de cosas en su butrón.* "The shoplifter had a lot of things in his inner pockets."

BUZO, *Car., n., crim.* Informer. (Lit. Diver.) *Un buzo causó la batida en que arrestaron a tu primo.* "A rat caused the roundup in which they arrested your cousin."

BUZÓN, *Spain, n.* Big mouth. (Lit. Mailbox.) *Ildefonso es el buzón de la barriada.* "Ildefonso is the big mouth of the neighborhood."

CA, *Spain, n., youth.* Home. (Abbreviation of "casa.") *Mi hermano está en ca de abuela.* "My brother is at Grandma's."

CABALLERO CUBIERTO, *Car., idiom.* Uncircumcised male. *Un productor de porno reclutaba caballeros cubiertos para una película.* "A porn producer was recruiting uncircumcised men for a movie."

CABALLISTA, *Spain, n., crim.* Prisoner with money, daddy. *A ese caballista no le falta nada.* "That daddy doesn't need a thing."

CABALLITO, 1. *L.Am./N, n.* Sanitary napkin. (Lit. Little horse.) *Matilde tuvo que ir corriendo a comprar caballitos ya que le vino la regla.* "Matilde got her period and had to run and get some sanitary napkins." **2.** *L.Am./N, n.* Merry-go-round. *Los niños quieren que les llevemos a los caballitos.* "The kids want us to take them to the merry-go-round."

CABALLITO DE BATALLA, *Car., idiom.* Same old argument. *Aquí viene Adán con su caballito de batalla. Lo hemos oído mil veces ya.* "Here comes Adam with the same old argument. We have heard it a thousand times already."

CABALLO, 1. *Car., n.* Virile or knowledgeable man. (Lit. Horse.) *La verdad es que la conferencia estuvo buenísima, ese tipo sabe un mundo, es un caballo.* "The truth is the conference was terrific. That guy knows a great deal— he is a top gun." **2.** *Spain, n., drugs.* Heroin. *Ella es adicta al caballo.* "She's hooked on horse." **3.** *L.Am./N, n.* Sanitary napkin. *Como se le bajó la regla, Mónica tuvo que ir a buscar caballos con las amigas.* "Her period started and Monica went to get sanitary napkins with her friends."

CABALLO BLANCO, 1. *Spain, n., crim.* Backer of suspicious ventures. *El estafador encontró un caballo blanco para su proyecto.* "The swindler found a backer for his project." **2.** *L.Am./N, n.* Chamber pot. *Allá en el rancho todavía usan caballo blanco en los dormitorios.* "Out at the ranch they still use chamber pots in the bedrooms."

CABALLÓN, LLONA, *U.S., adj., drugs.* High on drugs. *Cuidado con él, está bien caballón.* "Be careful with him; he is high on drugs."

CABALLOS, *L.Am./C, pl. n.* Pants. (Lit. Horses.) *Mamá, tienes que comprarme unos caballos nuevos.* "Mom, you have to buy me some new pants."

CABE, *Spain, n., sports.* Head shot in soccer. *Allí va González y da un cabe, la coge Jiménez y ¡gol!* "There goes Gonzalez, he makes a head shot, Jimenez get's it and scores!"

CABECITA NEGRA, *L.Am./S, idiom.* Black person. *El mejor amigo de Tomás es un cabecita negra.* "Tomas's best friend is a black person."

CABELLERA See SOLTARSE LA CABELLERA, TOMAR LA CABELLERA

CABER, *L.Am./S, v., youth.* To like, to dig, to get a kick out of. (Lit. To fit.) *A mí me cabe la nueva moda para esquiar.* "I get a kick out of the new ski fashions."

CABESTRO, *Spain, n., neg.* Cuckold. *El marido de esa tía es un cabestro.* "That broad's husband is a cuckold."

CABEZA, *U.S., n.* Black person. (Lit. Head.) *Hay muchas cabezas en ese barrio.* "There are a lot of blacks in that neighborhood."

CABEZA CUADRADA, *Spain, idiom.* Person with rigid mentality, blockhead. *Ese tío es una cabeza cuadrada.* "That guy is a blockhead."

CABEZA DE BÚFALO, *U.S., n.* Black person. *Entró una cabeza de búfalo preguntando por ti.* "A black guy came in looking for you."

CABEZA DE RODILLA, *L.Am./S, idiom.* Bald. *Mi tío Juan es un cabeza de rodilla.* "My Uncle John is as bald as a cue ball."

CABEZA RASPADA, *Spain, idiom.* Skinhead. *Hay que tener cuidado con las cabezas raspadas.* "You've got to be careful with those skinheads."

CABLE See **CRUZÁRSELE LOS CABLES A ALGUIEN**

CABRA, 1. *L.Am./C, n.* Sweetheart. (Lit. She-goat.) *Ana es la cabra de Javier.* "Ana is Javier's sweetheart." **2.** *Car., n.* Call girl. *Dicen que la hija de tu amiga es una cabra en Nueva York.* "They say that your friend's daughter is a call girl in New York." **See also ESTAR COMO UNA CABRA**

CABREARSE, 1. *Spain, prnl. v.* To get angry. *Se cabreó cuando le dije que no iba prestarle el dinero.* "He got pissed off when I told him I wasn't going to lend him the money." **2.** *L.Am./S, prnl. v.* To get bored. *Se cabreó de tanto esperar y se fue.* "He got bored of waiting and left."

CABRITO, 1. *Spain, n.* Cuckold. *¡Qué cabrito es José! Su esposa putea con todos.* "What a cuckold Jose is! His wife goes whoring with everybody!" **2.** *Spain, n.* Prostitute's customer, John. *Detuvieron a la putita y a su cabrito.* "They detained the little hooker and her John."

CABRO, RA, 1. *L.Am./S, n.* Young person. *Los cabros estarán contentos cuando les diga que los voy a llevar al cine.* "The boys will be happy when I tell them that I'll take them to the movies." **2.** *Car., n.* Good-looking man, a hunk. *El nuevo vecino es un cabro.¡Y es soltero también!* "The new neighbor is a hunk. And single too!"

CABRÓN, 1. *L.Am./C, n.* Expression used among men. Dude. *¡Oye cabrón! ¿Cuándo vamos a ir a ver un partido?* "Hey dude! When are we going to go see a game?" **2.** *Spain, n.* Cuckold, one whose wife is cheating on him. *Ese desgraciado es un cabrón, a su mujer la visita un amiguito durante el día.* "That poor slob is a wimp. His wife's boyfriend visits her during the day." **3.** *Spain, n.* Undesirable person. *¡Qué cabrón es ese taxista! Quería cobrarme el doble por un viaje corto.* "That taxi driver is a bastard! He wanted to charge me double for a short trip." **4.** *L.Am./N, n.* Nasty person. *Quique es muy cabrón con su vieja, no la deja salir ni a la esquina.* "Quique is a real bastard with his old lady; he doesn't let her go out of the house."

CABRONADA, *Spain, n.* Dirty trick. *Hicieron una cabronada a Ramón. Le quitaron todas las llantas del coche.* "They pulled a rotten trick on Ramon. They took all the tires off his car."

¡CACA!, *Spain, L.Am., interj.* Expression of disapproval. Crap! *"¿Qué te parece la idea de Román?" "¡Caca!"* " 'How does Roman's idea seem to you?' 'Crap!' "

CACA, *Spain, L.Am., n.* Worthless thing, crap. *Esa bicicleta es una caca.* "That bicycle is a piece of crap."

CACAHUATE, *U.S., n.* Pill. (Lit. Peanut.) *Yo le vi echarse un cacahuate antes de ponerse a manejar.* "I saw him take a pill before starting to drive."

CACALOTE, *L.Am./N, n.* Crow. *Dicen que si ves un cacalote a la izquierda es mala suerte.* "They say that if you see a crow on the left it's bad luck."

CACAO, *Spain, n.,* Confusion, disturbance, brouhaha. *Dijeron que hubo un cacao anoche en tu barrio.* "They say that there was a brouhaha in your neighborhood last night."

CACARIZO, *L.Am./N, adj.* Pockmarked. *Después de que le dio viruela, quedó todo cacarizo de la cara.* "After he got smallpox, his face was all pockmarked."

CACATÚA, 1. *Spain, n.* Ugly, weird, or eccentric woman. *La mujer del estanco es una cacatúa, no cambia de ropa nunca.* "The woman from the tobacco store is a weirdo, she never changes her clothes." **2.** *Car., adj.* Dull, stupid. *La mujer de Pepe es una cacatúa, por eso él es tan mujeriego.* "Pepe is such a womanizer because his wife is so stupid."

CACHA, *L.Am./S, n.* Head. *¿No te duele la cacha?* "Doesn't your head ache?"

CACHACO, 1. *L.Am./S, adj.* Native of Bogotá. *El papá de María es un cachaco de la cabeza a los pies.* "Maria's father is pure Bogotano from head to foot." **2.** *L.Am./S, n.* Soldier. *El hijo del compadre se metió de cachaco.* "My best friend's son went into the army."

CACHAPA, *Car., n.* Cunnilingus between lesbians. *Entraron y pescaron a las tortilleras haciendo cachapa.* "They went in and caught the dykes licking each other."

CACHAPEAR, *Car., v.* To practice cunnilingus between lesbians. *Se venden muchos videos en que cachapean dos mujeres.* "They sell a lot of videos in which two women are getting it on."

CACHAPERA, *L.Am., n.* Lesbian. *En el mundo de las cachaperas ella es la reina.* "In the world of the dykes, she is the queen."

CACHAPUTA, *Car., n.* Lesbian hooker. *Esa mujer tan atractiva es una cachaputa.* "That very attractive woman is a lesbian hooker."

CACHAR, 1. *L.Am./S, v.* To understand. *Víctor no cacha nada de lo que le dicen, creo que está sordo.* "Victor doesn't catch any of what you tell him, I think he's deaf." **2.** *L.Am./N, v., crim.* To catch, to grab, to trap, to capture. *La primera vez que me cachó la policía fue por robar una bicicleta.* "The first time the police caught me was for robbing a bike." **3.** *L.Am./N, v.* To catch by surprise. *Mi mamá me cachó con las manos en la masa.* "My mom caught me in the act." **4.** *Car., v., sports.* Baseball catcher.

El hermano de Lola va a cachar con los Rangers de Texas. "Lola's brother is going to catch with the Texas Rangers."

CACHARRA, 1. *Spain, n., crim.* Pistol. *Cuando cogieron al tipo tenía una cacharra escondida en la camisa.* "When they caught the guy he had a piece hidden in his shirt." **2.** *Car., n., crim.* Jail. *Jacobo lleva cuatro años en la cacharra.* "Jacobo has been in the clink for four years." **3.** *Car., n.* Old car, jalopy. *Es increíble que todavía ande la cacharra de tu abuelo.* "It's unbelievable that your grandfather's jalopy still runs."

CACHARRAS, 1. *L.Am./C, pl. n.* Woman's breasts, tits. *"¡Qué buenas cacharras tiene esa!" "¡Cuidado! Esa es mi mujer". "Te felicito".* " 'What nice ones that one has!' 'Be careful! That's my wife.' 'Good for you.' " **2.** *L.Am./S, pl. n.* Things. *Mi tía colecciona toda clase de cacharras.* "My aunt collects all kinds of stuff."

CACHARRAZO, 1. *Spain, n.* Smack, whack. *La muchacha le pegó un cacharrazo a Juanito porque él le dijo un piropo feo.* "The girl gave Juanito a whack because he gave her a left-handed compliment." **2.** *Spain, n.* Crash. *Estaba durmiendo yo cuando sentí el cacharrazo en la calle.* "I was sleeping when I heard the big crash out in the street."

CACHARREAR, *L.Am./S, v.* To fix things. *A mi papá le fascina cacharrear.* "My father loves to tinker."

CACHARRO, 1. *L.Am./S, Car., n.* Old car, wreck, jalopy. (Lit. Pot.) *El carro de Lucho es un cacharro.* "Lucho's car is a wreck." **2.** *Spain, n., crim.* Pistol. *¿Sabes dónde puedo conseguirme un cacharro? Tengo que defenderme.* "Do you know where I can get a rod? I have to defend myself." **3.** *Spain, n., drugs.* Joint of marijuana. *Cuando entré estaban sentados fumando un cacharro. El lugar apestaba.* "When I entered they were sitting and smoking a joint. The place stunk." **4.** *Car., n., crim.* Jail. *Están construyendo un cacharro nuevo en mi pueblo.* "They're building a new jail in my town." **5.** *Car., n.* Anus, ass, asshole.

A ese bubarrón le dolerá el cacharro de tanta actividad. "That fag probably has a sore asshole from so much activity."

CACHAS, *Spain, adj.* Muscular. *Jorge está cachas de tanto levantar pesas.* "Jorge is pumped up from lifting weights so much."

CACHAZA, *L.Am./C, n.* Nerve, cheek, chutzpah. *Adriana tuvo la cachaza de mentirme en la cara.* "Adriana had the nerve to lie to my face."

CACHÉ, *Car., n., youth.* Style, charisma. *La nueva novia de Armando tiene mucho caché.* "Armando's new girlfriend has a lot of cachet."

CACHEAR, *L.Am./N, v., crim.* To search, to frisk. *Los policías lo detuvieron y luego lo cachearon.* "The police officers detained him and right away they searched him."

CÁCHER, *Car., n.* Baseball catcher. *Mi hijo es el cácher de un equipo de las ligas menores.* "My son is the catcher on a minor-league team."

CACHETEAR BANQUETAS, *L.Am./N, idiom.* To love, to be wild about. *Desde que conoció a Paty anda cacheteando la banqueta.* "Since he met Patty he's been crazy about her."

CACHETEAR, *Car., v.* To freeload. *Hay personas que prefieren cachetear a pagar lo suyo.* "There are people who prefer to freeload than to pay their own way."

CACHETERO, RA, *Car., adj.* Person who freeloads drinks. *Martín es bien cachetero; nunca compra una bebida ni invita a los otros.* "Martin is a real freeloader; he never buys a drink nor does he invite others."

CACHETÓN, NA, 1. *L.Am./S, n.* Braggart. *La cachetona de Rosario dice que no hay mejor cocinera que ella.* "Bigshot Rosario says that there is no better cook than she." **2.** *L.Am./N, adj.* Fat. *Estaba tan cachetón que casi no se le veían los ojos.* "He was so chubby that you could hardly see his eyes." **3.** *L.Am./N, adj.* Spoiled. *Como no le* *exigen en su nuevo trabajo, la tienen bien cachetona.* "Since they don't demand much in her new job, they have her really spoiled."

CACHIPORRA, *L.Am./N, n.* Club, mace. *Los policías le daban tan tupido con las cachiporras que parecía marimba.* "The cops were hitting him so much with the clubs that it sounded like a marimba."

CACHO, 1. *L.Am./S, n.* Infidelity, cuckoldry. (Lit. Horn.) *A Rodolfo le montaron cacho cuando estaba de viaje.* "When Rodolfo went on a trip, they played around behind his back." **2.** *L.Am./S, n., drugs.* Marijuana joint. *Según Pedro, mejor cachos que pan.* "Pedro prefers joints to bread." **See also SER UN CACHO DE PAN**

CACHONDEO, 1. *Spain, n.* Levity, joking around, hell-raising, partying. *Todos lo pasamos muy bien en la feria. ¡Qué cachondeo!* "We all had a great time at the fair. What a ball!" **2.** *Spain, n.* Trouble, confusion, fuss. *Hubo un cachondeo hoy en el taller. Los trabajadores estaban protestando.* "There was a ruckus today at the shop. The workers were protesting." **3.** *Spain, n.* Runaround. *¿Qué cachondeo es esto? ¿No dijiste que mi coche estaría listo?* "Is this some kind of joke or something? Didn't you tell me that my car would be ready."

CACHONDO, DA, 1. *Spain, adj.* Sexually excited, aroused. *Le confesó a Pepe que estaba muy cachonda por él.* "She confessed to Pepe that she was hot for him." **2.** *Spain, adj.* Jovial, happy. *Mi amigo es un chico cachondo, siempre está dispuesto para la fiesta.* "My friend is a real fun guy; he is always ready for a party." **3.** *L.Am./N, adj.* Hot, cool, great. *Ricardo y Beatriz estaban bien cachondos bailando en la fiesta.* "Ricardo and Beatrice were real hot dancing at the party."

CACHOS, 1. *L.Am./C, pl. n.* Shoes. (Lit. Horns.) *Estos cachos nuevos me duelen.* "These new shoes hurt."

CACHÚ, CHÚA, *Car., adj.* Person with a fat posterior. *Roberto se ha puesto bien cachú en los últimos años.* "Roberto has become a fat ass in recent years."

CACHUCHA, 1. *U.S., n., crim.* Police force, police officer. *La cachucha le agarró con el dinero del banco.* "The cops grabbed him with the bank's money." **2.** *U.S., n., drugs.* Drug stash. *Tenía una cachucha de caballo en esa casa vieja.* "He had a drug stash in that old house."

CACHUQUEAR, *U.S., v.* To do poorly, to screw up, to mess up. *Ya cachuqueaste el año y vas a tener que repetir.* "You screwed up during the entire school year and now you'll have to do it again."

CACO, *L.Am., n.* Armed robber. *Un caco entró al almacén y se lo robó todo.* "An armed robber came into the warehouse and stole everything."

CACOMIXTLE, *L.Am./N, n.* Thief. *Ya era hora que arrestaran a ese cacomixtle.* "It was about time that they arrested that thief."

CACRIATO, TA, *Car., adj.* Wandering person. *Tomás es bien cacriato; no está quieto ni por cinco minutos.* "Thomas is a real wanderer; he can't be still for five minutes."

CACULEO, *Car., n.* Social butterfly. *A Bárbara le encanta el caculeo. Está metida en todo.* "Barbara loves the social world. She's into everything."

CACULERO, RA, *Car., adj.* Social climber. *Los Pérez son unos caculeros que siempre quieren tener roces con la alta sociedad.* "The Perezes are social climbers who always want to be in touch with high society."

CÁCULO SOCIAL, *Car., idiom.* Social butterfly. *La madre de Maruja es un cáculo social.* "Maruja's mother is a social butterfly."

CADAVERIZAR, *L.Am./N, v.* To kill, to murder. *Los narcos cadaverizaron a la competencia.* "The drug dealers got rid of the competition."

CADERAMEN, *Spain, n.* Woman's hips. *Fíjate en el caderamen de esa gachi.* "Look at the hips on that babe."

CAER, 1. *Spain, v.* To be detained. (Lit. To fall.) *Ya cayeron los dos ladrones de los pisos de la esquina.* "They finally picked up the two hoodlums from the apartments on the corner." **2.** *L.Am./N, v.* To propose. *Mañana le voy a caer a Patti.* "Tomorrow I'm going to propose to Patti."

CAER BIEN, *L.Am./S, idiom.* To like someone. *Tu amiga Isabel me cayó super bien.* "I really liked your friend Isabel."

CAER DE MADRE, *L.Am./N, idiom.* To honestly like. *La amiga de Juan me cae de madre.* "I really like Juan's girlfriend."

CAER EL VEINTE, *L.Am./N, idiom.* To realize, to understand. *Estuvo hablando un rato conmigo hasta que me cayó el veinte que era hermano de Tita.* "He was talking to me for a long time until I realized he was Tita's brother."

CAER EN EL AJO DE ALGO, *Car., idiom.* To be in the middle of something. *Tú te caíste en el ajo de algo y quiero saber qué.* "You fell into the middle of something and I want to know what."

CAER EN LA OLLA, *Car., idiom,* To guarantee success. *El contrato ya se cayó en la olla.* "The contract is in the bag."

CAER FRITO, *Car., idiom.* To be annoyed by someone or something. *Me cae frito ese muchacho. Siempre está fastidiando.* "I can't stand that fella. He is always annoying."

CAER GORDO, *L.Am./N, idiom.* To dislike. *Me cae gordo tener que hacer la tarea.* "I don't like to do the homework."

CAER MALA, *Car., idiom.* To menstruate. *Rogelio me dijo que en medio de su luna de miel su mujer cayó mala.* "Rogelio told me that right in the middle of his honeymoon his wife got her period."

CAERLE SURA A ALGUIEN, *U.S., idiom.* To dislike someone. *Me cae sura ese bato.* "I don't like that dude."

CAERSE CON ALGO, *L.Am./N, idiom.* To give money, to hand over. *Cáete con veinte pesos para los refrescos.* "Hand over twenty pesos for sodas."

CAERSE DE CULO, *Spain, idiom.* To be shocked. *Cuando me dijiste lo del arresto de Armando casi me caigo de culo.* "When you told me about Armando's arrest I almost fell on my ass."

CAERSE DE CULO Y ROMPERSE LA POLLA, *Spain, idiom.* To have disastrous luck. *Perder el trabajo y la novia a la vez es caerse de culo y romperse la polla.* "To lose your job and your girlfriend at the same time is like falling on your ass and breaking your dick."

CAERSE DE MORROS, *Spain, idiom.* To fall on one's face. *Estábamos paseando cuando de pronto Pablo se cayó de morros.* "We were taking a stroll when all of a sudden Pablo fell flat on his face."

CAERSE LOS CHONES, *L.Am./N, idiom.* To be amazed, to be surprised. *Se me cayeron los chones cuando nos encontró me mamá.* "I almost fell over when my mother found us."

CAFÉ CON LECHE, *Spain, idiom, n.* Homosexual, effeminate. *El dependiente de esa tienda es un café con leche.* "The clerk at that store is a fairy."

CAFECOLAO See YA ESTÁ EL CAFÉ COLADO

CAFELITO, *Spain, n.* Coffee. *Todas las tardes mi mujer me trae un cafelito y unas galletas.* "Every afternoon my wife brings me a little coffee and some cookies."

CAFETERA (RUSA), 1. *Spain, n.* Jalopy, piece of junk. *El coche de Paco es una cafetera rusa.* "Paco's car is a rattle trap." **2.** *Spain, adj.* Complaining old man. *El viejito de la esquina protesta más que una cafetera rusa.* "That old guy on the corner complains more that a noisy old coffee machine."

CAFIRO, *U.S., n.* Coffee, java. *Tengo sueño, necesito un poco de cafiro.* "I am sleepy. I need a little java."

CAFISIO, *Spain, n., crim.* Pimp. *A la fulanita esa le dio una paliza su cafisio.* "That little whore's pimp beat the hell out of her."

CAFRE, *Spain, n.* Crazy driver. *Me da miedo manejar con*

Victor, es un cafre. "I am afraid to ride with Victor; he is crazy."

CAFRE DEL VOLANTE, *L.Am./N, idiom.* Taxi, truck, or bus driver. *Lo más peligroso de manejar en el D.F. son los cafres del volante.* "The most dangerous part about driving in Federal District are the crazy drivers."

CAGACATRE, *Car., n.* Stupid person, dope. *Yo no voy a hacer un viaje con ese cagacatre. Tendría que explicarle todo.* "I am not going to take a trip with that jerk. I'd have to explain everything to him."

CAGADA, *Spain, L.Am., n.* Mistake, blunder, miss. *Hiciste una cagada hoy Antonio. No saludaste a tu futuro suegro.* "You pulled a boo-boo today, Antonio. You didn't say hello to your future father-in-law."

CAGADERO, *Spain, L.Am., n.* Toilet. (Lit. Shitter.) *"¿Dónde está Teodoro?" "Está en el cagadero"* " 'Where is Teodoro?' 'He is in the shitter.' "

CAGADO, DA, *Spain, L.Am., n.* Coward, chicken. *Tu primo es un cagado. ¿Viste cómo salió corriendo al ver la policía?* "Your cousin is a shitless coward. Did you see how he took off running when he saw the fuzz?"

CAGALERA, *Spain, n.* Fear. *Cuando vi que estaba solo con ese toro me entró una cagalera.* "When I saw that I was alone with that bull, I got the shits."

CAGAO, *L.Am./C, n.* Coward. *Ese tipo es un cagao.* "That guy is a chicken."

CAGAR, 1. *Spain, L.Am., v.* To crap, to shit. *Estaba en el baño tanto tiempo que parecía que estaba cagando un piano.* "He was in the bathroom so long it seemed that he was shitting a piano." **2.** *Spain, L.Am., v.* To ruin something. *Te dije que no jugaras con mi pluma y ya la cagaste.* "I told you not to play around with my pen and now you've ruined it." **3.** *Spain, L.Am., v.* To be surprised. *Cuando nos agarró el profe, aquél se cagó entero.* "When the prof caught us he was amazed."

CAGAR A PEDOS, *L.Am./S, idiom.* To scold, to chew out.

Mi novia me cagó a pedos cuando supo que salí con los amigos. "My girlfriend gave me an ass chewing when she found that I went out with the boys."

CAGAR EL PALO, *L.Am./N, idiom.* To bother, to pester. *Le pegué a mi hermano chico porque ya me cagaba el palo.* "I hit my little brother because he was pushing me."

CAGARLA, *Spain, L.Am., idiom.* To blunder, to make a mistake. *La cagaste Ramón. Te iban a dar el trabajo pero dijiste lo de la cárcel.* "You screwed up, Ramon. They were going to give you the job but you told them about the jail thing."

CAGARSE, 1. *Spain, prnl. v.* To be scared to death, to be scared shitless. *Me cagué de miedo al ver que el tipo me iba a atacar con la navaja.* "I was scared shitless when I saw the guy was going to attack me with the knife." **2.** *Spain, prnl. v.* To shit on something or someone. This expression is used with a variety of negative expressions and insults. *¡Me cago en la leche!* "Shit!" **3.** *L.Am./S, prnl. v.* To lose everything. *Se cagó Manuel, la policia lo agarró con las manos en la masa.* "Manuel screwed himself up, the police caught him red-handed."

CAGARSE EN DIEZ, *Spain, interj.* Expression of anger, rejection, dejection. ("Diez" is a euphemism for "Dios.") *¡Me cago en diez! No me llamaron para el trabajo.* "Shit! They didn't call me for the job."

CAGARSE EN LA HOSTIA, *Spain, interj.* Expression of anger, rejection, dejection; very sacrilegious. *¡Me cago en la hostia! ¡Me robaron el radio del coche!* "God damn it! They stole the car radio!"

CAGARSE EN LA MADRE QUE TE PARIÓ, *Spain, interj.* Exclamation of rejection, anger, admiration. *Me cago en la madre que te parió, que bueno ese chiste.* "I shit on the mother that bore you, that was a really good joke."

CAGARSE EN SU PUTA MADRE, *Spain, idiom.* Gross insult. *Me cago en tu puta madre.* "I shit on your whoring mother."

CAGARSE EN TRES TIEMPOS, *L.Am./S, idiom.* To get scared shitless. *Eduardo se cagó en tres tiempos cuando oyó que venía su padre.* "Eduardo shat a gold brick when he heard his father was coming."

CAGATINTA, *L.Am./N, n.* Attorney. (Lit. Ink-shitter.) *Vas a perder tu caso porque tienes un cagatinta pésimo.* "You're going to lose your case because you've got a shitty lawyer."

CAGATINTAS, *Spain, n.* Office worker. *Esos cagatintas del gobierno se dan importancia que se creen reyes.* "Those government clerks act so important because they think they are kings."

CAGÓDROMO, *Spain, n.* Toilet. *José lleva quince minutos en el cagódromo. Esperemos cinco minutos más.* "Jose has been in the shithouse for fifteen minutes. Let's wait for five more."

CÁGUENSE, *Spain, idiom, youth.* The most! *Ese club es el cáguense.* "That club is the most."

CAHUÍN, *L.Am./S, n.* Trouble. *Rodrigo metió a Carlos en un cahuín con la novia.* "Rodrigo got Carlos in trouble with his girlfriend."

CAÍDO DEL CATRE, *L.Am./S, idiom.* Stupid. *Ni le preguntes nada a ese retaco porque es un caído del catre.* "Don't ask Shorty anything, because he's stupid."

¡CAIFÁS!, *L.Am./N, interj.* Hand it over, right now! *Me vio el billete de a cien y me dice "¡caifás!"* "He saw the one-hundred-peso note and said, 'Quick, hand it over!' "

CAIREL, *L.Am./N, n.* Ringlet, loop. *Chela se hizo un chongo con un cairel a un lado.* "Chela did her hairdo with a ringlet on the side."

CAITEÁRSELAS, *L.Am./C, prnl. v.* To take off running. *Cuando me oyeron venir se las caitearon.* "When they heard me coming they hit the bricks."

CAITES, *L.Am./C, pl. n.* Old shoes. *Al padre de Adolfo le gusta andar con unos caites feos.* "Adolfo's father likes to walk around in old, ugly shoes."

CAJA DE DIENTES, *L.Am., n.* A complete set of dentures. *El dentista le dijo a mi abuelo que necesita una caja de dientes.* "The dentist told my grandfather that he needs a full set of teeth."

CAJA TONTA, *Spain, n.* Television. *Hoy en día los niños pasan demasiado tiempo delante de la caja tonta.* "Nowadays children spend too much time in front of the boob tube."

CAJA, *Car., n.* Handsome man, hunk. *Eduardo es un caja. Es el más guapo de la oficina.* "Eduardo is a hunk. He is the handsomest at the office."

CAJEARSE, *L.Am./N, prnl. v.* To receive a prize. *Ya me andaba cajeando cuando quebraron la ventana del salón de clases.* "I was receiving a prize when they broke the classroom window."

CAJETÓN, *Car., n.* A very handsome man, a real hunk. *El nuevo profesor de biología es un cajetón.* "The new biology professor is a hunk."

CAJETUDA, *U.S., adj.* Sexy. *La nueva secretaria está cajetuda.* "The new secretary is sexy."

CAJÓN, 1. *Spain, n., crim.* Jail. (Lit. Box.) *Pasó dos semanas en el cajón.* "He spent two weeks in the tank." **2.** *L.Am., n.* Coffin. *Estaba tan malo que ya andaba encargando el cajón.* "He was so sick that he was already ordering his coffin." **3.** *L.Am./N, n.* Parking space. *Perdí mi cajón frente a la oficina.* "I lost my parking space in front of the office."

CAJONERÍA, *U.S., n.* Funeral parlor. *Llevaron el cadáver a la cajonería.* "They took the body to the funeral parlor."

CALA See CALADA

CALA, *Spain, n.* Peseta. *Víctor está arruinado, perdió veinte millones de calas en la bolsa.* "Victor is ruined. He lost twenty million pesetas on the stock market."

CALABAZA, *Spain, n.* Head. (Lit. Pumpkin.) *¡Niño! ¿Cuándo vas a usar esa calabaza? Ya te fracasaron en* *dos asignaturas.* "Boy! When are you going to use that bean? Now they flunked you in two subjects."

CALACA, *L.Am./N, n.* Human skeleton. *Estaba tan flaco que le decían El Calaca.* "He was so skinny that they called him Bones."

CALADA, *Spain, n., drugs.* Drag of a cigarette, of a joint. *Guillermo dio una calada honda del porro y se desmayó.* "Guillermo took a deep drag of the joint and passed out."

CALANDRIA, *Spain, n.* Peseta. *¿Cuántas calandrias me va a costar la fiesta?* "How many pesetas is this party going to cost me?"

CALCAR, *Spain, v., crim.* To write a ticket. *El motoricón me calcó por exceso de velocidad.* "The motorcycle cop wrote me a ticket for speeding."

CALCETÍN, *Spain, n.* Condom. (Lit. Sock.) *No llevó Manolo un calcetín y ahora creen que tiene sida.* "Manolo didn't wear a rubber and now they think he has AIDS."

CALCETO, TA, *L.Am./S, n. or adj.* Unreliable. *Camilo es un calceto, me dejó esperando otra vez.* "Camillo is someone you can't count on."

CALCOS, *Spain, pl. n., crim.* Shoes. *Los calcos que nos dan en la cárcel son una mierda.* "The monkey boots that they give us in the clink are shitty."

CALDERA, *Spain, n., sports.* Stomach. (Lit. Boiler.) *A Trabadela le dieron una patada en la caldera.* "They kicked Trabadela in the stomach."

CALDERITA DE LATA, *L.Am./S, idiom.* Impatient, quick-tempered person. *La mujer del director es una calderita de lata, no la provoque Ud.* "The director's wife is hot-tempered, don't provoke her."

CALDO, *Spain, n.* Gasoline. (Lit. Broth.) *Espérame un momento, tengo que echar caldo a mi cafetera.* "Wait a minute for me, I have to put soup in my jalopy."

CALDO DE POLLO, *Car., idiom, drugs.* Heroin. (Lit. Chicken broth.) *El calentoso robaba para conseguir su* *caldo de pollo diario.* "The junkie stole to get his daily fix."

CALDO DE TETA, *Spain, n.* Milk. *El niño está llorando porque quiere el caldo de teta.* "The boy was crying because he wanted his momma's milk."

CALÉ, *Spain, n.* Gypsy. *Había muchos calés en la estación del metro hoy.* "There were a bunch of gypsies at the subway station today."

CALEFA, *L.Am./S, Spain, n.* Heater. *Tengo frío, me parece que no funciona la calefa.* "I'm cold; it seems to me that the heat isn't working."

CALENTAR, *Spain, L.Am., v.* To arouse, to excite sexually. *A esa gachi le gusta ir calentando a todo tío que ve.* "That babe likes going around heating up every guy she sees."

CALENTARSE, *Car., prnl. v.* To get angry. (Lit. To warm up oneself.) *Él se calentó cuando llegaste tarde esta mañana.* "The foreman got hot under the collar when you arrived late this morning."

CALENTÓN, 1. *Car., n.* Anger. *Mira Antoñita, me diste un calentón cuando te vi con ese maleante.* "Look Antoñita, you really pissed me off when I saw you with that hoodlum." **2. CALENTÓN, NA,** *Spain, adj.* Hot to trot. *¡Qué calentón es el marido de la Pepa! Quiere ligarse con todas las que ve.* "Pepa's husband is really hot to trot! He wants to lay everyone he sees."

CALENTORRO, RRA, *Spain, adj.* Hot, aroused. *Se pone calentorra bailando para los tíos en el puticlub.* "She gets hot dancing for the guys at the topless joint."

CALENTOSO, SA, *Car., n., drugs.* Drug addict. *Teodoro es un calentoso desgraciado. Ha dado su vida a la droga.* "Theodoro is a lowdown junkie. He has given his life over to drugs."

CALENTURA, *L.Am., n.* Sexual arousal. *Mujer, con ese vestido me vas a dar calentura.* "Girl, with that dress, you are going to give me a fever!"

CALES, *Spain, pl. n., crim.* Money, coins, dough. *En la cárcel no te dejan tener muchos cales.* "In the clink they don't let you have a lot of dough."

CALETA (DE ALGO), *L.Am./S, adv. or adj.* Much, many, very. *Tenía caleta de frío, por eso me puse el suéter.* "I was very cold; that's why I put on a sweater."

CALICATAS, *Spain, n.* Ass, butt. *Le duelen las calicatas de tanto estar sentado en la sala de urgencia.* "His cheeks hurt from sitting so long in the emergency room."

CALICHE, *L.Am./S, n.* Pejorative Venezuelan term for Colombian. *Muchos caliches frecuentan ese bar.* "A lot of clayheads frequent that bar."

CALIE, *Car., n.* A gossip. *Le contaste mi secreto a Inés. ¡Eres una calié!* "You told my secret to Inez. You're a big mouth!"

CALIENTABRAGUETAS, *Spain, n.* Cockteaser. *Las chicas que trabajan en ese puticlub no son más que calientabraguetas.* "The girls that work in that B joint are nothing more than cockteasers."

CALIENTAPICHAS See CALIENTABRAGUETAS

CALIENTAPOLLAS See CALIENTABRAGUETAS

CALIENTE, 1. *L.Am./S, adj.* Angry. (Lit. Hot.) *Mi mamá se puso caliente cuando vio mi cuarto desordenado.* "My mother got upset when she saw my messy room." **2.** *L.Am., Spain, adj.* Hot, aroused. *Amor mío, hazme eso, me pone tan caliente.* "Do that to me, baby, it gets me so hot!" **3.** *Spain, n., crim.* Criminal slang. *En la cárcel hablamos el caliente.* "In the slammer we speak jailhouse slang." **4.** *Spain, n.* Obsessed with sex. *Rubio es un caliente. Tiene obsesión con el sexo.* "Rubio is a sex maniac. He is obsessed with sex." **5.** *Car., adj., crim.* Stolen (item). *Unos jovencitos querían venderme una casetera caliente.* "Some kids wanted to sell me a hot cassette player."

CALIFORNIANO, *Spain, n., drugs.* Variety of LSD. (Lit. Californian.) *El californiano es más fuerte que el pro-*

ducto fabricado aquí. "Californian LSD is stronger than the product they make here."

CALIMOCHO, *Spain, n.* Combination of Coca-Cola and red wine. *Esta tarde voy a sentarme en el patio y voy a tomarme un calimocho.* "This afternoon I am going to sit down on the patio and have a 'calimocho'."

CALLE See ESCUPIR A LA CALLE

CALLO, *Spain, n.* Very ugly woman. (Lit. Corn.) *La mujer de Álvaro es un callo.* "Alvaro's wife is as ugly as a callus."

CALMADA, *L.Am./N, adj.* Calm. *Tú llévatela calmada y no te aceleres.* "Take it easy and don't get hyper."

CALÓ, 1. *Spain, n.* Gypsy, *Había un caló yendo de bar en bar veniendo chucherías.* "There was a gypsy going from bar to bar selling trinkets." **2.** *Spain, n.* Gypsy language. *George Borrow vendía la Biblia traducida al caló.* "George Borrow sold the bible translated into Romany." **3.** *L.Am./N, n.* Slang. *Los criminales tienen su propio caló.* "Criminals speak their own slang."

CALORRILLO, LLA, *Spain, adj. or n.* Little gypsy. *Estábamos comiendo cuando llegó un grupo de calorrillas a bailar rumbas.* "We were eating when a group of gypsy girls showed up to dance rumbas."

CALORRO, RRA, *Spain, n. or adj.* Gypsy. *En la feria se ven calorros por todas partes.* "At the fair you see gypsies all over the place."

CALUGAZO, *L.Am./S, n.* A big kiss on the lips. *Adelita le dio un calugazo a Gustavo delante de todos los profes.* "Adelita gave Gustavo a big kiss on the lips in front of all the profs."

CALVOROTA, *Spain, adj.* Bald. *Jorge se preocupa de que se va a quedar calvorota.* "Jorge is worried about going bald."

CALZÓN See HABLAR A CALZÓN QUITADO

CALZONAZOS, *Spain, n.* Condescending or snobbish

man. *No aguanto al calzonazos de Julio. Se cree mejor que nadie.* "I can't stand that snob Julio. He thinks he is better than everybody."

CALZONCILLOS See DEJAR EN CALZONCILLOS

CALZONES, *L.Am./N, pl. n.* Briefs, panties. *No encontré calzones limpios que ponerme esta mañana.* "I couldn't find any clean underwear this morning."

CAMA REDONDA, *Spain, idiom.* Sexual game with multiple partners. (Lit. Round bed, play on "round table.") *La mujer entró y pescó al marido en cama redonda con dos rubias.* "The wife went in and caught her husband playing in bed with two blondes."

CAMARETA, *Spain, n.* Waiter. *Oiga, dígale al camareta que no podíamos esperar más tiempo.* "Listen, tell the waiter that we couldn't wait any longer."

CAMARÓN, *L.Am./S, n.* A nap, a brief break. *Necesito un buen camarón después de comer.* "I need a good nap after I eat."

CAMARUTA, *Spain, n.* Waitress at a hostess bar. *¡Qué buenas camarutas tienen en este bar!* "What nice waitresses they have in this bar!"

CAMBIAR DE PALO PA' RUMBA, *Car., idiom.* To change one's beliefs. *Se las daba de muy católico, pero en cuanto triunfó la revolución cambió de palo pa' rumba.* "He put on that he was very Catholic, but when the revolution won he changed his shirt."

CAMBIAR EL AGUA AL CANARIO, *Spain, idiom, joc.* To urinate, to pee. *Con permiso, tengo que ir a cambiar el agua al canario.* "With permission, I have to go water the canary."

CAMBIAR EL AGUA AL RIÑÓN, *L.Am./N, idiom.* **See CAMBIAR EL AGUA AL CANARIO**

CAMBIAR EL AGUA DE LAS ACEITUNAS, See CAMBIAR EL AGUA AL CANARIO

CAMBIAR EL CALDO A LOS GARBANZOS, See

CAMBIAR EL AGUA AL CANARIO

CAMBIAR EL CHIP, *Spain, idiom, youth.* To change one's way of thinking. *Hay que cambiar el chip para adaptarse al mundo de la tecnología.* "You're going to have to change your chip to adapt to the world of technology."

CAMBIAR EL DISCO, *Car., idiom.* To change subjects. *Roberto, cambia el disco ya, estamos hartos de escuchar siempre lo mismo.* "Can it, Roberto, we are tired of hearing the same thing all the time."

CAMBIARSE A LA CIUDAD DE LOS CALVOS, *Spain, idiom.* To die. *¿Ya oíste? El papá de Alfredo ya se cambió a la ciudad de los calvos.* "Did you hear? Alfredo's dad kicked the bucket."

CAMELAR, 1. *Spain, v., youth.* To love. *Julio camela a Carmen.* "Julio is crazy about Carmen." **2.** *Spain, v.* To be a sycophant, to brownnose, to suck up to. *Mira como el nuevo empleado camela al jefe. ¡Qué pelotero!* "Look how the new employee sucks up to the boss. What a kiss-ass!" **3.** *Spain, v., youth.* To win over, to court. *Gustavo camelaba la novia durante cinco años y ella al fin le dejó.* "Gustavo dated his sweetheart for five years and finally she left him."

CAMELLAR, *L.Am./S, v.* To work. *Antes camellaba en el taller de Fermín.* "Before I worked at Fermin's shop."

CAMELLEAR, *Spain, v., drugs.* To sell drugs at the street level. *Detuvieron al ladrón por camellear caballo.* "They grabbed the hoodlum for hustling horse."

CAMELLO, 1. *L.Am./S, n.* Job. (Lit. Camel.) *Tengo un buen camello.* "I have a good job." **2.** *Spain, n., drugs.* Drug dealer. *Arrestaron al tío por ser camello.* "They arrested the guy for being a drug hustler."

CAMELO, *Spain, n., crim.* Swindle, deception. *Hay mucho camelo en la internet.* "There is a lot of conning on the internet."

CAMINAR, 1. *L.Am./N, v., crim.* To steal. (Lit. To walk.) *Héctor tuvo que caminar el dinero del lonche.* "Hector had to steal to have lunch money." **2.** *L.Am./N, v., crim.* To go to jail. *"Ahora sí, vas a caminar," le dijeron cuando le sacaron la pistola.* " 'Now you're really going to the slammer,' they said when they took away his pistol."

CAMIÓN, *L.Am./N, n.* Bus. (Lit. Truck.) *Invité mi novia al cine pero no tengo ni para el camión.* "I invited my girlfriend to the movies but I don't have money even for the bus." **See also ESTAR COMO UN CAMIÓN**

CAMISA, *Spain, n., drugs.* Wrapping of a heroin hit. (Lit. Shirt.) *Llevaba 15 camisas de heroína en su bolsillo cuando lo arrestaron.* "He had 15 hits of heroin in his pocket when they arrested him."

CAMÓN, *Car., n.,* Automobile rim. *Los ladrones me dejaron el carro en los camones.* "The thieves left my car on the rims." **See also ESTAR EN EL CAMÓN, IR AL CAMÓN**

CAMOTE, *L.Am./N, n.* Penis. *Ese tipo siempre anda jugando con el camote.* "That guy is always playing around with his dick."

CAMPANA See TOCAR LA CAMPANA

CAMPANEAR, *Spain, v.* To take a stroll, to go for a walk. *Vamos a campanear por el olivar.* "Let's go take a walk through the olive grove."

CAMPEONA DE NATACIÓN, *L.Am./N, n.* Shapeless girl. (Word play on "nada" meaning both "swims" and "nothing.") *Rebe es campeona de natación. Nada por delante, nada por detrás.* "Rebe is a shapeless girl. Nothing in front and nothing behind."

CAMPO See SER MÁS DE CAMPO QUE LAS AMAPOLAS

CANA, 1. *L.Am./S, n., crim.* Police. *La cana tardó dos segundos en llegar.* "The cops got there in two seconds." **2.** *L.Am./S, n.* Jail. *Lo metieron a la cana por ladrón.* "They put him in the clink for being a crook."

CAÑA, 1. *Car., n.* Dollar. *Ese servicio te va a costar cinco cañas.* "That service is going to cost you five bucks."

2. *Spain, n.* Glass of beer or wine. *Vamos al bar de los mellizos para tomarnos una caña de cerveza.* "Let's go to the twins' bar to have a glass of beer." **3.** *Car., n.* Moonshine rum. *Se emborrachó Pedro con media botella de caña. Es muy fuerte.* "Pedro got drunk on half a bottle of moonshine rum. It's real strong." **4.** *Car., n., sports.* Baseball bat. *Andrés colecciona las cañas de famosos bateadores.* "Andres collects the bats of famous hitters."

CANARIO, *Spain, n.* Penis. (Lit. Canary.) *¡Ciérrate la bragueta coño! o se te va a escapar el canario.* "Close your fly you fool, or the canary will get out."

CAÑAS, 1. *L.Am./C, pl. n.* Colones, Costa Rican money. *¿Sabes a cómo está el dólar a cambio de las cañas?* "Do you know what the exchange is between dollars and colones?" **2.** *L.Am./N, pl. n.* Legs. *Me duelen las cañas.* "My sticks hurt."

CAÑAZO, 1. *Car., n.* Double shot of a hard drink. *Estaba tomando cañazos de caña y lo tuvieron que llevar a casa. Es un borracho.* "He was drinking double shots of moonshine rum and they had to carry him home; he's a drunk." **2.** *Car., n., sports.* In baseball, a long hit. *García pegó un cañazo en la novena entrada pero era tarde.* "Garcia hit a long one in the ninth inning but it was too late."

CANCERBERO, *Spain, n., sports.* Goalie. *El equipo de Sevilla tiene un cancerbero nuevo.* "The Seville team has a new goalie."

CANCO, *Spain, n.* Homosexual, effeminate. *Esa calle está llena de bares de cancos.* "That street is full of gay bars."

CANDELA, 1. *Car., n.* A sparkling, bubbly, effervescent person. *Solita es una candela, es enérgica y sonriente siempre.* "Solita is a sparkler; she is always energetic and smiling." **2.** *Car., n.* A difficult job. *Esa reparación es candela. ¿Tú crees que puedes terminarla para mañana?* "This repair is tough. Do you think that you can finish it by tomorrow?"

CANDONGA, *Spain, n.* Peseta. *Oye Pepe, préstame unas candongas hasta el miércoles.* "Hey Pepe, lend me some moola until Wednesday."

CANEAR, *Spain, v.* To hit, to punch. *Joselito le caneó uno bueno al rafián.* "Joselito gave the hood a good punch."

CANECA, *L.Am./S, n.* Trash basket. *Lo encontré en la caneca.* "I found it in the trash basket."

CANECO, CA, *Car., adj.* Person who carries a flask of rum in order to take a sip at any time. *El Sr. Arredondo es un caneco, lleva su traguito en el bolsillo.* "Mr. Arredondo is a serious drinker; he always has his drink in his pocket."

CAÑERÍA, *Spain, n., drugs.* Vein where drug is injected. (Lit. Pipe.) *Toñio tenía el brazo todo picado donde pinchaba su cañería.* "Tonio had his arm all pockmarked at the places he mainlined."

CAÑERO, *Spain, adj., youth.* Fantastic, cool, super cool. *Esa canción es muy cañera.* "That song is too much."

CANGREJO, *Spain, n.* Twenty-five-peseta coin. (Lit. Crab.) *Un momento, se me cayó un cangrejo del bolsillo.* "Just a moment, a quarter fell out of my pocket."

CANGRI See CANGREJO

CANGRIO See CANGREJO

CANGURO, 1. *Spain, n., youth.* Babysitter. (Lit. Kangaroo.) *Tenemos un canguro nuevo para los pipiolos.* "We have a new sitter for the rugrats." **2.** *Spain, n., crim.* Police van for transporting prisoners. *El canguro llevaba seis presos cuando cayó por el terraplén.* "The police van was carrying six prisoners when it went over the cliff."

CANICAS, *Spain, n.* Testicles, balls (Lit. Marbles.) *Doctor, mi hijo tiene un sarpullido en sus canicas, ¿qué le puede recetar?* "Doctor, my son has a rash on his little balls, can you prescribe something?"

CANICO, CA, *Spain, n.* Old person. *A las tres llega el autobús con los canicos americanos.* "At three o'clock the bus arrives with the elderly Americans."

CANIJO, 1. *L.Am./N, adj.* Mean, despicable. *El hijo de Sandra es muy canijo. A diario anda haciendo diabluras.* "Sandra's son is real nasty. He's always getting into mischief." **2.** *L.Am./N, adj.* Hard, difficult. *Está canijo educar a tus hijos con lo caro que sale el colegio.* "It's tough to educate your children as expensive as school is."

CANILLA, *L.Am./S, n.* Newspaper hawker. *Compré el diario del canilla de la esquina.* "I bought the newspaper from the hawker on the corner."

CAÑIÑA, *Car., n.* Animal excrement, turds. *La calle delante de esa casa siempre está llena de cañiña.* "The street in front of that house is always full of dog turds."

CAÑITA, *Spain, n., drugs.* Thin marijuana joint. *Ramón estaba echando una cañita de gloria cuando entró su madre.* "Ramon was puffing on a thin joint when his mother came in."

CAÑÓN, 1. *Spain, adj., youth.* Great, to die for, something else. (Lit. Cannon.) *El concierto fue cañón.* "The concert was out of sight." **2.** *Spain, adj.,* Woman with great body. *Está cañón la novia de Julio.* "Julio's girlfriend is a ten." **3.** *L.Am./N, n.* Penis. *La puta me tuvo que inspeccionar el cañón antes de poder cogérmela.* "The hooker had to inspect my cannon before she would fuck me." **4.** *L.Am./N, adj.* Drunk. *Pedro ya está cañón otra vez. Siempre toma demasiado.* "Pedro is already drunk again. He always drinks too much." **5.** *L.Am./S, n.* Something positive. *La entrevista con el jefe salió como cañón.* "The interview with the boss went off like a cannon." **6.** *L.Am./N, adj.* Difficult. *Está cañón pagar la escuela de tus hijos cuando nunca aumentan el sueldo.* "It's difficult to pay for your children's schooling when you never get a raise."

CAÑONAZO, *Spain, n., sports.* Hard shot. *Rodríguez metió un cañonazo a la portería para ganar el partido.* "Rodriguez put a cannon shot into the goal to win the game."

CAÑONEAR, 1. *Car., v.* To cut in. *Como hay personas esperando, voy a tener que cañonear para pasar primero.*

"Since there are people waiting, I'll have to cut in in order to be first." **2.** *Car., v.* To fart. *Paco, deja de cañonear, vas a dejar la casa apestada.* "Paco, stop farting. You are going to smell up the house." **3.** *Car., v.* To have sex with a woman. *La mujer del abogado llegó cuando éste estaba cañoneando la secretaria.* "The lawyer's wife arrived when he was drilling the secretary."

CAÑONERAS, *Car., pl. n.* Marital difficulties. *Nuestros amigos Paquita y Javier están pasando por unas cañoneras.* "Our friends Paquita and Javier are going through some hard times in their marriage."

CANSÓN, NA, *L.Am./S, adj.* Bothersome, annoying person. *¡Qué cansón eres Diego! ¿Por qué no te vas a otra parte?* "What a pain you are Diego! Why don't you go somewhere else."

CANTADA, *Spain, n.* Mistake, error. *Hice una cantada en no ir a hablar con el profe. Creo que me canteó por eso.* "I blew it by not going to talk with the prof. I think that's why he failed me."

CANTALETA, *L.Am./S, n.* To scold, to read the riot act, to give a chewing out. *Cuando llegue mi hija le voy a dar una cantaleta por venir tan tarde.* "When my daughter gets here, I'm going to read her the riot act for coming home late."

CANTAMAÑANAS, *Spain, n.* Teller of tall tales. *Juanito es un cantamañanas. No sé si debo creerlé o no.* "Juanito is a bullshitter. I don't know if I should believe him or not."

CANTAR, 1. *Spain, L.Am., v., crim.* To confess, to squeal, to sing. (Lit. To sing.) *Una vez que se dio cuenta de la pena que enfrentaba cantó como un gallo.* "Once he became aware of the sentence that he was facing, he sang like a rooster." **2.** *Spain, v.* To smell bad. *¡Huy! ¡Cómo cantan las gambas! Están malas.* "Boy those shrimp stink! They are bad."

CANTAR EL GALLO, *Car., idiom.* The onset of menstruation. *"¿Cuántos años tenía Concha cuando le cantó el* *gallo?" "Doce años tenía".* " 'How old was Concha when she first had the menses?' 'She was twelve.' "

CANTAR FLOR, *L.Am./S, idiom.* To die. *Solita dijo que el caballo de Antonio cantó flor ayer.* "Solita said that Antonio's horse died yesterday."

CANTAR LA GUACARA, *L.Am./N, idiom.* To vomit. *No sé qué fue lo que le hizo daño, pero andaba cantando la guacara toda la noche.* "I don't know what made him sick, but he was throwing up all night."

CANTAR LAS CUARENTA A ALGUIEN, *Spain, idiom.* To scold, to berate. *Cuando Juan llegó tarde, el jefe le cantó las cuarenta.* "When Juan arrived late, the boss screamed at him."

CÁNTAROS, *Spain, pl. n.* Woman's breasts, jugs. (Lit. Jugs.) *¡Mira los cántaros que lleva esa!* "Look at the jugs she is carrying!"

CANTE, 1. *Spain, n., crim.* Confession, information. *El cree que con ese cante se va a salvar.* "He thinks that that song and dance is going to save him." **2.** *Spain, n.* Bad smell. *Hay un cante por aquí de algo podrido.* "There's a stink of something rotten here."

CANTIDAD, *L.Am./N, adv.* A lot. (Lit. Quantity.) *Amor mío, te quiero cantidad.* "Honey, I love you a bunch."

CANTIDUBI, *Spain, n.* A lot. *Había una cantidubi de gente en la emisora.* "There was a bunch of people at the radio station."

CANTIMPLORAS, *Spain, n.* Woman's breasts, jugs. (Lit. Canteens.) *¡Qué buenas cantimploras tienen esas chicas!* "What nice gazongas those girls have."

CANTÓN, *L.Am./N, U.S., n., youth.* Home, dwelling, apartment. *Nada más deja llegar a mi cantón antes de ir a la fiesta.* "Just let me stop off at my pad before going to the party."

CANTÚO, A, *Spain, adj.* Having a great body. *Josefa está cantúa.* "Josefa is luscious."

CANUTO, 1. *Spain, n., drugs.* Joint. *Joaquín siempre tiene un canuto en la boca.* "Joaquin always has a joint of maryjane in his mouth." **CANUTO, TA, 2.** *Car., n.* A slow learner. *El hijo menor de los Garza es un canuto. Le pusieron un maestro especial.* "Garza's youngest son is a slow learner. They gave him a special teacher."

CAO, *Spain, adj., sports.* Unconscious, out cold. *Pepe se quedó cao en el tercer asalto.* "Pepe was out cold in the third round."

CAPADOR, *Spain, n., crim.* Blackjack. *El policía le dio con un capador y se cayó al suelo.* "The police hit him with a blackjack and he fell to the ground."

CAPAO, *Car., n.* Coward. *¡No seas capao Luis! Reclama tus derechos.* "Don't be a chicken Luis! Claim your rights."

CAPICÚA, *Spain, adj. or n.* Ugly person, person whose face and ass match. *Ese muchacho es capicúa, tiene cara de culo.* "That guy is a palindrome. His face is just like his ass."

CAPIRULO, *Spain, n., mil.* Captain. *El capirulo canceló todos los permisos.* "The captain cancelled all leaves."

CAPISCAR, *Spain, v.* To understand, to comprehend. (From Italian "capire," to understand). *Capisco amigo, no me tienes que decir más.* "I get it. You don't have to tell me more."

CAPITALISTA, *Spain, n., sports.* Spontaneous bullfighter. (Lit. Capitalist.) *Se lanzó un capitalista a la rueda con el tercer toro y no hizo mal.* "An amateur jumped into the ring with the third bull and didn't do bad."

CAPO, 1. *L.Am./S, adj.* Intelligent, brilliant. (From Italian "capo" [chief].) *¡Qué capo! ¿De dónde sacaste la idea para ese cuadro?* "How cool! Where did you get the idea for that painting?" **2.** *L.Am., n.* Big boss, top man. *La policía capturó al capo del cartel de la droga.* "The police captured the head of the drug cartel."

CAPOTE, *L.Am./N, n.* Foreskin. *Al niño le hicieron la* *circunsición y le quitaron el capote.* "They circumcised the boy and took away his hood."

CAPRICHO, *Spain, n.* Young lover of older person, usually paid. (Lit. Fancy.) *Ese joven es el capricho de Doña Beatriz, la directora de la revista.* "That young man is the toy of Ms. Beatriz, the director of the magazine."

CAPULLADA, *Spain, n.* Stupid comment, nonsense. *Maribel siempre está diciendo capulladas.* "Maribel is always talking nonsense."

CAPULLO, 1. *Spain, n.* Foreskin. *Ese es más feo que el capullo de un pene.* "He is uglier than a dick's foreskin." **2.** *Spain, n.* Stupid, asshole, fuckup. *Yo no voy a dar más trabajo a ese capullo. Todo lo que toca sale mal.* "I am not going to give anymore work to that fuckup. Everything he touches turns out bad."

CAQUI See MARCAR EL CAQUI

CARA, *Spain, L.Am., n.* Brazeness, boldness. (Lit. Face.) *¡Qué cara tienes para decirme eso! Yo soy tu padre.* "You're pretty bold to say that to me. I'm your father."

CARA DE ALGUACIL, *Spain, idiom.* Somber-looking. *¿Qué le pasa a Jaime? Parece que tiene cara de alguacil.* "What's the matter with Jaime? He looks gloomier than an undertaker."

CARA DE CEMENTO See CARADURA

CARA DE CHISTE, *Spain, idiom.* Ridiculous, funny-looking. *Tienes cara de chiste con esa pintura. ¿Adónde vas a ir así?* "You look funny with that makeup! Where are you going like that?"

CARA DE CULO, *L.Am./S, idiom.* Bad expression, sourpuss. (Lit. Ass-face.) *No me pongas esa cara de culo.* "Don't give me that sourpuss."

CARA DE MALA LECHE, *Spain, idiom.* Mean look on one's face. *Cuidado con el jefe hoy. Ha llegado con cara de mala leche.* "Be careful with the boss today. He showed up with a mean look on his face."

CARA DE PIJO, *Spain, idiom.* Having the face of a clown of jokester. *¡Qué cara de pijo tiene el muchacho de la heladería!* "The kid from the ice cream shop really has a prankster's face!"

CARA DE PÓQUER, *Spain, idiom.* Poker face. *¿Te has fijado en la cara de póquer que tiene el padre de Paco? No cambia.* "Did you notice the poker face on Paco's father? It doesn't change."

CARA DE SARGENTO, *Spain, idiom.* Somber-looking. (Lit. Face of a sergeant.) *La nueva maestra tiene cara de sargento.* "The new teacher has a sergeant's face."

CARA O CRUZ, *L.Am., idiom.* Heads or tails. *Cara pago yo, cruz pagas tú.* "Heads I pay, tails you pay."

CARABA, *Spain, adj.* The most, far-out, the extreme (positive or negative). *Esa música es caraba. Nunca he oído algo así.* "That music is far-out. I've never heard anything like that."

CARABINA, *Spain, n., youth.* Companion, sidekick. (Lit. Carbine.) *Luisa siempre viene aquí con su carabina.* "Luisa always comes here with her sidekick."

CARACULO, *Spain, n.* Ass face. *Aquí viene caraculo. Mira qué feo es el tipo.* "Here comes ass-face. Look how ugly the guy is."

CARADURA, 1. *L.Am./S, adj.* Brassy, cheeky, bold. *Jorge es muy caradura con la gente que no lo conoce.* "Jorge is real brassy with people who don't know him." **2.** *Spain, n.* Boldness, brazeness. *Le dije que tenía un mensaje para el director y me dejó entrar. ¡Hay que tener caradura!* "I told her that I had a message for the director and she let me in. You've got to be bold." **3.** *Spain, n.* Shameless individual. *No quiero nada que ver con ese caradura. Es un sinvergüenza.* "I don't want anything to do with that wiseass. He's a bastard."

CARAJADA, *Spain, n.* Stupidity, dumb thing. *¡Ya metí la pata! Cometí una carajada en no escribirte.* "I put my foot in it! I did a dumb thing in not writing you."

CARAJADAS, *L.Am./C, pl. n.* Things or deeds. *Juan, deja de hacer carajadas para hacer rabiar a tu hermano.* "Juan, stop doing things to tease your brother."

CARAJILLO, 1. *L.Am./C, n.* Children. *Julieta y su marido llevaron los carajillos a la playa.* "Julieta and her husband took the kids to the beach." **2.** *Spain, n.* Drink made of coffee and a liquor. *Después de comer nos preparó Amparo un carajillo y conversamos por horas.* "After eating, Amparo prepared us a coffee with liqueur and we conversed for hours."

CARAJITO, *L.Am./S, n.* Child, kid. *Llevé los carajitos al parque esta mañana para jugar un rato.* "I took the kids to the park this morning to play for a while."

¡CARAJO!, *L.Am./N, interj.* Damn! *¡Carajo! Siempre me dejan el trabajo más pesado.* "Damn! They always leave me the heaviest job."

CARAJO, 1. *Spain, n.* Penis. *Su padre la pilló agarrada al carajo del novio.* "Her father caught her holding on to her boyfriend's prick." **2.** *Spain, n.* Conversational crutch. *Bueno, entonces me dió esta carajo cosa y me dijo que la guardara.* "Well, then he gave me this damn thing and told me to keep it." **3.** *Car., interj.* Expression of disgust, anger, joy, approval. *¡Carajo! Te dije que no quería que me llamaras al trabajo.* "Damn! I told you I didn't want you to call me at work." **4. CARAJO, JA,** *Spain, adj.* Gorked, dopey, out to lunch. *Adelita está caraja. Parece que está en otro mundo.* "Adelita is out to lunch. She seems to be in another world."

CARÁTULA, *L.Am./N, n.* Human face. *Se le veía en la carátula que le gustaba la muchacha.* "You could see on his face that he liked the girl."

¡CARAY!, *L.Am./N, interj.* Darn it! Rats! *¡Caray, don Melchor! No se le hace mucho pagar cien pesos?* "Darn it, Melchor, sir! Doesn't it seem like a lot to pay a hundred pesos?"

CARBÓN See SE ACABO EL CARBÓN

CARBURADOR UNIVERSAL, *L.Am./N, n.* Good stomach, digestive system. *A mí sírveme tequila o ron. Yo tengo carburador universal.* "Serve me tequila or rum, my gut will handle anything!"

CARBURAR, 1. *Spain, v.* To work properly. (Lit. To carburet.) *Ese aparato no carbura bien. Vas a tener que llevarlo al técnico.* "This thing isn't working right. You'll have to take it to a technician." **2.** *Spain, v.* To think. *Tú no estás carburando muy bien, Ricardo. Deja el asunto por algún tiempo.* "You're not thinking very well Ricardo. Leave the matter alone for a while."

CARCA, *Spain, adj.* Reactionary, ultra-conservative. *El padre de Elena es muy carca. ¡Y tú izquierdista! ¡Vaya dos!* "Elena's father is ultra-conservative and you a leftist! What a pair!"

CARCACHA, *L.Am./N, n.* Jalopy. *La carcacha de Sergio ya ha de tener unos diez años.* "Sergio's jalopy must be ten years old."

CARCAMÁN, NA, *Car., n.* Raggedy person. *Me parece que ese carcamán vive debajo del puente.* "I think that raggedy guy lives under the bridge."

CARCELARIO, *Spain, n., crim.* Jailhouse slang. *Hablando en carcelario, los chabolos de este cajón son chungos.* "Speaking in jailhouse slang, the rooms in this Hilton are crappy."

CARDÍACO, CA, *L.Am./N, adj.* Hyper. (Lit. Cardiac.) *María está siempre muy cardíaca, ¿estará tomando algo más que café?* "Maria is always real hyper. Could she be taking something more than coffee?"

CARDO, DA, *Spain, adj.* Cold, unaffectionate, antisocial person. *Estan cardo que no saluda ni a su madre.* "He's so cold he wouldn't greet even his mother."

CARETA, *L.Am./S, n.* Hypocritical person, false person. *¡Qué careta sos vos! Decís que sos muy religioso.* "What a hypocrite you are! You say you are very religious."

CARETO, *Spain, n., youth.* Face. *Siempre te pones ese* *careto cuando te pido un favor.* "You always get that face when I ask you for a favor."

CARGADA, *Spain, n., youth.* Failing grade. *¿Ya le dijiste a tu padre lo de la cargada?* "Did you tell your father about the failing grade?"

CARGAR, *Car., v.* To load the dice. (Lit. To load.) *Los cabrones cargaron los dados. Y por eso perdimos.* "The bastards loaded the dice and that is why we lost."

CARGAR LA BARRIGA, *Spain, n.* To get someone pregnant. *Mi hermano ya cargó la barriga de la novia y mis padres están negros.* "My brother knocked up his girlfriend and my parents are furious."

CARGAR LA CRUZ, *L.Am./N, idiom.* Hangover. *Se me pasaron las copas y ahora me toca cargar la cruz.* "I had a little too much to drink and now I have to bear the cross."

CARGAR MOCHILA, *L.Am./N, idiom.* Pregnant. *Ana se fue con el novio y ya carga mochila.* "Ana went off with her boyfriend and now she is carrying the package."

CARGARSE, 1. *Spain, v.* To break, to destroy, to ruin something. *Ya la cargaste hijo. Ya no va a funcionar.* "Now you broke it son. Now it is not going to work." **2.** *Spain, prnl. v.* To have sex with, to screw, to fuck. *Había varias parejas en el parque cargándose sin darse cuenta de nada.* "There were several couples in the park screwing, oblivious to everything." **3.** *Spain, prnl. v.* To dismiss, to fire. *Le cargaron a Carlos en el trabajo por llegar siempre tarde.* "They fired Carlos from work for always showing up late." **4.** *Spain, prnl. v., crim.* To kill. *Se cargaron al chalao por chivato.* "They killed the dude for being a squealer."

CARGÁRSELA CON TODO EL EQUIPO, *Spain, idiom, youth.* To make a serious mistake, to get into trouble. *La cargaste con todos por no decir la verdad.* "You fucked up royally by not telling the truth."

CARICORTAO, TA, *Car., n.* Scarface. *El caricortao en la* *esquina no es tan peligroso como parece.* "The scarface on the corner isn't as dangerous as he looks."

CARIOCA, *Car., n.* Puerto Rican shuttle van. *Voy al trabajo en la carioca todos los días.* "I go to work on the shuttle every day."

CARMELITA, *Car., adj.* Brown. (Lit. Carmelite.) *Ayer me compré un vestido carmelita que está monísimo.* "Yesterday I bought a brown dress that's real cute."

CARNAL, 1. *U.S., n.* Brother. *Mi carnal se fue para San José.* "My brother left for San Jose." **2.** *L.Am./N, n.* Brother, partner, friend, companion. *Voy a pedirle la bici a mi carnal Pedro.* "I am going to ask my bro Pedro for the bike."

CARNE See TENER MENOS CARNE QUE EL PUCHERO DE UNA GITANA

CARNICERO, *Spain, L.Am., n.* Incompetent surgeon. (Lit. Butcher.) *Ese carnicero operó a mi madre y le dejó el bisturí adentro.* "That butcher operated on my mother and left a scalpel inside."

CAROTA, *Spain, n.* Wise guy, smart-ass. *A ese carota no le invito más. Insultó a todos mis amigos.* "I'm not inviting that wiseass anymore. He insulted all my friends."

CARPA, *L.Am./S, n.* Stand, usually made of canvas. (Lit. Tent.) *Estaban vendiendo comida en una carpa en la feria.* "They were selling food from a stand at the fair."

CARRACUCA See SER MÁS FEO QUE CARRACUCA

CARRADA, *L.Am./S, n.* A lot of something. *Mi hijo tiene una carrada de juguetes que no sé dónde meterlos.* "My son has a truckload of toys and I don't know where to put them."

CARRANCEAR, *L.Am./N, v.* To rob, to steal. *El no trabaja, sólo sale a carrancear algo para venderlo después.* "He doesn't work; he just goes out to see what he can steal to sell later."

CARRANCHO, *Car., n.* Run-down, worn-out thing. *Ese*

carrancho anda bien todavía. "This old thing still runs well."

CARRERA, 1. *Spain, n.* Taxi ride. (Lit. Race.) *La carrera del centro hasta el aeropuerto tarda unos veinte minutos.* "The cab ride from downtown to the airport takes around twenty minutes." **2.** *Spain, n.* Prostitute's stroll. *La carrera de esa tía es cerca del río.* "That hooker's stroll is by the river." **3.** *Car., n.* Prostitution. *Esa putita lleva muchos años en la carrera.* "That little whore has been in the profession for many years."

CARRERITAS, *Car., pl. n.* Diarrhea. (Lit. Little races.) *Juan llamó para decir que no viene al trabajo porque tiene las carreritas.* "Juan called to say that he wasn't coming to work today because he had the runs."

CARRETA, 1. *L.Am./S, n.* Lie, exaggeration, tall tale. (Lit. Cart.) *No me vengas con esa carreta. La he oído antes.* "Don't come to me with that story. I've heard that one before." **2.** *L.Am./S, n.* Good friend. *El carreta Jorge Pérez ganó dinero como loco en su última presentación.* "My pal Jorge Perez made money like crazy on his last presentation."

CARRETE, *L.Am./S, n.* Fun. (Lit. Reel.) *Pasé una tarde estupenda; fue todo un carrete.* "I had a great afternoon. Everything was a blast!"

CARRETEAR, *L.Am./S, v.* To go out on the town. *Esta noche vamos a carretear hasta tarde.* "Tonight we are going partying until late."

CARRETILLERO, *L.Am./S, n.* Liar, bullshitter. *Tomás es un carretillero.* "Tomas is a bullshitter."

CARRILLUDO, *L.Am./N, n.* Critic, cynic. *Es muy carrilludo Humberto, nunca nos deja en paz.* "Humberto is a real cynic; he never leaves us alone."

CARRO See APEARSE DEL CARRO

CARROCERÍA, *Spain, n.* Figure, body. (Lit. Car body.) *La chica que vive en frente tiene buena carrocería.* "The girl that lives across the street has a nice body."

CARTELÚO, LÚA, *L.Am./S, adj.* Very good, excellent. *Ese retrato está cartelúo; se te parece un montón.* "That portrait is cool, it's a great likeness."

CARTILLA, *L.Am./N, n.* ID card. *Me pidieron la cartilla pero la dejé en casa.* "They asked for my ID card, but I left it at home."

CARTUCHO, CHA, 1. *L.Am./S, adj.* Old-fashioned, conservative. *Mis padres son muy cartuchos y creen que debemos estar en casa para las doce.* "My parents are behind the times and think we should be at home by twelve." **2.** *L.Am./S, n.* Virgin. *Anita se hace la vampiresa y yo estoy seguro de que es cartucha.* "Anita plays the vamp, but I am sure she's a virgin."

CASA, *Spain, n., sports.* Home field. (Lit. House.) *Este domingo Sevilla juega en casa.* "This Sunday Sevilla plays at home."

CASA CHICA, *L.Am./N, n.* House maintained by married man for his mistress. *Abel le puso casa chica a su amiguita.* "Abel set up a little love nest for his mistress."

CASA COLORADA, *L.Am./N, idiom.* Brothel, whorehouse. *Puras casas coloradas y cantinas hay en la zona de tolerancia.* "There are only red-light districts and bars in the tolerance zone."

CASA DE CITAS, 1. *L.Am./N, n.* Brothel. *Dicen que Carlos la conoció en una casa de citas.* "They say that Carlos met her at the brothel." **2.** *L.Am./S, n.* Sex motel. *En ciudades grandes la gente joven va a casas de citas con frecuencia.* "Young people often use sex motels in big cities."

CASA DE CUENTO, *Spain, n.* Whorehouse. *Esa rubia trabaja en una casa de cuento.* "That blonde works at a house of ill repute."

CASA DE PUTAS, *L. Am., Spain, n.* Whorehouse. *Lo primero que descubrieron los americanos en el pueblo era la casa de putas.* "The first thing the Americans discovered in the village was the whorehouse."

CASA GRANDE, 1. *L.Am./N, n., crim.* Prison, the big house. *Me tiré cinco años en la casa grande por robo menor.* "I pulled five years in the big house for a minor robbery." **2.** *L.Am./N, n.* Main home of a mistress's lover. *No se encuentra mi amigo. Tuvo que reportarse a la casa grande.* "My friend isn't here. He had to report in at home."

CASARSE DE PENALTY, *Spain, idiom.* To get married after discovering pregnancy. *Ellos no se querían, se casaron de penalty.* "They didn't love each other, but they had to get married."

CASASOLA, *Car., adj.* Loner. *Teresita es una casasola. Dice que no necesita a nadie.* "Teresa is a loner. She says that she doesn't need anybody."

CASCABELEAR, *L.Am./N, v.* To be ill, to feel unwell. *Me puse a cascabelear cuando me dieron las fiebres.* "I wasn't myself when I got the fever."

CASCABELES, *Spain, n.* Testicles. (Lit. Jingle bells.) *Ese hijo de puta no tiene los cascabeles para pelear conmigo.* "That son of a bitch does not have the balls to fight me."

CASCAR, 1. *L.Am./S, v.* To hit. *Vete rápido porque esos tipos te van a cascar.* "Get out of here fast because those guys are going to kick your butt." **2.** *Spain, v., crim.* To kill. *En Dallas, un hombre cascó a otro por un aparcamiento.* "In Dallas, a man bumped off another for a parking space."

CÁSCARA See NO HABER MÁS CÁSCARAS

CASCARLA, *Spain, idiom, crim.* To die. *El muchacho que fue apuñalado anoche la cascó esta mañana.* "The kid that was stabbed last night kicked the bucket this morning."

CASCARSE, *L.Am., Spain, prnl. v.* To break. *Se cascó la estatua. Ya no tiene arreglo.* "The statue broke. Now it can't be fixed."

CASCOS, *L.Am./S, pl. n.* Feet. (Lit. Hooves.) *Dice que le* *duelen los cascos de tanto caminar.* "He says his dogs are hurting from so much walking."

CASETA See MANDAR A LA CASETA

CASETA, *Spain, n., sports.* Locker room. *La polémica era sobre si las periodistas pueden entrar en la caseta.* "The argument was whether female reporters can enter the locker room."

CASETO, *Spain, n., youth.* Audio or videocassette player. *Le regalamos un caseto para el día de su santo.* "We gave him a cassette player for his saint's day."

CASILLERO, *Spain, n., sports.* Scorer. *Trabadela era un buen casillero en su día.* "In his day, Trabadela was a good scorer."

CASIMIRO, *Car., n.* Cross-eyed person. *Ese casimiro es el hermano de Lola.* "That cross-eyed guy is Lola's brother."

CASQUETE, *Spain, n.* Fornication, fuck. *¡Cómo se nota que has tenido un casquete! ¡Con esa cara de contento!* "With that happy face, you've had a great fuck!"

CASTAÑA, 1. *Spain, n.* Punch, slap. *La muchacha le soltó una castaña al muchacho que sonó por todo el pasillo.* "The girl gave the guy a whack that you could hear all the way down the hallway." **2.** *Spain, n.* Peseta. *No me quedan castañas para salir esta noche.* "I don't have any cash left to go out tonight." **3.** *Spain, n.* Drinking bout. *Después de la castaña anoche tengo una resaca que no veo.* "After last night's drinking, I have an unbelievable hangover."

CASTAÑAZO, *Spain, n., sports.* Roundhouse punch. *Iglesias le pegó un castañazo a Jiménez que terminó la pelea.* "Iglesias hit Jimenez with a roundhouse and finished the fight."

CASTILLA, *L.Am./N, n.* The Spanish language. *Al otro lado hay muchos lugares donde hablan la castilla.* "On the other side of the border there are a lot of places where they speak Spanish."

CATANO, NA, *L.Am./S, adj. or n.* Older person. *La mamá de Sandra es una catana muy alegre.* "Sandra's mom is a real happy senior."

CATAPLASMA, *Car., adj.* Sedentary, inactive person. (Lit. Poultice.) *Abuela, no seas cataplasma, vente con nosotros a la playa.* "Grandma don't be such a couch potato, come with us to the beach."

CATAPLINES, *Spain, n.* Testicles, balls. *Ese peleador tiene cataplines.* "That fighter has balls."

CATE, *Spain, n.* Failing grade. *Le dieron un cate en matemáticas.* "They failed him in math."

CATEADO, DA, *L.Am./N, adj.* Ruined, exhausted, run-down. *Yo lo vi muy cateado a Andrés después de su enfermedad.* "Andres looked real run-down to me after his sickness."

CATEAR, 1. *L.Am./N, v.* To frisk. *Me catearon cuando entré en ese club para ver si llevaba un arma.* "They searched me when I entered that club to see if I was carrying a weapon." **2.** *L.Am./N, v.* To search a place. *Los azules entraron y catearon toda la casa.* "The cops came in and searched the whole house." **3.** *Spain, v.* To fail. *Me catearon en inglés.* "They flunked me in English."

CATEDRO, *Spain, n.* Professor. *Juan, ¿conoces el nuevo catedro de historia?* "Juan, do you know the new history prof?"

CATETE, *L.Am./S, adj. or n.* Annoying, irksome, picky. *No seas tan catete. Ya te dije que no quiero ir contigo a la fiesta.* "Don't be such a pest. I told you that I don't want to go to the party with you!"

CATETEAR, *L.Am./S, v.* To annoy, to bother, to irk, to pester, to bug. *Tu hermano siempre me está cateteando.* "Your brother is always bugging me."

CATETO, *Spain, n.* Hick, yokel. *Hijo mío, quítate ese sombrero, pareces un cateto.* "Son, take off that hat. You look like a hillbilly."

CATINGA, *L.Am./S, n.* Body odor, stench. *Tengo que*

ducharme, tengo una catinga horrible. "I've got to shower; I stink."

CATIRO, RA, *L.Am./S, n.* Blonde. *Me encantan las catiras.* "I dig blondes."

CATORRAZO, *L.Am./N, n.* Hard fall, blow. *Se resbaló con algo y se dio un santo catorrazo.* "He slipped on something and had a hard fall."

CATRE See LLEVARSE AL CATRE

CATRINA, *L.Am./N, n.* Glass pulque mug. *Es tan bravo para el pulque que en un ratito se echó dos catrinas.* "He likes pulque so much that in just a short time he had two mugs."

CAYETANO, *L.Am./S, n.* Person of few words. *Abel es un verdadero don Cayetano hoy.* "Abel is a regular Mr. Quiet today."

CAZADORA, *L.Am./C, n.* Bus. (Lit. Huntress.) *La cazadora pasa por mi casa a las ocho.* "The bus comes by my house at eight."

CAZAR, *Spain, v., sports.* To attempt to kick one's opponent and not the ball. *Hoy los jugadores pasan más tiempo cazando la oposición que la pelota.* "Today the players spend more time trying to kick the opposition than the ball."

CAZO, *Spain, n., crim.* Pimp. *Ese cazo vive de cinco mujeres.* "That pimp lives off of five women."

CEBAO, BA, *Car., adj.* Obese person or animal. *¡Vaya cebaos que se ven en los Estados Unidos!* "What fat people you see in the United States!"

CEBOLLA, 1. *Spain, n.* Head. (Lit. Onion.) *Tú lo tienes metido en la cebolla que voy a salir contigo.* "You've got it into your skull that I am going out with you." **2.** *U.S., n.* Wristwatch. *Le robaron la cebolla a mi carnala.* "They stole my sister's wristwatch."

CEBOLLAZO, *Spain, n.* Blow to the head. *En el accidente me pegué un cebollazo contra el parabrisas.* "In the accident I hit my noggin against the windshield."

CEBOLLÓN, *Spain, n.* Binge on alcohol or drugs. *Armando no sirve para nada hoy después de su cebollón anoche.* "Armando is not worth a damn today after that drinking session last night."

CENCERRO See ESTAR COMO UN CENCERRO

CENSO, *Car., n.* Continuous expenditure of money. *Alvaro, no podemos continuar con este censo. Tenemos que controlarnos.* "Alvaro, we can't continue with this spending binge. We have to control ourselves."

CEPILLAR, 1. *Spain, v.* To apple-polish, to play up to someone, to suck up. (Lit. To brush.) *Mira como Elena le cepilla al jefe.* "Look at how Elena honeys up to the boss." **2.** *Spain, v.* To win at gambling, to take someone's shirt. *Me cepillaron anoche jugando póquer.* "I lost my shirt playing poker last night." **3.** *Spain, prnl. v., crim.* To kill. *Los mafiosos lo cepillaron por haberles robado la cocaína.* "The mafia guys bumped him off for having stolen their cocaine."

CEPILLERO, *L.Am./S, adj.* Sychopant, brownnoser, kiss ass. *Se ganó el aumento de sueldo por cepillero.* "He got a raise by being a brownnoser."

CEPILLÓN, *Spain, n.* Bootlicker, apple-polisher, brownnoser. *¡Qué cepillón es ese nuevo dependiente!* "What a brownnoser that new clerk is!"

CEPO DE LAS LIMOSNAS, *L.Am./N, n.* Toilet, head, john. *Fue a hacer un depósito en el cepo de las limosnas.* "He went to make a deposit at the crapper."

CERAPIO, *Spain, n.* Zero. *¿Sabes lo que te voy a dar por este trabajo mal hecho? Cerapio.* "Do you know how much I am going to give you for that bad job? Zero."

CERDADA, *Spain, n.* Bad move, dirty trick. *¡Vaya cerdada me has hecho! ¿Qué te he hecho para que me hagas eso?* "That's a rotten trick you pulled on me! What did I do to you to deserve this?"

CERDO, DA, *Spain, adj.* Rotten, mean. (Lit. Pig.) *Ese tipo* *fue muy cerdo conmigo. No voy a comprar más allí.* "That guy was real rotten to me. I am not going to buy there anymore."

CEREBRÍN, *Spain, n.* Mixed drink of cream, whiskey, peach liqueur, and red currant. *Después de comer se me apetece un cerebrín.* "After eating I feel like drinking a 'cerebrín.' "

CEREBRO, *Car., n.* The brains of an organization. (Lit. Brain.) *Ricardo es el cerebro y los otros son los mulos.* "Ricardo is the brain and the others are the mules."

CERO, *Spain, n., crim.* Police car. (Lit. Zero.) *Ya pasó un cero por aquí hace cinco minutos.* "A cop car came by here five minutes ago."

CERO-CERO, *Spain, adj.* High-quality (hashish). *La grifa que encontraron en el coche era cero-cero.* "The hashish they found in the car was top-notch."

CERRAMIENTO DEL CANO, *L.Am./N, n.* Blockage of urinary tract. *No pude orinar porque tenía un cerramiento del cano.* "I couldn't pee because my line was blocked."

CERRO A CERRO, *L.Am./N, interj.* Vulgar remark when someone breaks wind. *"¡Cerro a cerro!" le gritaron a Rodrigo cuando se echó un pedo.* " 'Light a match!' they yelled when Rodrigo farted."

CERUL, *L.Am./N, n., crim.* Uniformed police officer. *Andaba un cerul cuidando fuera del banco.* "There was a cop on guard outside the bank."

CHABOLA, 1. *Spain, n., youth.* House. *Vamos a tener la reunión en la chabola de José.* "We are going to have the meeting at Jose's pad." **2.** *Spain, n.* Prison cell. *Seis meses en una chabola es suficiente para cualquiera.* "Six months in a prison cell is enough for anybody."

CHABÓN, *L.Am./S, n.* Man, guy. *Ese chabón es policía.* "That guy is a cop."

CHACAL, *L.Am./S, adj.* Wonderful, marvelous, good. (Lit. Jackal.) *Enrique hizo una estatua chacal para la clase de* *escultura.* "Enrique made a cool statue for sculpture class."

CHÁCHARA, *L.Am./N, n.* Something of little value. *El tiene un puesto en el mercado donde vende puras chácharas.* "He has a stand in the market where he just sells trinkets."

CHACHARERO, *L.Am./N, n.* Vendor of used goods. *Dagoberto anda de chacharero en el tianguis.* "Dagoberto sells junk at the flea market."

CHACHI, *Spain, adj., youth.* Great, fantastic, the real thing, cool. *¡Niña! Qué chachi estás!* "Girl! You look fantastic!"

CHACUACO, *L.Am./N, n.* Chimney. *Mi padre fuma más que un chacuaco.* "My father smokes more than a chimney."

CHAFALOTE, *L.Am./N, adj.* Vulgar, ordinary. *No me gusta el novio de Lola, es muy chafalote.* "I don't like Lola's boyfriend. He is very vulgar."

CHAINEADO, DA, *L.Am./N, adj.* Clean, washed. *Daniel siempre se daba su chaineada antes de ir con la novia.* "Daniel always washed himself before seeing his girlfriend."

CHAIRA, *Spain, n., crim.* Pocket knife. *Encontraron una chaira en la chabola de Gómez.* "They found a pocket knife in Gomez's cell."

CHAIRO, RA, *U.S., n.* Sweetheart, lover. *Lulú es mi chaira.* "Lulu is my sweetheart."

CHALÁN, *L.Am./N, n.* Bricklayer's assistant. *El maestro albañil traía a sus tres chalanes cuando llegó a la obra.* "The bricklayer had his three assistants with him when he got to the job."

CHALARSE, *Spain, prnl. v.* To get silly, to go crazy. *Fernando se está chalando con su trabajo nuevo.* "Fernando is getting silly with the new job."

¡CHALE! 1. *L.Am./N, interj.* No! (General interjection.) *¡Chale José! Vamos con Celso a ver el partido.* "No, Jose! We're going with Celso to see the game."

2. *L.Am./N, n., pej.* Chinese person, chink. *Ese chale tiene tres negocios en Guadalajara.* "That chink has three businesses in Guadalajara."

¡CHÁLESE! *U.S., interj., youth.* Knock it off! Cut it out! Cool it! *¡Chale con el ruido! No puedo pensar.* "Cut out the noise! I can't think."

¡CHALECA!, *L.Am./S, interj.* Good-bye! *¡Chaleca viejo! Nos vemos el próximo mes.* "See you later alligator! We'll see each other next month."

CHALEQUEAR, *L.Am./S, v.* To make fun of someone. *A Ramona le gusta chalequear al profe.* "Ramona likes to make fun of the teacher."

CHALIMÁN, *Car., n., crim.* Gangster. *Ten cuidado con ese chalimán. Dicen que está conectado con la mafia.* "Be careful with that gangster. They say that he is connected with the Mafia."

CHALUPA, 1. *Spain, adj.* Silly or crazy person. *Isabel está chalupa, ya está hablando sola.* "Isabel is nuts. She is talking to herself." **2.** *Spain, adj.* Very much in love. *Mari Toni estaba chalupa por Ricardo.* "Mari Toni has flipped over Ricardo." **3.** *L.Am./N, n.* Corn-filled and fried tortilla. *Comí tres chalupas con carne y las acompañé con una cerveza.* "I ate three chalupas with meat and washed them down with a beer."

CHAMACO, *L.Am./N, n.* Child, young person. *Cuando era chamaco, vendía periódicos para ayudar a la familia.* "When I was a kid I sold newspapers to help the family."

CHAMAGOSO, SA, *L.Am./N, adj.* Dirty. *Fernando andaba todo chamagoso de cara.* "Fernando had a dirty face."

CHAMARRA, *L.Am./N, n.* Jacket. *Gerardo se compró una chamarra de piel.* "Gerardo bought a leather jacket."

CHAMBA, 1. *L.Am./N, n.* Job. *Ando buscando chamba de jardinero.* "I'm looking for a job as a gardener." **2.** *Car., n.* Temporary job. *Tengo una chamba en correos para la temporada de Navidad.* "I got a part-time job at the post office for the Christmas season."

CHAMBEAR, *L.Am./N, v.* To work. *Ni modo, a los pobres no nos queda más que chambear.* "No way, all we poor people can do is work."

CHAMBISTA, *L.Am./N, n.* Moonlighter. *El dependiente de noche es chambista.* "The night clerk is a moonlighter."

CHAMO, *L.Am./S, n.* Fella, guy. *Bueno chamo, estamos viendo.* "Ok guy, I'll be seeing you."

CHAMORRO, *Car., n.* Short person. *Miguelito es un chamorro simpático.* "Miguelito is a nice shorty."

CHAMULLAR, *Spain, v.* To talk. *Estábamos chamullando hasta las cinco de la mañana.* "We were chewing the fat until 5:00 A.M."

CHANAR, *Spain, v.* To know. *Jaime no chana nada de lo que pasa aquí.* "Jaime is out of the loop about what's going on here."

CHANCESITO, *L.Am./C, n.* Moment. *Un chancesito y te acompaño al cine.* "Give me a moment and I'll go with you to the movies."

CHANCHI, *Spain, adj., youth.* Good, fantastic, real, authentic. *Pedro, ese cuadro es chanchi. ¿Cuándo lo hiciste?* "That painting is cool, Pedro. When did you do it?"

CHANCLAS, *L.Am., n.* Shoes, slippers. *No hay nada más comodo que mis chanclas viejas.* "There is nothing more comfortable than my old shoes."

CHANDOSO, SA, *L.Am./S, adj. or n.* Mongrel. *Me voy a llevar a ese chandoso para la casa.* "I am going to take this mongrel home."

CHANELA, *Spain, n., youth.* Knowledgeable person. *Mercedes es una chica muy chanela de la música.* "Mercedes is a real savvy chick when it comes to music."

CHANELAR, *Spain, v., youth.* To understand, to comprehend. *No chanelo nada de lo que está haciendo Juan.* "I don't get what Juan is doing."

CHANGA, 1. *L.Am./S, n.* Little part-time job. *Esta changa me da para lo principal.* "This little job gives me enough for the essentials." **2.** *L.Am./N, n.* Prostitute. *La amiga de José se viste como changa de segunda.* "Jose's girlfriend dresses like a second-rate hooker."

CHANGADO, DA, *Spain, adj.* Broken. *Esta grabadora está changada.* "This recorder is screwed up."

CHANGARRO, *L.Am./N, n.* Small business, stand, shop. *Su papá tenía un pequeño changarro donde vendía refacciones.* "His father had a little shop where he sold spare parts."

CHANGO, 1. *L.Am./N, n.* Vagina. *Berta traía el pantalón tan apretado que se le veía hasta el chango.* "Bertha's pants were so tight that you could see her pussy." **2.** *U.S., n.* Young person. *Ese es el chango que me ayudó a cambiar la llanta.* "That's the kid who helped me change the tire." **3. CHANGO, GA,** *Car., n.* Person who is hard to please. Picky. *A Margarita no le gusta nada, es una changa.* "Margarita doesn't like anything; she is a picky person." **4.** *L.Am./N, adj.* Sharp, quick. *¡Ponte chango y nos robamos unas naranjas!* "Quick! Let's steal some oranges!"

CHANO, *L.Am./S, adj.* Coarse, vulgar. *A mi hijo le gusta andar con gente chana.* "My son likes to hang around with roughnecks."

CHANTA, *L.Am./N, adj.* Affected, conceited. *Sara es tan chanta que nadie la aguanta.* "Sara is so conceited that no one can stand her."

CHANTE, 1. *L.Am./C, n.* Laziness. *No me puedo quitar este chante. No tengo ganas de hacer nada.* "I can't get over this laziness. I don't feel like doing anything." **2.** *L.Am./C, n.* Place or field. *Nos encontraremos en el chante después del almuerzo.* "We'll get together at the field after lunch."

CHANZA, *L.Am./N, n.* Opportunity, chance. *Díle a mamá que nos dé chanza de ir al cine.* "Tell mom to give us a chance to go to the movies."

CHAPA, 1. *Spain, n.* Male homosexual prostitution. *El tipo* *ese está metido en la chapa. Dicen que gana bien como puto.* "That guy is involved in prostitution. They say he makes big bucks as a male hooker." **2.** *Spain, n., crim.* Plainclothes police badge. *El poli no quería enseñarme la chapa, hasta que llegó otro en uniforme.* "The cop didn't want to show me his badge until another arrived in uniform." **3.** *L.Am./S, n.* Nickname. *Los tiras lo tenían fichado con diferentes chapas.* "The detectives had them listed under different nicknames."

CHAPADO A LA ANTIGUA, *L.Am., idiom.* Old-fashioned. *Toda mi familia es chapada a la antigua.* "My whole family is old-fashioned."

CHAPAR, 1. *Spain, v., youth.* To work or study constantly. *Ramiro no tiene vida, chapa siempre.* "Ramiro doesn't have a life, he's always working." **2.** *Spain, v.* To stay until closing time. *Roberto cree que tiene que chapar el bar todas las noches.* "Roberto thinks that he has to close the bar every night."

CHAPARRO, RRA, *L.Am./N, n.* Short person. *¿De modo que aquel chaparro es el hermano de Estela?* "So that shorty is Stella's brother?"

CHAPE, 1. *L.Am./S, n.* Kiss. *Su mamá la encontró en un chape enorme.* "Her mother caught her in a wild kiss." **2.** *L.Am./S, n.* Slug. *¡Cuidado! No pises ese chape.* "Careful! Don't step on that slug."

CHAPERO, *Spain, n.* Male homosexual prostitute. *La calle estaba llena de chaperos buscando pareja.* "The street was full of male hookers looking for johns."

CHAPIRI, *Spain, n.* Hat. *Siempre llega el señor con el mismo chapiri verde.* "The gentleman always shows up with the same green hat."

¡CHAPÓ!, *Spain, interj.* Wow! *¡Chapó! ¡Qué jugada más buena!* "Wow! What a play!"

CHAPUCERO, RA, 1. *L.Am./N, adj. or n.* Cheat. *No me gusta jugar baraja con Edgar, es muy chapucero.* "I don't like to play cards with Edgar, he is a real cheat."

2. *L.Am./S, adj. or n.* Incompetent. *Tenemos que dejar de usar a ese mecánico porque es un chapucero.* "We have to stop using that mechanic because he's a nincompoop."

CHAPULÍN, *L.Am./C, n.* Young thief, thug, crook. *Entraron unos chapulines y robaron todo el dinero que había en caja.* "Some young thugs came in and stole all the money from the cash register."

CHAQUETERO, *L.Am./N, n.* Person who changes political ideas as easily as shirts. *Damián es tan chaquetero que nadie lo respeta.* "Damian has been switching sides so often that nobody respects him."

CHARCHINA, *L.Am./N, n.* Jalopy, wreck, junker. *Mi primer carro fue una charchina que tenías que empujar para arrancar.* "My first car was a junker that you had to push to get it started."

CHAROL, *Spain, adj.* Black person. (Lit. Patent leather.) *Hace tiempo que no veo a tu amigo charol.* "It has been a long time since I saw your black friend."

CHAROLA, 1. *L.Am./N, n., crim.* Police badge. *Cuando nos detuvieron, el que iba vestido de civil sacó su charola.* "When they stopped us, the one who was wearing civilian clothes took out his badge." **2.** *L.Am./N, n.* Tray. *Mayte nos sirvió las bebidas en charola de plata.* "Mayte served us drinks on a silver tray."

CHARRAR, *Spain, v.* To chat. *Julia y Pedro estaban charrando durante horas.* "Julia and Pedro were chatting for hours."

CHARRASCA, *L.Am./N, n.* Knife. *Arrestaron al cuate por llevar una charrasca.* "They arrested the guy for carrying a knife."

CHARRO, *L.Am., adj.* Flashy. *Eduardo es muy charro en su manera de vestir.* "Eduardo is real flashy in his way of dressing."

CHARRO CON SARTÉN, *L.Am./N, n.* Homosexual. *Como a Jaime no le gustaban las muchachas, sabíamos* *que era charro con sartén.* "Since he didn't like girls, we knew that he was a gay blade."

CHAS-CHAS, *L.Am./N, idiom.* Cash. *Roel pagó por el coche al chas-chas.* "Roel paid cash on the barrelhead for the car."

CHASÍS, *L.Am./C, n.* Skeleton. (Lit. Chassis.) *Hijo mío, te estás quedando en el chasís. Tienes que comer más.* "My son, you are getting down to the bone. You've got to eat more."

CHATA, *Spain, n., crim.* Pistol. *Tenía escondida una chata debajo del asiento del coche.* "He had a piece hidden under the car seat."

CHATARRA, 1. *Spain, n.* Small change. (Lit. Scrap iron.) *Tenía cinco billetes de 1,000 pesetas y 856 pesetas en chatarra.* "I had five 1,000 peseta notes and 856 pesetas in metal." **2.** *Spain, n.* Jewelry or decorations worn by a person. *El almirante tenía el pecho lleno de chatarra.* "The admiral had a chest full of lettuce." **3.** *L.Am., adj. or n.* Jalopy, junker. *Ese carro tuyo es una chatarra.* "That car of yours is a jalopy."

CHATEAR, *Spain, v.* To have drinks with friends. *Salimos anoche a chatear por el centro.* "Last night we went downtown to drink."

CHATEO, *Spain, n.* Having drinks. *Una de las cosas que me encantan de Madrid es el chateo.* "One of the things I like about Madrid is going out for drinks."

CHATI, *Spain, n.* Affectionate name, hon. *Oye, Chati, ¿me puedes traer un cortaíto?* "Hey hon, could you bring me a coffee with a little cream?"

CHATA, *L.Am./S, adj.* Drunk. *Me quedé bien chato anoche.* "I got real smashed last night."

CHATO, 1. *Spain, n.* Drink. *¡Paco! Echame un chato de ese vino que tienes de Montilla.* "Paco! Bring me a glass of that wine you have from Montilla." **2. CHATO, TA,** *Spain, n.* Affectionate name, pug. *Oye Chata, dame un beso.* "Hey pug, give me a kiss." **3.** *L.Am./S, n.* Midget. *El* *chato Mario resultó campeón de salto.* "Mario the midget ended up being champion jumper." **4.** *L.Am./N, n.* Pug-nosed kid. *Diego está chato de las narices.* "Diego is a pug-nosed kid." **5.** *L.Am./S, adj.* Tired, drowsy. *Juana estaba chata del viaje tan pesado.* "Juana was drowsy from the boring trip." **6.** *L.Am./S, adj.* Bored. *Mi padre estaba chatísimo durante la misa.* "My father was bored to death during the mass."

CHAUCHAU, *Car., adv.* Eating fast, chowing down. *Juan, siempre comes a chauchau.* "Juan, you are always eating in a rush."

CHAVO, 1. *Spain, n.* Boy. *El chavo pelirrojo es el hijo del joyero.* "The redheaded kid is the jeweler's son." **2.** *Spain, n.* Person. *Había unos chavos sospechosos chamullando en la esquina.* "There were some suspicious characters pushing drugs on the corner." **3.** *L.Am./N, n.* Boy, girl, youth. *Cuando era chavo tenía que vender chicles en la calle.* "When he was a boy he had to sell chewing gum in the street."

CHAVOS, *Car., pl. n.* Money. *Voy a pedirle unos chavos prestados a mi papá.* "I am going to ask my dad to loan me some bread."

¡CHE!, *L.Am./S, interj.* Hey! *¡Che, mirá a ese borracho!* "Hey, look at that drunk!"

CHE, 1. *Spain, L.Am./S, n.* Person from Valencia or Argentina. (Comes from the use of "Che" with the person to whom one is speaking.) *Los ches pueden ser de Valencia o de Argentina.* "The 'ches' can be either from Valencia or from Argentina." **2.** *Spain, L.Am./S, n.* Expression used by person from Valencia or Argentina when addressing another. *Che, ¿cuándo vamos a ir a ver un partido?* "Che, when are we going to go see a game?"

CHECAR, 1. *L.Am./N, v.* To check. *Tengo que checar mi horóscopo para ver si es mi día de suerte.* "I've got to check my horoscope to see if it's my lucky day." **2.** *L.Am./N, v.* To check in. *Cuando andaba con Iris, tenía* *que checar a las nueve.* "When I was going out with Iris I had to check in at nine."

CHÉCHERE, *L.Am./S, n.* Things. *Mi cajón vive lleno de chécheres, no encuentro nada.* "That drawer is full of stuff; I can't find a thing."

CHEIRA, *Spain, n., crim.* Penknife. *Llevaba una cheira en el bolsillo y una pis en la chaqueta.* "He had a blade in his pocket and a pistol in his jacket."

CHELA, *L.Am., n.* Beer. *No hay nada mejor que ver el fútbol y tomar unas chelas bien heladas.* "There is nothing better that watching soccer and having a couple of icy beers."

CHELFA, *L.Am./S, n.* Girl, young woman. *¡Qué buena está la chelfa!* "That fox is fantastic!"

CHELI, *Spain, n.* Affectionate term used in Madrid. *Cheli, vente con nosotras al cine.* "Cheli, come with us to the movies."

CHEPA(S), 1. *Spain, adj. or n.* Hunchbacked, hunchback. *El hermano de Juan se está poniendo chepas. Es una forma de artritis, ¿no?* "Juan's brother is getting hunchbacked. It's a form of arthritis, isn't it?" **2.** *L.Am., n.* Pure luck. *El gol que metió Julio fué de puras chepas.* "The goal that Julio made was pure luck."

CHEPE, *L.Am./C, n.* Capital of Costa Rica. *Eduardo es de Chepe.* "Eduardo is from San Jose."

CHERNA, *Car., n.* Homosexual, fairy, fag. *Ese tipo es un cherna. No ves su manera de hablar? Parece una mujercita.* "That guy is a fairy. Don't you see the way he talks? He looks like a little woman."

CHERO, *L.Am./N, n.* Hick. *Tengo un primo bien chero que se crió en el rancho.* "I've got a real hick cousin who was raised on a ranch."

CHÉVERE, *L.Am., adj.* Good, great, cool. *No es raro que la hayas pasado bien. Yo te dije que mi amigo era chévere.* "It's not strange that you had a good time. I told you that my friend was a neat guy."

CHIBOLO, *L.Am./S, n.* Child. *Los chibolos del barrio tiran pelota que da miedo.* "The neighborhood kids play ball so well that it's unbelievable."

CHICABACHO, CHA, *U.S., n.* Mexican-American, Chicano, Chicana, Latino, Latina. *Cuando fui a mi clase me encontré con otros chicabachos.* "When I went to my class I found myself with other Latinos."

CHICANERO, NERA, *L.Am./N, adj. or n.* Tricky, crafty. *¡Cuidado! Ese vendedor es muy chicanero.* "Look out! That salesman is real tricky."

CHICANO, *L.Am./N, n.* Chicano. *Mi primo Reymundo es chicano, nacido en Los Angeles.* "My cousin Reymundo is a Chicano; he was born in L.A."

CHICAS PATAS, *U.S., idiom.* Mexican. *Muchas chicas patas van a ese club.* "Many Mexicans go to that club."

CHICATO, *L.Am./S, n.* Person with poor vision who uses glasses, four-eyes. *Oye chicato, ¿por qué no te compras lentes de contacto?* "Hey, four-eyes, why don't you buy contact lenses?"

CHICHA, 1. *Car., n.* Vagina. *Ten cuidado con esa mujer. Siempre está rascándose la chicha.* "Be careful with that woman. She is always scratching her pussy." **2.** *Car., n.* Drink made of rum and anisette. *Te invito a una copa de chicha.* "I invite you to a drink of chicha." **3.** *L.Am./N, n.* Drink made of the fermentation of corn in sugary water. **4.** *L.Am./S, n.* Drink made from fermentation of apples or grapes.

CHICHAR, *Car., v.* To have sexual intercourse. *Amor, vamos a tu casa para chichar a gusto.* "Love, let's go to your house to make love with pleasure."

CHICHARO, *L.Am./N, n.* Assistant. *Tenía su chicharo para ayudarlo en la oficina.* "He had his assistant to help him at the office."

CHICHARRA, *L.Am./N, n., drugs.* Marijuana butt, roach. *Estaban pasando una chicharra de uno a otro para tomar una calada.* "They were passing a roach from one to another for a drag."

CHICHARRÓN, NA, *L.Am./N, adj.* Pockmarked or very wrinkled. (Lit. Pork rind.) *Tenía la piel como chicharrón por tanto trabajar en el campo.* "His skin was all wrinkled from working in the field."

¡CHICHELA!, 1. *Car., interj.* Get out of here! *¡Chichela Pepe! No te creo.* "Get out of here Pepe, I don't believe you." **2.** *Car., interj.* Go ahead! *¡Chichela! Ud. tiene la verde.* "Go, go! You've got the green light."

CHICHES, *L.Am./N, n.* Woman's breasts, tits, boobs, gozongas. *Estaba tan escotado el vestido de Raquel que ya se le salían las chiches.* "Raquel's dress had such a neckline that her boobs were about to pop out."

CHICHÍ, 1. *L.Am./C, n.* Baby. *Isidora y Miguel tienen un chichí tan bonito.* "Isidora and Miguel have such a pretty baby." **2.** *Spain, n.* Vagina. *La puta se levantó la falda en plena calle y mostró el chichí.* "The whore lifted up her skirt right out in the street and showed her pussy." **3.** *L.Am./N, n.* Woman's breast. *Cuando frenó el camión, un pelado me agarró la chichí.* "When the bus braked, a kid grabbed my boob." **4.** *L.Am., n.* Penis. *Manolo tiene el chichí chiquitico.* "Manolo has a tiny dick." **5.** *L.Am., n.* Urine. *El niño se volvió a hacer chichí en la cama.* "The boy made pee-pee in bed again."

CHICHINABO, *Spain, n.* Something of little importance. *Este chichinabo me costó menos de nada.* "This little thingamabob hardly cost me anything."

CHICHIPATO, TA, *L.Am., adj.* Tightwad, stingy. *Ese chichipato no me regaló nada en mi cumpleaños.* "That tightwad didn't give me anything for my birthday."

CHICHO, CHA, 1. *U.S., adj.* Crazy. *Cuidado con esa muchacha; está bien chicha.* "Be careful with that girl, she is real crazy." **2.** *L.Am./N, adj.* Nice, neat, cool. *Me cae bien tu hermano, es muy chicho.* "I like your brother; he is cool." **3.** *L.Am./N, adj.* Talented. *Mi nieto es muy chicho para la música.* "My grandson is very talented with music."

CHICHÓN 1. *Car., n.* Inconvenience, difficulty. (Lit. Bump.) *El chichón fue que no podía renovar mi pasaporte en un día.* "The problem was that I couldn't renew my passport in one day." **2. CHICHÓN, NA,** *Car., adj.* Bothersome, annoying. *Al chichón de Juancho no lo aguanta ni su mamá.* "Not even his mother can stand that pain in the ass Juancho."

CHICHONA, *L.Am./N, adj.* Having big breasts, stacked. *Desde que tenía unos quince años María ya estaba bien chichona.* "When she was fifteen Maria was already stacked."

CHICHONEAR, *Car., v.* To bother, to annoy. *Si me sigues chichoneando te vas a arrepentir.* "If you keep bugging me you're going to be sorry."

CHICHONERA, *L.Am., n.* Crowd. *Había una chichonera terrible en el centro comercial.* "There was an awful crowd in the mall."

CHICHONERÍA, *Car., n.* Bother, disturbance, annoyance. *Tanta chichonería de estos muchachos ya me tiene cansado.* "All the screwing around by these guys got to me."

CHICLE, *L.Am./N, n.* Hanger-on. (Lit. Chewing gum.) *Todo el día anda Judith con Ramón, pegada como chicle.* "Judith is Ramon's hanger-on. She sticks to him like chewing gum."

CHIDO, *L.Am./N, adj.* Fantastic, great, cool, awesome. *El grupo que tocó en la fiesta estaba bien chido.* "The group that played at the party was awesome."

CHIFLIS, *L.Am./S., adj. or n.* Crazy, nuts. *Sandra se volvió chiflis de pena.* "Sandra went crazy from the pain."

CHILANGO, *L.Am./N, n.* Person born in Mexico City. *Por el habla se nota que es chilango.* "From his accent you can tell that he is from the capital."

CHILANGOLANDIA, *L.Am./N, n.* Mexico City. *Dicen que hay unos veinte millones de habitantes en Chilan-*

golandia. "They say that there are twenty million inhabitants in chilangoland."

CHILLA, *L.Am./N, n.* Poverty. *Antonio y su familia andan en la chilla desde que perdió su trabajo.* "Antonio and his family are experiencing poverty since he lost his job."

CHILLÓN, *L.Am./N, n.* Radio, receiver. (Lit. Squealer.) *Alvaro lleva su chillón a todas partes.* "Alvaro takes his squawk box everywhere."

CHILPAYATE, *L.Am./N, n.* Baby. *A los cuatro años de casados ya tenían cinco chilpayates.* "After four years of marriage they already had five rugrats."

CHIMBO, 1. *L.Am./S, adj.* Worthless, fake. *El reloj que lleva Edgar es un Rolex chimbo.* "The watch Edgar is wearing is a fake Rolex." **2.** *L.Am./S, adj.* Ugly, terrible, lousy. *Ese carro es chimbo, no lo compres.* "That car is lousy, don't buy it."

CHIMENEA, *Spain, n.* Head. (Lit. Chimney.) *Javier, no estás carburando en la chimenea.* "Javier, you're not all right upstairs."

CHIMISTURRIA, *L.Am./N, n.* Useless thing, something of little value. *Se me paró el coche porque se quebró una chimisturria.* "My car broke down because a thingamajig broke."

CHIMUELO, LA, *L.Am./N, adj.* Toothless. *El abuelo de Roberto está todo chimuelo.* "Roberto's grandfather is toothless."

¡CHIN!, *L.Am./N, interj.* Expression of disgust or disappointment. *¡Chin! ya se acabaron los refrescos.* "Shoot! There are no more sodas."

CHIN, *Car., n.* A little bit. *Solo quiero un chin de pan y nada más.* "I just want a little piece of bread and that's all."

CHINA, 1. *L.Am./C, n.* Babysitter. (Lit. Chinese.) *La china llega a las ocho y se va a las seis, no se queda la noche.* "The babysitter arrives at eight and leaves at six, she doesn't stay over." **2.** *Spain, n.* Enough marijuana to roll

143

a joint. *Estaban fumando la chicharra porque no tenían china para un porro.* "They were smoking a roach because they didn't have enough grass for a joint."

CHINAMO, *L.Am./C, n.* Small stand. *Vamos a tomar un refresco en ese chinamo.* "Let's go have a soft drink at that stand."

CHINAR, *Spain, v., crim.* To cut, to knife. *Al pobre muchacho lo chinaron y lo dejaron desangrar en la calle.* "They knifed the poor boy and left him bleeding in the street."

CHINARSE, *Spain, prnl. v.* To cut one's own face. *Se chinó la cara para tener una cicatriz como los esgrimadores alemanes.* "He cut his face to have a scar like the German fencers."

CHINAZO, *Spain, n.* Cut on the face made with the point of a knife. *Anoche, a Mario, un ratero le hizo un chinazo en la cara.* "Last night, a hoodlum gave Mario a slash on the face."

CHINCHOSO, *L.Am., adj.* Person who gets upset over anything. *Te estás volviendo tan chinchoso que no se te puede ni hacer una broma.* "You're getting so touchy that you can't even take a joke."

CHINEAR, *L.Am./C, v.* To be affectionate, to spoil, to treat nice. *César chinea mucho a su mujer.* "Cesar really spoils his wife."

CHINERA, *Spain, n., crim.* Stash box. *Guardó el drogata su hierba en la chinera.* "The pothead put the grass away in his stash box."

CHINGA, *L.Am./C, n.* Cigarette butt. *Cuando fumaba, si no tenía cigarrillos buscaba hasta chingas que fumar.* "When I smoked and didn't have any cigarettes I even looked for butts to smoke."

CHINGAR, 1. *L.Am., v.* To fuck. *Ese tipo chinga más que un perro.* "That guy fucks more than a dog." **2.** *L.Am./N, v.* To pester. *El niño de José siempre está chingando. Molesta mucho.* "Jose's boy is always screwing around. He's a real bother." **3.** *L.Am./N, v.* To damage, to ruin. *Juan me* *chingó la bicicleta.* "Juan fucked up my bicycle."

CHINGAZO, *U.S., n.* Slap. *Su marido le pegó un chingazo delante de todo el mundo.* "Her husband gave her a slap in front of everybody."

CHINGO, GA, 1. *L.Am./C, adj.* Naked, nude. *A nuestros amigos les gusta andar chingos en casa cuando están solos.* "Our friends like to go around naked at home when they are alone." **2.** *Car., adj.* Animal without a tail. *Todos los cachorritos de mi perra salieron chingos.* "All my dog's puppies turned out without a tail."

CHINGÓN, NA, *Car., adj.* Troublemaker, bastard, bitch. *¡Qué chingona eres, muchacha! Te gusta fastidiar.* "What a bitch you are, girl! You love to cause trouble."

CHINGOS, *L.Am./C, pl. n.* Panties. *La minifalda dejaba ver los chingos, la moda nueva no.* "The mini-skirt let you see the panties, the new fashions don't."

CHINGUE, *L.Am./C, n.* Fun thing. *El nuevo centro de tiendas es un chingue, hay tanto que hacer.* "The new commercial center is a blast, there is so much to do."

CHINGUERO, *L.Am./N, n.* A lot, loads of, a large quantity. *Encontraron un chinguero de juana en una bodega.* "They found loads of marijuana in a warehouse."

CHINGUETAS, *L.Am./N, n.* Smug individual, smart-ass. *No tolero ese hombre, es un chinguetas.* "I can't stand that man—he is a smart-ass."

CHINITA, 1. *L.Am./N, n.* Term of affection, honey, sugar, sweetheart. *Ay chinita mía, cuánto te quiero.* "Oh my honey, how I love you!" **2.** *Spain, n., drugs.* Piece of hashish. *Cuando registraron el coche, encontraron una chinita liada en un papel.* "When they searched the car they found a piece of pot wrapped in paper."

CHINO, 1. *L.Am./S, n.* Child. (Lit. Chinese.) *Los chinos de José fueron a visitar a la abuela.* "Jose's kids went to visit their grandmother." **2.** *Spain, n., crim.* Razor blade or knife used by pickpockets to cut clothing to lift a wallet. *Los carteristas usan un chino para cortar el bol-*

sillo donde se lleva la cartera. "The pickpockets use a shiv to cut the pockets where people carry their wallets." **3.** *L.Am., n.* Any oriental person. *En el Perú, los chinos son muy activos en la política.* "In Peru, the orientals are very active in politics." **4.** *L.Am./N, adj.* Curly-haired. *¡Qué chino tienes el pelo Mari! ¿Te hiciste una permanente?* "Your hair is so curly Mari! Did you get a perm?"

CHINORRI, *Spain, n.* Child. *La niñera aprovechó la oportunidad para llevar los chinorris al parque.* "The babysitter took advantage of the opportunity and took the kids to the park."

CHIPE, *L.Am./N, n.* Youngest child. *Mario es el chipe de la familia.* "Mario is the youngest of the family."

CHIPÉN, *Spain, adj., youth.* Super, fantastic, cool. *Oye, Juanita, tu nueva moto es chipén.* "Hey, Juanita, your new motorcycle is cool!"

CHIPICHUSCA, *Spain, n.* Whore. *Esa chipichusca llega a esa casa a la misma hora cada sábado.* "That bimbo arrives at that house at the same time every Saturday."

CHIPILE, *L.Am./N, n.* Crybaby. *No seas chipile, Nachito.* "Don't be a crybaby, Nachito."

CHIPOCLUDO, DA, *L.Am./N, adj.* Great, fantastic, cool. *Ese carro es bien chipocludo.* "That car is totally cool."

CHIQUEADO, DA, *L.Am./N, adj.* Spoiled. *Tu niño está muy chiqueado porque le das todo.* "Your boy is very spoiled because you give him everything."

CHIQUILÍN, *L.Am., n.* Boy, kid. *Ese chiquilín juega muy bien al fútbol.* "That kid is good at playing football."

CHIQUITERO, *Spain, n.* One who enjoys going out to have glasses of wine. *¡Qué chiquitero es Álvaro! Será por eso que tiene la nariz tan roja.* "What a nipper Alvaro is! That's probably why he has such a red nose."

CHIRI, *Spain, n., drugs.* Marijuana joint. *Joselito estaba liándose un chiri cuando entró la madre.* "Joselito was rolling a joint when his mother walked in."

CHIRIMBOLO, *Spain, n., drugs.* Marijuana joint. *El tenía suficiente gloria en el piso para liar 200 chirimbolos.* "He had enough pot on the floor to roll two hundred joints."

CHIRINGUITO, *Spain, n.* A small food or drink stand. *Había un chiringuito en la playa donde comprábamos algo de comer y beber.* "There was a little stand on the beach where we bought something to eat and drink."

CHIRIPA, *L.Am., n.* Luck. *El gol que metió de media cancha sólo fue de chiripa.* "The goal he made from half field was just pure luck."

CHIRLA, 1. *Spain, n., crim.* Penknife. *Guárdate la chirla Paco. Aquí no la necesitas.* "Put the knife away Paco. You don't need it here." **2.** *Spain, n., crim.* Robbery with a knife. *Ayer le hicieron una chirla a Manolo en pleno día.* "Yesterday they robbed Manolo with a knife in broad daylight." **3.** *Spain, n.* Vagina. *En ese puticlub las tías le echan las chirlas en la cara de uno.* "At that nightclub the broads put their gashes right on your face."

CHIRLAR, *Spain, v., crim.* To rob with a knife. *Estaba andando por la calle cuando me chirló un maleante.* "I was walking down the street when a hood robbed me with a knife."

CHIRLO, *Spain, n., crim.* Knife cut, scar from knife cut. *El tipo tenía un chirlo en la mejilla.* "The guy had a knife scar on his cheek."

CHIRO, *L.Am./N, adj.* With it, cool. *El profesor de inglés es bien chiro.* "The English professor is very cool."

CHIROLA, 1. *L.Am./S, n.* Coin. *No me queda ni una chirola.* "I don't have one red cent." **2.** *Car., n.* Jail. *Por fin metieron a ese mafioso a la chirola.* "They finally put that mafioso in the clink."

CHIRONA, *Spain, n., crim.* Jail. *Ricardo lleva dos años en la chirona.* "Ricardo has been in the clink for two years."

CHIRRI, *Spain, n., drugs.* Marijuana joint. *Ibamos en el metro cuando vimos este ratero fumando un chirri tan* *tranquilo.* "We were on the subway when we saw this hoodlum smoking a joint without a worry in the world."

CHISME, 1. *Spain, n.* Sexual organ, penis or vagina. (Lit. Gizmo.) *Hoy en día en las playas desnudas la gente anda con los chismes al aire.* "These days at the nude beaches the people walk around showing their gizmos." **2.** *Spain, n.* Alcoholic drink. *¿Cómo se llama este chisme? Es un destornillador.* "What do you call this gizmo? It's a screwdriver."

CHISPA(S), *Spain, n.* Nickname commonly used for electricians. (Lit. Sparks.) *Tuvimos que llamar al chispas para que viniera a arreglar la luz.* "We had to call Sparks so that he could come fix the light."

¡CHISPAS!, *U.S., interj.* Wow! (Lit. Sparks.) *¡Chispas! ¡Qué casa más grande!* "Wow! What a big house!"

CHISPEAR, *L.Am./S, Car., v.* To drizzle. *Mejor lleva la sombrilla porque ya está chispeando.* "You're better off taking an umbrella because it has started to drizzle."

CHISTE ALEMÁN, *L.Am./S, Car., adj., hum.* Bad joke. (Lit. German joke.) *Arturo pasó la noche contando chistes alemanes.* "Arturo spent the night telling bad jokes."

CHIVA, *L.Am./C, adj.* Cool, awesome. *El nuevo CD de Enrique Iglesias es muy chiva.* "Enrique Iglesias' new CD is super cool."

CHIVAR, 1. *Spain, v.* To fuck. *En ciertos videos se ve chivar hasta a aficionados.* "On certain videos you even see amateurs fucking." **2.** *Spain, v., crim.* To squeal, to inform. *Lo vi en la comisaría chivando a la poli.* "I saw him at the police station squealing to the cops."

CHIVATA, *Spain, n.* Flashlight. *Tengo una pequeña chivata que uso para iluminar el candado de la puerta.* "I have a little flashlight that I use to light up the lock on the door."

CHIVATEAR, *Car., v.* To inform, to squeal, to rat. *Pepito le escupió al niño de la camisa azul y su compañero lo chivateó a la maestra.* "Pepito spit on the kid with the blue shirt and his buddy squealed on him to the teach."

CHIVATO, TA, 1. *Car., n.* Gossip. (Lit. Young goat.) *Qué señora tan chivata, todo lo cuenta.* "That lady is such a gossip—she tells everything." **2.** *Spain, n., crim.* Informer. *La policía tenía que tener un chivato para atrapar a los camellos.* "The police had to have a rat to trap the dealers." **3.** *Spain, n., crim.* Peephole in jail cell. *El guardia miraba al preso por el chivato.* "The guard looked at the inmate through the peephole." **4.** *Spain, n.* Pilot light. *Se había apagado el chivato y el piso se llenó de gas asfixiando a la gente.* "The pilot light had gone out; the apartment filled with gas and asphyxiated the people." **5.** *Spain, n.* Taxi light indicating whether it is free or occupied. *El taxista tenía el chivato puesto indicando que estaba libre.* "The taxi driver had his light on indicating he was free." **6.** *Spain, n.* Time clock. *Según el chivato, José llegó a trabajar a las 10:30.* "According to the time clock, Jose came to work at 10:30."

CHIVIADO, DA, *L.Am./S, adj.* Worthless, fake. *Compré un diamante de ese joyero y luego descubrí que era chiviado.* "I bought a diamond from that jeweler and later found that it was fake."

CHIVO, 1. *L.Am./C, n.* Pimp. (Lit. Goat.) *Esa puta tiene su chivo.* "That whore has her pimp." **2.** *Car., n.* Cheat sheet. *Cuando llegó el día del examen se llevó un chivo en el bolsillo.* "When test day arrived he took a cheat sheet with him in his pocket." **3.** *Car., n.* Fraud. *Ese negocio es todo un chivo.* "This business is a rip-off." **4.** *Car., n.* Imperfection or defect in a piece of work. *Esta mesa tiene un chivo, yo no voy a comprarla así.* "The table has a defect. I am not going to buy it like that." **5.** *L.Am./S, n.* Big shot. *Ricardo tiene amistad con un chivo de la embajada norteamericana.* "Ricardo is friends with a big shot at the American Embassy." **6.** *Car., n.* Odd job. *Todos los trabajos que consigue mi novio son chivos.* "All the jobs that my boyfriend gets are part-time." **7.** *Car., adj.* Suspicious, distrustful, skeptical. *Carlos está chivo; parece que se dio cuenta que salí con Iván la otra noche.* "Carlos is suspicious; it seems that he found out that I went out with

Ivan last night." **8.** *Spain, n.* Person who takes the blame for others. *Armando es un chivo, siempre toma la culpa de lo que hacen otros.* "Armando is a wimp; he always takes the blame for what other people do." **9.** *L.Am./N, n.* Day's wages. *A Pedro no le pagaron el chivo.* "They didn't pay Pedro his daily wages." **10.** *U.S., adj.* Afraid. *Mi hijo está bien chivo del perro.* "My son is very afraid of the dog." **11.** *U.S., n.* Ten-dollar bill. *¿Tienes cambio de un chivo?* "Do you have change for a ten-dollar bill?"

¡CHÓCALA!, *Car., interj.* OK! Right on! *¡Chócala! Qué plan tan bueno, todo va a salir muy bien.* "Okay! What a good plan. Everything is going to turn out all right."

CHOCHA, *Car., n.* Vagina. *Bájate la falda, hija. Te van a ver la chocha.* "Lower your skirt, daughter. They are going to see your pussy."

CHOCHETE See CHOCHITO

CHOCHÍN See CHOCHITO

CHOCHITO, *Spain, n.* Child's vagina. *"Niña ven aquí, te voy a limpiar el chochito". "Si mami".* " 'Come here girl, I am going to clean your little fanny.' 'Yes mommy.' "

CHOCHO, 1. *Spain, n.* Vagina. *Si así tiene las uñas ¿cómo tendrá el chocho de sucio?* "If her nails were like that, how dirty would her pussy be?" **2.** *Spain, n.* Lupino bean. *Nos sirvieron vino blanco y platitos de chochos.* "They served us white wine and little plates of lupino beans."

CHOCHOLOCO, *Spain, n.* Crazy woman. *Cuidado con esa chocholoco. A esa tía le falta un tornillo.* "Be careful with that crazy cunt. That broad is missing a screw."

CHOCHONA, *Spain, adj.* Effeminate homosexual. *Lalo es una chochona. Tiene ademanes de reina.* "Lalo is a flaming fag. He behaves like a queen."

CHOCHOTRISTE, *Spain, n.* Dull woman; overly pious woman, holier than thou. *La mujer de mi amigo es una chochotriste y por eso él busca niñas alegres.* "My friend's wife is a sad sack. That is why he is looking for jolly girls."

CHOCOLATE, *Spain, n., drugs.* Hashish. (Lit. Chocolates.) *Los civiles incautaron 300 kilos de chocolate afgano en Sevilla hoy.* "The fuzz seized 300 kilos of Afgan hashish in Seville today."

CHOCOLATERA, *Spain, n., drugs.* Little leather pouch worn around one's neck to carry a stash. *El tipo llevaba una chocolatera llena de hashish y dos monedas de oro.* "The guy had a little stash bag full of hash and two gold coins."

CHOLA, 1. *L.Am./S, n.* Maid. *La chola se puso de acuerdo con su amiguito para robar la casa.* "The maid got together with her boyfriend to rob the house." **2.** *Car., n.* Head. *Tú como que estás mal de la chola, te portas muy raro.* "You seem to be a little sick in the noodle. You're acting real strange."

CHOLLO, *Spain, n.* Bargain. *El coche nuevo de Manolo fue un chollo.* "Manolo's new car was a steal."

CHONCHO, CHA, 1. *Car., adj. or n.* Short, stocky person. *Mariela se casó con un choncho millonario.* "Mariela married a stocky little millionaire." **2.** *L.Am./N, adj.* Serious. *Este asunto se está poniendo bien choncho.* "This matter is getting very serious."

CHONES, *U.S., n.* Underwear. *Mario, súbete los pantalones, se te ven los chones.* "Mario, pull up your pants. You can see your underwear."

CHONTRIL, *L.Am./S, n.* Guy. *Ese chontril es buena gente.* "That dude is a nice person."

CHOPANO, *Spain, n., crim.* Jail cell. *René está en el chopano 23 horas diarias. Le dejan afuera por una hora.* "René is in his cell 23 hours a day. They let him out for one hour."

CHOPO, *Spain, n., crim.* Rifle. *Antes de subir al avión le encontraron un chopo en su equipaje.* "Before he got on the plane, they found a rifle in his luggage."

CHORAR, *Spain, v., crim.* To rob, to steal. *El sinvergüenza estaba chorando de todos los vecinos.* "The bastard was ripping off all the neighbors."

CHORBO, BA, *Spain, n.* Individual. *Ese chorbo es el primo de Alvaro.* "That dude is Alvaro's cousin."

CHORCHI, *Spain, n., mil.* Recruit. *¿Cómo se notan los chorchis? Todos están pelados y llevan uniformes grandes.* "How can you tell the recruits? They all have shaved heads and wear uniforms that are too large."

CHOREADO, DA, *L.Am./S, adj.* Bored. *Pepe se queda choreado cuando la novia le obliga ir al ballet.* "Pepe gets bored when his girlfriend makes him go to the ballet."

CHOREAR, *L.Am./S, v.* To rob. *En sus narices le chorearon la cartera y ella ni se dio cuenta.* "They robbed her purse right under her nose and she didn't even notice."

CHORI See CHORIZO

CHORICERO, *L.Am./C, n.* Trinket vendor, illegal vendor. *Llegó un choricero que quería vendernos unos anillos.* "A street hustler arrived who wanted to sell us some rings."

CHORIZAR, *Spain, v. crim.* To rob, to steal. *Mantiene su adicción chorizando de una tienda y otra.* "He supports his addiction ripping off one store and another."

CHORIZO, 1. *Spain, n.* Penis. (Lit. Sausage.) *El viejo no piensa en otra cosa más que meter el chorizo en el bollito.* "The old guy didn't think of anything else but putting his sausage in the crack." **2.** *Spain, n.* Hoodlum, criminal. *Cada ciudad tiene su barriada de chorizos.* "Every city has its hoodlum neighborhood. **3.** *Spain, n.* Turd. *Esa gente no respeta a nadie, dejan los chorizos de sus perros en la calle.* "Those people don't respect anybody; they leave their dogs' turds on the street."

CHORLITO, 1. *Spain, n., crim.* Unsuspecting person, mark. *Ese estafador está buscando un chorlito. Prefiere a los ancianos.* "That swindler is looking for a mark. He prefers the elderly." **2.** *Spain, n.* Prostitute's john. *Arrestaron a la pindonga y a su chorlito.* "They arrested the hooker and her john."

CHORO, RA, 1. *L.Am./S, n.* Thief. *En el centro de la ciudad hay choros por todo lado.* "Downtown, there are thieves all over the place." **2.** *L.Am./S, adj.* Aggresive, hostile, violent. *Cuidado con Emilio, es un tipo choro y se pone furioso por nada.* "Be careful with Emilio; he's hot-tempered and gets furious over nothing." **3.** *L.Am./S, adj., youth.* Great, neat, cool. *El concierto anoche fue bien choro.* "Last night's concert was super cool."

CHORRA, *Spain, n.* Penis. *¡Ciérrate la cremallera! Se te va a escapar la chorra.* "Close your zipper! Your dick is going to run away."

CHORRADA, *Spain, n.* Stupidity, dumb thing. *Cometiste una chorrada. Dejaste las llaves en el coche y ya lo robaron.* "You screwed up. You left the keys in the car and now they've stolen it."

CHORREAR, *Spain, v.* To scold, to reprimand, to chew out. *El dueño de ese taller siempre está chorreando a los trabajadores.* "The owner of that shop is always chewing out the workers."

CHORREO, *Spain, n.* Scolding, reprimand, chewing out. *Cuando Tomás estropeó la pieza el jefe le metió un chorreo.* "When Thomas broke the part, the boss gave him a chewing out."

CHORRO, RRA, *L.Am./S, n. crim.* Criminal, delinquent, hood, thug. *Hay muchos chorros en ese lugar.* "There are a lot of hoods at that place."

CHOTA, 1. *Spain, n., crim.* Squealer. *Hay una chota en ese grupo pero no saben quién es.* "There is a rat in that group, but they don't know who it is." **2.** *Car., n.* Sparring partner. *Rodrigo es el chota del campeón.* "Rodrigo is the champion's sparring partner."

CHOTEARSE, *Spain, prnl. v.* To make fun of, to joke about. *Juan, deja a tu hermano en paz. Siempre te* *choteas de él.* "Juan, leave your brother alone. Quit making fun of him."

CHOZA, *L.Am./C, n.* House, home. (Lit. Hut.) *Buenas noches amigos, me voy pa' la choza.* "Goodnight friends, I'm going to my crib."

CHUBASQUERO, *Spain, n.* Condom. (Lit. Raincoat.) *Dijo que no le gustaba echar un polvo con chubasquero y ahora tiene el SIDA.* "He said that he didn't like to fuck with a raincoat and now he's got AIDS."

CHUCHA, 1. *L.Am./S, n.* Pussy, twat. *La chucha de María es muy peluda.* "Maria's pussy is very hairy." **2.** *L.Am./S, n.* Perspiration odor. *Teresa huele a chucha.* "Theresa smells like sweat." **3.** *Spain, n.* Peseta. *No tienes las chuchas para comprarme la moto.* "You don't have the coins to buy my motorcycle."

CHUCHA DE TU MADRE, *L.Am./S, idiom.* Gross insult. (Lit. Your mother's twat.) *¡Chucha de tu madre! ¿Cómo se te ocurre hacer eso?* "Fuck you! How could you do that?"

CHUCHEAR, *L.Am./S, v.* To insult. *Hay gente que siempre está chucheando a los demás.* "There are people who are always cutting down others."

CHUCHÍN, *Car., adj.* Good person or thing. *El sacerdote Manuel es un chuchín, lo estimo mucho.* "Manuel, the priest, is a good guy; I really appreciate him."

CHUECO, CA, *L.Am., adj.* Deceptive, two-faced, crooked. *Diego es un tipo chueco, no es de fiar.* "Diego is a two-faced one; he's not to be trusted."

CHULA, 1. *L.Am./S, n.* A person who hangs with another just for the person's money. *Maribel es una chula con Marcos.* "Maribel is just after Marcos's money." **2.** *Spain, adj.,* Nice, elegant, stylish. *Bego, que chula estás esta noche. ¿Adónde vas tan elegante?* "Bego, you look so nice tonight. Where are you going so dressed up?"

CHULADA, *Spain, n.* Something pretty or nice. *Esa falda* *que llevas es una chulada.* "That skirt you are wearing is really cute."

CHULEAR, 1. *Spain, v.* To live off several women. *Ese tipo no trabaja—sólo chulea de las pietas.* "That guy doesn't work, he just pimps off the hookers." **2.** *Car., v.* To act and dress flashy. *Para llamar la atención Fabiola se la pasa chuleando en las fiestas.* "To get attention, Fabiola spends her time being flashy at parties."

CHULEARSE, *L.Am./S, prnl. v.* To hang with people for their money or favor. *José se está chuleando a su amigo Arnulfo.* "Jose is leaching off his friend Arnulfo."

CHULETA, 1. *Spain, n.* Pimp, dandy. (Lit. Pork chop.) *Pedro es un chuleta.* "Pedro is a pimp." **2.** *Spain, n., sports.* Divit. *Cuando ese juega al golf levanta muchas chuletas.* "When that guy plays golf he picks up a lot of divits." **3.** *Spain, n., youth.* Crib sheet, cheat sheet. *Con la chuleta que te preparé, claro que saliste bien.* "Sure you passed, with that cheat sheet I prepared for you." **4.** *L.Am./S, n.* Blow, hit. *Le pegué una chuleta por estúpido.* "I gave him a whack for being stupid."

CHULO, *L.Am./S, adj.* Coarse, vulgar, in poor taste. *Guillermo sólo sabe contar chistes chulos.* "Guillermo only knows how to tell dirty jokes."

CHUMENDO, *Spain, n., crim.* Kiss. *Allí estaban los dos tan tranquilos dándose un chumendo en plena calle.* "There they were, the two of them, calm as can be, kissing in the middle of the street."

CHUMINGA, *L.Am./S, adj.* Poor. *Lorena es la niña más chuminga de la escuela.* "Lorena is the poorest girl of the school."

CHUMINO, *Spain, n.* Vagina. *Ella estaba en el escenario mostrando el chumino a todos.* "She was on the stage showing her beaver to everybody."

CHUN, CHUN, CHUN, *Car., adv.* Sneakily. *Julio entró chun, chun, chun en el cuarto de Matilde.* "Julio went tiptoeing into Matilde's room."

CHUNCHE, *L.Am./C, n.* Thing, object. *¿Qué es ese chunche que tienes en la mano?* "What is that thing you have in your hand?"

CHUNCHERO, *L.Am./C, n.* Pile of things. *Adela siempre tiene un chunchero en medio de su casa.* "Adela always has a pile of junk lying around at her house."

CHUNGO, GA, 1. *Spain, adj.* Bad. *Estas gambas están chungas.* "These shrimp are rotten." **2.** *Spain, adj.* Sick. *Me siento chungo hoy. Será algo que he comido.* "I am feeling rotten today; it must be something I ate."

CHUNGÓN, NA, *Spain, adj.* Joking, teasing. *Marta es muy chungona, no se sabe cuando está de broma o en serio.* "Martha is a real teaser, you don't know when she is joking or serious."

CHUPA, *L.Am./S, n.* Traffic police. *Iba manejando tan rápido que lo paró el chupa y le puso un parte.* "He was going so fast that the traffic cop stopped him and gave him a ticket."

CHUPACHARCOS, 1. *U.S., n.* Athletic shoes. *Le robaron los chupacharcos a Luís.* "They stole Luis's athletic shoes." **2.** *U.S., n.* Homosexual. *Dicen que el dependiente nuevo es un chupacharcos.* "They say that the new clerk is a fag."

CHUPACHUP, *Spain, n.* Street vacuum cleaner. (Lit. Lollipop.) *El chupachup pasa por esta calle a las cinco de la mañana.* "The street cleaner comes down this street at five in the morning."

CHÚPAME UN COJÓN, *Spain, idiom.* Expression of anger or rejection. (Lit. Suck my nut.) *Si no te gusta lo que te digo, chúpame un cojón.* "If you don't like what I am telling you, suck my balls."

CHUPAMEDIAS, *L.Am./S, n.* Bootlicker, apple-polisher, brownnoser, ass-kisser. *Lupita es una chupamedias y por eso le gusta a la directora.* "Lupita is an apple-polisher, that's why the principal likes her."

CHUPAPINGA, *Car., n.* Cocksucker. *El gobierno se hunde* *por ese chupapinga.* "The government is sinking because of that cocksucker."

CHUPAR, 1. *L.Am./S, v.* To drink. (Lit. To suck.) *Esos son unos borrachines que se lo pasan chupando todo el fin de semana.* "They are a bunch of boozers who spend all weekend drinking." **2.** *L.Am., v.* To perform cunnilingus or fellatio, to eat pussy, to suck cock. *Ese tipo sólo habla de chupar coño.* "All that guy talks about is eating pussy." **3.** *L.Am./S, Spain, v.* To live off the government or someone else. *Nosotros tenemos que trabajar mientras que ellos chupan del estado.* "We have to work while they suck off the government's tit."

CHUPAR BANQUILLO, *U.S., idiom, sports.* To be on the bench for most of the game. *Tuvieron a Roldán chupando banquillo por todo el partido.* "They had Roldán warming the bench for the whole game."

CHUPAR EL BOTE, *Spain, idiom.* To take advantage of the system without working. *Hay gente que realmente sabe chupar el bote.* "There are people who really know how to suck off the system."

CHUPAR RUEDA, *Spain, idiom, sports.* To run or cycle behind another racer to benefit from reduced wind resistance. (Lit. To suck wheel.) *González chupó rueda hasta el último minuto y salió a ganar la carrera.* "Gonzalez was riding the drag up to the last minute and then he came out to win the race."

CHUPARLE EL RABO A LA JUTÍA, *Car., idiom.* To drink. *Antes se pasaba el día chupándole el rabo a la jutía, pero ahora está asistiendo a reuniones de Alcohólicos Anónimos.* "Before, he used to spend all day hitting the bottle, but now he goes to Alcoholics Anonymous."

CHUPATINTAS, *Spain, n.* Bureaucrat, office worker, clerk. *Ese chupatintas me cae como un tiro. Es muy desagradable.* "I can't stand that petty bureaucrat. He is very unpleasant."

CHUPE, *Spain, n.* Baby's pacifier. *Dicen que los chupes* *estropean los dientes.* "They say that pacifiers damage teeth."

CHUPENDO, *Spain, crim.* Kiss. *Vaya chupendo que dio el preso a su amigo.* "What a kiss the prisoner gave his friend."

CHUPETA, *Car., n.* Government job. *Esta chupeta me tiene aburrido porque es lo mismo todos los días.* "This cushy job bores me because every day it's the same thing."

CHUPETE, *Car., n.* Kiss. *Soñé toda la noche con el chupete que me diste.* "I dreamed all night about the kiss you gave me."

CHUPI, *L.Am./S, n.* Alcoholic drink. *Voy a tomarme unos chupis con mis amigos.* "I am going to have a few drinks with my friends."

CHUPINAZO, *Spain, n., sports.* Powerful shot or kick. *Dio tal chupinazo a la pelota que metió un gol.* "He gave the ball such a powerful kick that he made a goal."

CHUPITO, *Spain, n.* Small glass of a liqueur. *Dame un chupito de Cuarenta y Tres, por favor.* "Give me just a sip of Cuarenta y Tres, please."

CHUPO, *L.Am., n.* Baby's pacifier. *Danny dejó el chupo cuando tenía dos años.* "Danny stopped using his pacifier when he was two."

CHUPÓN, 1. *L.Am./S, n.* A big kiss on the lips. *El chupón que me diste me dio tiritones.* "That kiss of yours gave me shivers." **2.** *L.Am./S, Car., n.* Hickey. *La chica tenía un chupón en el cuello.* "The girl had a hickey on her neck."

CHUPOTERO, *Spain, n.* Person who works little but has several salaries, a double- or triple-dipper. *Tu cuñado es muy chupotero, cobra de todas partes y no da ni golpe.* "Your brother-in-law is a real hustler. He gets paid everywhere and he doesn't do a thing."

CHURIMANGAR, *Spain, v., crim.* To steal, to rob. *Esa gente no hacen más que churimangar. Son unos bandidos.* "Those people do nothing but rob. They're hoodlums."

CHURRETA, *L.Am., n.* Diarrhea. *Siempre que cambio de agua me da churreta.* "Whenever I have a change in drinking water I get the runs."

CHURRO, *L.Am./S., adj. or n.* Handsome man or pretty woman. *El actor que protagoniza esa película es un churro.* "The actor in that movie is a hunk."

CHUSCO, CA, 1. *Spain, adj.* Audacious, quick, sassy. *Tu hermana es muy chusca, tiene una respuesta para todo.* "Your sister is real sassy, she's got an answer for everything." **2.** *L.Am./S, adj.* Pretty, nice, pleasant. *Adelfa tiene una familia muy chusca.* "Adelfa has a very nice family."

CHUSMA, 1. *L.Am./S, n.* Gossip. *¡Cuidado con Matilde, es una chusma! Contará todo lo que le dices.* "Be careful with Matilde, she's a gossip! She will tell everything you say to her." **2.** *L.Am./S., adj. or n.* Low-class people. *Los nuevos vecinos son pura chusma.* "The new neighbors are pure rednecks."

CHUSQUERO, *Spain, n., mil.* Commander. *El chusquero dio la orden de cancelar todos los permisos.* "The commander gave the order to cancel all leaves."

CHUTA, *Spain, n., drugs.* Hypodermic needle. *Usó una chuta sucia y ahora está bajo tierra.* "He used a dirty harpoon and now he is six feet under."

CHUTAR, *Spain, v.* To work, to function. *Este motor no chuta.* "This motor doesn't work."

CHUTAZO, *Car., n., drugs.* Drug injection. *Los adictos a la heroína se dan unos chutazos que estropean los brazos.* "Heroin junkies give themselves shots that mess up their arms."

CHUTE, *Spain, n., drugs.* Injection of heroin or other drug, fix. *Se metió un chute de caballo y cuando llegó la coz se desmayó.* "He gave himself a shot of horse and when the rush arrived he passed out."

CIEGAMACHOS, *Car., n.* Woman who lures married men into extramarital relationships. *Cuidado, que la nueva* *administradora es una ciegamachos.* "Careful, the new administrator is a home-wrecker."

CIEGAYERNOS, *Car., n.* Woman who looks for a husband for her daughter. *La madre de Olga es una ciegayernos y te está echando el ojo.* "Olga's mother is a husband-catcher and she's got her eye on you."

CIEGO, *Spain, n., drugs.* Stoned or smashed on drugs or alcohol, respectively. (Lit. Blind.) *Llevaba Julio un ciego encima que no se mantenía de pie.* "Julio was so blind drunk that he couldn't stay on his feet."

CIERTAS HIERBAS, *L.Am./S, idiom.* Euphemism employed so as not to mention a person's name. *Ciertas hierbas no cerraron la puerta cuando salieron.* "Certain people didn't close the door when they left."

CIERVO, *Spain, n.* Cuckold. (Lit. Deer [because of the horns that are the symbol of the cuckold].) *Felipito es un ciervo, su mujer se acuesta con todos.* "Felipito is a cuckold; his wife goes to bed with everybody."

CINCO CONTRA UNO, *Spain, idiom.* Male masturbation. *Muchos hombres prefieren los cinco contra uno que arriesgar el SIDA.* "Many men prefer Lady Palm and her five daughters than the risk of AIDS."

CIPOTE, 1. *Spain, n.* Prick. *¡Qué cipote es el policía ese! Quiere dar de porrazos a todos los jóvenes.* "What a prick that cop is! He wants to club all the young people." **2.** *Spain, adj.* Jerk, idiot. *El dueño de ese bar es un cipote. No sabe tratar a sus clientes.* "The owner of that bar is a jerk. He doesn't know how to treat his customers."

CIPOTEAR, *Spain, v.* To fuck. *Lo único que le interesa a ese hombre es cipotear.* "The only thing that interests that man is fucking."

CIRI, *Spain, n.* One-hundred-peseta coin. *Oye, Manolo, dame un ciri.* "Hey Manolo, give me a 'ciri'."

CIRIO, *Spain, n.* Scandal, commotion. *Montaron un cirio en la feria anoche.* "They raised hell at the fair last night."

CIRUELO, *Spain, n.* Fool, jerk. (Lit. Plum tree.) *El nuevo profesor de empresariales es un ciruelo.* "The new professor of business administration is a jerk."

CLAQUE, *Car., n.* Political follower. *Los claques del candidato favorito son muy apasionados.* "The groupies of the favorite candidate are very hot-headed."

CLARA, *Spain, n.* Beer with white soda, shandy. *"¿Qué desea Ud.?" "¿Me puede preparar una clara?"* " 'What would you like?' 'Can you prepare a shandy for me?' "

CLARINETE, *Spain, adj.* Clear, evident. (Lit. Clarinet.) *"Creo que Guillermo está medio loco". "¡Eso está clarinete!"* " 'I believe that Guillermo is half-crazy.' 'That is for sure!' "

CLAVAR, *Spain, v., neg.* To charge, to collect. (Lit. To nail down.) *Anoche nos clavaron por la comida. Ese restaurante es muy caro.* "Last night they nailed us for the meal. That restaurant is very expensive."

CLECA, *Car., adj.* Awkward at sports. *Carolina es tan cleca que no la dejaron ser parte del equipo.* "Carolina is so clumsy that they didn't let her be part of the team."

CLISOS, *Spain, pl. n., crim.* Eyes. *Los guardias echaron espré a los clisos de los presos.* "The guards sprayed the prisoner's peepers."

COA, *L.Am./S, n., crim.* Criminal slang. *Esos ladrones sólo hablan en coa y nosotros no entendemos nada.* "Those thieves speak in their slang only, and we don't understand a thing."

COBA See DAR COBA

COBANI, *L.Am./S, n., crim.* Police, cops. *Cuando entró el cobani todos los cabros salieron por las ventanas.* "When the cops entered the kids went out through the windows."

COBRARSE ALGO EN ESPECIES, *Spain, idiom.* To take back in trade, usually referring to repayment of debt with sex. *Le vendí un sofa a una ramera y quería que le cobrara en especies.* "I sold a sofa to a hooker and she wanted me to take payment back in pussy."

COCA, *L.Am., Spain, n., drugs.* Cocaine. *Los civiles confiscaron 300 kilos de coca de un barco en Marbella.* "The cops confiscated 300 kilos of coca from a boat in Marbella."

COCERSE, *L.Am., Spain, prnl. v.* To get drunk. (Lit. To get boiled.) *Joaquín dijo que iba a cocerse en la fiesta esta noche.* "Joaquin said that he was going to get plastered at the party tonight."

COCHAMBROSO, *Spain, adj.* Filthy, cruddy. *Esa gente siempre lleva una ropa cochambrosa.* "These people always wear cruddy clothes."

COCHARCAS, *L.Am./S, n.* Old lady. *La pobre Lucía ya está bien cocharcas.* "Poor Lucia is quite old by now."

COCHINCHINA, *Car., n.* Faraway place. *Mi hijo Marcos trabaja en la cochinchina.* "My son Marcos works at the end of the earth."

COCHINERA, *Spain, n., crim.* Police car. *Cuando los ladrones vieron llegar la cochinera arrancaron a perderse.* "When the hoodlums saw the patrol car they hit the road."

COCHINERO, RA, *L.Am./S, n.* Joker. *Ya pues, no seas cochinero y dime la verdad.* "Hey, stop being a joker and tell me the truth."

COCÍO, CÍA, *L.Am./S, adj.* Drunk. (Lit. Cooked, from the Spanish word "cocido.") *Pablo vino cocío a casa.* "Pablo came home stewed."

COCO, 1. *Spain, n.* Molotov cocktail. (Lit. Coconut.) *Un etarra tiró un coco al cuartel de la guardia civil.* "A Basque terrorist threw a Molotov cocktail at the civil guard barracks." **2.** *L.Am., n.* Head. *Me duele el coco.* "I have a headache."

COCOLO, *Car., n.* Afro-British immigrant. *En la casa del frente vive un cocolo muy amistoso.* "A very friendly *cocolo* lives across the street."

COCOMACACO, *Car., adj.* Very ugly. *Ese hombre es un cocomacaco, pero tiene tremenda suerte con las mujeres.* "That man is butt-ugly, but he is really lucky with women."

CÓCONO, 1. *U.S., n.* Gigolo. *Dicen que tu hermano es el cócono de la Sra. López.* "They say that your brother is Mrs. Lopez's gigolo." **2.** *U.S., n.* Turkey. *Nos regalaron un cócono para el Día de Acción de Gracias.* "They gave us a turkey for Thanksgiving."

COCOROCO, CA, *Car., n.* High executive, big shot. *El esposo de Juana es un cocoroco y gana cantidades de plata.* "Juana's husband is a big shot and makes a bundle of money."

COCORRICO, *Car., n.* Soda pop with the flavor of coconut milk. *No hay nada mejor que un cocorrico para refrescarse en un día caliente.* "There is nothing better than a *cocorrico* to cool off on a hot day."

COCOS, *Spain, pl. n.* Testicles. (Lit. Coconuts.) *Deja de rascarte los cocos. La gente te está viendo.* "Stop scratching your balls. People are watching you."

COCOTEO, *Car., n.* Fistfight. *Mira, se armó otro cocoteo en el bar de la esquina.* "Look, another fistfight broke out at the corner bar."

COCOTÚ, TÚA, 1. *Car., adj.* Big-headed person. *No encontré sombrero de tu talla, eres una cocotúa.* "I didn't find a hat your size, you're a big-headed one." **2.** *Car., adj.* Inflexible (person), strong, rigid (character). *Ya sabes lo inflexible que es mi padre, siempre igual de cocotú.* "You know how inflexible my father is: always hardheaded."

COGER, *L.Am./S, v.* To fuck. (Lit. To grab.) *La mujer entró y pescó al marido cogiendo con la amiguita.* "The wife went in and caught her husband fucking his girlfriend."

COGER ASANDO MAÍZ, *Car., idiom.* To catch someone by surprise. *Hace tiempo que Jorge se robaba el dinero sin que nadie lo supiera, pero ese día lo cogieron asando* *maíz.* "Jorge had been stealing money for a long time without anybody knowing, but that day they caught him by surprise."

COGER BERRO, *Car., idiom.* To get angry. *¡Qué berro cogí al ver el montón de mentiras que me estaba diciendo!* "I got so angry on seeing the pack of lies that he was telling me!"

COGER BRISA, *Car., idiom.* To flee. *Los criminales cogieron brisa antes de que llegara la policía.* "The criminals took off before the police arrived."

COGER COTORRA, *Car., idiom.* To be convinced. *El jurado cogió cotorra y me dejaron libre.* "The jurors were convinced and they let me go free."

COGER DE ATRÁS PA' 'LANTE, *Car., idiom.* To catch by surprise. *Con la pregunta que le hice, lo cogí de atrás pa' 'lante.* "With the question I asked him, I caught him off-guard."

COGER FIAO, *Car., idiom.* To have premarital sex. *Nadie se espera ahora al matrimonio, todos cogen fiao.* "Nobody waits for marriage anymore—they all have sex ahead of time."

COGER FUERA DE BASE, *L.Am., idiom.* To get caught by surprise. *No sé qué contestarte, me cogiste fuera de base.* "I don't know how to answer you. You caught me off-guard."

COGER MARGARITAS, *Car., idiom.* To be effeminate. *El caminadito del vecino me hace pensar que coge margaritas.* "My neighbor's cute way of walking makes me think he is on the other team."

COGER ZUMBO, *Car., idiom.* To disappear. *Rogelio cogió zumbo, no lo he visto en semanas.* "Rogelio disappeared. I haven't seen him in weeks."

COGERLA, *Spain, v.* To get drunk. *Hoy es mi día y la voy a coger bien esta noche.* "Today is my day and I am going to tie one on tonight."

COGERLE EL GOLPE A ALGO, *Car., idiom.* To pick up

on how to do something, to catch on. *Me llevó tres semanas de aprendizaje, pero al fin le pude coger el golpe al trabajo.* "I've been in training for three weeks, but finally I was able to catch on to the job."

COGERLE LA BAJA A ALGUIEN, *Car., idiom.* To get an advantage. *Tienes que enfrentar la situación de una vez y para siempre. No puedes permitir que ese guapetón te coja la baja.* "You've got to face the situation once and for all. You can't let that smart-ass get ahead of you."

COGIOGUERO, RA, *Car., n., crim.* One who accepts bribes. *Verás como te arregla la multa ese cogioguero.* "You'll see how that guy fixes your ticket."

COIMA, *L.Am./S, n.* Bribe. *El policía me pidió una coima pero no se la di.* "The cop asked me for a bribe but I didn't give it to him."

COIMERO, *L.Am./S, n.* One who gives or takes a bribe. *Ese subdirector tiene fama de coimero en esta compañia.* "That assistant director is known for taking bribes in this company."

COJÓN, *n.* Testicle. *¿Oíste que al Ramírez le dieron una patada en los cojones?* "Did you hear that they kicked Ramírez in the balls?"

COJONADA, *Spain, n.* Stupidity. *Me parece que hiciste una cojonada cuando no le diste el pésame a Juan.* "It seems to me that you screwed up when you didn't pay your respects to Juan."

COJONAMEN, *Spain, n.* Testicles. *¡Qué cojonamen! ¡Qué boxeador!* "What balls! What a boxer!"

COJONAZOS, *Spain, n.* Condescending jerk. *Yo no tolero a ese cojonazos. Se cree superior a todo el mundo.* "I can't stand that snob. He thinks he is better than anybody."

¡COJONES!, *Spain, interj.* Exclamation of anger, joy, affirmation, indignation. Balls! *¡Cojones! Te dije que no le dijeras nada del despido.* "Balls! I told you not to tell anybody about the firing."

COJONUDAMENTE, *Spain, adv.* Fantastically, terrifically. (Lit. Ballsy.) *Tomás, hiciste ese gol cojonudamente.* "Thomas, it was cool the way you made that goal."

COJONUDO, DA, *Spain, adj.* Great, fantastic, cool, the most, super cool. (Lit. Ballsy.) *La nueva canción de Manolo es cojonuda.* "Manolo's new song is cool."

COLA, *L.Am./S, adj.* Homosexual. (Lit. Tail.) *El peluquero me dijo que es cola.* "The barber told me that he is gay."

COLADO, DA, *L.Am./S, adj. or n.* Party crasher. *Ese tipo que está parado junto al sofá es un colado, nadie lo llamó.* "That guy standing next to the sofa is a party crasher, no one invited him."

COLALOCA, *Spain, n.* Coca-Cola. *Paco, dame un cubalibre con ColaLoca, por favor.* "Paco give me a Cuba Libre with Coke, please."

COLARSE, *L.Am./S, v.* To cut in ahead of others in a line. *Felipe se coló en la fila del cine y todo el mundo se enfureció con él.* "Felipe cut into the line at the movies and everybody got mad at him."

COLECTIVO, *L.Am./S, n.* Bus. (Lit. Collective.) *Nos fuimos en colectivo al centro comercial.* "We took the shuttle bus to go downtown."

COLEGA, *Spain, n.* Friend. (Lit. Colleague.) *Hola Ramón, quiero presentarte a mi colega Javier.* "Hi Ramon, I want to introduce you to my buddy, Javier."

COLGADO, DA, *Spain, adj., drugs.* Drugged. (Lit. Hung.) *Mira a ese pobre desgraciado, va colgado en caballo.* "Look at that poor slob, he is hooked on horse."

COLGAR, *Spain, v., youth.* To fail tests. (Lit. To hang.) *Me colgaron en historia y economía.* "They flunked me in History and Economics."

COLGAR LAS BOTAS, *Spain, idiom, sports.* To retire from the game. *Rodríguez va a colgar las botas después de esta temporada.* "Rodriguez is gonna hang up his boots after this season."

COLGAR LOS GUANTES, *L.Am./S, idiom.* To die. (Lit. To hang up the gloves.) *Cuando el tirano viejo colgó los guantes, la nación dio gracias a Dios.* "When the old tyrant kicked the bucket, the country gave thanks to God."

COLGAR LOS TENIS, *L.Am./C, idiom.* To die. *Cuando cuelgue yo los tenis quiero que echen mis cenizas al mar.* "When I croak I want them to throw my ashes into the sea."

COLIMBA, *L.Am./S, n.* Soldier. *Mandaron a mi primo, el colimba, a pelear en el Oriente Medio.* "They sent my GI cousin to fight in the Middle East."

COLLERA, *L.Am./S, pl. n.* Friends. (Lit. Cuff link.) *Lo invité a él solamente pero se vino con toda su collera.* "I just invited him but he came with his whole crowd."

COLMENA, *Spain, n.* Public urinal. (Lit. Beehive.) *Había una cola para entrar en la colmena, así que meé detrás de un árbol.* "There was a line to get into the public urinal, so I peed behind a tree."

COLOCADO, DA, 1. *Spain, adj., youth.* Tipsy, high. (Lit. Placed.) *Estuviste bien colocado en la fiesta anoche, ¿verdad Miguel?* "You were feeling pretty good at the party last night, right Miguel?" **2.** *Spain, adj.* Detained. *Me tuvieron colocado toda la noche hasta que vino mi amigo para sacarme.* "They had me locked up all night until my friend came to get me out."

COLOCAR, *Spain, v., crim.* To detain, to pick up, to arrest. (Lit. To place.) *La poli lo colocó anoche, pero lo soltó en seguida.* "The police grabbed him last night, but they cut him loose right away."

COLOCARSE, *Spain, prnl. v., drugs.* To get high on alcohol or drugs. *Todos los días Alvaro se colocaba con el espid.* "Alvaro got high on speed every day."

COLOMBIANA, *Spain, n., drugs.* Colombian marijuana. *Dicen que la colombiana lo eleva mejor a uno.* "They say that Colombian pot gives you a better high."

COLOQUETA, *Spain, n., crim.* Police roundup. *El asesino fue recogido en la coloqueta de la poli.* "The murderer was picked up in a police dragnet."

COLOR, *Spain, n.* Atmosphere. (Lit. Color.) *Esa sala de fiestas tiene mucho color.* "That nightclub has a lot of atmosphere."

COLORADO, 1. *Spain, n.* Gold. (Lit. Colored.) *Algunas personas todavía no confían en los bancos e invierten en el colorado.* "Some people don't trust banks and invest in gold." **2.** *L.Am./S, n.* Red. *Tengo un lápiz verde y otro colorado.* "I have a green pencil and a red one."

COLUMPIARSE, *Spain, prnl. v.* To err, to stick one's foot in one's mouth. *Te columpiaste tonto. El padre de Lola no sabía que ella iba a vivir conmigo y tú lo comentaste.* "You really screwed up, you fool. Lola's father didn't know that she was going to live with me, and you mentioned it."

COMADREJA, *Car., adj. or n.* (Lit. Weasel.) Woman who prefers married men. *Cuida a tu marido, porque su secretaria tiene fama de comadreja.* "Watch your husband, because his secretary has a reputation as a home wrecker."

COMAY, *Car., n.* Short for "comadre" (godmother or close friend). *¡Hola, comay! Cuánto tiempo sin verla.* "Hi dear! It's been a long time since I saw you."

COMECOCOS, 1. *Spain, n.* Confidence man, conman. *Cuidado, Francisco es un comecocos y te venderá algo que tú no quieres.* "Francisco is a conman. Be careful, or he will sell you something you don't want." **2.** *Spain, n.* Pacman®. *Mis hijos están enloquecidos con el juego de comecocos.* "My children are crazy with the Pacman® game."

COMEDOR, *Spain, n.* Nursing breasts. (Lit. Dining room.) *El niño está llorando porque quiere visitar el comedor de su mamá.* "The child is crying because it wants to visit his momma's chow line."

COMEHOSTIAS, *Spain, adj.* Holier than thou. (Lit. Hosteater.) *Esa mujer es una comehostias, se cree una santa total.* "That woman is holier than thou; she thinks she is a total saint."

COMEMIERDA, *L.Am., Spain, n.* Despicable person. (Lit. Shit-eater.) *Ese comemierda amarga la vida a cualquiera.* "That shit-eater would embitter anyone's life."

COMER, *L.Am./S, v.* To have sexual relations. (Lit. To eat.) *Julián me contó que se quiere comer a Blanca.* "Julian told me that he wants to get into Blanca."

COMER ARROZ CON PERICOS, *Car., idiom.* To talk too much. *No le digas nada a Josefa, ella come arroz con pericos.* "Don't say anything to Josefa; she's a real chatterbox."

COMER BANCO, *Car., idiom, sports.* To be benched. *Mi sobrino pasó todo el partido comiendo banco.* "My nephew spent the whole game on the bench."

COMER CABLE, *Car., idiom.* To be in a difficult economic situation. *Estábamos comiendo cable cuando el banco nos hizo el préstamo.* "We were at the end of our rope when the bank gave us a loan."

COMER CANDELA, *Car., idiom.* To be daring, bold, brazen. *Alvaro come candela, no se echa pa' 'tras con nadie.* "Alvaro is a live wire; he doesn't back down for anybody."

COMER CARNE DE BURRO, *Car., idiom.* To have homosexual relations. *La policía confiscó unos vídeos de maricas comiendo carne de burro.* "The police confiscated some videos of fags fucking."

COMER CEREBRO, *Car., idiom.* To brainwash. *Claudia se cambió de religión porque el novio le comió el cerebro.* "Claudia changed her religion because her boyfriend brainwashed her."

COMER EL COCO, *Spain, idiom.* To brainwash. *Marta, te están comiendo el coco con esos anuncios, piensa un poco.* "Marta, those ads are brainwashing you; think a little."

COMER GOFIO, *Car., idiom.* To kill time. *Estábamos todos sentados comiendo gofio, esperando las noticias.* "We were all sitting around, killing time while waiting for the news."

COMER JOBOS, *Car., idiom.* To play hooky. *Te van a expulsar de la escuela si sigues comiendo jobos.* "They are going to kick you out of school if you keep playing hooky."

COMERCIO, *Spain, n., youth.* Food. (Lit. Trade.) *Había mucho comercio y bebercio en la reunión.* "There was a lot to eat and drink at the party."

COMERLE A UNO EL SESO, *Car., idiom.* To indoctrinate someone, to brainwash. *A los viejos les comieron los sesos con la publicidad.* "Advertising brainwashed the elderly."

COMERSE A ALGUIEN, *Car., idiom, crim.* To swindle someone. *Se comieron al viejo por todos sus ahorros.* "They swindled the old man of all his savings."

COMERSE LA COLORÁ, *Car., idiom.* To run a red light. *Le multaron a Pepe por comerse la colorá.* "They fined Pepe for running a red light."

COMERSE UN ÁCIDO, *Spain, idiom, drugs.* To take acid. *Estaban comiéndose un ácido cuando uno empezó a alucinar.* "They were doing acid when one of them began to hallucinate."

COMERSE UN GARRÓN, *L.Am./S, idiom.* To put up with something. *Me comí un garrón esperándote, che.* "It was a real drag waiting for you, guy."

COMÉRSELO ENTERITO, *L.Am./S, idiom.* To believe something, to fall for something. *Ella se lo comió enterito y se cree muy inteligente.* "She fell for it completely, and thinks she's real bright."

COMETA, *L.Am./S, n., crim.* Bribe. (Lit. Comet.) *Mi primo le dio una cometa al oficial para que me dejara ir.* "My cousin gave a bribe to the officer to let me go."

COMETERO, *L.Am./S, n., crim.* Person who bribes or

takes a bribe. *Fue expulsado de la policía por cometero.* "He was kicked out by the police for taking bribes."

¿CÓMO ANDAMIO?, *L.Am./S, idiom,* How are we doing? (From the Italian "Come andiamo?") *¿Cómo andamio, compadre?* "How are we doing, pal?"

¿CÓMO LE QUEDÓ EL OJO?, *L.Am./S., idiom.* What do you think? *Gané la competencia. ¿Cómo le quedó el ojo?* "I beat the competition. What do you think?"

COMODÍN, *Car., n.* Jack-of-all-trades. (Lit. Wild card.) *Mis hijos son unos comodines. Saben hacer de todo.* "My sons are jacks-of-all-trades. They know how to do everything."

COMPADRE, *L.Am./S, Car., n.* Friend, buddy, pal. (Lit. Godfather.) *Ven acá, compadre. Necesito que me aclares esta duda.* "Come here pal. I need you to clear up a doubt that I have."

COMPAI See COMPAY

COMPAÑEROS, *Car., pl. n.* Testicles. (Lit. Comrades.) *Me duelen los compañeros después de la patada que me dieron.* "My balls hurt after the kick they gave me."

COMPAY, *Car., n.* Short for "compadre" (godfather or close friend). *Compay! ¿Adónde vamos a pescar mañana?* "Bro! Where are we going fishing tomorrow?"

COMPRAR GATO ENTRE SACO, *Car., idiom.* To buy something sight unseen. *Mi marido compró la joya al amigo como comprar gato entre saco.* "My husband bought the jewel from a friend without even looking at it."

COMPUTARSE, *L.Am./S, prnl. v.* To think about oneself. *Justino se computa lo máximo porque ya tiene carro.* "Justino thinks he is the greatest because now he has a car."

CON CARPA, *L.Am./S, idiom.* Surreptitiously, on the quiet, *Le di el dinero con carpa al oficial.* "I slipped the official the money."

CON EL CULO A DOS MANOS, *L.Am./S, idiom.* Very

frightened, scared shitless. *Mañana tengo que ir al médico y tengo el culo a dos manos.* "Tomorrow I have to go to the doctor and I'm scared shitless."

CON EL CULO FUERA, *L.Am./S, idiom.* Angry, pissed off. *El jefe llegó esta mañana con el culo fuera, no sé por qué.* "The boss arrived this morning all pissed off, I don't know why."

CON LOS CHICOTES CRUZADOS, *L.Am./S, idiom.* Ill-humored, in a bad mood. *Ni te le acerques mucho porque amaneció con los chicotes cruzados.* "Don't get too close to him, because he got up on the wrong side of the bed."

CON TODA LA PATA, 1. *L.Am./C, idiom.* Completely satisfied or recovered. *"¿Te mejoraste del dolor?" "¡Con toda la pata! Me siento de maravilla."* " 'Did you get over your pain?' 'Completely! I feel wonderful.' " **2.** *L.Am./C, idiom.* Good, in good health. *"¿Cómo está tu padre?" "Con toda la pata."* " 'How's your father?' 'OK.' "

CON TODOS LOS HIERROS, *Car., idiom.* With everything, the works. *Me acabo de comprar un carro con todos los hierros.* "I just bought a car with the works."

CONCHO, CHA 1. *L.Am./C, n.* Hick, yokel. *¡No seas concho Guillermo! Ponte otra camisa.* "Don't be a hick, Guillermo! Put on another shirt." **2.** *Car., n.* Shuttle taxi. *Me tocará irme en concho hasta donde mi abuelita.* "I'll have to take the shuttle taxi to my grandmother's."

CONCHUDO, DA, *L.Am./S., adj.* A person who takes advantage of others. *Quiere que todo lo haga yo, es un conchudo.* "He wants me to do everything, he's very selfish."

CONCRETAR, *L.Am., v.* To score. *Y allí va López y concreta, ¡gol!* "And there goes Lopez and he scores, goal!"

CONDORO, *L.Am./S, n.* Mistake, error. *Cometí un condoro gordo.* "I made a big boo-boo."

CONEJA, *Car., n.* Woman who gives birth frequently. (Lit. Rabbit.) *La señora de Hinojosa es una coneja, tiene ocho* *hijos en ocho años.* "Mrs. Hinojosa is a rabbit; she has had eight children in eight years."

COÑETE, *L.Am./S, n.* Tightwad, stingy person. *Ese tipo es un coñete, no come un plátano por no botar la cáscara.* "That guy is a tightwad—he doesn't eat bananas because he doesn't want to throw away the peel."

CONGO, GA, *Car., adj.* Short person. *Felipe es congo pero muy apuesto.* "Felipe is a short guy but he is very dapper."

CÓNSUL, *Car., adj., crim.* Partner in crime. (Lit. Consul.). *Ese hombre tuvo un cónsul que le ayudó a secuestrar al ministro.* "That man had a partner who helped him kidnap the minister."

CONTROL, LA, *U.S., n., crim.* Boss, leader. (Lit. Control.) *Los pandilleros hacen todo lo que les dice su control.* "The gang members do everything their boss says."

CONTROLA, *U.S., n.* Wife. *La controla de Juan no le deja salir a jugar al póquer.* "Juan's wife doesn't let him go out to play poker."

COOPERASTE, *L.Am./S, idiom.* Expression used when one willingly goes along with another to one's own disadvantage. (Lit. Cooperated.) *Tú le prestaste el dinero y ahora no te paga. ¡Cooperaste!* "You lent him the money and now he won't pay you. You cooperated!"

COPADO, DA, 1. *L.Am./S, adj.* Happy, excited. *Isabel está muy copada con su auto nuevo.* "Isabel is bonkers with her new car." **2.** *L.Am./S, adj.* A lot of fun, a blast. *Se ve que el partido del domingo va a estar copado.* "You can tell that Sunday's game is going to be a blast."

COPAR, *L.Am./C, v.* To visit one's sweetheart. *Pablo está copando con la novia.* "Pablo is visiting his girl."

COPETE, *L.Am./S, n.* Drink, shot, glass. *Tomemos un copete antes de que te vayas.* "Let's have a glass before you go."

COPIETAS, *L.Am./S, n.* Copycat. *La copietas de Diana siempre se viste como yo.* "Diana is a copycat, and is always dressing like me."

COPUCHA, *L.Am./S, n.* Gossip. *¿Le contaste la copucha de Isidro y Lola a tu madre?* "Did you tell your mom the choice bit about Isidro and Lola?"

COPUCHENTA, *L.Am./S, adj.* Nosy, gossipy. *No puedo tolerar a esa señora, es tan copuchenta.* "I can't stand that lady, she is so nosy."

CORA, *U.S., n.* Twenty-five-cent coin, quarter. (From English "quarter.") *Ya necesitamos más que una cora para el teléfono.* "Now we need more than a quarter for the telephone."

CORCHADO, DA, *L.Am./S., adj., youth.* To not know the answer. *Quedó corchado con la segunda pregunta.* "He got stuck on the second question."

CORCHAR, *L.Am./S., v., youth.* To ask someone something that they don't know. *El profesor lo corchó con la segunda pregunta.* "The professor caught him on the second question."

CORNETA, 1. *Car., adj.* Stupid, fool. (Lit. Bugle.) *No seas corneta, tienes que saber esta materia para mañana.* "Hey stupid, you've got to know this material for tomorrow." **2.** *Car., n.* Cuckold. *El marido de Lola es un corneta. Ella tiene un amante.* "Lola's husband is a cuckold. She has a lover."

COROTO, *L.Am./S, n.* Any object or thing, stuff. *Recogí mis corotos y me largué.* "I picked up my stuff and split."

CORRALÓN, *L.Am./N, n.* Car impound lot. *Ya me llevaron el carro al corralón.* "They already took my car to the impound lot."

CORRECORRE, *Car., n.* Stampede of people. *¡Hubo un correcorre en el centro hoy! Pensaban que había una bomba.* "There was a stampede downtown today. They thought there was a bomb."

CORRER MANO, *L.Am./S, idiom.* To paw, to feel up. (Lit. To run the hand.) *A ese viejo verde le gusta correr mano a todas la mujeres.* "That dirty old man likes to paw all the women."

CORRERSE, 1. *Car., prnl. v.* To be disrespectful. *Armando se corrió cuando estaba hablando con el jefe.* "Armando went too far when he talked to the boss." **2.** *L.Am./S, prnl. v.* To slip away. *Juan se corrió a última hora y no me acompañó en el viaje.* "Juan slipped away at the last minute and didn't go with me on the trip." **3.** *Spain, prnl. v.* To come, to have an orgasm. *Con María me corro en un minuto.* "With Maria I come in one minute."

CORRERSE LAS TEJAS, *L.Am./C, idiom.* To go crazy, to get turned around. *Al padre de Tomás se le corrieron las tejas y lo tuvieron que ingresar.* "Tomas's father went nuts and they had to hospitalize him."

CORRIDA, *Car., n.* Nightlife. *A mi hijo le encanta la corrida de San Juan.* "My son loves San Juan's nightlife."

CORRONCHO, CHA, 1. *L.Am./S, n.* A hick or yokel from the coast. *El vecino corroncho se va a casar pronto.* "Our coastal yokel neighbor is going to get married soon." **2.** *L.Am./S, adj.* Tacky. *¡Qué música tan corroncha!* "What hickish music!"

CORTAR CHAQUETAS, *Car., idiom.* To gossip. *Lo único que haces cuando te reúnes con tus amigas es cortar chaquetas.* "The only thing you do when you get together with your friends is to gossip."

CORTAR TRAJES, *Spain, idiom.* To talk about someone, to gossip. *Las mujeres estaban tomando café y cortando trajes.* "The women were having coffee and gossiping."

CORTARLE A UNO LAS PATAS, *Car., idiom, crim.* To place restrictions on a prisoner, to take away privileges. *Ya le cortaron las patas a Jiménez. Había insultado a un guardia.* "They've reined Jimenez in. He had insulted a guard."

CORTE, *Spain, n.* Sudden comeback, quick insult. (Lit. Court.) *¡Qué corte tiene Gustavo! No se queda atrás con nadie.* "What a quick comeback Gustavo's got! He doesn't get left behind with anybody."

CORTO, 1. *L.Am./S, Spain, n.* Short film. (Lit. Short.)

Echaron un corto antes de poner la película principal. "They showed a short film before screening the main picture." **2. CORTO, TA,** *L.Am./S, Spain, adj. or n.* Shy, slow starter. *Eugenio es muy corto. No dice mucho.* "Eugenio is very shy. He doesn't say much."

COSA MALA, *Spain, idiom.* Much, many, a lot, large. (Lit. A bad thing.) *La cantidad de comida que tenían era una cosa mala.* "The amount of food they had was something out of sight."

COSCOLINO, NA, *L.Am./N, adj.* Sensitive, touchy. *Oye, no seas tan coscolina conmigo.* "Listen, don't be so touchy with me."

COSTAR UN OJO DE LA CARA, *L.Am./S, Car., idiom.* To be very expensive, to cost an arm and a leg. *Esta casa me costó un ojo de la cara.* "That house cost me an arm and a leg."

COSTILLA, 1. *U.S., Spain, n.* Wife. (Lit. Rib.) *¿Alvaro, cuándo nos vas a presentar la costilla?* "Alvaro, when are you going to introduce us to your better half?" **2.** *U.S., L.Am./S, n.* Sweetheart. *La costilla de Juan le estaba poniendo los cachos en sus narices y él ni cuenta se daba.* "Juan's significant other was cheating on him right under his nose and he didn't even notice."

COTISUELTO, TA, *Car., n.* Person who wears the tail of the shirt outside his or her pants. *Hay muchos cotisueltos en ese club.* "There are a lot of rednecks in that club."

COYOTEAR, *U.S., v.* To hang out, to goof off. *Esos batos estaban coyoteando frente a la escuela.* "Those dudes were hanging out in front of the school."

COYUNTOS, TAS, 1. *Car., pl. n.* Persons who are related. *¿Sabe Ud. que Juan López y Javier son coyuntos?* "Do you know that Juan Lopez and Javier are related?" **2.** *Car., pl. n.* Half siblings. *Alvaro López Rodondo y Juan López Alvarez son coyuntos.* "Alvaro Lopez Rodondo and Juan Lopez Alvarez are half brothers." **3.** *Car., pl. n.* Children raised as siblings. *Esos muchachos son coyuntos, se* *criararon juntos pero no son hermanos.* "Those boys are like brothers; they were raised together but are not relatives."

COZ, *Spain, n., drugs.* Heroin rush. (Lit. Kick.) *Los drogatos se pinchan por la coz que reciben.* "The junkies stick themselves for the rush they get."

CRACK, *Spain, n., drugs.* Treated cocaine smoked in a pipe, crack. *El crack da una colgada más intensa.* "Crack gives a more intense high."

CREERSE LA MUERTE, *L.Am./S, idiom.* To consider one's self superior, the best. *Inés se cree la muerte.* "Ines thinks she's the living end."

CRIAR GUSANOS See CRIAR MARGARITAS

CRIAR MARGARITAS, *Spain, idiom.* To be dead, to be pushing up daisies. *Si no deja Tomás de tomar drogas, pronto va a estar criando margaritas.* "If Thomas doesn't stop taking drugs soon he's going to be pushing up daisies."

CRONO, *Spain, n., youth.* Watch. *Mis padres me regalaron un crono.* "My parents gave me a watch for a present."

CRUZARLE LOS CABLES A ALGUIEN, *Spain, idiom.* To get confused, to get one's wires crossed. *Juan me cruzó los cables y llegué tarde para nuestra cita.* "Juan got my wires crossed and I was late for our appointment."

CUADRADO, *Spain, adj.* Overweight, fat. *Enrique está muy cuadrado. ¿Cuándo le dio por comer?* "Enrique is real fat. When did he get into eating?"

CUADRANGULAR, *Car., n.* Home run. *Rodolfo pegó un cuadrangular para ganar el partido.* "Rodolfo hit a homer to win the game."

CUADRAO, *L.Am./N, adj.* Drunk. *Pablo bebió tanto que se quedó cuadrao.* "Pablo drank so much that he got plastered."

CUADRARSE, *L.Am./S, v.* To become somebody's boyfriend or girlfriend. *Me cuadré con Andrés ayer y* *estoy dichosa.* "I became Andres's girlfriend yesterday and I am happy."

CUADRILLA, *Spain, n., youth.* Group of friends. *Mamá, voy a salir con la cuadrilla.* "Mom, I am going out with the gang."

CUADRO, *L.Am./S, n.* Soccer team. *¿Con qué cuadro juegas vos?* "What team do you play with?"

CUAJO, *L.Am./N, n.* Lie, fib. *El niño me contó un cuajo.* "The boy told me a fib."

¿CUÁL BOLSA?, *L.Am./C, idiom.* Interrogative expression indicating doubt. *¿Cuál bolsa? Yo no hice nada.* "What are you talking about? I didn't do anything."

CUARTA, *Car., n.* Sidekick. *A mi cuarta Solita le gusta ir conmigo a los museos.* "My sidekick Solita likes to go with me to the museums."

CUARTOS, *Car., pl. n.* Money. *Si no tienes suficientes cuartos, no vas a poder comprar ese carro.* "If you don't have enough moola, you won't be able to buy that car."

CUÁS, *L.Am./N, n.* Best buddy. *María, quiero presentarte a mi cuás.* "Maria, I want to introduce you to my best pal."

CUBANO, *Spain, n.* Masturbation with the penis placed between the woman's breasts. (Lit. Cuban.) *Siempre que iba al burdel pedía hacer el cubano.* "Whenever he went to the brothel he would ask for the Cuban special."

CUBATA, *Spain, n.* Rum and Coca-Cola. *Después de tres cubatas estoy para irme a casa.* "After three rum and cokes I am ready to go home."

CUCA, *L.Am./S., n.* Vagina. *En esas revistas todas muestran la cuca.* "They show pussy in all those magazines."

CUCO, CA, 1. *Car., adj.* Lively (elderly person). *Mi padre es bien cuco. Tiene la actividad de un hombre más joven.* "My father is real lively. He acts like a younger man." **2.** *L.Am./S, adj.* Cute, pretty. *La bebita de Natalia es muy cuca y se parece al papá.* "Natalia's baby girl is very cute and she looks like her daddy."

CUCOS, *L.Am./S, n.* Panties. *No te sientes así que se te ven los cucos.* "Don't sit that way, one can see your panties."

CUENTO CHINO, *Spain, idiom.* Tall tale, bull. *No te creo. Lo que tú dices es un cuento chino.* "I don't believe you. What you say is a crock."

CUERDA, *Car., n.* Anger. (Lit. Rope.) *Cuando supo que su mujer lo engañaba, le dio una cuerda terrible.* "When he found out that his wife was cheating on him he got truly pissed."

CUERO, 1. *L.Am./S, n.* Prostitute. (Lit. Leather.) *Anoche la calle estaba llena de cueros de para allá y para acá.* "Last night the street was full of whores back and forth." **2.** *L.Am./S, adj.* Attractive. *¡La prima de Chantal es un cuero!* "Chantal's cousin is a real hunk!"

CUERVO, 1. *L.Am./S, n.* Pejorative term for attorney. (Lit. Crow.) *El cuervo me cobró un dineral por los trámites del divorcio.* "The shark charged me a bundle for handling the divorce." **2.** *Spain, n.* Priest. *Vi al cuervo muy temprano yendo para la iglesia.* "I saw the priest going very early to the church." **3.** *U.S., n.* African-American. *El nuevo maestro es un cuervo.* "The new teacher is a black person."

CUEVA DEL INDIO, *Car., idiom, crim.* Jail cell. *¡Qué tristeza pasar los días metido en su cueva del indio!* "How sad it is to spend one's days in a cell!"

CUICO, *L.Am./S, n. or adj.* Big shot. *Todos los cuicos se reúnen en ese club los viernes por la tarde.* "All the preppies get together at that club every Friday afternoon."

CUITEAR, *U.S., v.* To quit. (From English "to quit.") *Ayer Juan cuiteó su trabajo.* "Yesterday Juan quit his job."

CULEBRA, *L.Am./S, idiom.* Debt. (Lit. Snake.) *Tengo tantas qulebras que no sé lo que voy a hacer.* "I've got so many debts that I don't know what I'm going to do."

CULEBRO, *L.Am./S, n.* Debt collector. *Si no pagas esa cuenta vas a tener una visita del culebro.* "If you don't pay that bill you'll have a visit from the bill collector."

CULEBRÓN, *Car., n.* Pejorative term for strong black man. (Lit. Augmentative for "serpent.") *Luis le pegó al jefe por haberle llamado culebrón.* "Luis hit the boss for calling him a big black snake."

CULETE, *Spain, n.* Child's behind. *Ven aquí niño, te tengo que lavar el culete.* "Come here boy, I have to wash your butt."

CULIBAJO, JA, *Car., adj.* Having a low-slung posterior. *Como eres tan culibaja esos pantalones no te quedan bien.* "Since you have such a flop-ass, these pants aren't going to fit you."

CULICAGAO, *Car., n.* Adolescent, teenager. *Estás muy culicagao para meterte en conversaciones de adultos.* "You're too much of a snot nose to get involved in adult conversations."

CULICHUMBO, BA, *Car., adj.* Having hardly any buttocks. *La niña de Rosario salió igual de culichumba a ella.* "Just like her mother, Rosario's girl has hardly any butt at all."

CULIFLACO, CA, *Car., adj.* Having a skinny rear. *No me gustan las mujeres culiflacas.* "I don't like skinny-assed women."

CULIFLOJO, JA, *Car., adj.* Cowardly. *El culiflojo de Omar salió corriendo cuando empezó la pelea.* "That scaredy-cat Omar took off running when the fight started."

CULIPANEAR, *Car., v.* To look for excuses for not meeting obligations. *Ese empleado tiene la costumbre de culipanear, yo no le creo nada.* "That employee is in the habit of making up excuses. I don't believe him at all."

CULO, 1. *Spain, n.* Buttocks, rear end, butt, behind, ass. *Niño, si no me escuchas te voy a dar una guantada en el culo.* "Boy, if you don't listen to me I'm going to give you a smack on your behind." **2.** *L.Am., n.* Anus, asshole. *Si no le gusta dile que se lo meta por el culo.* "If he doesn't like it, tell him to stick it up his ass. **3.** *L.Am./S, n.* Luck.

No tengo culo para el juego. "I don't have the luck for gambling."

CULO PAJARERO, *Spain, idiom.* Naked behind. *En las playas las niñas y las mujeres pasean con el culo pajarero.* "On the beaches girls and women walk by showing their naked butts."

CULÓN, NA, 1. *L.Am./S, n.* Lucky or fortunate person. *¡Qué culón es Roberto! Ganó la lotería por un millón.* "What a lucky guy Roberto is! He hit the lottery for a million." **2.** *Spain, n.* Person having big buttocks. *Antonio se ha puesto muy culón desde que lo vi la última vez.* "Antonio has become big-butted since I've seen him last.

CUMA, *L.Am./S, n.* Low-class individual, bum. *No hay más que cumas en ese bar.* "There's nothing but lowlifes in that bar."

CUMECO, CA, *Car., n., drugs.* Drug addict. *El cumeco robaba para mantener su adicción.* "The junkie stole to support his addiction."

CUMPA, *L.Am./S, n.* Godfather or close friend. *Mi cumpa tiró la casa por la ventana por su aniversario.* "My buddy went all out for his anniversary."

CUMPLIR, *Spain, v.* To fulfill one's sexual duty with one's partner. *Ella ya no tenía ganas, pero le hizo el amor por cumplir.* "She didn't feel like it, but she made love out of duty."

CUÑAO, *L.Am./S, n.* Good friend. *Cuñao mío, vamos a tomar un trago.* "My buddy, let's go have a drink."

CUORA, *U.S., n.* Twenty-five-cent piece, quarter. (From English "quarter.") *Préstame una cuora.* "Lend me a quarter."

CUQUEAR, *Car., v.* To flirt. *Tienes que cuquear más para atraer a los hombres.* "You've got to flirt more to attract men."

CUQUERÍA, 1. *Car., n.* Flirting. *Tanta cuquería tuya ya está fastidiando a Alberto.* "All your flirting is bothering Alberto." **2.** *L.Am., n.* Cute thing. *Qué cuquería de muñe-*

quita la que le regalaste a Lili. "What a cute little doll you gave Lili."

CUQUERO, RA, *Car., n.* Flirt. *Marcela es definitivamente la más cuquera del grupo.* "Marcela is definitely the biggest flirt of the group."

CURADO, *L.Am./S, adj.* Drunk. *Aurelia quedó curada en la fiesta.* "Aurelia tied one on at the party."

CURARSE, *Car., prnl. v.* To feel mellow from drugs. *Al principio a uno le gusta curarse con la droga, pero después uno paga.* "At first one feels mellow with the drug, but later one has to pay."

CURDA, 1. *L.Am./S, n.* Drinking bout. *Nos pusimos una buena curda anoche.* "We really got smashed last night." **2.** *L.Am./S, n.* Drunk. *No eres más que un curda.* "You're nothing but a drunk."

CURRA, *Spain, n., crim.* Penknife. *Tenía una curra escondida en la bota.* "He had a shiv hidden in his boot."

CURRADOR, *L.Am./S, n., crim.* Dishonest person, crook. *El que me vendió el reloj era un currador, el reloj es falso.* "The guy who sold me the watch was a crook; the watch is fake."

CURRANTE, *Spain, n.* Worker. *Hay cuarenta currantes en la fábrica de mi tío.* "There are forty workers in my uncle's factory."

CURRAR, *Spain, v., crim.* To hit, to strike a blow. *Le curró a Carlos por haberle insultado a su mujer.* "He socked Carlos for having insulted his wife."

CURRO, 1. *L.Am./N, n.* Andalusian Spaniard. *Los curros son muy simpáticos, me encanta como hablan.* "Andalusians are very likable. I love the way they talk." **2.** *L.Am./N, n.* Elegant person, sharp dresser. *¿Quién es ese curro sentado con Luisa?* "Who is that sharp dude sitting with Luisa?"

DABUTE(N), *Spain, adj., youth.* Cool, great, fantastic. *Tu coche nuevo es dabute. ¿Cuándo lo compraste?* "Your new car is awesome. When did you buy it?"

DAGA, *Car., n.* Cutting tongue. (Lit. Dagger.) *La mujer del alcalde tiene una daga que deja a cualquiera humillado.* "The mayor's wife has a sharp tongue that humiliates anybody."

DAIME, *U.S., n.* Ten-cent coin. (From English "dime.") *Mira, encontré un daime en el suelo.* "Look, I found a dime on the ground."

¡DALE!, 1. *Spain, interj.* O.K.!, Affirmative!, Let's do it! *"¿Los parece bien si vamos al boliche?" "¡Dale!"* " 'How about if we go to the bar?' 'Let's do it!' " **2.** *L.Am./S, Spain, interj.* Hit it!, Go, go! *¡Dale, Rodriguez! Necesitamos un gol.* "Hit it, Rodriguez! We need a goal."

DANONE, *Spain, n., crim.* White patrol car. *Allí está el danone. ¿Dónde estarán los polizontes?* "There's the patrol car. Where would the coppers be?"

DAR A LA LENGUA, *L.Am./N, idiom.* To talk a lot. *A Isabel le gusta dar a la lengua. Nunca para.* "Isabel likes to wag her tongue. She never stops."

DAR BÁSCULA, *U.S., idiom, crim.* To frisk. *Nos bascularon antes de dejarnos visitar al amigo.* "They frisked us before letting us visit our friend."

DAR BATERÍA, *U.S., idiom.* To bother, to give a hard time. *Oye Pepe, no quiero darte batería, pero me debes dinero.* "Listen Pepe, I don't want to give you a hard time but you owe me money."

DAR BOLA, *L.Am./S, idiom.* To pay attention, to follow advice. *Amigo mío, nunca le das bola a lo que te digo.* "My friend, you never pay attention to what I tell you."

DAR BOLILLA See DAR BOLA

DAR CANDELA, 1. *Car., idiom.* To misbehave. *El niño de esa pareja da candela. No sé cómo lo aguantan.* "That couple's boy is a pain. I don't know how they stand him." **2.** *Spain, idiom.* To spank. *Niño, como no me dejes en paz, te voy a dar candela.* "Boy, if you don't leave me alone, I am going to warm your behind."

DAR CARRERAS, *Car., idiom.* To run all over the place doing something. *El está dando carreras para obtener el pasaporte antes de su viaje al extranjero.* "He is running all over the place trying to get his passport before his trip abroad."

DAR CEREBRO, *Car., idiom, crim.* To plan a robbery. *Los cinco se juntaron para dar cerebro acerca del robo del banco.* "The five got together to plan the bank robbery."

DAR COBA, *Car., idiom.* To flatter for some hidden purpose. *Me gustaría saber lo que quiere mi mujer, lleva varios días dándome coba.* "I'd like to know what my wife wants; she's been buttering me up for several days now."

DAR COTORRA, *Car., idiom.* To pester. *Le di cotorra hasta que por fin me dio un beso.* "I pestered her until she finally gave me a kiss."

DAR CUARTEL, *Spain, idiom.* To help, to give aid, to lend a hand. *Oiga, señor, ¿nos puede dar cuartel aquí por favor?* "Listen sir, could you give us a hand here, please?"

DAR CUERDA, 1. *L.Am./S, idiom.* To show interest. *No le des cuerda o nos tocará oír su historia por tres horas.*

"Don't pay any attention to him or we'll have to hear his story for three hours." **2.** *Car., idiom.* To make someone angry. *No me des cuerda porque te vas a arrepentir.* "Don't get me started or you will be sorry."

DAR DAGA, *Car., idiom.* To have sexual intercourse. *Prendí la tele y allí estaba una pareja dando daga como si no fuera nada.* "I switched on the TV and there was a couple fucking as if it were nothing."

DAR EL AGUA, *Spain, idiom.* To warn that the police are coming or of some danger, to put on alert. *Pablo dio el agua y todos se fueron corriendo.* "Pablo gave the alarm and everybody took off."

DAR EL BOTE, *Spain, idiom.* To dismiss someone. *No sé lo que vamos a hacer. Le dieron el bote a José.* "I don't know what we are going to do. They canned Jose."

DAR EL BRAGUETAZO, *Spain, idiom.* Marriage of a poor man with a rich woman. *Gustavo dio el braguetazo con Lourdes.* "Gustavo struck gold with Lourdes."

DAR EL CALLO, *Spain, idiom.* To work. *"¿Dónde está tu hermano?" "Dando el callo en el taller."* " 'Where is your brother?' 'Getting calluses at the shop.' "

DAR EL DEDO, *Car., idiom.* To give the finger. *Cuando lo despedimos nos dio el dedo y se fue.* "When we dismissed him, he gave us the finger and left."

DAR EL PALO, *Car., idiom.* To make a good impression. *Cuando entró Pedro para la entrevista dio el palo y ganó el puesto.* "Pedro came in, knocked our socks off, and won the job."

DAR EL PASAPORTE, 1. *Spain, idiom, crim.* To kill. *El jefe le dijo que diera el pasaporte al chivato.* "The boss said to give the squealer a send-off." **2.** *Spain, idiom.* To fire from a job. *Ayer le dieron el pasaporte a cincuenta empleados de la fábrica.* "Yesterday they gave the walking papers to fifty employees from the factory."

DAR EL QUEO, *Spain, idiom, crim.* To alert, to warn. *Pablo no me dio el queo y cuando vi la poli era tarde.*

"Pablo didn't give me the warning signal, and when I saw the police it was too late."

DAR EL SANTO, *Spain, idiom, crim.* To provide information on a place that has been cased for a possible robbery. *Su cuñado conocía el lugar y dio el santo si por acaso lo queríamos robar.* "His brother-in-law knew the place, so he gave us the layout in case we wanted to rob it."

DAR JABÓN, *Car., idiom.* To flatter, to soft-soap. *Carlos está dándole jabón a mi mamá para poder salir conmigo.* "Carlos is softening up my mother so he can go out with me."

DAR LA BLANCA, *Spain, idiom, mil.* To get discharged from military service. *A mí me dieron la blanca en 1961.* "They gave me my papers in 1961."

DAR LA BRONCA, *Spain, idiom.* To bother, to pester. *¡Niño! ¡Deja de dar la bronca ya!* "Boy! Stop pestering already!"

DAR LA NOTA, *Spain, idiom.* To get attention with something outlandish. *A la mujer del alcalde le gusta dar la nota con los peinados que lleva.* "The mayor's wife likes to get attention with her hairdos."

DAR LEÑA, *Car., idiom.* To try hard, to give one's best shot. *¡Dale leña y sacarás ese proyecto adelante!* "Hit it hard and you will pull that project off!"

DAR MADERA, *U.S., idiom.* To flatter. *Julia siempre le está dando madera al jefe.* "Julia is always flattering the boss."

DAR MENTE, *Car., idiom.* To think, to reflect. *No sabemos donde nos casaremos. Todavía le estamos dando mente.* "We don't know where we will get married. We are still wracking our brains."

DAR MICO, *Car., idiom.* To consume without paying. *Si vuelves a dar mico no te van a dejar entrar más al restaurante.* "If you leave without paying again they'll never allow you to come back to the restaurant."

DAR MUELA, *Car., idiom.* To try to convince someone. *Mariela le sigue dando muela a su novio para que le* *compre el anillo.* "Mariela keeps after her boyfriend so he will buy her a ring."

DAR O METER UNA MUELA, *Car., idiom.* To talk excessively to someone. *¡Qué muela me metió tu amiga! Por poco me duermo en el teléfono.* "Did your friend bend my ear! I almost fell asleep on the telephone."

DAR PÁJARA, *Car., idiom, crim.* To deceive. *Ese tipo nos dio pájara y terminó estafándonos a todos.* "That guy conned us and ended up swindling everybody."

DAR PALO, *L.Am./S, idiom.* To beat. *A los colombianos les dieron palo en el partido del sábado.* "The Colombians were beaten in Saturday's game."

DAR PAPAYA, *L.Am./S, idiom.* To give reason for ridicule. *No quiero reirme de ti, pero tú mismo das papaya con las tonterías que dices.* "I don't want to laugh at you, but you give me reason to do it with the dumb things you say."

DAR PELOTA, 1. *L.Am./C, idiom.* To go along with someone. *Yo no le hago caso cuando habla así, le doy pelota y ya.* "I don't pay attention when she talks like that; I just go along with her." **2.** *L.Am., idiom.* To pay attention to someone. *Patricia no le da pelota a la profesora y por eso terminó castigada.* "Patricia did not pay attention to the teacher and ended up punished."

DAR PIE CON BOLA, *Car., idiom.* To figure out. *Por más que me esfuerzo no logro dar pie con bola. Esas fórmulas de física son muy difíciles.* "As much as I try I can't figure it out. These physics formulas are difficult."

DAR PIREY, *Car., idiom.* To dismiss, to get rid of. *Nena no estaba verdaderamente enamorada del novio y en cuanto se le presentó una oportunidad le dio pirey.* "Nena wasn't really in love with her boyfriend, and when the chance came she gave him the boot."

DAR POTE, *Car., idiom.* To study with interest. *Luisa estaba dando pote a los libros de cocina.* "Luisa was studying the cookbooks hard."

DAR PUPILA, *Car., idiom.* To eyeball. *El tipo estaba*

dando pupila a mi reloj. Ya me tenía nervioso. "The guy had his eye on my watch. He was making me nervous."

DAR UN CORTE, *Car., idiom.* To give a clue. *Pablo, dame un corte para solucionar este rompecabezas.* "Pablo, give me a clue to solve this puzzle."

DAR UN MÍNIMO TÉCNICO, *Car., idiom.* To give a lesson in the basics. *Te voy a dar un mínimo técnico para que el trabajo te quede bien.* "I am going to give you some basic training so that the job turns out all right for you."

DAR UN PALO, *Spain, idiom, crim.* To hold up, to rob. *Anoche les dieron un palo en la tienda de Fernando.* "Last night they held up the people at Fernando's store."

DAR UN TAJO, *Car., idiom.* To swindle. *El sinvergüenza dio el tajo con los ahorros de los viejos.* "The bastard conned the old people out of their savings."

DAR UN TIMBRAZO, *Car., idiom.* To make a telephone call. *Oye, te daré un timbrazo mañana.* "Hey, I'll give you a ring tomorrow."

DAR UN TOQUE, *Car., idiom.* To give a reminder. *¿Me puedes dar un toque un día o dos antes de la fiesta?* "Can you give me a reminder a day or two before the party?"

DAR UNA MANO, *L.Am./S, idiom.* To help. *Los amigos le dieron una mano cuando estaba pobre.* "His friends gave him a hand when he was poor."

DAR UNA TROVA, *Car., idiom.* To talk, to get a load off. *El pobre hombre no tiene a nadie y cuando se encuentra con una persona que lo escucha le da una trova tremenda.* "The poor man doesn't have anybody, so when there's a chance for someone to listen to him, he really unloads."

DARLE A LA SIN HUESO, *Car., idiom, hum.* To chat, to wag tongues. *Juana y yo estuvimos una hora dándole a la sin hueso.* "Juana and I were wagging our tongues for an hour."

DARLE A LOS CAITES, *L.Am./C, idiom.* To walk fast, to

hurry. *Vamos Lalo, dale a los caites a ver si llegamos a tiempo.* "Let's get a move on Lalo, see if we can make it on time."

DARLE A UNO EL/UN PUNTO, *Spain, idiom.* To do something on impulse. *Me dio el punto de comprarme un coche nuevo.* "I got an urge to buy a new car."

DARLE CUERDA, *Spain, idiom.* To egg on. *A mi hijo le gusta darle cuerda a los sobrinos cuando éstos discuten.* "My son likes to egg his cousins on when they are arguing."

DARLE DE LADO A ALGUIEN, *Car., idiom.* To no longer associate with someone, to kiss someone off. *Cuando te encuentres con Pepe, dale de lado porque estafa a todos.* "When you run into Pepe, don't deal with him; he's been cheating everybody."

DARLE LA PÁLIDA, *L.Am./S, idiom.* To faint. *Le dio la pálida cuando le dieron las noticias.* "She passed out when they gave her the news."

DARLE LAS TABAS, *Spain, idiom, crim.* To run. *Le dieron las tabas en cuanto vio a los policías.* "He hit the bricks when he saw the fuzz."

DARLE POR, *L.Am./S, idiom.* To have a mind to do something. *Le dio por ver televisión a la madrugada.* "He took to watching television in the wee small hours."

DARSE EL BISTEC, *Spain, idiom.* To kiss inserting the tongue into the other's mouth, to French kiss. *La pareja estaba dándose el bistec.* "The couple was sucking face."

DARSE EL BOTE, *Spain, idiom.* To take off, to flee, to escape. *Juanito ya no está en la cárcel, se dio el bote.* "Juanito isn't in the clink anymore. He booted out of there."

DARSE EL CALENTÓN, *Spain, idiom.* To caress erotically. *Estaban sentados detrás de la sala, besándose y dándose el calentón.* "They were seated in the back of the room, kissing and getting each other hot."

DARSE EL PIRO, *Spain, idiom.* To leave, to take off.

Estábamos hablando y de pronto Daniel se dio el piro sin decir ni adiós. "We were talking and all of a sudden Daniel took off without saying good-bye."

DARSE LIJA, *Car., idiom.* To be conceited, to be stuck up. *Betty se da tremenda lija, se cree la princesa del barrio.* "Betty is really stuck up; she thinks she is the neighborhood princess."

DARSE UN PINCHO, *Spain, idiom, drugs.* To inject a drug into a vein. *No sé cómo pueden darse un pincho con jeringas sucias.* "I don't know how they can stick themselves with dirty needles."

DARSE UN VOLTIO, *Spain, idiom.* To take a stroll. *Bueno amigos, me voy a dar un voltio.* "Well friends, I am going for a walk."

DARSE UNA PIÑA, *L.Am./S, idiom.* To have an automobile accident. *La hermana de Alejandro se dio una piña el sábado.* "Alejandro's sister had an auto accident on Saturday."

DÁRSELAS, *L.Am./S, prnl. v.* To show off. *Nubia se las da de que es muy inteligente.* "Nubia fancies herself to be very intelligent."

DÁTILES, *Spain, pl. n.* Fingers. (Lit. Dates.) *¿Has visto los dátiles tan largos que tiene Catarina?* "Have you seen how long Catherine's fingers are?"

DE BOLA, *L.Am./N, idiom.* Sure, certainly. *"¿Está Ud. seguro que viene?" "¡De bola!"* " 'Are you sure he's coming.' 'You've got it!' "

DE CAMPEONATO, *Spain, idiom.* Super-cool, fantastic, out of sight. *Esa moto es de campeonato. ¿Cuándo la compraste, Pepe?* "That motorcycle is super-cool. When did you buy it, Pepe?"

DE GRATÉN, *Car., idiom.* Free. *Ese tipo es un descarado. Le encanta salir con los amigos y comer de gratén.* "That guy has balls. He loves to go out with his friends and eat for free."

DE GUAGUA, *Car., idiom.* Free. *Este perfume me lo dieron* *de guagua en la tienda.* "They gave me this perfume for free at the store."

DE GUILLETÉN, *Car., idiom.* Sneakily, on the sly. *Salió de guilletén mientras la maestra estaba mirando la pizarra.* "He snuck out while the teacher was turned to the blackboard."

DE INFARTO, *L.Am., idiom.* Breathtaking. *Guillermo me regaló unas rosas de infarto.* "Guillermo gave me some roses to die for."

DE LA GRAN SIETE, *L.Am./S, idiom.* Enormous, tremendous, out of sight. *Tengo un hambre de la gran siete. ¿Cuándo vamos a comer?* "I've got a gigantic hunger. When are we going to eat?"

DE LA PLANTA, *L.Am./S, idiom.* Exellent, top-notch. *Esa moto es de la planta. Ud. la mantiene muy bien.* "That motorcycle is top-notch. You maintain it very well."

DE LUNA, *L.Am./C, idiom.* Ill-humored. *Araceli está de luna y no quiere hablar con nadie.* "Araceli's in a bad mood and doesn't want to talk to anyone."

¡DE MÁS!, *L.Am./S, interj.* Of course! OK! *"¿Qué te parece una vuelta por la playa?" "¡De más!"* " 'How about a stroll on the beach?' 'OK!' "

DE MIEDO, *L.Am./S, idiom.* Great, very good, excellent. *Ese vestido te queda de miedo.* "That dress looks great on you."

DE MUERTE See DE INFARTO

DE PAPAYITA, *L.Am./S, idiom.* Just at the right time. *No me salía la palabra que buscaba y de papayita la escuché en la tele.* "I couldn't get the word I was looking for and right then I heard it on the TV."

DE POSTA, *L.Am./S, adj.* True, reliable, legitimate, authentic. *La familia Chávez tiene un Picasso de posta en su casa.* "The Chavez family has an authentic Picasso in their home."

DE PREPO, *L.Am./S, idiom.* Obligatorily. *De prepo me*

puse el traje de gaucho. "It was mandatory that I put on my gaucho outfit."

DEBERLE A LAS VÍRGENES, *Car., idiom, hum.* To have a lot of debt. *Marta tiene tres tarjetas de crédito cargadas hasta el tope y además le debe a las vírgenes.* "Marta has three credit cards maxed out and besides she owes everybody."

DEDAL, *U.S., n.* Finger. (Lit. Thimble.) *Me duele el dedal.* "My finger hurts."

DEDOCRÁTICO, CA, *Spain, adj.* (Lit. "Fingercratic.") Undemocratic appointment of governmental positions. *No había voluntarios, así que la selección de personal fue muy dedocrática.* "There were no volunteers, so finger-pointing selected the personnel."

DEFEÑO, *L.Am./N, n.* Person from Mexico City. *Ignacio es defeño, se nota por el acento.* "Ignacio is from Mexico City; you can tell by his accent."

DEFENSA ESCOBA, *Spain, idiom, sports.* Player who backs up the defense line, defensive sweep. *Ricardo está jugando la defensa escoba.* "Ricardo is playing the defensive sweep."

DEJAR CON EL PAQUETE, *Spain, idiom.* To leave a woman pregnant. *Guillermo dejó la novia con el paquete y se fue para América.* "Guillermo left his girlfriend with a little package and he went to America."

DEJAR CON LOS CRESPOS HECHOS, *L.Am./S, idiom.* To miss an appointment. *El idiota de Jorge siempre me deja con los crespos hechos.* "That idiot George always stands me up."

DEJAR EN CALZONCILLOS, *L.Am./S, Spain, idiom.* To leave without money, to take the shirt off someone's back. *En ese juego me dejaron en calzoncillos.* "In that game they took my shirt."

DEJAR LA ESCOBA, 1. *L.Am./S, idiom.* To lose one's temper, to make a fuss. (Lit. To leave the broom.) *Si no llego a la hora, el jefe deja la escoba.* "If I don't arrive on time my boss raises hell." **2.** *L.Am./S, idiom.* Disaster, major accident. *¡Chocaron dos trenes y quedó la escoba!* "Two trains collided; what a fuckup!"

DEJAR LOS COJONES EN CASA, *Spain, idiom.* To show cowardice. *Ese torero dejó los cojones en casa hoy. Seguro que no le van a dar una oreja.* "That bullfighter left his balls at home today. They sure aren't going to give him an ear."

DEJAR METIDO, DA, *L.Am./S, idiom.* To miss an appointment. *Juan me invitó a salir anoche y me dejó metida.* "Juan invited me to go out last night and left me standing."

DEJARLO A UNO EN PELO, *L.Am./N, idiom.* To leave somebody without money. *Los caballos me dejaron en pelo.* "The horses left me flat broke."

DEJARSE DE JODER, 1. *L.Am./S, idiom.* To stop giving the runaround. *El vendedor no se dejaba de joder así que fuimos a otra tienda.* "The salesman wouldn't stop giving us the runaround so we went to another store." **2.** *L.Am./S, idiom.* To stop bothering. *Déjese de joder o llamo al guardia.* "Stop bothering me or I'll call the guard."

DEL CODO, *L.Am./S, idiom.* Cheap, avaricious. *Bernardo es bien del codo y no quiere regalarle nada a nadie.* "Bernardo is a real tightwad and doesn't want to give presents to anybody."

DEL DEMONIO, *Spain, idiom, youth.* Fantastic, wonderful. *Mari, ese traje es del demonio. ¿Dónde lo compraste?* "Mari, that outfit is the wildest. Where did you get it?"

DEL OTRO EQUIPO, *L.Am./S, adj.* Homosexual. (Lit. From the other team.) *Nunca lo veo con mujeres, parece que es del otro equipo.* "I never see him with women; it looks like he's from the other team."

¡DELE! See ¡DALE!

DEPÓSITO, *Car., n.* Police custody. (Lit. Warehouse.) *Anoche pasé la noche en el depósito por la borrachera* *que tenía.* "I spent last night in the tank because I was stewed."

DESAHOGARSE, *Car., prnl. v.* To have an orgasm. *Y precisamente en el momento en que iba a desahogarme, me desperté.* "Just at the moment I was going to come, I woke up."

DESBRAGUETADO, *Spain, adj.* Poor, unfortunate. *Ese pobre desbraguetado no encuentra trabajo en ninguna parte.* "That poor devil can't find work anywhere."

DESCAPULLAR, *Car., v.* To deflower a virgin. (Lit. To remove the bud.) *Ese viejo verde quiere descapullar a la vecinita de enfrente.* "That dirty old man wants to get the cherry off the neighbor across the street."

DESCOJONARSE, *Spain, prnl. v.* To break up laughing. (Lit. To lose one's balls.) *Nos descojonamos viendo las películas antiguas de Cantinflas.* "We cracked up watching the old Cantinflas movies."

DESCOSER, *Car., v.* To keep the opposition from scoring for nine innings. (Lit. To unstitch.) *Los Rangers de Texas descosieron a los de Kansas City.* "The Texas Rangers shut out Kansas City."

DESCUACHARRANGADO, *U.S., adj.* Broken. *No puede ir con nosotros porque su carro está descuacharrangado.* "He can't go with us because his car is broken down."

DESCUACHARRANGAR, *U.S., v.* To break. *Si no tienes cuidado vas a descuacharrangar el plato favorito de tu madre.* "If you aren't careful, you are going to break your mother's favorite plate."

DESCUADRAR, *Car., v.* To upset the relationship between two people. *Voy a hacer todo lo posible por descuadrar a esos dos.* "I am going to do everything possible to break those two up."

DESECHABLE, *L.Am./S, n.* Street person, bum, homeless person. (Lit. Disposable.) *Encontraron un desechable muerto en la calle.* "They found the homeless person dead in the street."

DESEMARSE, *Spain, prnl. v.* To hide, to disguise. *El creía que se desemaba bien pero todo el mundo lo reconoció en seguida.* "He thought he had a good disguise, but everybody recognized him right away."

DESENGANCHARSE, *Spain, prnl. v., drugs.* To stop using drugs. *Queremos ayudarle a Alfredo a desengancharse de su adicción.* "We want to help Alfredo to kick his habit."

DESGOMARSE, *Car., prnl. v.* To have bad tires on a car. *Tengo que comprar gomas nuevas, ya se desgomó el auto mío.* "I've got to buy new tires; my car is out of rubber."

DESGRANARSE, *Car., prnl. v.* To become incapacitated due to age. *Me da mucho pesar ver como se desgrana mi abuelita.* "It's real hard for me to see how my grandmother is just wasting away."

DESHUEVARSE, *Spain, prnl. v.* To die laughing, to crack up laughing. *Cuando le dije lo que pasó se deshuevó con ganas.* "When I told him what happened, he cracked up laughing."

DESLECHARSE, *Car., prnl. v.* To masturbate. *Esos viejos verdes entran en esa tienda porno para deslecharse.* "Those dirty old men go into that porn shop to whack off."

DESMADRARSE, *Spain, prnl. v.* To go too far. *Ya te desmadraste. Siempre tienes que meter la pata.* "Now you went too far. You've always got to stick your foot in it."

DESMADRE, *Spain, n.* Chaos, commotion. *Se armó la desmadre anoche en la fiesta de Pablo.* "All hell broke loose at Pablo's party last night."

DESORTIJARSE, *Car., prnl. v.* To return the engagement ring, to break up. *Faltando un mes para la boda, nos desortijamos.* "We broke up a month before the wedding."

DESPACHARSE, *L.Am., prnl. v.* To consume. *Eloy se despachó tres tacos seguiditos.* "Eloy put away three tacos in a flash."

DESPAPAYE, *L.Am./N, n.* Disorder, confusion. *Hubo*

mucho despapaye con la reventa de los boletos para el concierto. "There was an utter mess with the resale of the concert tickets."

DESPEDIRSE A LA INGLESA, *Spain, idiom.* To leave without saying good-bye. *Estoy enfadado contigo. Cuando te fuiste te despediste a la inglesa.* "I am mad at you. When you left you didn't even say good-bye."

DESPELOTADO, DA, *Spain, adj.* Naked, nude. *Estaban despelotadas todas las niñas en la playa.* "All the babes on the beach were in their birthday suits."

DESPELOTARSE, *Spain, prnl. v.* To get undressed, to get naked. *El oficial le mandó despelotarse. Quería encontrar alguna droga.* "The officer ordered him to get undressed. He wanted to find some drug."

DESPELOTE, 1. *L.Am./S, n.* Commotion. *Se armó el despelote cuando descubrieron a Paco robándose la plata de la caja.* "All hell broke loose when they found Paco stealing money from the cash register." **2.** *Spain, n.* Nakedness. *El despelote se ha puesto de moda en las telenovelas.* "Nakedness has become stylish in soap operas."

DESPIOLE, *L.Am./S, n.* Trouble, disturbance, agitation. *Hubo un despiole en la oficina esta mañana.* "There was a commotion at the office this morning."

DESTARTALADO, DA, *L.Am./S, adj.* Run-down. *Mi pobre bicicleta cada vez está más destartalada.* "My poor bike gets more run-down as time goes by."

DESTERNILLARSE, *Spain, prnl. v.* To go crazy laughing. *Me desternillé de risa cuando escuche la cinta de Pepe da Rosa.* "I broke up laughing when I heard the Pepe da Rosa tape."

DESTORNILLADOR, *Spain, n.* Vodka and orange juice. (Lit. Screwdriver.) *Oiga, ¿puede prepararme un destornillador con vodka rusa?* "Listen, can you make me a screwdriver with Russian vodka?"

DESVIRGAR, *Spain, v.* To use for the first time. (Lit. To deflower.) *Eulalio está desvirgando su coche nuevo. ¡Qué contento está!* "Eulalio is enjoying his new car. Look how happy he is."

DETALLE, *Spain, n.* Courtesy. (Lit. Detail.) *José tuvo un detalle con nosotros. Nos llevó a cenar en Valdilecha.* "Jose was real nice to us; he took us to dinner at Valdilecha."

DEX, *Spain, n., drugs.* Dexedrine. *Cuando le registraron encontraron gloria, coca y dex.* "When they searched him they found grass, coke, and dex."

DÍA DE RAYA, *L.Am./N, idiom.* Payday. *¿Me puedes prestar un poco de guita hasta el día de raya?* "Can you lend me a few bucks until payday?"

DIABLITO, *L.Am./N, n.* Illegal device that stops water or electric meters. (Lit. Little devil.) *Nos estábamos robando la luz con un diablito.* "We were stealing electricity with a meter-cheater."

DIARREA MENTAL, *Spain, idiom.* Confusion, disturbed mental processes. *Conchita, esa manera de pensar es una diarrea mental.* "Conchita, that way of thinking suggests bats in the belfry."

DICHA, *L.Am./C, n.* Luck. (Lit. Happiness.) *Por dicha traía mi otra llave en el bolsillo y pude abrir el carro.* "By luck I had my other key in my pocket and I could open the car."

DIEGO, *L.Am./S, n.* Euphemism for ten. A ten-percent bribe. *"¿Cuánto le diste?" "Un diego."* " 'How much did you give him?' 'A ten-spot.' "

DIEZ CON HUECO, *L.Am./C, idiom.* To fool, to deceive. (Lit. A ten with a hole in it, alluding to a worthless ten-colon perforated coin.) *El creía que me iba a meter un diez con hueco pero yo no soy tan tonto.* "He thought he was going to stick me with a Hong Kong Rolex, but I'm not so stupid."

DIFERENCIAL, *L.Am./N, n.* Buttocks. *Ese señor está muy ancho del diferencial.* "That man's got a wide butt."

DIÑARLA, *Spain, v., crim.* To die. *¿Te dijeron que Ignacio la diñó anoche? Tragó unas anfetas malas.* "Did they tell you that Ignacio bought the farm last night? He swallowed some bad speed."

DINERAL, *L.Am., n.* A lot of money. *Esa pulsera debió costarte un dineral.* "That bracelet must have cost you a bundle."

DINERO CONTANTE Y SONANTE, *Spain, L.Am., idiom.* Cash. *Yo no necesito crédito, tengo dinero contante y sonante.* "I don't need credit; I've got cash."

DISCO, *Spain, n.* Something said or done over and over again. (Lit. Record.) *Ahora viene el pesado de Eduardo para ponernos el disco de su nuevo trabajo.* "Here comes that bore Eduardo to play us that broken record about his new job."

DISPARAR, *L.Am./N, v.* To pick up the bill. (Lit. To shoot.) *Dispárame la comida, que no traigo dinero.* "Pick up the bill for the meal; I didn't bring any money."

DÍVER, *Spain, adj.* Fun, entertaining. *La fiesta de Piri fue muy díver.* "Piri's party was a real blast."

DOBLAR, *Spain, v.* To work. (Lit. To bend.) *Tu cuñado no dobla para nada. ¿Qué le pasa?* "Your brother-in-law doesn't do squat. What's the matter with him?"

DOBLARLA, *Spain, idiom.* To die. (Lit. To double it.) *Tres drogatos la doblaron anoche cuando explotó su laboratorio.* "Three junkies died last night when their lab blew up."

DOBLE, 1. *Spain, n.* Large glass of beer, double of any drink. (Lit. To double.) *¡Vaya día de trabajo! Juan, échame un doble.* "What a workday! Juan, give me a double." **2.** *Spain, n., crim.* Warden. *El doble vino a mirar a Rodríguez por el chivato.* "The warden came to look at Rodriguez through the peephole."

DOLOROSA, *Spain, n.* The bill. *Camarero, la dolorosa por favor.* "Waiter, the bad news, please."

DOMINGUERO, *Spain, n.* Sunday driver. *Vamos a llegar*

tarde si no se quita del medio el dominguero que va de-lante. "We are going to be late if that Sunday driver up front doesn't get out of the way."

DOÑA, *Car., n.* Wife. *Tengo que llegar temprano porque si no, la doña se enfurece.* "I have to get home early because, if not, the old lady will go through the roof."

DOÑA BLANCA, *L.Am./N, n.* Cocaine. *Te mandaron 100 gramos de doña Blanca.* "They sent you a hundred grams of Snow White."

DOÑA MANUELA, *L.Am./N, n.* Masturbation. *Ese muchacho demacrado conoce demasiado bien a doña Manuela.* "That skinny fart knows Lady Palm and her five daughters all too well."

DOÑAJUANITA, *U.S., n., drugs.* Marijuana. *Apesta a Doñajuanita aquí.* "It stinks of pot here."

DOPARSE, *Spain, prnl. v., drugs.* To use drugs. (Lit. To dope oneself.) *Ese muchacho siempre está dopándose. No va a tener gran porvenir.* "That fella is always getting doped out. He is not going to have much of a future."

DORMIR LA MONA, *L.Am./S, Spain, idiom.* To sleep it off. *Después de la parranda anoche, Antonio está durmiendo la mona.* "After last night's partying, Antonio is sleeping it off."

DOS-TRES, *L.Am./N, idiom.* More or less, regular, so-so. *Fui al cine pero la película no era más que dos-tres.* "I went to the theater but the movie was just so-so."

DRAGA, *Car., adj.* Gluttonous. *No seas draga, mujer, tienes que perder peso.* "Don't be so voracious, woman! You've got to lose weight."

DROGA, 1. *Car., n.* Cheat sheet. (Lit. Drug.) *No habría salido bien del examen si no fuera por la droga que llevó.* "He wouldn't have passed the test if it weren't for the cheat sheet he took." **2.** *L.Am./N, n.* Debt. *Ya no veo claro con tanta droga y tan poco sueldo.* "I no longer see clearly with so much debt and so little salary."

DROGATA, *Spain, n., drugs.* Drug addict. *Esa drogata*

roba para comprar su caballo. "That junkie steals to buy her horse."

DROGUERO, 1. *L.Am./N, n., drugs.* Drug dealer. *Mataron al droguero y a toda su familia.* "They killed the dealer and all his family." **2.** *L.Am./N, n.* Person who is heavily in debt. *Federica es muy droguera, todo lo compra a crédito.* "Federica is a real shopping queen; she buys everything on credit."

DUARTE, *Car., n.* Dominican peso. *Ese hombre me debe mil duartes.* "That man owes me a thousand bucks."

DÚPLEX, *Spain, n.* Lesbian act. (Lit. Duplex.) *Todas las noches en esa sala ponen un dúplex y atraen a las lesbianas.* "Every night at that club they have a duplex show to attract the dykes."

DURA, *L.Am./S, n.* Truth. (Lit. Hard.) *La dura es que tenemos que trabajar esta noche.* "The hard truth is that we have to work tonight."

DURACO, CA, *Car., adj.* Dedicated student. *Afortunadamente mis dos hijos son unos duracos.* "Fortunately my two boys are hard-studying students."

DURO, RA, *Spain, n.* Five-peseta coin. (Lit. Hard.) *Ese coche está muy viejo, no vale ni un duro.* "That car is very old; it is not worth a nickel."

¡ECHA EL FRENO, MAGDALENO!, *Spain, idiom, interj., youth.* Calm down! *Tú te emocionas demasiado, ¡echa el freno, Magdaleno!* "You get too emotional. Put on the brakes, you flake!"

ECHADO PA'LANTE, *Spain, adj.* Daring, decisive, aggressive. *Tu hijo es muy echado pa'lante. No es ni corto ni perezoso.* "Your son is a real mover. He is not shy or lazy."

¡ÉCHALE COJONES!, *Spain, idiom.* Expression of admiration for a good performance. *¡Échale cojones Tomás! ¡Otro gol para nosotros!* "What balls, Tomas! Another goal for us!"

¡ÉCHALE GALLETA!, *L.Am./N, idiom.* Hit hard! *¡Échale galleta Ramón! Tú le puedes ganar.* "Hit him hard Ramón! You can beat him."

ECHAR CABEZA, *L.Am./S, idiom.* To think. *Le he echado cabeza todo el día al problema y todavía no encuentro la solución.* "I have been putting my head to the problem all day and I am still without a solution."

ECHAR CARRETA, *L.Am./S, idiom.* To joke. *Anoche la pasé muy bien echando carreta con los compañeros.* "Last night I had a good time joking around with my buddies."

ECHAR CEPILLO, *L.Am./S, v.* To act in an obsequious manner. *Ruth vive echándole cepillo al jefe para que le dé* *un aumento.* "Ruth is always sucking up to the boss so he will give her a raise."

ECHAR CHISPAS, *Spain, L.Am., idiom.* To be angry. *No le hables ahora porque está echando chispas.* "Don't talk to him now because he is hot under the collar."

ECHAR DE CABEZA, *L.Am./N, idiom.* To squeal on someone. *Imelda me echó de cabeza con mis papás.* "Imelda ratted on me to my parents."

ECHAR EL BOFE, *Car., idiom.* To work like a dog. *Toda esta semana me ha tocado echar el bofe sin parar.* "I've had to work like a dog all week."

ECHAR EL CIERRE, *Spain, idiom.* To shut up. *Echa el cierre ya mamón, has dicho bastante y nadie te está escuchando.* "Close your trap already, you jerk. You said enough and nobody is listening to you."

ECHAR EL DÍA, *Car., idiom.* To spend the day. *Hoy no voy a trabajar, voy a echar el día en la playa.* "I am not going to work today. I'll spend the day at the beach."

ECHAR EL OJO, *L.Am./S, idiom.* To want. *Ese tipo le está echando el ojo a mi reloj; me lo quiere robar.* "That guy is drawing a bead on my watch; he wants to steal it from me."

ECHAR FLORES, *L.Am., idiom.* To compliment. *Me fascina cuando me echan flores bonitas por la calle.* "I love it when they throw me compliments out on the street."

ECHAR LA CREMALLERA, *Spain, idiom.* To shut up, to zip it up. *No podía aguantar el rollo que echaba Juan y le dije que echara la cremallera.* "I couldn't stand the long story Juan was telling and I told him to zip it up."

ECHAR LA SAL, *U.S., idiom.* To cause bad luck, to jinx. *Mis amigos me echaron sal al proyecto.* "My friends jinxed the project."

ECHAR LA ÚLTIMA PAPILLA, *Car., idiom.* To vomit. *Me sentía muy mal de la resaca. Pensaba que iba a echar* *la última papilla.* "I felt so bad with the hangover, I thought I was going to throw up my guts."

ECHAR LEÑA, *Spain, idiom.* To punish, to spank. *Te van a echar leña si descubren que rompiste el vidrio.* "You are going to get it when they find out that you broke the glass."

ECHAR LOS DIENTES, *Car., idiom.* To get experience from an early age. *Juan echaba los dientes en política.* "Juan was cutting his teeth in politics."

ECHAR LOS PERROS, *L.Am./S, idiom.* To court, to woo someone. *Luis le anda echando los perros a Matilde.* "Luis is going after Matilde like a hound after a fox."

ECHAR LOS RAYOS, *Spain, idiom.* To get an X ray. *Dicen que mi padre tiene piedras en el riñón. Ahora se fue a echar los rayos.* "They said that my father has kidney stones. Now he went to get X rays."

ECHAR LOS TEJOS, *Spain, idiom.* To court someone. *Paco le está echando los tejos a Trini. Se ve que está loco por ella.* "Paco is chasing after Trini. You can see that he is nuts about her."

ECHAR MANO, *Car., idiom.* To take something that doesn't belong to you. *Elisa no estuvo en casa ni cinco minutos cuando echó mano a mi CD.* "Elisa wasn't in my house for five minutes when she pinched my CD."

ECHAR OJO, *L.Am./S, idiom.* To watch over. *Échale ojo a la comida para que no se queme, ya vengo.* "Keep an eye on the food so that it doesn't burn; I'll be right there."

ECHAR PAPA, *L.Am./N, idiom.* To eat. *Vamos a echar papa a la fonda de la calle Venecia.* "Let's get some chow on Venecias Street."

ECHAR PORRAS, *L.Am./N, idiom.* To cheer on. *Vamos al partido a echarle porras al equipo de la escuela.* "Let's go to the game to cheer on the school team."

ECHAR UN CASQUETE See ECHAR UN POLVO

ECHAR UN CLAVO See ECHAR UN POLVO

ECHAR UN COHETE See ECHAR UN POLVO

ECHAR UN FONAZO, *L.Am./N, idiom.* To telephone. *Échame un fonazo si tus papás te dejan ir a la fiesta.* "Give me a ring if your parents let you go to the party."

ECHAR UN PALO See ECHAR UN POLVO

ECHAR UN PIE, *Car., idiom.* To dance. *Anoche estuvimos echando un pie hasta las tantas.* "Last night we were shaking until late."

ECHAR UN POLVO, *Spain, L.Am./S, idiom.* To have sexual intercourse, to fuck. *Eres un obsesionado. Sólo piensas en echar un polvo.* "You're obsessed. All you think about is fucking."

ECHAR UNA BRONCA, *Spain, idiom.* To scold severely, to chew out royally, to give an ass-chewing. *Cuando llegué tarde el jefe me echó una bronca.* "When I arrived late the boss read me the riot act."

ECHAR UNA CANITA AL AIRE, *Spain, L.Am., idiom.* To have a fling. (Lit. To pitch a white hair to the wind.) *Dicen que a cierta edad todo casado tiene que echar una canita al aire.* "They say that at a certain age every married man has to have a little fling."

ECHAR UNA CARTA, *Car., idiom.* To have a bowel movement, to crap, to shit. *¿Armando? Me parece que está en el baño echando una carta.* "Armando? I think he is in the bathroom, laying eggs."

ECHAR UNA FIRMA, *L.Am./N, idiom.* To urinate, to piss. *Ahorita vengo, voy a echar una firma.* "I'll be right there; I have to sign the water."

ECHAR UNA MANO, *L.Am., Spain, idiom.* To lend a hand. *Oye, Guillermo, ¿puedes echarme una mano con esta mesa?* "Hey Guillermo, can you give me a hand with this table?"

ECHARLE A UNO EN CARA, *L.Am., Spain, idiom.* To throw in one's face. *Siempre me echa en cara que yo dije que sería millonario.* "She is always throwing in my face that I said I would be a millionaire."

ECHARLE A UNO LAS CACAS, *Car., idiom.* To accuse, to blame. *Cuando llegó el inspector todos le echaron las cacas a Bernardo.* "When the inspector arrived everybody put the crap on Bernardo."

ECHARLE A UNO UN BAÑO DE AGUA FRÍA, *L.Am., Spain, idiom.* To throw cold water on someone's plans. *Isabel siempre le echa un baño de agua fría a las ilusiones de su marido.* "Isabel is always throwing cold water on her husband's dreams."

ECHARLE LA CARA, *L.Am./N, idiom.* To face, to confront, to dare. *Me dijeron lo que dijo de mí y ahora tengo que echarle la cara.* "They told me what he said about me and how I have to confront him."

ECHARSE AL MONTE, *Spain, idiom.* To rebel. *Su padre era muy estricto y por eso un día se echó al monte.* "His father was very strict, so one day he rebelled."

ECHARSE (o MARCAR) EL CAQUI, *Spain, idiom, mil.* To enlist in the military service. *Alfredo se echó el caqui ayer.* "Alfredo signed up for the service yesterday."

ECHARSE LA BOLITA, *L.Am./N, idiom.* To put the responsibility on another, to pass the buck. *Cuando le agarraron con las manos en la masa, él se echó la bolita a otro.* "When they caught him red-handed, he put the blame on another guy."

ECHARSE UNA MANO DE GATO, *L.Am./S, idiom.* To touch up one's makeup. *Tengo que echarme una mano de gato, ya viene mi novio.* "I've got to touch up my face; my boyfriend is coming already."

ECO, *Spain, interj.* Expression of agreement. (From Italian "ecco.") *"Yo creo que deben retirar a ese jugador." "¡Eco!"* " 'I believe they ought to retire that player.' 'Right on!' "

EFECTUAR UN ANÁLISIS DE CONCIENCIA, *L.Am./N, idiom.* To defecate, to shit. *Ahorita vengo, tengo que efectuar un análisis de conciencia.* "I'll be right there; I've got to do some thinking on the throne."

EL BACÁN, *Car., n.* The man, the cool guy, the dude. *Manolo se cree el bacán, piensa que todas las mujeres se enamoran de él.* "Manolo thinks he's the man; he believes that all the women are in love with him."

EL DEDO, *Spain, n.* Expression of rejection used instead of showing the middle finger. (Lit. The finger.) *"¿Quieres guardarme este paquete?" "¡El dedo!"* " 'Do you want to keep this package for me?' 'The finger!' "

EL DESCUEVE, *L.Am./S, idiom.* The greatest, the most. *¡Los muebles que compró Nora son el descueve!* "The furniture that Norma bought is awesome!"

EL DUEÑO DE LOS CABALLITOS, *Car., idiom.* Boss, leader. *No nos queda más remedio que pedirle permiso, porque él es el dueño de los caballitos.* "We have no choice but to ask for his permission because he's the boss."

EL HERMANO PEQUEÑO, *Spain, n.* Penis. *¡Uy! Cuando te veo, el hermano pequeño quiere ponerse grande.* "Oh! When I see you, little brother feels like growing up."

EL OTRO LADO, *L.Am./N, idiom.* The United States. *Luis fue al otro lado para ganar dólares.* "Luis went across the border to make some bucks."

EL PRE, *Car., n., youth.* Senior high school. *Ya terminé el noveno grado, ahora voy para el pre.* "I finished the ninth grade; now I am going to senior high."

EL TATA, *L.Am./S, n.* God. *Pídele al Tata que te ilumine.* "Ask the Man upstairs to light your way."

EL ÚLTIMO MONO, *Spain, idiom.* Person at the bottom of the scale. *Cerraron la fábrica y despidieron hasta al último mono.* "They closed the factory and fired every last soul."

¡ELE!, *Spain, interj.* Exclamation of agreement or approval. *¡Ele! Así se hace, muchacho.* "Right on! That's how you do it fella!"

ELEBEPE, *Car., idiom.* Free on own recognizance. (Lit.

The pronunciation of the acronym L.B.P. [Libertad Bajo Palabra].) *El juez me dejó salir en elebepe.* "The judge let me out on my own recognizance."

ELEMENTO, TA, *Car., n.* Pejorative for individual. (Lit. Element.) *Entraron dos elementos que tenían aspecto de criminales.* "Two characters who looked like criminals came in."

ELIMINAR, *Spain, v., crim.* To kill, to murder. *Dicen que la mafia tenía la orden de eliminar a Fidel.* "They say that the Mafia had orders to eliminate Fidel."

EMBAJADOR, *Spain, n.* Cunnilinguist. (Lit. Ambassador.) *Las chicas del bar le llaman embajador a tu tío.* "The girls at the bar call your uncle a muff diver."

EMBALADO, DA, *L.Am./S, adj.* Absorbed, engrossed. *Estaba tan embalado en sus pensamientos que no vio el semáforo.* "He was so absorbed in his thoughts that he didn't see the traffic light."

EMBALAO, LÁ, *Car., adj.* High on drugs. *Los elementos estaban embalaos con no sé qué drogas.* "The characters were high on I don't know what drugs."

EMBALARSE, *L.Am./S, prnl. v.* To be engrossed, absorbed in something. *Mi hija se embala en las novelas románticas.* "My daughter gets hooked on romantic novels."

EMBARCAR, *Car., v.* To keep waiting, to stand up. (Lit. To ship.) *Te espero mañana a las diez. Por favor, no me embarques.* "I'll wait for you tomorrow at ten. Please don't stand me up."

EMBARRADA, *L.Am./S, n.* Dumb thing. *¡Qué embarrada! Dejé la sombrilla en la casa y me voy a mojar.* "What a dumb thing! I left my umbrella at home and I am going to get wet."

EMBARRARLA, *L.Am./S, v.* To make a mistake. *José la embarró con Paula, no se acordó del aniversario.* "Jose screwed up with Paula. He didn't remember their anniversary."

EMBASAR, *Car., v., sports.* To get to base on a ball. *Ahora*

está embasado Rodríguez y esperamos un jit o un jonrón.
"Now Rodriguez is on base and we are waiting for a hit
or a homer."

EMBASARSE, *Car., prnl. v., sports.* To get to base on a hit.
*Jiménez batea y es un jit, debe ser suficiente para em-
basarse, ¡y es!* "Jiménez swings and it's a hit; it should be
enough to get on base, and it is!"

EMBOLADO, DA, *L.Am./S, adj.* Bored. *Ya me quiero ir,
estoy embolado.* "I want to go now; I am bored."

EMBOLILLADO, DA, *Spain, adj., drugs.* Drugged. *No se
puede hablar con él. Está embolillado y alucinando.*
"You can't talk with him. He's doped out and hallucinating."

EMBONAR, *L.Am./N, v.* To suit, to fit, to favor. *Oye, ¡qué
bien te embona ese sombrero!* "Hey, that hat fits you to
a tee."

EMBOTELLAR, *Spain, v., sports.* (Lit. To bottle up.) To
surround the opposing team in their defensive area. *Y
ahora Sevilla tiene embotellado a los del Betis.* "And now
Seville has the Betis team in a bottle."

EMBRAGUE See PATINAR EL EMBRAGUE

EMBRETARSE, 1. *Car., prnl. v.* To get in trouble, to get in
a jam. *Ya te embretaste. Tu padre va a estar enojadísimo.*
"Now you did it. You're father is going to be very angry."
2. *Car., prnl. v.* To shack up. *Fernando y Lola se embre-
taron hace un año. Dicen que se casarán luego.* "Fernando and Lola shacked up a year ago. They say they will
get married later."

EMBRISCARSE, *Car., prnl. v.* To escape, to flee. *Cuando
entré en el cuarto el ladrón se embriscó por la ventana.*
"When I entered the room the thief took off through the
window."

EMBUTE, *L.Am./N, n.* Illicit profits. *El empleado del gobierno denunció el embute del contratista.* "The government employee denounced the illicit profit made by the
contractor."

EME, *Spain, n.* Shit. Letter used when one doesn't want to say the whole word. (Lit. The letter "M" for "mierda.") *¡Eme! ¡Qué tonto soy! Salí de casa sin mis tarjetas de crédito.* "Shit! I am so stupid! I left home without my credit cards."

EMERGENTE, *Car., n.* Pinch-hitter. (Lit. Emerging.) *Gómez viene a batear ahora como emergente.* "Gomez is coming up to bat now as a pinch-hitter."

EMILIO, *Spain, n.* Email. *Tío, acabo de recibir tu emilio de ayer.* "Uncle, I just received your email from yesterday."

EMPACAR, *L.Am./N, v.* To eat. (Lit. To pack.) *Vamos a empacar unos tacos.* "Let's put away some tacos."

EMPALMADO See ESTAR EMPALMADO

EMPANADA, *Car., n.* Flat tire. *Voy a llegar tarde porque el carro tiene una empanada.* "I am going to arrive late because the car has a flat."

EMPANADA MENTAL, *Spain, idiom.* Confusion. *Hay tantas cosas en el internet que se me forma una empanada mental.* "There are so many things on the Internet that I get a mental block."

EMPAQUETAR, 1. *Car., v.* To deceive, to tell tall stories. *Ya te conozco y no me vas a volver a empaquetar.* "I know you already and you are not going to put one over on me again." **2.** *Spain, v., crim.* To fine or to punish. *Le empaquetaron con tres años en el chiquero.* "They sent them up the river for three years."

EMPARANOIADO, *Spain, adj.* Worried. *Me tienen emparanoiado con los rumores de la quiebra.* "They got me all paranoid with the bankruptcy rumors."

EMPEDARSE, *L.Am./N, prnl. v.* To get drunk. *Yo me vine temprano porque los demás se estaban empedando.* "I came home early because everyone else was getting a jag on."

EMPELOTADO, DA, 1. *L.Am./N, adj.* In love. *Gilberto estaba bien empelotado cuando andaba con Elisa.* "Gilbert was really in love when he was going out with Elisa."

2. *L.Am./N, adj.* Naked, nude. *El marido entró y pescó a su mujer y al amante empelotados en la cama.* "The husband walked in and caught his wife and her lover naked in bed."

EMPIJADO, DA, *L.Am./S, adj.* Very busy. *Estamos muy empijados con este proyecto. Tenemos que terminarlo para el viernes.* "We are very involved with this project. We have to finish it by Friday."

EMPILTRARSE, *Spain, prnl. v.* To go to bed. *Me empiltré temprano porque me dolía todo.* "I went to bed early because I ached all over."

EMPINARSE, *Spain, prnl. v.* To get an erection. *Cada vez que Martín piensa en Marta se pone empinado.* "Every time Martin thinks about Marta he gets a hard-on."

EMPIÑATADO, *L.Am./S, adj.* Crazy about. *Sole está muy empiñatada con su perrita.* "Sole has a real soft spot for her dog."

EMPLANTILLADO, DA, *Spain, adj., crim.* Hidden, stashed. *Tiene la hierba emplantillada en un garaje cerca del centro.* "He has the grass stashed in a garage close to the downtown area."

EMPLEOMANÍA, *Car., n.* Group of employees. *Cuando sonó la alarma se formó una empleomanía delante del edificio.* "When the alarm sounded, the group of employees formed in front of the building."

EMPLUMAR, *Spain, v., crim.* To arrest, to fine. *Le emplumaron a Jorge por no pagar las multas que tenía.* "They picked George up for not paying the fines he had."

EMPORRADO, DA, *Spain, adj., drugs.* High on grass. *Estaban todos emporrados cuando entraron los uniformados.* "They were all high when the fuzz came in."

EMPORRARSE, *Spain, prnl. v., drugs.* To get high on grass. *A mi hermano le gustaba emporrarse cuando era joven.* "My brother liked to get high when he was young."

EMPREÑADOR, *Spain, n.* Bothersome, annoying. *El sobrino tuyo es muy empreñador. Anda, dale algo para que* *se vaya.* "Your nephew is a real pain in the butt. Here, give him something so he will go away."

EMPREÑAR, *Spain, v.* To bother, to annoy. *¡Deja de empreñar coño!* "Stop screwing around, asshole!"

EMPUJAR, *L.Am./N, v.* To drink continuously. *Estábamos empujando los jaiboles.* "We were guzzling the highballs one after the other."

EMPURAR, *Spain, v., mil.* To fine, to impose punishment. *Al Sargento Rodríguez le empuraron dos meses de calabozo.* "They gave Sergeant Rodriguez two months in the stockade."

EMPUTECERSE, 1. *Spain, prnl. v.* To prostitute oneself. *En mi opinión, si aceptamos esas condiciones estamos emputeciéndonos.* "In my opinion, if we accept these conditions we are prostituting ourselves." **2.** *L.Am./S, prnl. v.* To get very angry. *Me emputecí cuando llegó la cuenta.* "When the invoice arrived I blew up."

EN CHINGA, *L.Am./N, idiom.* Fast, quick. *Me vine en chinga para no perder la clase.* "I really flew so I wouldn't miss class."

EN CORITATIS, *Spain, idiom.* Naked, nude. (Lit. Latin for "en cuero" [naked, nude].) *Abrí la puerta y allí estaba ella, totalmente en coritatis.* "I opened the door and there she was, totally naked."

EN CUEROS, *L.Am./S, adj.* Naked. *Al pobre se le cayó el traje de baño y quedó en cueros.* "The poor guy's swimsuit fell off and he was left naked."

EN CUEROS VIVOS, *Spain, idiom.* Stark naked, nude. *Los padres de Lola encontraron al novio en cueros vivos en el cuarto de ella.* "Lola's parents found her boyfriend in her room, stark naked."

EN EL CARRO DE FERNANDO, *L.Am./C, idiom.* On foot. *"¿Cómo vas a ir a la casa de Rogelio?" "En el carro de Fernando."* " 'How are you going to Rogelio's?' 'On the ten-toed taxi.' "

EN EL CULO DEL MUNDO, *Spain, idiom.* Far away.

Ramón se fue a vivir en un pueblo que está en el culo del mundo. "Ramón went to live in a town that's at the end of the earth."

EN EL QUINTO COÑO, *Spain, idiom.* Far away. *No quiero ir allí. Ese bar está en el quinto coño.* "I don't want to go there. That bar is too fucking far."

EN MENOS QUE CANTA UN GALLO, *L.Am./N, idiom.* Right away, immediately. *Terminamos la tarea en menos que canta un gallo.* "We finished the job in the blink of an eye."

EN NADA, *L.Am./S, idiom.* Boring. *"¿Y qué tal la fiesta?" "Toda la noche estuvo en nada."* " 'How was the party?' 'Boring the entire night.' "

EN PALETA, *L.Am./C, idiom.* Much, great, great amount. *El profesor tiene premios en paleta y ahora sacó el premio Nobel.* "The professor has a bunch of prizes and now he got the Nobel Prize."

ENANITO, *Spain, n.* Very small child. (Lit. Dwarf.) *Llevaron a todos los enanitos de la escuela a una excursión.* "They took all the little rugrats from school on an excursion."

ENCABRONARSE, *L.Am./N, prnl. v.* To get angry, to get pissed off. *No le cuentes lo ocurrido, no vaya a ser que se encabrone con nosotros.* "Don't tell him what happened unless you want him getting pissed at us."

ENCAJADOR, RA, *Spain, adj.* Boxer who can take a punch. *Hay unas boxeadoras americanas que son muy encajadoras.* "There are some American women boxers who can really take a punch."

ENCAJOSO, *L.Am./N, n.* Moocher. *Aquí viene el encajoso de tu vecino.* "Here comes that moocher neighbor of yours."

ENCAMARSE, *Spain, prnl. v.* To bed someone, to have sexual relations. *El dependiente de la ferretería está encamándose con la dueña.* "The hardware store clerk is bedding down with the owner."

ENCANASTAR, *Car., v., sports.* To make a basket, to score in basketball. *Magic encanastó un total de 42 puntos.* "Magic made baskets for a total of 42 points."

ENCARGO, *Car., n.* Pregnancy. *Me ha ido muy bien con este segundo encargo.* "This second pregnancy has been going very well for me."

ENCARTAR, *Spain, v., crim.* To inform on someone during interrogation. *Ese hijo de puta encartó a todos sus compañeros cuando le interrogaron.* "That son of a bitch gave up all his friends when they interrogated him."

ENCATRINARSE, *L.Am./N, prnl. v.* To get dressed up, to get decked out, to get dolled up. *Pepita se encatrina por cualquier cosa.* "Pepita gets all dressed up for anything."

ENCERRAR, *Spain, v., crim.* To follow someone to find out where they live. (Lit. To lock up.) *Encerraron al tipo usando tres agentes y así encontraron su escondite.* "They tailed the dude using three agents and that's how they found his hideout."

ENCHILADO, *L.Am./N, adj.* Annoyed, angry. *Mi papá andaba super enchilado cuando supo lo del accidente.* "My father was super pissed off when he found out about the accident."

ENCHILARSE, *L.Am./N, prnl. v.* To get angry, to get mad, to get pissed off. *¿No te enchilas si te digo una cosa de tu novia?* "You're not going to get upset if I tell you something about your girlfriend?"

ENCHILOSO, *L.Am./N, adj.* Hot, spicy. *No me gusta ese plato por enchiloso.* "I don't like that dish because it is too spicy."

ENCHIQUERAR, *Spain, v., crim.* To jail. *La jueza le enchiqueró por dos años.* "The judge sent him up for two years."

ENCHUFADO, DA, *Spain, adj.* Connected. (Lit. Plugged.) *Tengo un primo bien enchufado en el ayuntamiento. Él te puede ayudar.* "I have a cousin who is well-connected at city hall. He can help you."

ENCHUFAR, *L.Am./N, v.* To have sex. (Lit. To plug in.) *Tengo ganas de enchufar a la vecina de al lado.* "I feel like plugging into our neighbor next door."

ENCHUFE, *Spain, n.* Connection. (Lit. Plug.) *¿Tienes un enchufe en el almacén que me pueda recomendar para el trabajo?* "Do you have a connection at the store who can recommend me for the job?"

ENCHUMBAO, Á, *Car., adj.* Soaked, soaking wet. *Llovió tanto que llegué al trabajo todo enchumbao.* "It rained so much that I got to work soaking wet."

ENCOÑADO, DA, *Spain, adj.* Very much in love, very attracted to. *Juanito está muy encoñado con Isadora.* "Juanito is crazy about Isadora."

ENCOÑAMIENTO, *Spain, n.* Falling in love, becoming sexually attracted to. *Ella va de novio en novio. Creo que le gusta el encoñamiento.* "She goes from boyfriend to boyfriend. I believe that she likes falling in love."

ENCOÑARSE, *Spain, prnl. v.* To fall in love, to become sexually atracted to. *Me parece que tu hermano está encoñándose con mi hermana.* "I think your brother has the hots for my sister."

ENCUERADO, DA, *L.Am./N, adj.* Naked, nude. *Rogelio estaba encuerado cuando salió del baño.* "Rogelio was in his birthday suit when he got out of the bath."

ENCUERATRIZ, *L.Am./N, n.* Topless dancer. *Silvia se metió de encueratriz en el cabaret.* "Silvia got a job as a topless dancer at a cabaret."

ENCULAR, *Spain, v.* To have anal sex, to give it in the ass, to shaft. *Cuidado con esa gente. Cuando menos lo piensas te están enculando.* "Look out for those people. When you least think about it, you get shafted."

ENCULARSE, *L.Am./S, prnl. v.* To get angry. *Juan se enculó con su jefe hoy.* "Juan got pissed off at his boss today."

ENDILGAR, *Spain, v.* To lecture, to berate. *Luego tuve que esperar mientras el jefe me endilgaba por llegar tarde.*

"Later I had to wait while the boss gave me a lecture on coming late."

ENDIÑAR, *Spain, v.* To give it to someone, to lecture, to slap. *Cuando llegó Alvaro a casa su mujer le endiñó bien.* "When Alvaro got home his wife really let him have it."

ENDOMINGAR, *U.S., v.* To dress up. *Ese hombre se endominga todos los días. ¡Qué formal!* "That man gets dressed up every day. How formal!"

ENDROGARSE, *Car., prnl. v., youth.* To prepare for a test. *Jorge pasó toda la noche endrogándose para el examen.* "Jorge spent the night hitting the books for the test."

ENE, *L.Am./S, adj.* Much, too much, a lot. *Yo le di ene de pena a mi madre cuando era joven.* "I gave my mother a lot of grief when I was young."

ENFARLOPADO, DA, *Spain, adj.* Drugged. *Damián estaba muy enfarlopado cuando lo vi.* "Damian was really out of it when I saw him."

ENFRIAR, *L.Am./N, v.* To kill. (Lit. To cool.) *Al comandante lo enfriaron tres asesinos jóvenes.* "Three young murderers put the commander on ice."

ENFRIARSE, *L.Am./N, prnl. v.* To die. (Lit. To cool oneself off.) *Aparentemente se enfrió de un ataque de plomo.* "Apparently he died of a lead attack."

ENFUNDARLA, *Spain, idiom.* To put one's penis back in one's pants. *El hombre sacó la picha, meó, la sacudió, la enfundó y se fue.* "The man pulled out his stick, he peed, he shook it off, he put it back in its holster, and he left."

ENGANCHADO, DA, *Spain, adj., drugs.* To be addicted to drugs. (Lit. Hooked.) *Lulú no tiene remedio. Está muy enganchada con la coca.* "Lulu has no remedy. She is very hooked on horse."

ENGANCHARLA, *Spain, idiom.* To get drunk or high. (Lit. To hook it.) *Yo la enganché bien anoche y ahora tengo la resaca.* "I got smashed last night and now I have a hangover."

ENGANCHARSE, *Car., prnl. v.* To get a good job or position. (Lit. To get hooked.) *Jorge está feliz pues se enganchó con una compañía buenísima.* "Jorge is happy because he got hooked up with an excellent company."

ENGANCHE, 1. *Car., n.* Good job. *Este enganche ofrece un gran entrenamiento.* "This job offers great training." **2.** *L.Am., n.* Down payment. *Compre su casa con sólo el 10% de enganche.* "Buy your house with just 10% down."

ENGATILLADO, DA, *L.Am./S, adj., youth.* Involved with, going with, going steady. *Teresa está engatillada con el hijo de mi vecino.* "Teresa is involved with my neighbor's son."

ENGENDRO, *Spain, n.* Ugly person. *¿Tú ves a ese engendro allí? Pues es el novio de Isabel.* "Do you see that ugly character there? Well, that's Isabel's boyfriend."

ENGRASAR, *L.Am., Spain, v., crim.* To bribe. *Perdió porque no engrasó a quién debía de engrasar.* "He lost because he didn't grease the right palm."

ENGRASE, *L.Am., Spain, n., crim.* Bribe. *Después de dar un poquito de engrase me dejaron entrar.* "After a little palm grease they let me in."

ENGRIFARSE, *Spain, prnl. v., drugs.* To get high on grass. *Esos grifotas no hacen más que pasar el día engrifándose.* "Those potheads don't do anything else but spend their day getting high on grass."

ENGRINGOLARSE, *Car., prnl. v.* To dress well. *Me voy a engringolar para ir a la entrevista del viernes.* "I am going to get decked out to go to the interview on Friday."

ENGRUPIR, 1. *L.Am./S, v.* To win over. *Por fin Isabel engrupó a Ricardo.* "Isabel finally won Ricardo over." **2.** *L.Am./S, v.* To lie, to fool. *Alvaro está engrupiendo, yo no dije eso.* "Alvaro is kidding you; I didn't say that."

ENGUARAPARSE, *Car., prnl. v.* To get drunk. *Es la segunda vez que te enguarapas esta semana.* "This is the second time you have tied one on this week."

ENGUARETARSE, *Car., prnl. v.* To become defiant. *Si te enguaretas así vamos a terminar peleando.* "Don't get smart with me or we'll end up fighting."

ENJABONADA, *Car., n.* Flattery. *María estaba dándole una enjabonada al jefe para que le diera un aumento.* "Maria was buttering up the boss so that he would give her a raise."

ENLATAO, TÁ, *Car., adj.* Canned, as in video program. *No me gustan los programas con las risas enlatás.* "I don't like programs with canned laughter."

ENROLLADO, DA, *Spain, adj.* Involved. (Lit. Rolled-in.) *Tu primo está muy enrollado en el ambiente de la tele, ¿verdad?* "Your cousin is real involved in the TV world, right?"

ENROLLAR, 1. *Spain, v.* To involve, to entangle. (Lit. To roll.) *Le dije a Adela que no me enrollara en sus asuntos.* "I told Adela not to involve me in her affairs." **2.** *Spain, v.* To like, to enjoy. *A mí me enrollan las reuniones políticas.* "I really get into political meetings."

ENROLLARSE, 1. *Spain, prnl. v.* To have a one-night stand. (Lit. To roll oneself.) *Anoche se enrolló con una y no llegó hasta la mañana siguiente.* "Last night he had a one-night stand and he didn't get home until the following morning." **2.** *Spain, prnl. v.* To run on. *Cuando empieza a hablar el profe se enrolla y no sabe terminar.* "When the prof starts to talk he gets on a roll and doesn't know when to quit." **3.** *Spain, v.* To get involved, to get into. *Pedro se enrolla mucho en las cuestiones del barrio.* "Pedro gets very wrapped up in neighborhood matters."

ENSALADA, *Spain, n.* A lot of something. (Lit. Salad.) *Había una ensalada de productos vendiéndose en la feria.* "There was a bunch of products sold at the fair."

ENSARDINAO, NA, *Car., adj.* To be packed in like sardines. *Estuvimos ensardinaos en el ascensor hasta la planta trece.* "We were packed like sardines in the elevator up to the thirteenth floor."

ENSEÑAR LA CAJETILLA, *Car., idiom.* To smile. *Alina siempre está enseñando la cajetilla para congraciarse con la gente.* "Alina is always showing her pearly whites to get along with people."

ENTALEGAR, *Spain, v., crim.* To jail. *"¿Cuándo te entalegaron?" "Hace dos años."* " 'When did they send you up?' 'Two years ago.' "

ENTERADILLO, LLA, *Spain, n.* Know-it-all. *Rubio es un enteradillo. Tiene que comentar sobre todo.* "Rubio is a know-it-all. He's got to comment on everything."

ENTERARSE POR LA BRAGUETA, *Spain, idiom.* To misunderstand. *David se enteró por la bragueta y le pegó.* "David misunderstood and hit him."

ENTERITO, TA, *Car., adj.* Having all of one's faculties. *Tus padres están enteritos para la edad que tienen.* "Your parents are at 100% for their age."

¿ENTÓS QUÉ, LOCO?, *L.Am./N, idiom.* Challenging greeting. What's with you! *¿Entós qué, loco? ¿Ves algo que no te gusta o qué?* "What's with you? Do you see something you don't like or what?"

ENTREPIERNA, *Spain, n.* Female genitals, beaver. *La tipa estaba mostrando la entrepierna a todos los que estábamos allí.* "The broad was showing her beaver to all of us there."

ENTRETENIDA, *Spain, n.* Kept lover, mistress. (Lit. Entertained.) *El tío tenía a la entretenida en un piso nuevo en Los Remedios.* "The guy had his mistress set up at a new apartment in Los Remedios."

ENTROMPARSE, *Spain, prnl. v.* To get drunk. *Anoche nos entrompamos para festejar el fin del curso.* "Last night we got plastered when we celebrated graduation."

¡EPA!, *Car., interj.* Greeting. Hi! *¡Epa compay! ¿A qué debo esta visita?* "Hi brother! To what do I owe this visit?"

¡ESA ONDA!, *L.Am./S, idiom, interj.* Affirmation. Right on! *"¡Vamos a divertirnos esta noche!" "¡Esa onda!"* " 'Let's go have some fun tonight!' 'Right on!' "

¡ESA(LE)!, ¡ESE(LE)!, *U.S., interj.* Hey! Hey you! *¡Esele! Quítese del medio que no veo.* "Hey you! Get out of the way; I can't see."

ESCABIAR, *L.Am./S, v.* To have a drink. *Vamos a escabiar esta noche.* "Let's go drinking tonight."

ESCABIO, *L.Am./S, n.* Alcoholic drink. *Tomamos un escabio todas las noches después del trabajo.* "We have a drink every night after work."

ESCALADOR, *Spain, n.* Cyclist who specializes in mountainous terrain. (Lit. Climber.) *El hijo de Mario es un escalador.* "Mario's son is a mountain biker."

ESCAMA, *L.Am./N, n., drugs.* Cocaine. (Lit. Scale.) *Todavía tenía la escama en el bolsillo cuando lo detuvieron.* "He still had the coke in his pocket when they detained him."

ESCAMAR, *L.Am./N, v.* To scare, to frighten. *A mí me escama salir muy tarde por la noche.* "It scares me to go out late at night."

¡ESCAMPA!, *Spain, interj.* Get out of here! *¡Escampa! Y no quiero verte por aquí más.* "Get the hell out of here! I don't want to see you around here anymore."

ESCANDALOSA, *L.Am./N, n., crim.* Radio patrol car, popcorn machine. (Lit. Scandalous.) *Todos los chiquillos estaban alrededor de la escandalosa.* "All the kids were around the patrol car."

ESCAPARATE, *Spain, n.* Woman's breast. (Lit. Store window.) *Esa preciosa tiene un escaparate de miedo.* "That chick has a great showcase."

ESCAQUEARSE, *Spain, prnl. v.* To avoid work. *Ese tipo siempre se escaquea cuando tenemos algo que hacer.* "That guy always pulls away when we have something to do."

ESCAQUEO, *Spain, n.* Avoidance of work. *Trabaja más con el escaqueo que haciendo lo que tiene que hacer.* "He works more trying to get out of work than doing what he has to do."

ESCOBA, *Spain, n.* Thin woman. (Lit. Broom.) *La mujer de Raimundo es una escoba. Si engordara estaría más bonita.* "Raymundo's wife is a broomstick. If she'd gain weight she would be prettier."

ESCOÑADO, DA, 1. *Spain, adj.* Broken. *Mi ordenador está escoñado y no puede navegar en el internet.* "My computer is screwed up and I can't navigate on the internet." **2.** *Spain, adj.* Very tired. *Después de subir la escalera con ese sofá estarás escoñado del todo.* "After climbing the stairs with that sofa you're probably exhausted."

ESCOÑAR, *Spain, v.* To break, to ruin. *El niño me ha escoñado el radio y ahora no puedo oír el partido.* "The kid screwed up my radio and now I can't listen to the game."

ESCOÑARSE, *Spain, v.* To break down. *Se escoñó el cajero automático justo cuando quería sacar dinero.* "The ATM broke down just when I wanted to withdraw money."

ESCOPETA, *L.Am./N, n.* Hypodermic syringe, nail. (Lit. Shotgun.) *Los drogatos a veces se pinchan con escopetas sucias y se enferman.* "Sometimes the drug addicts stick themselves with dirty nails and get sick."

ESCOPETEADO, DA, *Spain, adj.* In a rush, in a hurry. *Conchita salió tan escopeteada que dejó su bolso en la silla.* "Conchita took off so fast she left her purse on the chair."

ESCOPETEO, *Car., n.* Backfiring of a car. *No nos dimos cuenta del tiroteo porque pensábamos que era un escopeteo.* "We didn't pay attention to the shootout because we thought it was a car backfiring."

ESCRIBIDOR, DORA, *Spain, n.* Writer, scribbler. *Antonia es escribidora de notas. Siempre me manda notas de sus ideas.* "Antonia is a note scribbler. She's always sending me notes about her ideas."

ESCUÁTER, *U.S., Spain, n.* Squatter. *El piso se quedó* *vacío por un mes y pronto llegaron los escuáteres.* "The apartment was vacant for a month and soon the squatters came in."

ESCUÍNCLE, *L.Am./N, n.* Small child. *Andaban unos escuíncles vendiendo periódicos en la esquina.* "There were some kids selling newspapers on the corner."

ESCUPIR, *Spain, v., crim.* To confess. (Lit. To spit.) *Tarde o temprano ese maleante va a escupir todo lo que hizo.* "Sooner or later that hoodlum is going to spit out everything he did."

ESCUPIR A LA CALLE, *Spain, idiom.* Interrupted coitus. (Lit. To spit in the street.) *Algunos creen que pueden evitar embarazar a la mujer escupiendo a la calle.* "Some men believe that they can avoid getting a woman pregnant by coming on the sheets."

ESCURRIRSE, *Spain, prnl. v.* To ejaculate, to have an orgasm. *Amor, tienes que ver al médico, no aguantas y te escurres en seguida.* "Honey, you have to see the doctor, you can't hold it and you come right away."

¡ESFÚMATE EN LA NIEBLA!, *Spain, idiom.* Get out of here! *¡Esfúmate en la niebla, hijo de puta! No te queremos por aquí.* "Disappear, you son of a bitch! We don't want you around here."

ESNIFADA, *Spain, n., drugs.* Sniff of cocaine or other drug. (From English "a sniff.") *Tenía polvo blanco alrededor de la nariz despues de una esnifada de coca.* "He had white powder around his nose after a sniff of coke."

¡ESO ES MEAO!, *Car., idiom, interj.* That's terrible! *¿Cómo se te ocurrió darle trabajo a ese tipo? ¡Eso es meao!* "How did you get the idea to hire that guy? That's terrible!"

ESO ES UN JAMÓN, *Car., idiom.* That's easy, it's a cinch, it's a piece of cake. *Ese trabajo que te asignaron es un jamón.* "This job they assigned you is a piece of cake."

¡ESO VA A MISA!, *Spain, idiom, interj.* Expression of certainty. You can take that to the bank! *Jaime va a entregar ese trabajo mañana. ¡Eso va a misa!* "Jaime is going to deliver that job tomorrow. You can bank on it!"

ESPACIAO, CIÁ, *Car., adj.* High on drugs, spaced-out. *Hay tantos jóvenes conduciendo espaciaos que es un peligro para todos.* "So many young people are driving while spaced-out that it is a danger for everybody."

ESPADA, *Spain, n.* Skeleton key, picklock. (Lit. Spade.) *Encontraron al ladrón en la puerta de la casa con una espada en la mano.* "They found the thief at the door of the house with a picklock in his hand."

ESPADISTA, *Spain, n., crim.* Picklock (person). *La pandilla reclutó a Germán porque tenía fama de espadista.* "The gang recruited Germán because he was famous as a picklock."

ESPANTACIGÜEÑAS, *L.Am./N, n.* Abortionist. (Lit. Stork frightener.) *Los doctores militares tienen fama de espantacigüeñas.* "Military doctors are well-known abortionists."

ESPARRABAR, *Spain, v., crim.* To commit burglary. *Anoche esparrabaron la tienda de mi cuñado pero no se llevaron nada.* "Last night they broke into my brother-in-law's store but they didn't take anything."

ESPARRABO, *Spain, n., crim.* Break-in. *Hubo un esparrabo en la agencia de viajes anoche.* "There was a break-in at the travel agency last night."

ESPECIALISTO, *Spain, n., hum.* Know-it-all. (Lit. A play on "especialista" [specialist] and "listo" [smart].) *Aquí viene el especialisto José. Ahora vamos a oír el rollo.* "Here comes Jose the specialist. Now we are going to hear a full load."

ESPERPENTO, *L.Am., adj.* Very ugly (person). *Ese pobre hombre es un esperpento.* "That poor man is a fright."

ESPESO, SA, *L.Am./C, adj.* Difficult, problematic. (Lit. Thick.) *Las cosas están un poco espesas en casa.*

"Things are kind of tough at home."

ESPETA, *Spain, n., crim.* Police inspector. *Hoy vino el espeta y quería hablar contigo del robo de anoche.* "Today the inspector came and wanted to talk to you about the robbery last night."

ESPICHARLA, *Spain, idiom.* To die. *El caballo de Marisa la espichó ayer. Tenía una infección de pulmones.* "Marisa's horse kicked the bucket yesterday. It had a lung infection."

ESPIRAL, *Spain, n.* Intrauterine device. (Lit. Spiral.) *El tocólogo de Paula le dijo que usara el espiral.* "Paula's gynecologist told her to use the coil."

ESPONTÁNEO, *Spain, n., sports.* Fan who jumps into the bullring during a bullfight. (Lit. Spontaneous.) *No me gusta cuando los espontáneos saltan al ruedo durante una corrida.* "I don't like it when the fans start jumping into the ring during a bullfight."

ESPUELA, *Spain, n.* One for the road. *Bueno amigos, es tarde, vamos a tomar la espuela.* "Well, friends, it's late; let's have one for the road."

ESQUELETO See MENEAR EL ESQUELETO

ESQUITE, *L.Am./N, n.* Popcorn. *Lo mejor de la película fue el esquite.* "The best thing about the movie was the popcorn."

ESTÁ EN NOTA, *Car., idiom.* To be drunk or high. *Se tomó diez cervezas y está en nota.* "He had ten beers and he is tipsy."

ESTAR A CIEN, *Spain, idiom, drugs.* To be very high on alcohol or drugs. *Ahora mismo Pablo está a cien y no carbura. Hablaremos con él mañana.* "Right now Pablo is flying a mile a minute and he is not thinking. We'll talk to him tomorrow."

ESTAR A MEDIA VELA, *Spain, idiom.* To be drunk. *El conductor del camión estaba a media vela cuando pasó el accidente.* "The truck driver was three sheets to the wind when the accident happened."

223

ESTAR AL LORO, *Spain, idiom.* To be ready, to be on the alert. *Quiero que todos estén al loro por si regresa el director temprano.* "I want everybody to be on the alert in case the director comes back early."

ESTAR (ALGO) QUERIDO, *Car., idiom.* Done. *No te preocupes por lo que me pediste. Eso ya está querido.* "Don't worry about what you asked me. Consider it done."

ESTAR ALTO, *Spain, idiom, drugs.* To be high, to be at the height of pleasure or effect of drugs or alcohol. *¿Qué le pasa a Fernando? Me parece que está alto de la coca.* "What's the matter with Fernando? I think he's high on coke."

ESTAR ARMADO, *Spain, adj.* To have an erection. (Lit. To be armed.) *El tipo estaba armado.* "The guy had a hard-on."

ESTAR ARRIBA, *Spain, idiom, crim.* To be in jail. *José está arriba hace ya tres años por robo.* "Jose has been up the river now for three years for robbery."

ESTAR BAJO, *Spain, idiom, drugs.* To be down. *Terminado su viaje con anfetas, Álvaro está ahora bajo.* "Now that he finished his speed trip, Alvaro is feeling down."

ESTAR BERZA, *Spain, idiom.* To be slow, dull. *Está berza hoy Tomás. ¿Qué le pasa?* "Thomas is dull today. What's the matter with him?"

ESTAR BIEN AGARRADO, *Spain, idiom.* To have good connections. *Mi cuñado está bien agarrado.* "My brother-in-law is well-connected."

ESTAR BIEN ARMADO, *Spain, idiom.* To have a large penis. *Su primo trabaja en películas porno porque está bien armado.* "His cousin works in porno movies because he has a big dick."

ESTAR BIEN PARADO, *L.Am./N, idiom.* To be well-connected. *Pídele trabajo a Joel, él está bien parado con el alcalde.* "Ask Joel for a job; he is well-connected with the mayor."

ESTAR BIMBO, *Car., idiom.* To be full after a meal. *No puedo comer postre, estoy bimbo.* "I can't eat dessert; I'm full."

ESTAR BOMBA, *Spain, idiom.* To have a great body. *Anoche salí con una chica que está bombísima.* "Last night I went out with a girl who has a body to die for."

ESTAR BRUJO, JA, *Spain, idiom.* To be broke. *No me pidas dinero en estos días porque estoy bruja.* "Don't ask me for money these days because I am flat broke."

ESTAR BUENO, NA, *L.Am., Spain, idiom.* To have a sexually attractive body. *¡Qué buena está esa chica!* "That girl is luscious!"

ESTAR CAGADO, DA, 1. *Spain, idiom.* To be scared to death, to be scared shitless. *Cuando vio echarse encima el camión, Jaime estaba cagado.* "When he saw the truck coming down on him, Jaime was scared shitless." **2.** *L.Am., idiom.* To be in a hopeless situation. *Mañana van a revisar los libros de la compañía, así es que estamos cagados.* "Tomorrow they'll check the company's books, so we are screwed."

ESTAR CANIJO, *L.Am./N, idiom.* To be difficult, to be complicated. *Va a estar canijo pasar de año si no estudias.* "It's gonna be tough to pass the year if you don't study."

ESTAR CARGADO, DA, *Spain, idiom.* Drunk. *Paco estaba cargado anoche en la feria.* "Paco was plastered last night at the fair."

ESTAR CHIFLAO, *Car., idiom.* To be crazy. *Este tonto está tan chiflao como siempre.* "This fool is as crazy as ever."

ESTAR COGÍO, 1. *Car., idiom.* To be crazy about somebody. *Tomás está cogío con Marta, anda atrás de ella como un bobo.* "Thomas has flipped over Marta; he runs after her like an idiot." **2.** *Car., idiom.* To have venereal disease. *David está cogío. Una puta le dio la gonorrea.* "David got a case of clap. A whore gave it to him."

ESTAR COLGADO, DA, 1. *Spain, idiom.* To be crazy, to be off one's rocker. *Rosario está colgada. Me llamó tres veces hoy creyendo que yo era Fernán.* "Rosario is nuts. She called me today three times thinking that I was Fernan." **2.** *Spain, idiom, drugs.* To be high on drugs. *Ramón estuvo colgado en la heroína durante años. Se desenganchó hace poco.* "Ramon was hooked on heroin for years. He got off only a short time ago."

ESTAR COMO AGUA PARA CHOCOLATE, *L.Am./N, idiom.* Angry, steaming, in a bad mood. *Beatriz está como agua para chocolate desde que supo que la engañas.* "Beatrice is steaming since she found out you are cheating."

ESTAR COMO CAÑA DE ENERO, *Car., idiom.* To have a voluptuous body, to be luscious. *Amanda está como caña de enero.* "Amanda is like a juicy peach."

ESTAR COMO LAS VACAS, *L.Am./C, idiom.* To be dopey, to be slow. *Esteban está como las vacas, hay que decirle las cosas tres veces.* "Esteban is slow as an ox; you've got to tell him things three times."

ESTAR COMO QUIERE, *Spain, idiom.* To have a good figure. *Pepa está como quiere. Hay que ver cómo se mantiene.* "Pepa is in great shape. It's awesome how she keeps herself."

ESTAR COMO UN BACALAO, *Car., idiom.* To be thin. *Estoy flaca como un bacalao.* "I am as skinny as a rail."

ESTAR COMO UN CAMIÓN, *Spain, idiom.* To have a great body. *Esa muchacha está como un camión.* "That girl is really stacked."

ESTAR COMO UN CENCERRO, *Spain, idiom.* To be crazy, to be off one's rocker. *Curro está como un cencerro. Dice que va a Hollywood a meterse en películas.* "Curro is nuts. He says he's going to Hollywood to get into movies."

ESTAR COMO UN CLAVO, *Spain, idiom.* To be very thin. *Tu hermano ha perdido mucho peso. Está como un* *clavo.* "Your brother has lost a lot of weight. He looks like a nail."

ESTAR COMO UN TITÍ, *L.Am./S, idiom.* To be angry. (Titi is a small screaming monkey in the South American jungle.) *Papá se puso como un tití cuando le dije que me reprobaron.* "Pop became a howling monkey when I told him that they failed me."

ESTAR COMO UN TREN, *Spain, idiom.* Very attractive. *Mi esposa cree que Antonio Banderas está como un tren.* "My wife thinks that Antonio Banderas is a hunk."

ESTAR COMO UNA CABRA See ESTAR COMO UNA CHIVA

ESTAR COMO UNA CHIVA, *Spain, idiom.* To be crazy, silly. *Pepita está como una chiva. Siempre se olvida de los nombres de la gente.* "Pepita is silly. She is always forgetting people's names."

ESTAR COMO YESCA, *Car., idiom.* To be sleeping soundly. *Daniel está como yesca en el sofá.* "Daniel is out like a light on the sofa."

ESTAR CON BOMBO, *Spain, idiom.* Pregnant. *María está con bombo.* "Maria is carrying a belly."

ESTAR CON EL AGUA AL CUELLO, *L.Am., Car., idiom.* To be heavily in debt. *Hay muchos matrimonios jóvenes que están con el agua hasta el cuello.* "There are many young marriages that are up to their necks in debt."

ESTAR CON EL CULO AL AIRE, *L.Am./S, Car., idiom.* To be in a difficult situation, to be poor. *Con la pérdida de su trabajo Ramón está con el culo al aire.* "With the loss of his job Ramon has his ass in a sling."

ESTAR CON EL CULO PRIETO, *Spain, idiom.* To be afraid. *Carlos ha estado con el culo prieto desde que le amenazaron de muerte.* "Carlos has been scared off his ass since they threatened him with death."

ESTAR CON UNA MANO DELANTE Y OTRA DETRÁS, *Spain, idiom.* To not have a pot to piss in.

Salieron de España con una mano delante y otra detrás. "They left Spain without a pot to piss in."

ESTAR CORTADO, *Spain, idiom.* To be in a difficult situation in terms of money, friends, love, drugs. *Cuando éramos jóvenes siempre estábamos cortados de dinero.* "When we were young we were always short on money."

ESTAR CORTO, *L.Am., idiom.* To have little money. *Hoy no tengo mucha plata, estoy corto.* "I don't have much money; I'm a little short."

ESTAR CURDA, *Car., idiom.* To be drunk. *Paco está curda, se ha tomado media botella de ron.* "Paco is plastered. He's had half a bottle of rum."

ESTAR DADO AL CUÁS, *L.Am./N, idiom.* To be broken down. *Lo vi muy dado al cuás a Tito desde que perdió el trabajo.* "Tito looks worn out since he lost his job."

ESTAR DE BOYA, *Car., idiom.* To be in a good mood. *Hoy estoy de boya, mi mujer sale del hospital con nuestro hijo nuevo.* "I am in a great mood; today my wife gets out of the hospital with our new son."

ESTAR DE LA NUCA, *L.Am./S, idiom.* To be crazy. *Josefa está de la nuca, quiere tener diez hijos.* "Josefa is off her rocker; she wants to have ten kids."

ESTAR DEL TOMATE, *L.Am./S, idiom.* Crazy, nuts, off one's rocker, out of one's mind. *Dicen que estoy de tomate porque quiero dejar mi trabajo.* "They say that I'm out of my mind because I want to leave my job."

ESTAR DETRÁS DEL PALO, *L.Am./C, idiom.* To not know, to not understand. *Cuando hablamos de computadoras se nota que Abel está detrás del palo.* "When we talk about computers you can tell that Abel is out of it."

ESTAR DURO, RA, *Car., idiom.* To be sharp, bright, good-looking. *Teresa está bien dura: además de guapa es muy inteligente.* "Teresa is terrific—besides being beautiful she is intelligent."

ESTAR EMPALMADO, *Spain, idiom.* To have an erection. *No sé como los artistas de cine pueden trabajar cuando* *están empalmados.* "I don't know how movie stars can work when they have a hard-on."

ESTAR EN BRAGAS, *Spain, idiom.* Broke, without money. (Lit. To be in one's panties.) *No puedo salir esta noche, estoy en bragas.* "I can't go out tonight because I am flat broke."

ESTAR EN CANA, *L.Am./S, Car., idiom.* To be in jail. *Beto está en cana. Le echaron dos años por malversación de fondos.* "Beto is in the big house. They gave him two years for misappropriation of funds."

ESTAR EN CARNE, *Car., idiom.* To be broke. *No tengo ni un centavo. Estoy en carne.* "I don't have a cent. I'm strapped."

ESTAR EN EL CAMÓN, *Car., idiom.* To be worn-out, to be exhausted. *Después del maratón Juan está en el camón.* "After the marathon Juan was like a wet rag."

ESTAR EN EL CULO DEL MUNDO, *L.Am./S, Car., idiom.* To be in a terrible place, at the end of the world. *El pueblo donde vive mi hijo está en el culo del mundo.* "The town where my son lives is at the end of the earth."

ESTAR EN EL QUINTO COÑO, *Spain, idiom.* To be very far away. *El bar La Paloma está en el quinto coño.* "La Paloma bar is out in the boondocks."

ESTAR EN LA INOPIA, 1. *Car., idiom.* To be broke. *Hoy no puedo prestarte dinero, estoy en la inopia.* "I can't lend you any money today; I am out of cash." **2.** *Spain, idiom.* To be in another world. *La madre de Manolo está en la inopia. Necesita atención continua.* "Manolo's mother is in another world. She needs continuous attention."

ESTAR EN LA LIPIDIA, *L.Am./C, idiom.* To be broke, to be poor. *Tenemos que ayudarlos porque están en la lipidia.* "We've got to help them because they are hurting."

ESTAR EN LA LONA, *L.Am./S, idiom.* Broke. *Me botaron del trabajo y estoy en la lona.* "I got fired from the job and I am down and out."

ESTAR EN LA LUNA, *L.Am., Car., idiom.* To be out of one's mind, to be in another world. *María no se da cuenta de nada, está en la luna.* "Maria isn't aware of anything; she is in another world."

ESTAR EN LA OLLA, *L.Am./S, idiom.* To be broke. *Mi familia está en la olla. No tenemos ni para la renta.* "My family is in the hole; we don't even have enough for the rent."

ESTAR EN LA ONDA, *L.Am./S, idiom.* To be with it. *Me encanta Julieta, siempre está en la onda.* "I really like Julieta; she is with it."

ESTAR EN LAS GRANDES LIGAS, *Car., idiom.* To be in the penitentiary. *El hermano de Juan está en las grandes ligas por robo de auto.* "Juan's brother is in the big house for auto theft."

ESTAR EN LAS LIGAS MENORES, *Car., idiom.* To be in jail. *Le mandaron a las ligas menores por cometer un delito menor.* "They sent him off to the minors for a misdemeanor."

ESTAR EN LAS MAJADAS, *Car., idiom.* To be making good money. *Con ese negocio Gloria está en las majadas.* "With this business Gloria is rolling in dough."

ESTAR EN LAS PAPAS, *Car., idiom.* To be well-off. *Nuestros vecinos están en las papas ya que tocaron la lotería.* "Our neighbors are rolling in clover since they hit the lottery."

ESTAR EN OTRA, *L.Am./S, idiom.* To not pay attention. *Alfredo está en otra, parece muy preocupado por algo.* "Alfredo is somewhere else; it seems he's worried about something."

ESTAR EN PELOTA, *Spain, L.Am., idiom.* To be naked, to be nude. *Cuando me llamaron estaba yo en pelota y no podía salir.* "When they called me I was stark naked and couldn't go out."

ESTAR EN TRES Y DOS, *Car., idiom.* To be between a rock and a hard place. *No sé qué hacer, estoy en tres y* *dos.* "I don't know what to do; I am between a rock and a hard place."

ESTAR EN UNA LLAMITA, *L.Am./C, idiom.* To be worried. *Mi madre estuvo en una llamita toda la noche hasta que llegó mi hermano.* "My mother was worried all night until my brother arrived."

ESTAR FINITO, *Car., idiom.* To be short on money. *Hoy no puedo gastar mucho porque estoy finito.* "I can't spend much today because I am short on cash."

ESTAR FRITO, TA 1. *Car., idiom.* To be a failure, to be disgraced. *Tomás está frito desde que lo cogieron estafando a la compañía.* "Thomas is ruined since they caught him swindling the company." **2.** *Spain, idiom.* To be broke, to not have something. *Estoy frito Paco, ¿me puedes prestar unas pesetas hasta el lunes?* "I'm broke Paco; can you lend me some pesetas until Monday?" **3.** *Spain, idiom.* To be exhausted. *Después de la carrera José quedó frito.* "After the race, José was wasted." **4.** *L.Am./S, idiom.* To be in big trouble. *Estamos fritos, el bote se hunde.* "We're screwed; the boat is sinking."

ESTAR GACHAS, *Spain, idiom.* To be strong and muscular. *Armando está gachas. ¿Levantará pesas?* "Armando looks diesel. Do you think he lifts weights?"

ESTAR GASEADO, *Car., idiom.* To be broke. *No puedo ir contigo al cine porque estoy gaseado.* "I can't go to the movies because I am broke."

ESTAR GUILLAO, *Car., idiom.* To be crazy about. *Me han dicho que Fernando está guillao por ti.* "They told me that Fernando is crazy about you."

ESTAR HACHA, *L.Am./N, idiom.* To be attentive. *Se puso bien hacha cuando le dijeron que podía perder su casa.* "He was all ears when they told him he could lose his house."

ESTAR HASTA EL COÑO See ESTAR HASTA LAS NARICES

ESTAR HASTA EL MOÑO See ESTAR HASTA LAS NARICES

ESTAR HASTA LAS NARICES, *Spain, idiom.* To be fed up. *El jefe estaba hasta las narices de las tonterías en el trabajo.* "The boss was up to his ears with the shenanigans at work."

ESTAR HASTA LOS COJONES See ESTAR HASTA LAS NARICES

ESTAR HECHO POLVO, *Spain, idiom.* To be exhausted. *Estoy hecho polvo después de la carrera.* "I am wrung out after the race."

ESTAR HECHO PURÉ See ESTAR HECHO POLVO

ESTAR HECHO UN MULO, *Spain, idiom.* To be strong. *Manolo estaba hecho un mulo cuando entró en el concurso.* "Manolo was as strong as an ox when he entered the contest."

ESTAR HECHO UN TRAPO, *Spain, idiom.* To be very tired, to be wrung out. *Mi hermano estaba hecho un trapo cuando llegó del trabajo.* "My brother looked like a wet rag after he got back from work."

ESTAR IDO, *L.Am., idiom.* To be high on drugs. *Tadeo está ido otra vez.* "Tadeo is high again."

ESTAR LIMPIO, *Spain, idiom, crim.* To not have a record, to be clean. *Pedro estaba limpio cuando fue arrestado.* "Pedro had a clean record when he was arrested."

ESTAR MALA, *Spain, idiom.* To be menstruating, to have one's period. *No hay nada que hacer esta noche Pedro, estoy mala.* "There is nothing to do tonight Pedro; I'm having my period."

ESTAR MAL DEL COCO, *Spain, idiom.* To be crazy. *Tu hermano está mal del coco. No carbura bien.* "Your brother is a little off upstairs. He's not thinking right."

ESTAR MÁS COMBINAO QUE UNA PAPELETA, *Car., idiom.* To color-coordinate one's clothes with extreme care. *Siempre estás más combinao que una papeleta,* *pareces maniquí.* "You're so color-coordinated you look like a mannequin."

ESTAR MÁS PUESTO QUE UN CALCETÍN, *L.Am./N, idiom.* To be ready to go. *Estoy más puesto que un calcetín para ir al paseo.* "I am readier than a dog waiting for its walk."

ESTAR METIDO CON, *Car., idiom.* To be in love with. *Juan está metido con mi prima y quiere que yo le hable bien de él.* "Juan is head over heels for my cousin and wants me to put in a good word for him."

ESTAR METIDO HASTA LOS COJONES, *Spain, idiom, crim.* To be completely involved in something. *El detective dijo que Juan estaba metido en el robo hasta los cojones.* "The detective said that Juan was involved in the robbery up to his balls."

ESTAR MOLIDO, DA, *L.Am., Spain, idiom.* To be very tired. *Luisa estaba completamente molida después del proyecto.* "Luisa was completely wiped out at the end of the project."

ESTAR MORMADO, *L.Am./N, idiom.* To be hoarse. *Estoy mormado desde que me dio gripe.* "I am hoarse since I got the flu."

ESTAR MOSCA, *Spain, idiom.* To be alert. *Mi madre ha estado mosca desde que le dijeron que me iban a entrevistar.* "My mother had her antenna up ever since they told her they were going to interview me."

ESTAR NEGRO, RA, *Spain, idiom.* To get angry, to get annoyed. *Estoy negro contigo porque no me llamaste cuando llegaste al aeropuerto.* "I am pissed off because you didn't call me when you got to the airport."

ESTAR PARADO DE PESTAÑAS, *L.Am./N, idiom.* To be enraged. *Manuel estaba parado de pestañas cuando supo que lo habían demandado.* "Manuel was super pissed when he found out they had sued him."

ESTAR PIPA, *Spain, idiom.* To be in great shape. *Carmen está pipa. Todos los días corre cinco kilómetros.*

"Carmen is in fine shape. She runs five kilometers every day."

ESTAR SENTADO EN EL BAÚL, *Car., idiom.* To be henpecked. *Luis está sentado en el baúl. Su mujer no le deja ir a ninguna parte.* "Luis is henpecked. His wife doesn't let him go anywhere."

ESTAR SIN UN CINCO, *L.Am./S, Spain, idiom.* To be broke. *No sé lo que voy a hacer. Estoy sin un cinco y tengo que pagar la renta.* "I don't know what I am going to do. I don't have a dime and I have to pay the rent."

ESTAR TOCADO DEL ALA, *Spain, idiom.* To be a little crazy. *El está tocado del ala.* "He's flipped."

ESTIRAR LA PATA, *L.Am., Spain, idiom.* To die. *Mi pobre perrito estiró la pata anoche.* "My poor dog kicked the bucket last night."

ESTO HUELE A QUESO, *Car., idiom.* Expression of suspicion, something stinks. *Este asunto me huele a queso.* "Something doesn't smell right about this matter."

ESTO PINTA MAL, *Car., idiom.* This looks bad. *Esto pinta mal. Yo creo que el enfermo no llega a mañana.* "This looks bad. I don't think the patient will make it till tomorrow."

ESTONASO, *L.Am./S, n.* Drug addict. *El pobre de Enrique, cada vez que lo veo está estonaso.* "Poor Enrique, every time I see him he is stoned."

ESTRECHO, CHA, *Spain, adj.* Sexually repressed, narrow-minded. *El padre de Alicia es muy estrecho de pensamiento.* "Alicia's father is very narrow-minded."

ESTRENAR, *Spain, v.* To deflower. *Dicen que los reyes tenían el derecho de estrenar a las novias de otros.* "They say that kings had the right to break in other men's new brides."

ESTUCHERO, *L.Am./N, n., crim.* Safe-cracker. *Ese robo fue trabajo de un estuchero profesional.* "That robbery was the work of a professional safe-cracker."

ESTUFEAR, *U.S., v., drugs.* To sniff cocaine. *No salgo con Roberto porque siempre está estufeando.* "I don't go out with Roberto because he is always sniffing coke."

ESTUPA, *Spain, n., crim.* Narcotics officer, narc. *Entraron las estupas y apresaron a todos los drogatos.* "The narcs came in and grabbed all the junkies."

ETARRA, *Spain, n.* Militant member of the ETA (organization for Basque independence). *Los etarras tienen la responsabilidad de muchos asesinatos en España.* "The Etarras are responsible for many killings in Spain."

EX, *L.Am., Spain, adj.* Ex-wife, ex-husband. *Javier todavía se lleva bien con su ex.* "Javier still gets along with his ex."

EXCUSADO, *L.Am., n.* Toilet. *Necesito ir al excusado ahora mismo.* "I need to go to the head right now."

EXÓTICA, *L.Am./N, n.* Stripper. *Esa chica lleva tres años de exótica en México.* "That girl has been a stripper in Mexico for three years."

EXPERTA EN ARTES CULINARIAS, *L.Am./N, n.* Prostitute. *A Estela no le quedó más que hacerse experta en artes culinarias.* "Estella had no alternative but to become a hooker."

EXPRIMIR EL CHAYOTE, *L.Am./N, idiom.* To think, to meditate. *Por más que exprimo el chayote, no se me ocurre como arreglarlo.* "As much as I rack my brain, I can't figure out how to fix it."

ÉXTASIS, *Spain, n., drugs.* Ecstasy, variety of LSD. *Los estupas lo encontraron muerto con restos de éxtasis en la mesa.* "The narcs found him dead with the remains of ecstasy on the table."

FACHA, *Spain, n.* Fascist. *Esos muchachos son unos fachas. Están medio locos.* "Those fellas are fascists. They're half-crazy."

FACHADA, *L.Am./N, n.* Face. (Lit. Front of a building.) *Le dieron un trancazo en la fachada.* "They hit him one right in the puss."

FACHENTO, *L.Am./C, adj.* Ridiculous-looking person. *Marino siempre se presenta tan fachento a las funciones.* "Marino always shows up at the shows looking so ridiculous."

FACHOSO, SA, *L.Am./N, adj.* Exaggerated, ridiculous. *No me gusta Raúl por fachoso.* "I don't like Raul because he is all show."

FAITE, *L.Am./N, n.* Fighter. (From English "fighter.") *César es un buen faite. Será campeón algún día.* "Cesar is a good fighter; someday he will be a champion."

FAJADOR, *Spain, idiom.* Aggressive boxer. *Roberto Rodríguez es un gran fajador. Tiene la posibilidad de llegar lejos.* "Roberto Rodriguez is a great fighter. He could go far."

FAJE, *L.Am./N, n.* Heavy petting. *Anoche Olga y yo estuvimos dándonos unos fajes rebuenos.* "Last night Olga and I were getting it on real heavy."

FALOCRACIA, *Spain, n.* Male domination in public

236

affairs. (Lit. Phallocracy.) *Hoy en día las feministas protestan contra la falocracia en el trabajo.* "Nowadays the feminists protest against phallocracy at work."

FALÓCRATA, *Spain, n.* Supporter of male domination in public affairs. *Mi hermano Martín es falócrata. No le gusta la competencia femenina.* "My brother Martin is a phallocrat. He doesn't like female competitiveness."

FALOCRÁTICO, *Spain, adj.* Pertaining to male domination in public affairs. *Algunas personas creen que España es un país falocrático, pero no es así.* "Some people believe that Spain is a phallocratic country, but that isn't so."

FALOPA, 1. *L.Am./S, n.* Bad-quality cocaine. *Esos mafiosos están traficando con falopa.* "Those mafiosi are trafficking in bad coke." **2.** *Spain, n., drugs.* Cocaine. *La guardia civil confiscó 300 kilos de falopa en Cádiz.* "The civil guard confiscated 300 kilos of coke in Cadiz."

FALTAR UN TORNILLO, *L.Am., Spain, idiom.* To be crazy. *A Daniel le falta un tornillo. Le gusta vestirse como vikingo.* "Daniel has a screw missing. He likes to dress like a Viking."

FAMILIA, *Car., n.* Police. *A dos cuadras queda la estación de la familia.* "The police station is two blocks from here."

FANDANGO, *L.Am., n.* Argument. *Todas nuestras conversaciones terminan en fandango.* "All our conversations end up in a yelling match."

FANDUCA, *Car., n.* Vagina. *En ese bar las chicas bailan con la fanduca al aire.* "At that bar the girls dance with their bushes up in the air."

FANFA, *Spain, n.* Braggart. *Jorge es un fanfa. Siempre está hablando de sí mismo.* "Jorge is a braggart. He is always talking about himself."

FARDAR, *Spain, v.* To show off, to be flashy. *A Alicia le gusta fardar en las reuniones, lleva ropa extravagante.* "Alicia likes to show off at parties by wearing extravagant clothing."

FARMACIA See TENER LA FARMACIA ABIERTA

FAROLAZO, *L.Am./N, n.* Alcoholic drink. *Ayer me eché unos farolazos de tequila.* "Last night I threw down some tequila shots."

FAROLES, *L.Am./S, pl. n.* Eyes. (Lit. Lanterns.) *El sol me hace doler los faroles.* "The sun hurts my eyes."

FAROLILLO ROJO, *Spain, idiom.* Last in a competition. *Bernardo era el farolillo rojo en la última carrera.* "Bernardo was last in the recent race."

FAROLÓN, *L.Am./N, n.* Braggart. *Edmundo es muy farolón y eso que no tiene ni de qué presumir.* "Edmundo is a real boaster and the thing is that he doesn't have a reason to show off."

FAROS, *Spain, pl. n.* Eyes. (Lit. Headlights.) *¡Qué faros más bonitos tiene esa muchacha!* "What beautiful peepers that girl has!"

FARRA, *L.Am./S, Car., n.* Party. *Me dieron una farra de despedida que fue divertidísima.* "They gave me a going-away party that was wild."

FARRISTA, *Car., adj.* Party guy or gal. *Carlos es el más farrista de nuestros amigos.* "Of our friends, Carlos is the biggest party guy."

FATO, *L.Am./S, n.* Affair. *Me contaron que mi jefe y su secretaria tuvieron un fato.* "I was told that my boss and his secretary had a thing going."

FATULO, LA, *Car., adj.* Worthless. *Ese tipo me compró la tele con un cheque fatulo.* "That guy bought the TV from me with a rubber check."

FAYUCA, *L.Am./N, n.* Street sales, contraband. *Mi hermana iba a Los Angeles a traer fayuca.* "My sister would go to Los Angeles to get contraband."

FAYUQUEAR, *L.Am./N, v.* To sell on the street. *Con la crisis, muchos tuvieron que fayuquear para sobrevivir.* "With the crisis, many people had to hustle things to survive."

FAYUQUERO, *L.Am./N, n.* Peddler, huckster. *Fernando se metió de fayuquero de aparatos electrónicos.* "Fernando became a hustler of electronic appliances."

FECA, *Car., adj.* Bad, incompetent, stupid. *Ese vendedor feca no entiende lo que quiero.* "That stupid vendor doesn't understand what I want."

FEDERICO, *L.Am., n., crim.* FBI. *Ya cogió Federico al que robó el banco ayer.* "The FBI already caught the guy who robbed the bank."

FELICIANO, *Spain, n.* Copulation, fuck. *Los muchachos están en la casa de putas esperando un feliciano.* "The fellas at the whorehouse are waiting for a quickie."

FELINA, *L.Am./N, n.* Maid, servant. (Lit. Feline.) *Dile a la felina que vaya por las tortillas.* "Tell the maid to go for tortillas."

FELIZ COMO UNA LOMBRIZ, *L.Am./N, idiom.* Very happy. *Gerardo está feliz como una lombriz desde que le compraron la bicicleta.* "Bernardo is as happy as can be since they bought him the bicycle."

FENÓMENO, NA, 1. *Car., n., crim.* Police. (Lit. Phenomenon.) *Se embriscaron los ladrones cuando vieron llegar a los fenómenos.* "The thieves took off when they saw the fuzz arrive." **2.** *L.Am./S, Spain, adj., youth.* Fabulous. *"¿Qué tal el nuevo CD de Enrique?" "Fenómeno."* " 'How's Enrique's new CD?' 'Phenomenal.' "

FERIA, 1. *L.Am, n.* Promotional gift, incentive. (Lit. Fair.) *En nuestra tienda siempre le damos feria al que compra un reloj.* "At our store we always give a little bonus to the person who buys a watch." **2.** *L.Am./N, n.* Change, money. *No le di limosna al mendigo porque no traía feria.* "I didn't give the beggar anything because I didn't have any change."

FERMÍN, *Spain, n.* Private chauffeur. *Alvaro triunfó tanto que podía tener un fermín que le llevara a todas partes.* "Alvaro was such a success that he could afford a private chauffeur to take him everywhere."

FETÉN, *Spain, adj., youth.* Fantastic, cool, wild, great. *El concierto de Chayán fue fetén.* "Cheyenne's concert was wild."

FETO, *Spain, n.* Very ugly person. (Lit. Fetus.) *El tipo allí es un feto. Nunca he visto a una persona tan fea.* "That guy there is a Quasimodo. I've never seen anyone so ugly."

FIACA, 1. *L.Am./S, adj.* Lazy. *Mi hermana es bien fiaca, no le gusta trabajar para nada.* "My sister is very lazy; she doesn't like to work at all." **2.** *L.Am./S, n.* Laziness, lazy feeling. *Hoy no voy al trabajo porque tengo mucha fiaca.* "Today I'm not going to work because I feel like loafing."

FIAMBRE, *L.Am., Spain, n.* Cadaver. (Lit. Cold cut.) *Entramos en la morgue y tenían tres fiambres esperando autópsias.* "We entered the morgue and they had three cold ones awaiting autopsies."

FIAMBRERA, *Spain, n.* Coroner's van, hearse. (Lit. Container for cold cuts.) *La fiambrera llegó para llevar las víctimas de la explosión.* "The meat wagon arrived to carry the explosion victims away."

FIBRA, *L.Am./N, n.* Strength, vigor. (Lit. Fiber.) *Hay que tener mucha fibra para acabar la carrera.* "You've got to put forth a lot of effort to finish the race."

FICHA, *Spain, n.* Criminal with a long record. *Los fichas se guardan en un edificio especial.* "The prisoners with long records are kept in special buildings."

FICHAR, 1. *L.Am., Spain, v.* To be under investigation or suspicion, to have one's number. *A Hernando lo tienen fichado y si se descuida lo descubren.* "They've got Hernando's number and, if he isn't careful, they will find out about him." **2.** *L.Am./N, v.* To dance or entertain in a night club. *Vi a la ex-esposa de Esteban fichando en el cabaret.* "I saw Esteban's ex dancing at the cabaret."

FIEBRE, *L.Am., n.* Urge, spontaneous desire to do something. (Lit. Fever.) *Acércate, que tengo fiebre de darte un beso.* "Come close, I've got an urge to give you a kiss."

FIERRO, *L.Am./S, n.* Gun, pistol, revolver, rod, piece. (Lit. Iron.) *Tenía un fierro debajo del saco.* "He had a piece under his jacket."

FIGURÓN, RONA, *Car., adj. or n.* Person with high social visibility. *Mario se volvió un figurón desde que protagonizó la telenovela.* "Mario has become a celebrity since he starred in the soap opera."

FIJADO, DA, *L.Am./N, adj.* Hypercritical. *No seas tan fijada y deja a tu hijo disfrutar su matrimonio.* "Don't be so hypercritical and let your son enjoy his marriage."

FILDEAR, *Car., v., sports.* To play the position of fielder in baseball. *Pepe Valdez fildea para los Cardenales.* "Pepe Valdez fields for the Cardinals."

FÍLDER, *Car., n., sports.* Fielder. (From English "fielder.") *El sobrino de Julio es un fílder con los Yankees.* "Julio's nephew is a fielder with the Yankees."

FILO, *L.Am./S, n.* Hunger, appetite. (Lit. Edge.) *Me da mucho filo después de correr.* "Running makes me hungry."

FILTRAR UN MAZO, *Car., idiom.* To learn fast. *Hazme caso, porque en estas cosas yo filtro un mazo.* "Do what I do, because in these things I learn fast."

FINO CAÑERÍA, *Spain, idiom.* Glass of tap water. *Échame un vaso de ese fino cañería que tienes.* "Pour me a glass of that tap wine you have."

FIRME, *L.Am./S, n.* Truth. *¿Saliste con Roberto? ¡La firme! ¿Sí o no?* "Did you go out with Roberto? The truth, yes or no?"

FIRMÓN, *L.Am./N, n.* Lawyer who will sign anything, shyster. *Cuidado con ese abogado, es un firmón.* "Be careful with that lawyer; he is one who will sign anything."

FITIPALDI, *Spain, n.* Humorous nickname for one's driver. *Fitipaldi, a ver si me puede tener en el aeropuerto en veinte minutos.* "Fitipaldi, see if you can get me to the airport in twenty minutes."

FLACA, *Spain, n.* Young svelte woman. (Lit. Skinny.) *Oye flaca, tienes los ojos más grandes que los pies.* "Hey skinny, your eyes are bigger than your feet."

FLACO, 1. *L.Am./S, n.* Dude. (Lit. Skinny.) *Oye flaco, pásate un par de cervezas.* "Hey dude, pass me a couple of beers!" **2.** *L.Am./S, n.* Informal way of addressing someone. *Flaco, ayúdame a levantar este bulto.* "Hey Slim, give me a hand with this bundle."

FLAI, *Spain, n., drugs.* Marijuana joint. *"¿Este flai es tuyo?" "No, no sé nada de eso."* " 'Is this joint yours?' 'No, I don't know anything about it.' "

FLAMA, 1. *Car., adj. or n.* Attractive person. *Diana es muy inteligente y además una flama.* "Diana is very intelligent and also a beauty." **2.** *Spain, n.* Heat reflecting from the street. *Al caminar la flama de la calle casi me asfixiaba.* "While I was walking, the heat from the street was almost smothering me."

FLAMENCO, CA, *Spain, adj.* Sassy, aggressive, bold. *No te pongas flamenco conmigo sobre esto. Yo no te estoy criticando.* "Don't get smart-ass with me about that. I am not criticizing you."

FLAN, *Car., adj.* Conceited. (Lit. Caramel custard.) *Ahí viene el flan de Luis a ostentar con su nuevo carro.* "Here comes that hot-shot Luis to show off his new car."

FLANEAR, *Car., prnl. v.* To show off. *Lola nos invitó a su casa para flanear con sus antigüedades.* "Lola invited us to her house to show off her antiques."

FLANERO, RA, *Car., n.* Show-off. *Sandra es una flanera que compra cosas sólo para ostentar.* "Sandra is a show-off who buys things just to show them off."

FLAUTA, 1. *Spain, n.* Submarine sandwich. (Lit. Flute.) *Quisiera una flauta de chorizo y queso por favor.* "I would like a sausage and cheese sub please." **2.** *Spain, n.* Penis. *El exhibicionista estaba en el escaparate con la flauta en la mano, ¡qué loco!* "The exhibitionist was in the store window with his flute in his hand; what a weirdo!"

FLAY, *Car., n., sports.* Fly ball. *López cogió el flay para cerrar la entrada.* "Lopez caught the fly to end the inning."

FLECHADOR, DORA, *Car., adj.* Seducer, seductress. *Esa mujer es una flechadora y me quitó el novio.* "That woman is such a slut that she took my boyfriend away."

FLECHERA, *Car., adj.* Flirt. *Todos los hombres andan a sus pies porque es una flechera.* "All the men are at her feet because she is a flirt."

FLETERA, *Car., n.* Loose woman, prostitute. *Marta anda con uno hoy y con otro mañana, es una verdadera fletera.* "Martha is with one guy today and another tomorrow. She is a real swinger."

FLICHE, *Car., adj.* Skinny. *Siempre he sido fliche y no puedo engordar.* "I've always been skinny and I can't gain weight."

FLIPADO, DA, *Spain, adj., youth.* Stunned, surprised. *Vaya, yo quedé flipado cuando me dijeron que me estaban despidiendo.* "Wow, I was stunned when they told me they were dismissing me."

FLIPANTE, *Spain, adj., youth.* Stunning, shocking, fabulous. *El estilo de los nuevos cantantes de rock es muy flipante.* "The style of the new rock singers is shocking."

FLIPAR, *Spain, v., youth.* To like, to enjoy. *Me flipa la música punk.* "I flip over punk music."

FLIPAR(SE), 1. *Spain, v., drugs.* To get stoned. *Los drogatos siempre están flipándose en esa casa.* "The druggies are always getting stoned in that house." **2.** *Spain, v., youth.* To be stunned, to be surprised. *Me fliparon las noticias de su padre.* "The news about your father flipped me out."

FLIPIADORA, *Car., n.* Pinball machine. *Cuando yo era joven me volvían loco las flipiadoras.* "When I was young I would go crazy over pinball machines."

FLOJERA, *L.Am./S, n.* Laziness. *Tengo una flojera terrible, no voy a cocinar hoy.* "I am feeling very lazy. I am not going to cook today."

FLOJO, JA, *L.Am./S, adj.* Lazy. *¡Qué flojo eres Jaime! Le-vántate y ayúdame con este sofá.* "You're so lazy Jaime! Get up and help me with this sofa."

FLOR FINA, *Car., idiom.* Gonorrhea. *Las putas esas son muy bonitas pero, cuidado, te pueden dar la flor fina.* "Those whores are very pretty, but be careful, they can give you the clap."

FLOR ROJA DE COLOMBIA, *Car., idiom.* Marijuana. *La flor roja de Colombia se consigue aquí a buen precio.* "I can get Colombian grass here at a good price."

FLORÓN, NA, *Car., adj.* Good-looking person with limited intelligence. *¿De qué le sirve la belleza a Lucy si es una florona?* "What good is beauty to Lucy if she is so slow?"

FLOTA, *L.Am./S, n.* Long-distance bus. (Lit. Fleet.) *Se fueron todos en flota para el pueblo.* "They all went to the village on the bus."

FLOTADORES, *L.Am./S, pl. n.* Love handles. (Lit. Floats.) *Con la dieta se me han acabado los flotadores.* "With the diet, I got rid of the love handles."

FLUS, *Spain, n., youth.* Money. *"¿Tienes un poco de flus para prestarme?" "Es que ando sin un cobre".* " 'Do you have a little cash you can lend me?' 'The thing is, I don't have a penny.' "

FOCA, *Spain, n.* Fat and ugly person. (Lit. Seal.) *Esa tía es una foca. Comerá como una bestia.* "That broad is a whale. She probably eats like an animal."

¡FOCHE!, *Car., interj.* Yuck! *¡Foche! ¡Qué comida más asquerosa!* "Yuck! What a rotten meal."

FOCO, *L.Am./N, n.* Light bulb. *Viven en un cuartito con un solo foco.* "They live in a little room with one light bulb."

FODONGO, GA, *L.Am./N, adj.* Sloppy. *La esposa de Claudio es muy fondonga y tiene la casa sucia.* "Flavio's wife is a real mess and her house is dirty."

FOLKLORE, *Spain, n.* Commotion, racket, fuss. *No pude* *dormir toda la noche con el folklore que tenían arriba.* "I couldn't sleep all night with the racket going on upstairs."

FOLLADA, *Spain, n.* Fuck. *Con la follada de anoche la novia estará muy contenta hoy.* "With last night's fucking, the bride should be very happy today."

FOLLADOR, RA, *Spain, n.* Fucker. *Paquita es muy folladora, se encarama en todos.* "Paquita is a real fucker; she climbs over everybody."

FOLLAJE, *Spain, n.* Fuck. *A Víctor le gusta mucho el follaje, pero el trabajo, nada.* "Victor really likes fucking, but work? No way!"

FOLLAPOSTES, *Spain, n.* Telephone or electrical worker who climbs telephone or electrical poles. (Lit. Pole-fucker.) *Llegó el follapostes para cambiar la línea de teléfono.* "The pole-climber arrived to change the telephone line."

FOLLAR, 1. *Spain, v.* To fuck. *Comer, follar y dormir, ¡vaya vida que tienes!* "Eating, fucking, and sleeping, what a life you have!" **2.** *Spain, v.* To bother, to pester, to annoy. *Pedro, no folles tanto, ya me estás molestando.* "Pedro, don't screw around so much; now you are bothering me." **3.** *Spain, v.* To cause grave injury. *A Eugenio le folló el accidente que sufrió con el camión.* "The accident Eugenio had with the truck fucked him up."

FOLLÓN, *Spain, n.* Commotion, disturbance, racket. *Anoche se armó un follón en la estación de camiones.* "Last night there was a row at the truck depot."

FOLLONERO, RA, *Spain, n.* Troublemaker, one who is always arguing. *Despidieron a Rodrigo por ser muy follonero. Siempre discutía con los jefes.* "They fired Rodrigo for being a real shitkicker. He always argued with the bosses."

FOLLONISTA See FOLLONERO

FOROFO, FA, *Spain, n., sports.* Fan. *Los forofos del Real Madrid son los más fieles que hay en el mundo.* "Real Madrid fans are the most faithful in the world."

FORRARSE, *Spain, prnl. v.* To get rich. *Juan y Josefa se fueron a Alemania, donde se forraron.* "Juan and Josefa went to Germany, where they made it big."

FORRO, 1. *L.Am./N, n.* Good-looker, knockout. (Lit. Lining.) *La amiga de Cristóbal es un forro.* "Cristobal's girlfriend is a knockout." **2.** *L.Am./S, n.* Quandary, distress. *Mis dos novias se enteraron de la verdad. Estoy en un forro.* "My two girlfriends found out the truth. I'm in deep shit."

FÓSIL, *L.Am./S, adj. or n.* Adult, older person. (Lit. Fossil.) *Al paseo no va a ir ningún fósil, sólo sardinos.* "No fossils are going on the tour, just minnows."

FOTERO, RA, *Spain, n., youth.* Photographer. *El fotero llegó tarde para la boda y no sacó muchas fotos.* "The photographer arrived late for the wedding and didn't take many pictures."

FOTINGO, GA, *Car., L.Am./N, n.* Old car, jalopy. *Te invitaría a viajar conmigo, pero es que voy en mi fotingo.* "I would invite you to travel with me, but the thing is that I am going in my bucket of screws."

FRACATÁN, *Car., n.* Many, a lot of. *En el parque hay un fracatán de niños jugando.* "In the park there's a crowd of kids playing."

FRAJO, *U.S., n.* Cigarette. *Oye Carlos, siempre te veo con un frajo en la mano.* "Listen, Carlos, I always see you with a cigarette in your hand."

FRAJO DE SEDA, *U.S., n., drugs.* Marijuana joint. *En medio de la calle el alumno estaba fumando un frajo de seda.* "The student was smoking a joint in the middle of the street."

FRANCÉS, *Spain, n.* Fellatio, blow job. (Lit. French.) *La puta le cobró seis mil pesetas por un francés.* "The whore charged him six thousand pesetas for a blow job."

FRANCHUTE, TA, *Spain, n., youth.* French. *Había un grupo de franchutes en nuestro hotel.* "There was a group of Frenchies staying at our hotel."

FRANELEAR, *L.Am./S, v.* To engage in heavy petting. *Carlos estaba franeleando con Mari en el parque.* "Carlos was getting it on with Mari in the park."

FREGADO, DA, *L.Am./N, n.* Screwed, messed up. (Lit. Scrubbed.) *Anda muy fregado el hermano de Lorenzo desde que perdió el trabajo.* "Lorenzo is a real mess since he lost his job."

FREGAO, GÁ, *Car., n.* Loser. *Pancho es un fregao y no puede ofrecerte un buen futuro.* "Pancho is a fuckup and he can't offer you a good future."

FREGAR, 1. *L.Am., v.* To bother, to bug, to trouble. (Lit. To scrub.) *El hermanito de Chelo anda fregando todo el tiempo.* "Chela's little brother is always going around bothering people." **2.** *L.Am./N, v.* To screw up, to fuck up. *Apreté mucho la tapa y la fregué.* "I really tightened the cover and I screwed it up." **3.** *L.Am./N, v.* To harm, to screw. *¿Te acuerdas de la vecina? Ya la fregaron.* "Do you remember the neighbor? They did a nasty thing to her."

FREGARSE, *L.Am./S, prnl. v.* To have one's plans ruined. *Se fregó porque no le iba a prestar el carro.* "He was screwed because I wasn't going to lend him the car."

FREGÓN, NA, *L.Am./N, adj.* Cool, neat, super. *El hermano de Chayo es bien fregón para el beis.* "Chayo's brother is super at baseball."

FREÍR, *Spain, v.* To riddle with bullets. (Lit. To fry.) *La poli frió a los ladrones al salir éstos del banco.* "The cops cut down the thieves as they came out of the bank."

FRESCO, CA, *Car., adj. or n.* Freshman. (Lit. Fresh.) *Vamos a hacerle una bienvenida a los frescos.* "Let's give a good welcome to the frosh."

FRÍA, *Car., n.* Beer. (Lit. Cold.) *Sírveme una fría, que tengo tremenda sed.* "Give me a cold one; I am really thirsty."

FRITO, TA, *Car., adj.* Annoyed. (Lit. Fried.) *Estoy frito con tanto ruido que hacen los vecinos.* "I am bent out of shape with all the noise the neighbors make." **See also ESTAR FRITO**

FRONDOSA, *Car., adj.* Buxom. (Lit. Luxuriant.) *Qué novia tan frondosa la que tiene ahora Pepe.* "What a well-endowed girlfriend Pepe has now."

FROTÁRSELA, *Spain, v.* To masturbate (male). (Lit. To rub one's own.) *Esos desgraciados entran en ese cine para ver follar y frotársela.* "Those poor bastards go into that movie to watch fucking and jack off."

FUCA, *L.Am./S, n.* Firearm, gun, rod. *Ese hombre allí lleva una fuca.* "That man there is packing a rod."

¡FUCHI!, *L.Am./N, interj.* Yuck! *¡Fuchi! Aquí huele a zorrillo.* "Yuck! It smells like a skunk here."

FUERCIORIS, *L.Am./N, adv.* Obligatorily. *Tuve que acompañar a mi hermana a fuercioris.* "I was forced to accompany my sister."

FUERTE LO TUYO, *L.Am., idiom.* Expression used to sympathize with another's difficulties. *"Y ahora María no me quiere ver ni pintado." "¡Fuerte lo tuyo!"* " 'And now Maria doesn't want to see me at all.' 'What a shame!' "

FULA, *Car., n.* Shit. *En esa casa de drogadictos había fula por todas partes.* "There was shit all over the place in those junkies' house."

FULERO, RA, *Spain, n.* Liar, bragger, bullshitter. *Martín es muy fulero, no puedes creer nada de lo que te dice.* "Martin is a real bullshitter; you can't believe anything he says."

FULINGA, *Car., n.* Shit. *Ay, esta mañana encontré la fulinga del perro en la alfombra.* "Oh, this morning I found the dog's shit on the rug."

FULL DE TO', *Car., idiom.* Very good, cool, super cool. *"¿Qué tal el concierto?" "¡Full de to'!"* " 'How was the concert?' 'Cool!' "

FUMA, *Car., n.* Drag on a cigarette. *Dame una fuma de tu cigarillo.* "Give me a drag of your cigarette."

FUMADERO, *Car., n., drugs.* Pot house. *La casa de en-*

frente parece ser un fumadero. "The house across the street seems to be a pot house."

FUMADO, DA, *Spain, adj., drugs.* Under the influence of hashish or marijuana. (Lit. Smoked.) *Ahora Jorge está fumado, cuando baje podremos hablar con él.* "Right now Jorge is high; when he comes down we can talk to him."

FUMAR COMO UN CARRETERO, *L.Am./S, Spain, idiom.* To smoke a lot. *Cuando era más joven yo fumaba como un carretero. Menos mal que lo dejé.* "When I was younger I smoked like a train. It's a good thing I quit."

FUMAR COMO UN CHACUACO, *L.Am./N, idiom.* To smoke like a chimney. *El primo de Adán fuma como un chacuaco.* "Adam's cousin smokes like a chimney."

FUMETA, *Spain, n., drugs.* Pothead. *El hermano de Álvaro es una fumeta, siempre está fumando porros.* "Alvaro's brother is a pothead; he is always smoking joints."

FUMIGADO, DA, *L.Am./N, adj.* Very drunk. (Lit. Fumigated.) *Andrés estaba fumigado cuando lo encontré fuera de la cantina.* "Andrew was drunk as a skunk when I found him outside the bar."

¡FUNA!, *L.Am./S, interj.* Look! *¡Funa, primo, que ahí vienen los payasos!* "Look cousin, here come the clowns!"

FUNCIONAR, *Spain, v.* To maintain sexual potency. (Lit. To function.) *El viejito ya no funcionaba y su mujer le pidió una receta de Viagra.* "The old guy wasn't getting it up and his wife asked for a Viagra prescription."

FUNDA, *Spain, n.* Condom. (Lit. Sheath.) *Hoy en día no se puede joder sin funda, si lo haces te estás jugando la vida.* "Nowadays you can't screw without protection; if you do, you are risking your life."

FUNDÍRSELE LOS PLOMOS, *Spain, idiom.* To go crazy. *A Joaquín se le fundieron los plomos y ahora le mandaron al manicomio.* "Joaquin blew his fuses and they sent him to the insane asylum."

FÚRICO, CA, *L.Am./N, adj.* Furious. *Anacleto estaba*

fúrico cuando encontró a la esposa con otro. "Anacleto was furious when he found his wife with another."

FURRIS, *L.Am./N, adj.* Cheap. *No me gusta este vestido porque se ve muy furris.* "I don't like that dress because it looks too cheap."

FURRUSCA, *L.Am./S, n.* Fight. *En el bar se armó una furrusca y nos tocó irnos a toda carrera.* "A riot broke out at the bar and we had to get out of there fast."

FUSCA, *L.Am./N, n., crim.* Pistol. *Cuando nos asaltaron, Max sacó una fusca.* "When they jumped us, Max pulled out a piece."

FUSCO, 1. *Spain, n.* Sawed-off shotgun. *Los fuscos están prohibidos en muchos países.* "Sawed-off shotguns are prohibited in many countries." **2. FUSCO, CA,** *Spain, n.* Pistol. *El tipo llevaba un fusco debajo de la chaqueta.* "The guy had a rod underneath his jacket."

FUSIL, *Spain, n.* Penis. (Lit. Rifle.) *Ya no sirve el abuelo, su fusil ya no tiene balas.* "Granddad can't do it anymore; his rifle doesn't have any bullets."

FUSILAR, *Spain, v.* To plagiarize. (Lit. To execute by firing squad.) *El periodista fusiló un reportaje sobre las drogas y los jóvenes.* "The journalist plagiarized a report on drugs and young people."

FUSILERO, *L.Am./N, n.* Plagiarist. (Lit. Gunner.) *Lalo nunca crea nada, es un fusilero.* "Lalo never creates anything; he's a copycat."

FUSTÁN, *L.Am./C, n.* Slip. *Tuve que acompañar a mi mujer a comprar un fustán.* "I had to accompany my wife to buy a slip."

FUTBOLERO, RA, *Spain, n., sports.* Soccer fan. *Fernando es muy futbolero, no se pierde un partido.* "Fernando is a real soccer fan; he doesn't miss a game."

GABACHO, 1. *L.Am./N, n.* Foreigner. *Mañana llegará un barco lleno de gabachos.* "Tomorrow a ship full of foreigners will arrive." **2.** *Spain, adj.* French person. *Los gabachos que llegan acá son muy pendencieros.* "The Frenchies that come here are real brawlers."

GABARDINA, *Spain, n.* Condom. *Por no llevar gabardina el idiota tiene gonorrea.* "For not wearing a rubber, the idiot now has gonorrhea."

GABARDINO, NA, *U.S., n.* Foreigner. (Euphemism for "gabacho.") *¿Por qué ahora vienen tantos gabardinos a este barrio?* "Why are so many foreigners coming to this neighborhood now?"

GABILO, *Spain, n., youth.* Overcoat. *¡Qué frío hace! ¿Dónde está tu gabilo?* "It's really cold! Where's your overcoat?"

GACHÍ, *Spain, n.* Woman, girl. *La gachí me preguntó por el pacorro, y yo le pregunté si se refería al parroco.* "The chick asked me for 'el pacorro,' and I asked her if she was referring to 'el parroco,' the parish pastor."

GACHÓ, *Spain, n.* Man, guy. *Este gachó se levantó y dijo "Viva España."* "This guy got up and said 'Long live Spain.' "

GACHO, CHA, 1. *Car., adj. or n.* One-eared person. *El gacho de la esquina le coquetea a mi hija.* "The one-eared guy on the corner flirts with my daughter."

251

2. *L.Am./N, adj., neg.* Mean, terrible, foul, rotten. *Mi abuelo es muy gacho, nunca regala nada en Navidad.* "My grandfather is very mean; he never gives presents at Christmas."

GACHUPÍN, *L.Am./N, n.* Mexican pejorative term for Spaniard. *El dueño de la tienda de abarrotes es un gachupín.* "The owner of the grocery store is a Spaniard."

GAFUDO, DA, *Spain, adj.* Person who wears glasses. *José, vino un hombre gafudo para verte hoy. Le dije que no estabas.* "Jose, a man wearing glasses came to see you today. I told him you weren't in."

GALLETA, *Spain, n.* Slap. (Lit. Cookie.) *Luisa le dio una galleta en la cara. Tenía que doler.* "Luisa gave him a slap on the face. It had to hurt."

GALLINA, 1. *Spain, n.* Girl who has sex with all the members of a group. (Lit. Hen.) *Esa gallina conoce bien a todos los muchachos de la barriada.* "That chickie really knows all the boys in the neighborhood." **2.** *L.Am., Spain, n.* Coward. *¡Qué gallina eres Pepe! Tienes que pedir tus derechos.* "What a chicken you are Pepe! You've got to demand your rights."

GALLITO, *L.Am./C, n.* Small portion of food, a bite. (Lit. Little rooster.) *Mamá, voy a comer un gallito con los amigos antes de ir a casa.* "Mom, I'm going to have a bite with the boys before coming home."

GAMBA, 1. *L.Am./S, n.* Argentine monetary unit. (From Italian "gamba.") *Sólo me quedan veinte gambas.* "I just have twenty bucks left." **2.** *L.Am./S, n.* Leg. *Me duele la gamba derecha.* "My right gam hurts."

GAMÍN, NA, *L.Am./S, adj. or n.* Street children. *Es increíble cómo se ha multiplicado la cantidad de gamines en el centro de la ciudad.* "It's unbelievable how the number of street kids has multiplied downtown."

GANADO, *Spain, n.* Crowd of whores, gang of hookers. (Lit. Cattle.) *Venía un ganado por la calle, de todos colores, tamaños y, supongo, precios.* "A gang of hookers came down the street, of all colors, sizes, and, I suppose, prices."

GANCHO, *Spain, n., sports.* Hook. (Lit. Hook.) *El campeón le pegó un gancho y terminó la pelea en seco.* "The champion hit him with a hook and the fight was over in an instant."

GANDALLA, *L.Am./N, n.* Scrounger, sponger, opportunist. *Pánfilo es muy gandalla, siempre nos tima el dinero para los refrescos.* "Panfilo is a scrounger; he always cheats the soda money away from us."

GANDUL, LA, *Spain, n.* Lazybones, loafer. *Eres muy gandula Pepa. ¿Cuándo vas a limpiar la casa?* "You're a real lazy bones Pepa. When are you going to clean the house?"

GANDULITIS, *Spain, n.* Laziness. *Estoy sufriendo de la gandulitis, no tengo ganas de hacer nada.* "I am suffering from a bout of laziness. I don't feel like doing anything."

GANDUMBAS, *Spain, n.* Testicles, balls: *¡Vaya gandumbas tiene ese tío! No le da miedo de nada.* "What a pair of balls that guy has! He's not afraid of anything."

GANGA, *Car., n.* Gang. *El sobrino de Lalo pertenece a una ganga y ha dejado la escuela.* "Lalo's nephew belongs to a gang and has dropped out of school."

GANGUISTA, *Car., n.* Gang member. *En la escuela de mi hija hay muchos ganguistas.* "At my daughter's school there are a lot of gang members."

GARAÑÓN, *L.Am./N, n.* Womanizer, ladies' man, cockhound. (Lit. Stud jackass.) *Tito tenía un tío muy garañón con las mujeres.* "Tito had an uncle who was a real ladies' man."

GARBANCERO, *L.Am./N, n.* Spanish storekeeper. (Lit. Garbanzo seller.) *Don Manolo es el garbancero del pueblo.* "Don Manolo is the town's Spanish storekeeper."

GARGAJO, *Car., adj. or n.* Low-life person. *Todos los amigos de Marcos son unos gargajos.* "All of Marco's friends are scuzzos."

GARIBOLO, *Spain, n., youth.* Garbanzo, chickpea. *Mi madre me mandó comprar los garibolos para el cocido.* "My mother sent me to buy garbanzos for the stew."

GARIMBA, *Spain, n., crim.* Beer. *Los presos hacían su propia garimba en el cajón.* "The prisoners made their own beer in the clink."

GARPAR, *L.Am./S, v.* To pay. (Word made by jumbling the letters of the word "pagar" [to pay].) *A mí me toca garpar la curda esta noche.* "It's my turn to pay for the binge tonight."

GARRA, *L.Am./N, n.* Ugly woman. (Lit. Claw.) *Tomás trae una garra de novia.* "Thomas has an ugly girlfriend with him."

GARRANCHO, CHA, *Car., adj.* Senile. *Mi abuelo cada día está más garrancho.* "Every day my grandfather is more senile."

GARRAPATA, *L.Am./N, n.* Streetwalker. *Cuando pasamos por la cantina, salieron las garrapatas a dar lata.* "When we walked by the bar, the streetwalkers came out to pester us."

GARRÓN, *L.Am./S, n.* Problem, difficulty, unfulfilled intention. *¡Qué garrón! No pude arreglar la tele para ver el partido.* "What a letdown! I couldn't fix the TV to see the game."

GARRONEAR, *L.Am./S, v.* To mooch. *No puedo ver a Damián, siempre anda garroneando.* "I can't stand Damian; he's always going around mooching."

GARRONERO, *L.Am./S, n.* Moocher. *Julio es un garronero, quiere que le invitemos cuando vamos a algún sitio.* "Julio is a moocher; he wants us to invite him when we go somewhere."

GARRULO, LA, *Spain, n.* Hick, yokel, lout. *Llegó este garrulo preguntando por el autobús para Almensilla.* "This yokel arrived asking for the bus to Almensilla."

GARÚA, *Car., n.* Fight, ruckus. *Vámonos de aquí antes que* *empiece la garúa.* "Let's get out of here before all hell breaks loose."

GASEADO, DA, 1. *Car., adj.* Exhausted. (Lit. Gassed.) *Esta caminata me dejó gaseada.* "That walk wore me out." **2.** *Car., adj.* Out of work. *Llevo dos meses gaseado y estoy desesperado.* "I've been out of work for two months and I am desperate." **3.** *Car., adj.* Undergoing hard times. *Desde que se divorció, Laura está gaseada.* "Since she got a divorce, Laura is having hard times."

GASOFA, *Car., n.* Gasoline. *Tengo que echar gasofa a mi auto.* "I've got to put gas in my car."

GASOLERO, 1. *L.Am./S, n.* Diesel car. *Mi gasolero es muy económico.* "My dieseler runs cheap." **2.** *L.Am./S, n.* Person who knows how to have a good time on little money. *Nicolás es un gasolero, siempre lo pasa bien con menos de nada.* "Nicolas knows how to stretch a buck. He has a good time on less than nothing."

GATA, 1. *Car., adj. or n.* Prostitute. (Lit. Cat.) *Fernando va donde las gatas todos los fines de semana.* "Fernando goes to where the hookers are every weekend." **2.** *L.Am./N, n.* Maid, servant. *Díle a la gata que no barrió la calle en frente de la casa hoy.* "Tell the maid that she didn't sweep in front of the house today."

GATÍGRAFA, *L.Am./N, n.* Typist. *Cuando María se vino del campo, su primer trabajo fue de gatígrafa.* "When Maria came in from the country, her first job was as a typist."

GATILLERO, *L.Am./N, n., crim.* Gunman, triggerman. (Lit. Triggerman.) *Nunca encontraron al gatillero que acribilló a mi padre.* "They never found the triggerman who riddled my father."

GATO, TA, *L.Am./C, n.* Green- or blue-eyed person. (Lit. Cat.) *Mi madre es gata pero mi padre no.* "My mother is green-eyed, but not my father."

GAUCHADA, *L.Am./S, n.* Favor. *Nadie se arruina haciendo gauchadas.* "Nobody goes broke doing favors."

GAUCHO, *Car., adj. or n.* Womanizer. (Lit. Gaucho.) *Me contaron que ese actor es un gaucho.* "They told me that that actor is a ladies' man."

GAVETA, *Spain, n., crim.* Jail chow. (Lit. Drawer.) *La gaveta que sirven a los presos es horrible.* "The chow they serve the inmates is horrible."

GAVETERO, *Spain, n., crim.* Inmate who serves jail chow. *Me tocó trabajar de gavetero durante un mes.* "It was my turn to work as chow server for a month."

GAVILÁN, *Car., n.* Older man looking for younger women. (Lit. Sparrowhawk.) *¡Qué gavilán es el tío de Roberto! Es un Don Juan viejito.* "What a womanizer Robert's uncle is! He is an old Don Juan."

GAVIOTA, *L.Am./N, n.* Moocher, freeloader. (Lit. Seagull.) *Rufino es muy gaviota, siempre llega a la hora de comer.* "Rufino is a freeloader; he always arrives at mealtime."

GAY, *Spain, adj.* Homosexual. (Lit. Gay.) *Los hombres y mujeres gay reclaman mejor tratamiento y consideración.* "Gay men and women demand better treatment and consideration."

GAYUMBAS, *Spain, n.* Panties. *Ana dejó las gayumbas en el coche de Paco.* "Ana left her panties in Paco's car."

GAYUMBOS, *Spain, n.* Men's shorts. *Tengo unos gayumbos con los colores del Betis.* "I have shorts with the Betis team colors."

GEBA, *Car., n.* Girlfriend, chick, babe. *La geba de Martín es feísima, yo no sé qué le ve.* "Martin's girl is a dog. I don't know what he sees in her."

GENA, *Spain, n.* Hashish-cutting agent. *La poli confiscó el hashish, la gena, unas bolsitas de plástico y el dinero.* "The police confiscated the hashish, the cutter, some plastic bags, and the money."

GENERAL, LA, *Car., adj. or n.* Bossy person. (Lit. General.) *La esposa de Beto es una generala y es la que manda en la casa.* "Beto's wife is a bossy woman and is the one in charge at home."

GENERALA, *L.Am./N, n.* Madam. *Si quieres llevarte a una de las chavas, tienes que hablar con la generala.* "If you want to take some chicks with you, you have to talk to the madam."

GENIAL, *L.Am., adj.* Very good, fantastic, cool. (Lit. Inspired.) *El concierto de Madonna estuvo genial.* "Madonna's concert was cool."

GENTE GORDA, *Spain, idiom.* Influential people, fat cats. *La gente gorda se reunía en el hotel y los trabajadores protestaban afuera.* "The big shots met at the hotel and the workers protested outside."

GEVA, *Car., n.* Young, good-looking woman. *La geva que se sienta junto a mí en clase me fascina.* "I dig the babe that sits next to me in class."

GEVO, *Car., n.* Handsome man. *El gevo que me presentaste me pidió el teléfono.* "The hunk you introduced me to asked me for my telephone number."

GIL See HACER EL GIL

GILA, *L.Am./S, n.* Sweetheart. *Pepe y su gila se prenden cada noche con unos buenos pititos.* "Pepe and his girlfriend light up some good joints every night."

GILI, *Spain, adj.* Silly, dumb. *Maruja está media gili. Se olvida de todo.* "Maruja is halfway stupid. She forgets everything."

GILIPOLLADA, *Spain, n.* Stupid or dumb thing. *Me hiciste una gilipollada ayer. Dejaste la plancha puesta.* "You pulled a stupid thing yesterday—you left the iron on."

GILIPOLLAS, *Spain, n.* Stupid person. *Antonio es un gilipollas. No sabe tratar a sus amigos.* "Antonio is a jerk. He doesn't know how to treat his friends."

GINE, *Spain, n.* Gynecologist. *Mi mujer fue a ver el gine hoy y dijo que todo está bien.* "My wife went to see the gynecologist today and he said everything was fine."

GIS, *L.Am./N, adj.* Drunk. *Higinio se puso gis con puro mescal.* "Higinio got bombed on nothing but mescal."

GLOBO, *L.Am./N, n.* Condom, rubber. (Lit. Globe.) *No me la pude llevar al hotel porque se me olvidaron los globos.* "I couldn't take her to the hotel because I forgot my rubbers."

GLORIA, *Spain, n., drugs.* Marijuana. (Lit. Glory.) *Encontraron 50 kilos de gloria en el piso.* "They found 50 kilos of grass in the apartment."

GOBI, *Spain, n., crim.* Police station. *Esposaron a Fernando y lo llevaron a la gobi.* "They handcuffed Fernando and took him to the police station."

GOBIERNO, 1. *Car., n.* Prison guard. (Lit. Government.) *Los gobiernos de esa cárcel maltratan a los presos.* "The guards at that jail mistreat the inmates." **2.** *Car., n.* Domineering spouse. *Mi gobierno no me deja salir ni a la esquina sin pedirle permiso.* "The boss doesn't like me to go out even to the corner without asking her permission."

GOLETA, *Car., n.* Marijuana joint. (Lit. Schooner.) *Todos los jóvenes en la fiesta estaban fumando goletas.* "All the kids at the party were smoking joints."

GOLFA, *Spain, n.* Whore. *La golfa le preguntó si quería la vuelta al mundo.* "The whore asked him if he wanted an around the world."

GOLFERAS See GOLFA

GOLONDRO, *Spain, n., crim.* Night watchman. *Cuando pasó el golondro los maleantes salieron corriendo.* "When the watchman passed by, the hoodlums took off running."

GOLPE, *Car., n.* Astute observation. (Lit. Hit, strike.) *Los golpes de José son siempre muy apropiados e inteligentes.* "All of Jose's remarks are appropriate and intelligent."

GOLPE DE ALA, *L.Am./S, idiom.* Bad body odor. *Andrés no usa desodorante y vive con un golpe de ala fatal.* "Andres doesn't use deodorant and he lives with a terrible B.O."

GOMA, 1. *L.Am./S, n.* Nothing, not anything. (Lit. Gum, rubber.) *Él no sabe ni una goma de música.* "He doesn't know a damn thing about music." **2.** *L.Am./S, n.* Pejorative term for someone who does things to curry favor. *El pasante del Juez Rodríguez es un goma.* "Judge Rodriguez's clerk is a brownnoser." **3.** *L.Am./C, n.* Hangover. *Después de la fiesta de anoche tengo una goma que no se me quita.* "After last night's party, I have a hangover that won't go away." **4.** *Car., n.* Tire. *Había vidrio en la carretera y se me pinchó una goma.* "There was glass on the road and I got a flat tire." **5.** *Spain, n.* Condom, rubber. *Ricardo dijo que iba a comprar algunas gomas.* "Ricardo said that he was going to buy some rubbers." **6.** *Spain, n.* Police club. *La poli le pegó una paliza con las gomas.* "The cops beat the hell out of them with their clubs." **7.** *Spain, n., drugs.* Marijuana joint. *Paco compró una goma de un traficante y la fumó en su casa.* "Paco bought a joint from a dealer and smoked it at home."

GOMAS, *L.Am./S, pl. n.* Woman's breasts. (Lit. Rubbers.) *¿Viste la belleza de gomas que tiene Catalina?* "Did you see how nice Catalina's boobs are?"

GOMELO, LA, *L.Am./S, n.* Child of a wealthy family, a preppy. *Ese colegio es para los gomelos. Cuesta una fortuna.* "That school is for preppies. It costs a fortune."

GOMÍA, *L.Am./S, n.* Friend. *Carlos es gomía de Raúl.* "Carlos is a friend of Raul."

GORDINFLAS, *Spain, n.* Fat guy. *Ese gordinflas va a tener problemas de corazón.* "That fatty is going to have heart problems."

GORDINFLÓN, NA, *L.Am., adj. or n.* Fat person. *El gordinflón no puede encontrar camisas de su talla.* "Fatty can't find shirts his size."

GORILA, 1. *L.Am., Spain, n.* Bodyguard. (Lit. Gorilla.) *Dicen que Madonna no va a ninguna parte sin sus gorilas.* "They say that Madonna doesn't go anywhere without her gorillas." **2.** *Car., n.* Abusive police officer. *Nos arrestó un gorila y parece que se divertía pegándonos.* "A gorilla arrested us and he got his kicks by hitting us."

GORREAR, *L.Am./S, v.* To be unfaithful. *No sé cómo Juan puede gorrearle a la mujer de esa manera.* "I don't know how Juan can fool around behind his wife's back that way."

GORRERO, RA, *L.Am./N, n.* Person who always allows others to pay. *Nunca paga por nada, es un gorrero.* "He never pays for anything. He is a moocher."

GORRÓN, *L.Am./N, n.* Moocher, deadbeat. *Fidel es tan gorrón que nunca trae para el bus.* "Fidel is such a moocher that he never brings money for the bus."

GOTA, *U.S., n.* Gasoline. (Lit. Drop.) *Tengo que echar una gota a mi carro.* "I have to put gas in my car."

GOTA QUE DERRAMA EL VINO (LA), *L.Am./N, idiom.* The straw that broke the camel's back, the last straw. *Cuando vio a Pedro con otra fue para Luisa la gota que derrama el vino.* "Seeing Pedro with another woman was for Luisa the last straw."

GOZQUE, *L.Am./S, adj. or n.* Mongrel, mutt. *Ceci alimenta a todos los gozques que viven en su barrio.* "Ceci feeds all the mongrels that live in her neighborhood."

GRADO DOS, *L.Am./S, idiom.* Second level (petting stage). *Paco ya llegó al grado dos con Amparo.* "Paco now got to second base with Amparo."

GRADO TRES, *L.Am./S, idiom.* Third level (copulation stage). *Pronto Paco y Amparo entrarán en el grado tres.* "Soon Paco and Amparo will be on third and heading home."

GRADO UNO, *L.Am./S, idiom.* First level (kissing stage). *Paco y Amparo ya se graduaron del grado uno.* "Paco and Amparo have already graduated from first grade."

GRATAROLA, *L.Am./S, adj.* Free. *En ese lugar la entrada es gratarola.* "At that place the admission is free."

GRIEGO, *Spain, n.* Anal sex. (Lit. Greek.) *Los homosexuales practican el griego.* "Homosexuals do it the Greek way."

GRIFA, *Spain, n., drugs.* Marijuana. *La venta de grifa se ha acelerado en España.* "The sale of hashish has increased in Spain."

GRIFEAR, *Spain, v., drugs.* To smoke pot. *Vamos a grifear a la azotea de la casa.* "Let's smoke on the roof of the house."

GRIFO, FA, *L.Am./N, adj.* High on drugs. *Arnoldo a diario anda grifo.* "Arnoldo is always tripping."

GRIFOTA, *Spain, n., drugs.* Pothead. *Los grifotas se juntan debajo del puente para fumarse unos porros.* "The pot-heads get together under the bridge to smoke joints."

GRILLA, *Car., n.* Marijuana butt, roach. *Encontré una grilla en el cuarto de mi hijo. ¡Qué pena me da!* "I found a roach in my son's room. It really saddens me!"

GRILLERA, *Spain, n., crim.* Police van. *Llevaron a cinco adictos en la grillera.* "They carried off five addicts in the paddy wagon."

GRILLOS, *Spain, pl. n., crim.* Handcuffs. *El preso le dijo que los grillos estaban demasiado apretados.* "The prisoner said that the cuffs were too tight."

GRIMA, *Spain, n.* Disgust, repugnance, repulsion. *Cuando fui a su casa me pusieron una comida que daba grima.* "When I went to her house, they put a disgusting meal in front of me."

GRINGO, GA, *L.Am., adj. or n.* Person from the United States. *En esta época el hotel se llena de gringos.* "During this season the hotel fills up with gringos."

GRINGOLANDIA, *L.Am./N, n.* United States. *Tengo ganas de ir a Gringolandia en mis próximas vacaciones.* "I feel like going to Gringoland on my next vacation."

GRONCHO, CHA, *L.Am./S, adj. or n.* Black person. *En la isla sólo se ven gronchos.* "On the island you only see blacks."

GRUESO, SA, *L.Am./N, adj.* Tremendous. (Lit. Thick.) *Los Rolling Stones tienen un show grueso.* "The Rolling

Stones have a fantastic show."

GRUPI, *Spain, n., rock.* Groupie. (From English "groupie.") *Los rockeros siempre son perseguidos por sus grupis.* "The rockers are always followed by their groupies."

GUA GUA, *L.Am./N, n.* Traffic cop. *Ese gua gua me dio una boleta por pasar un semáforo que no existía.* "That traffic cop gave me a ticket for going through a nonexistent traffic light."

¡GUÁCALA!, *L.Am., interj.* Yuck! *¡Guácala! Esto sabe a podrido.* "Yuck! This tastes rotten."

GUACAREAR, *L.Am./N, v.* To vomit, to throw up. *Tomé tanto vino en la fiesta que ya me daban ganas de guacarear.* "I drank so much wine at the party that I felt like throwing up."

GUACHAR, *L.Am./N, v.* To watch, to look at, to observe (From English "to watch.") *Yo estaba guachando el partido por la tele.* "I was watching the game on TV."

GUACHE, *L.Am./S., adj. or n.* Bad person. *Pobre Lucía, el esposo en un guache.* "Poor Lucia, her husband is a bastard."

GUACHIMÁN, *L.Am., n.* Watchman, car watcher, guard. (From English "watchman.") *Si le das unas monedas, el guachimán te cuidará el carro.* "If you give him some coins, the watchman will look after your car."

GUACHO, 1. *L.Am./N, n., mil.* Soldier. *Los guachos estaban patrullando fuera del pueblo.* "The grunts were patrolling outside of town." **2.** *L.Am./S, n.* Orphan. *Después de la guerra, El Salvador está lleno de guachos.* "After the war, El Salvador is full of orphans."

GUAGUA, 1. *L.Am./S, n.* Baby. *Rosalinda y Alvaro ya tienen guagua en casa.* "Rosalinda and Alvaro now have a rugrat at home." **2.** *Car., n.* Bus. *Esa guagua viene repleta.* "That bus is full." **3.** *Car., n.* Cheap hooker. *Por andar con guaguas se le pegó el SIDA.* "For going out with cheap hookers, he got AIDS." **SEE also DE GUAGUA**

GUAI See GUAY

GUAIFA, *U.S., n.* Wife. (From English "wife.") *Mi guaifa me está esperando.* "My wife is waiting for me."

GUAJE, *Spain, n.* Boy, young man. *Ese guaje es de Constantina.* "That boy is Constantina's."

GUAJOLOTE, *L.Am./N, n.* Turkey. *Aquí acostumbramos comer guajolote en Navidad.* "Here, we're accustomed to turkey on Christmas."

GUALDRAPÓN, ONA, *Spain, n.* Raggedy person. *Se me acercó una gualdrapona y me pidió una limosna.* "This raggedy lady came up to me and asked for a handout."

GUAMAZO, *L.Am./N, n.* Blow, punch. *Porfirio le dio un guamazo en la panza a Rolando.* "Porfirio gave Rolando a sock in the belly."

GUÁMBITO, *L.Am./S, n.* Child. *Jorge y Lilí tienen tres guámbitos.* "Jorge and Lili have three tadpoles."

GUANAJITA, *Car., n.* Money saved, nest egg. *Tengo una guanajita echá pa' la boda de mi hija.* "I've got a little nest egg set aside for my daughter's wedding."

GUANDOCA, *L.Am./S, n.* Jail. *Lo metieron a la guandoca por robar el banco.* "They put him in the clink for robbing a bank."

GUANGO, *L.Am./N, adj.* Soft, spongy. *¿Cómo vas a competir si estás todo guango?* "How are you going to compete if you are so soft?"

GUANTE See HACER GUANTES

GUAPACHOSO, *L.Am./N, adj.* Upbeat, rhythmic. *Esta música guapachosa es buena para bailar.* "This bumpin' music is cool for dancing."

GUAPERAS, *Spain, adj.* Handsome, vain. *El novio de Alicia es muy guaperas.* "Alicia's boyfriend is very good-looking."

GUAPO, PA, *Spain, adj., youth.* Good, interesting. *Tu coche ha quedado bien guapo después de lavarlo.* "Your car looks real handsome after washing."

GUARANGADA, *L.Am./S, n.* Rude comment or action. *Lo*

que dijo Carmelo fue una guarangada. "What Carmelo said was a rude remark."

GUARANGO, GA, 1. *L.Am./S, adj.* Coarse, nasty. *Julio es bien guarango, no le importa a quién ofende.* "Julio is very nasty; he doesn't care who he offends." **2.** *L.Am./S, n.* Jerk, idiot. *Tu nuevo amigo es un guarango.* "Your new friend is a jerk."

GUARDAPOLVOS, *Spain, n.* Vagina. *La puta ganaba bastante de su guardapolvos.* "The hooker made quite a bit from her gash."

GUARDIA, *Car., n.* Drug pad, drug den. *Diego pasaba horas en la guardia con sus amigos fumando marihuana.* "Diego spent hours in the drug den with his friends smoking pot."

GUARDIA TUMBADO, *L.Am./N, n.* Speed bump. *Instalaron guardias tumbados en nuestra colonia.* "They installed speed bumps in our neighborhood."

GUARES, *Car., n.* Twins. *Los Gómez tuvieron guares y están dichosos.* "The Gomezes had twins and are happy."

GUARO, *L.Am./C, n.* Costa Rican firewater. *No se puede ir a San José sin probar el guaro.* "You can't go to San José without trying their firewater."

GUARURA, *L.Am./N, n.* Bodyguard. *Toño consiguió trabajo de guarura; cuidará a un político.* "Toño got a job as a bodyguard; he'll look after a politician."

GUASA, *L.Am./N, n.* Joke. *No te enojes, es pura guasa.* "Don't get mad, it's just a joke."

GUATAQUEAR, *Car., v.* To apple-polish, to brownnose, to kiss ass. *Alfredo siempre le está guataqueando a su jefe.* "Alfredo is always brownnosing his boss."

GUATÓN, NA, *L.Am./S, adj.* Fat. *Gonzalo se puso muy guatón después de la universidad.* "Gonzalo got real heavy after college."

GUAY, *Spain, adj., youth.* Fantastic, tremendous, cool. *Esa* *blusa es muy guay, Julia.* "That blouse is the coolest, Julia."

GUAYABO, 1. *Spain, n.* Pretty girl. *A los viejitos les gusta sentarse en la calle a ver pasar los guayabos.* "The old men like to sit outside watching all the cute girls go by." **2.** *L.Am./S, n.* Hangover. *Después de la fiesta tenía un guayabo tremendo.* "After the party I had a terrible hangover." **3.** *L.Am./N, n.* Vagina. *Anoche subí al guayabo.* "Last night I climbed the bush."

GÜELEFLOR, *Car., adj.* Stupid, dumb. *La pobre Sofía es una güeleflor y le va muy mal en los estudios.* "Poor Sofia is not too swift, and she is not doing well in her studies."

GÜELEPEGA, *Car., n.* Inhalant user, gluehead. *Antes vivía un güelepega en la casa de al lado. Ya está en el manicomio.* "A glue-sniffer used to live in the house next door. Now he is in an asylum."

GÜERA, *Car., n.* Prostitute. *Dicen que la hija de tu amigo es una güera en Nueva York.* "They say that your friend's daughter is a hooker in New York."

GÜERO, RA, *L.Am./N, n.* Blonde. *El hermano de Aníbal era güero de ojos azules.* "Anibal's brother was blonde with blue eyes."

GÜEVÓN See HUEVÓN

GÜILA, *L.Am./C, n.* Small child. *Ese parque siempre está lleno de güilas.* "That park is always full of little tykes."

GUILLADO, DA, *Spain, adj.* Crazy, nuts, silly. *Ramón está muy guillado. Hay que ver las cosas locas que hace.* "Ramón is very silly. You've got to see the crazy things he does."

GÜINCHA, 1. *Car., n.* Paddy wagon. *Llevaron a todos los muchachos a la cárcel en la güincha.* "They carried all the boys off to jail in the paddy wagon." **2.** *Car., n.* Police drunk tank. *Pedro estaba tan borracho que le dejaron en la güincha hasta la mañana.* "Pedro was so drunk that they left him in the tank until the morning."

GÜINCHAR, *Car., v.* To throw in the drunk tank. *Le güincharon a Pepe por borracho.* "They threw Pepe in the tank for being drunk."

GUINDAR, *Spain, v., crim.* To rob, to steal. *Anoche guindaron la tienda de Guillermo.* "Last night they hit Guillermo's store."

GUINDE, *Spain, n.* Robbery. *Hay mucho guinde en esa barriada.* "There are a lot of robberies in that neighborhood."

GUINDÓN, *Spain, n.* Thief. *Cogieron al guindón enseguida y vieron que llevaba el dinero encima.* "They caught the crook right away and saw that he had the money on him."

GUIRI, *Spain, n.* Foreigner, tourist. *Los maleantes prefieren robar a los guiris porque son muy despistados.* "The hoodlums prefer to rob foreigners because they don't know what is going on."

GUIRILANDIA, *Spain, n., crim.* Abroad. *Gregorio se fugó para guirilandia y no ha vuelto desde entonces.* "Gregorio fled abroad and hasn't returned since."

GUISO, 1. *Car., n.* Theft, robbery. (Lit. Cooked dish.) *Nadie sabe quién cometió ese guiso.* "Nobody knows who pulled that job." **2. GUISO, SA,** *L.Am./S, adj.* Ignorant, uncultured. *La novia de Manolo es tan guisa que ni sabe cómo combinar la ropa.* "Manolo's sweetheart is such a clod that she doesn't even know how to put her clothes together."

GUITA, 1. *L.Am./N, n., crim.* Money. *A los presos no les dejan tener mucha guita en el talaguero.* "They don't let the inmates have much cash in the slammer." **2.** *Spain, n., youth.* Guitar. *¿Sabes tocar la guita Fernán?* "Do you know how to play the guitar, Fernan?"

GUITARRA, 1. *Spain, n., crim.* Machine gun. (Lit. Guitar.) *Encontraron cinco pistolas, un rifle y una guitarra en la furgoneta.* "They found five pistols, a rifle, and a machine gun in the van." **2.** *L.Am./S, n.* Money. *No puedo ir,* *no tengo guitarra.* "I can't go; I don't have any dough."

GÜITOS, *Spain, pl. n.* Testicles, balls. *Los que no tienen güitos sacan sus agresiones con sus mujeres.* "Those who don't have balls get rid of their aggression on women."

GURI, *Spain, n.* Police officer. *El guri los arrestó por hacer aguas en la vía pública.* "The cop arrested them for peeing in the public thoroughfare."

GURÚ, *Spain, n.* Leader of a community. (Lit. Guru.) *Alvaro es el gurú de su barriada.* "Alvaro is the guru of his neighborhood."

HABICHUELA, *Car., n.* Clitoris. (Lit. Bean.) *Dicen que a las moritas les cortan la habichuela. ¡Qué horror!* "They say that they cut off the clits of Moorish women. How horrible!"

HABITANTE, *Spain, n.* Louse. (Lit. Inhabitant.) *Me parece que varios estudiantes tienen habitantes en el pelo.* "It seems to me that several students have lice in their hair."

HABLAR A CALZÓN QUITADO, *Spain, idiom.* To speak openly. *Aquí no hay secretos, todos pueden hablar a calzón quitado de todo.* "There are no secrets here; everyone can speak openly."

HABLAR A MEDIAS, *Car., idiom.* To insinuate, to say things halfway. *Silvia siempre está hablando a medias y no sé lo que está insinuando.* "Silvia is always leaving things halfway and I don't know what she is insinuating."

HABLAR EN CHINO, *Car., idiom.* To speak unintelligibly. *A Carmen no le entiendo nada, como si me estuviera hablando en chino.* "I don't understand Carmen at all; it was as if she was speaking to me in Chinese."

HABLAR MIERDA, *Car., idiom.* To say stupid things, to talk shit. *Álvaro, deja de hablar mierda. Estás diciendo tonterías.* "Alvaro, stop talking shit. You're saying stupid things."

HABLAR PAJA, *L.Am./S, idiom.* To talk a lot without saying anything. *Marisa siempre está hablando paja. Ya no* *la escucho siquiera.* "Marisa is always talking nonsense. I no longer even listen to her."

HABLAR PATO, *Car., idiom.* To talk like a fairy. *Nuestro amigo es graciosísimo cuando se pone a hablar pato.* "Our friend is really funny when he starts talking like a fairy."

HABLAR SIN PELOS EN LA LENGUA, *L.Am., idiom.* To talk straight. *Ceci es muy sincera y habla sin pelos en la lengua.* "Ceci is very sincere and talks straight."

HACE UN TOCO, *L.Am./S, idiom.* Ages ago. *Hace un toco que no tomo licor.* "It's been some time since I drank liquor."

HACE UNA PUNTA DE AÑOS, *L.Am./S, idiom.* Years ago. *Hace una punta de años que no veo a mi mejor amigo.* "I haven't seen my best friend for years."

HACER A PLUMA Y A PELO, *Spain, idiom.* To be bisexual. *Dicen que al joyero le gusta hacer a pluma y a pelo.* "They say that the jeweler is a switch-hitter."

HACER ALGO COMO AGUA, *U.S., idiom.* To do something with ease. *Mi madre hacía todo como agua.* "My mother did everything with ease."

HACER ARROZ CON CULO, *Car., idiom.* To raise hell. *Hicieron un arroz con culo anoche en la taberna.* "They raised hell in the bar last night."

HACER BOLLOS, *Spain, idiom.* To practice lesbianism. *Esa es una de aquellas que les gusta hacer bollos.* "She is one of those who like to get it on with other women."

HACER BUCHES, *Car., idiom.* To be on the verge of crying. *Se veía que el presidente estaba haciendo buches, pero no lloró.* "You could see that the President looked as if he were going to cry, but he didn't."

HACER BUENA LETRA, *L.Am./S, idiom.* To be on good behavior to impress someone. *Isabel siempre hace buena letra cuando están los jefes.* "Isabel is always Goody Two-Shoes when the bosses are here."

HACER CHANGUITOS, *L.Am./N, idiom.* To cross one's fingers for good luck. *Yo estoy haciendo changuitos para sacarme la lotería.* "I'm crossing my fingers to win the lottery."

HACER CHAPAS, *Spain, idiom.* To perform homosexual prostitution. *A veces los maricas tienen que hacer chapas para sobrevivir.* "Sometimes the fairies have to prostitute themselves in order to survive."

HACER CUCO (A ALGUIEN), *L.Am./N, idiom.* To make fun of someone. *Me estaban haciendo el cuco por la ropa que llevaba.* "They were making fun of me for the clothes I was wearing."

HACER DE CHIVO LOS TAMALES, *L.Am./N, idiom.* Cheat on one's spouse. *Laura estaba haciendo de chivo los tamales a Pablo.* "Laura was stepping out on Pablo."

HACER DEDO, *L.Am./S, Spain, idiom.* To hitchhike. *Carlos dio la vuelta a España haciendo dedo.* "Carlos went all around Spain hitchhiking."

HACER EL ARTÍCULO, *Spain, idiom.* To appraise someone. (Lit. To make the article.) *Se acercó a ella, le hizo el artículo y se fue.* "He approached her, gave her the once-over, and left."

HACER EL AVIÓN, *Spain, idiom, crim.* To deceive, to defraud. *Me hizo el avión y se arrancó.* "He shafted me and took off."

HACER EL CÁLIZ, *U.S., idiom.* To attempt, to try, to give it a shot. *Voy a hacer el cáliz para ver si puedo entrar en el equipo de básquetbol.* "I am going to try my best to get on the basketball team."

HACER EL CANDADO, *Spain, idiom.* To hang out. *Tu hermano pasa todo el día en el casino haciendo el candado. ¡Qué flojo!* "Your brother spends all day at the casino hanging out. How lazy!"

HACER EL CUATRO, *L.Am./S, idiom.* To stand on one leg while bending the other. Sobriety test demanded by highway police. *A ver, mírame fijo y haz el cuatro.* "Let's see, look at me straight and do a four."

HACER EL DOS, *L.Am./S, idiom.* To do a favor. *Oye Luisa, hazme el dos de traerme una cervecita, por favor.* "Hey Luisa, do me a favor and bring me a little beer, please."

HACER EL OSO, *L.Am./S, v.* To be embarrassed. *Adriana hizo el oso cuando se cayó en pleno desfile.* "Adriana was mortified when she fell in the middle of the parade."

HACER EL VIACRUCIS, *Spain, idiom.* To go bar hopping. *Anoche hice el viacrucis con los amigos y ya no me queda ni una moneda.* "Last night I went bar hopping with my friends and now I don't have a dime left."

HACER EL ZURI, *Spain, idiom.* To flee, to take off. *En cuanto le dijimos que había trabajo que hacer, se hizo el zuri.* "As soon as we told him that there was work to do, he disappeared."

HACER GARRAS, *L.Am./N, idiom.* To tear to pieces. *Si tú le dices eso a tu mujer te va a hacer garras.* "If you say that to your wife, she'll tear you to pieces."

HACER GORRO, *L.Am./S, idiom.* To lie around doing nothing. *Si sigues haciendo gorro se nos va a hacer tarde.* "If you keep loafing around, we are going to be late."

HACER GUANTES, *Spain, idiom.* To spar. *Estaba haciendo guantes con Jorge cuando me rompió el colmillo.* "I was sparring with Jorge when he broke my tooth."

HACER HOYOS DONDE HAY TIEZAS, *L.Am./N, idiom.* To reinvent the wheel. *¿Por qué te estás matando, haciendo hoyos donde hay tiezas?* "Why are you killing yourself trying to reinvent the wheel?"

HACER LA BARBA, *L.Am./N, idiom.* To brownnose, to kiss ass. *Pepe no trabaja, pero bien que le hace la barba al jefe.* "Pepe doesn't work but he sure kisses the boss's ass."

HACER LA BUFANDA, *Spain, idiom.* To perform fellatio or cunnilingus. *Hoy en día hay más escenas de gente* *haciendo la bufanda en el cine.* "Nowadays there are more movie scenes of people licking each other."

HACER LA CARA NUEVA, *Spain, idiom.* Beat someone in the face. *Si ése me dice algo más acerca de eso le voy hacer la cara nueva.* "If he says something to me about that, I am going to make him a new face."

HACER LA CARRERA, *Spain, idiom.* To work as a prostitute. *Esa puta lleva años haciendo la carrera.* "That whore has been hooking for years."

HACER LA CUSQUI, *Spain, idiom.* To bother, to pester, to annoy. *Deja de hacer la cusqui, Pepita. Tú sabes que eso me molesta.* "Stop screwing around Pepita. You know that that bothers me."

HACER LA GAMBA, *L.Am./S, idiom.* To stick by one's friend, to be there for someone. *Mi amigo Paco me hizo la gamba cuando perdí mi trabajo.* "My friend Paco was there for me when I lost my job."

HACER LA PELOTA, *Spain, idiom.* To brownnose, to suck up to someone for favors. *Mira como Rosita le hace la pelota al jefe.* "Look how Rosita sucks up to the boss."

HACER LA PINTA, *L.Am./N, idiom.* To play hooky. *Todos hicimos la pinta el último día de clases.* "We all played hooky the last day of class."

HACER LA PIRULA, 1. *Spain, idiom, crim.* To deceive, to swindle. *Lo arrestaron por hacerles la pirula a unos ancianos.* "They arrested him for conning some elderly people." **2.** *Spain, idiom.* To cut corners, to skip a procedure. *Juan, tienes que hacerlo bien, no se puede hacer la pirula con este trabajo.* "Juan you have to do it right. You can't be cutting corners on this job!"

HACER LA PUÑETA, *Spain, idiom.* To bother, to do wrong, to screw up. *¡Coño! Ahora me hicieron la puñeta en el banco con sus equivocaciones.* "Damn! Now the bank has screwed me up with their mistakes."

HACER LA SOPA, *L.Am./N, idiom.* To mix the dominoes

before playing. *Como ganaste, ahora te toca hacer la sopa.* "You won, so now you have to mix them up."

HACER LA VACA, *L.Am./S, idiom.* To cut school, to play hooky. *Tenía una flojera fatal de ir al colegio e hice la vaca.* "I felt so lazy about going to school that I played hooky."

HACER LA VISTA GORDA, *Spain, idiom.* To pretend not to notice something, to look the other way. *No podían defraudar la compañía sin que nadie hiciera la vista gorda.* "They couldn't defraud the company without someone looking the other way."

HACER LOS MANDADOS, *L.Am./N, idiom.* Expression of inferiority. (Lit. To run the errands.) *No le tengo miedo a Victor, a mí me hace los mandados.* "I am not afraid of Victor; he runs my errands."

HACER MEME, *L.Am./N, idiom.* To sleep, to catch Zs. *Es la hora de la siesta, hay que hacer meme.* "Siesta time, time to catch some Zs."

HACER O HACERSE TACO, *L.Am./N, idiom.* To wrap oneself or somebody else up. *Me hice taco con una cobija.* "I wrapped myself up with the blanket."

HACER PERRO MUERTO, *L.Am./S, idiom.* To leave without paying. *A Paco le gusta mucho comer en restaurantes y después hacer perro muerto.* "Paco likes to eat in restaurants and leave without paying the check."

HACER PINTA, *L.Am./N, idiom.* To play hooky. *El día antes del Día de la independencia, hicimos la pinta.* "The day before Independence Day, we played hooky."

HACER PIPÍ, *L.Am., idiom.* To urinate. *Papá, para el coche, tengo que hacer pipí.* "Daddy, stop the car; I have to go pee."

HACER PIS, *Spain, idiom.* To urinate. *Doctor, creo que tengo algo del riñón, no puedo hacer pis.* "Doctor, I believe I have something wrong with my kidney; I can't pee."

HACER POR LA PATRIA, *Car., idiom.* To eat. *Dile que*

después lo llamo, que ahora estoy haciendo por la patria. "Tell him I'll call him later. Right now I am putting on the feed bag."

HACER PUENTE, 1. *Spain, idiom.* To take a day off to have a long weekend. (Lit. To bridge.) *Aprovechamos el Día de San José para hacer puente e irnos a la playa.* "We took advantage of St. Joseph's Day to make it a long weekend and go to the beach." **2.** *Spain, idiom, crim.* To hot-wire a car. (Lit. To bridge.) *El ladrón me robó el coche haciendo puente a los cables de encendido.* "The hoodlum stole my car by hot-wiring the ignition cables."

HACER ROÑA, *L.Am./S, idiom.* To wallow. *Voy a hacer roña otro poquito antes de levantarme.* "I am going to loaf around a little bit before I get up."

HACER ROSCA, *Car., idiom.* To have sex, to fuck. *A ese doctor lo encontraron haciéndole rosca a su paciente.* "They found that doctor screwing his patient."

HACER SOMBRA, *Spain, idiom, sports.* To shadowbox. *Antonio se cree boxeador; siempre está haciendo sombra.* "Antonio thinks he is a boxer; he is always shadow-boxing."

HACER UN CRUZADO, *L.Am./N, idiom.* Arm in arm. *Los dos compadres brindaron haciendo un cruzado.* "The two friends made an arm-in-arm toast."

HACER UN JALÓN, *L.Am./N, idiom.* To help, to go along with. *Pide a Alejandro que te haga el jalón de hablar con el jefe.* "Ask Alejandro to back you up by talking to the boss."

HACER UN PAQUETE, *Spain, idiom.* To get a woman pregnant. *¡Qué sinvergüenza! Le hizo un paquete a la novia y se largó.* "The bastard! He knocked his girlfriend up and took off."

HACER UN POZO, *L.Am./S, idiom.* To gather money for immediate use. *Ya se acabó la cerveza, vamos a hacer un pozo.* "We are out of beer; let's pitch in."

HACER UN RETRATO See HACER UNA FOTO

HACER UNA FOTO, *Spain, idiom.* For a woman to show her genitals, to give a beaver shot. *La mujer sentada en la otra mesa nos está haciendo una foto.* "The woman seated at the other table is giving us a beaver shot."

HACER UNA GUARANGADA, *L.Am./S, idiom.* To respond rudely, to insult or to be rude. *Lola hizo una guarangada, le contestó al profe con mala lengua.* "Lola pulled a nasty one; she answered the prof in a bad way."

HACER UNA PONINA, *Car., idiom.* To take up a collection. *Vamos a hacer una ponina para comprarle regalos a la mujer de Pepe que está embarazada.* "Let's pitch in to buy a present for Pepe's pregnant wife."

HACER UNA RADIOGRAFÍA, *Spain, idiom.* To grope, to paw or to feel up a person. (Lit. To do an X ray.) *Me dijo María que en el metro un tipo le hizo una radiografía.* "Maria told me that a guy pawed her in the subway."

HACER ZAPPING, *Spain, idiom, youth.* To change channels. *Mi padre me vuelve loco cuando empieza a hacer zapping.* "My father drives me crazy when he starts channel-surfing."

HACERLA DE TOS, *L.Am./N, idiom.* To place obstacles. *No me gusta pedir permiso a mi papá, siempre la hace de tos.* "I don't like to ask my father for permission; he always causes difficulties."

HACERLE AGUA LA CANOA, *L.Am./N, idiom.* Homosexual. *A aquél se le hace agua la canoa.* "That one over there is on the other team."

HACERLE AL MONJE, *L.Am./N, idiom.* To play dumb. *¡No te hagas al monje, tú sabes lo que te digo!* "Don't play dumb; you know what I am talking about!"

HACERLE AL OSO, *L.Am./N, idiom.* To dance. *Vamos a la fiesta a hacerle al oso.* "Let's go to the party to cut a rug."

HACERLE AL VENENO, *L.Am./N, idiom.* To drink. *En la*

boda tuve que hacerle al veneno. "At the wedding I had a drink."

HACERLE CHIVO LOS TAMALES (A ALGUIEN), *L.Am./N, idiom, crim.* To defraud someone, to take someone to the cleaners. *Cuando vendieron ese carro a mi hermano le hicieron chivo los tamales.* "When they sold that car to my brother, they took him to the cleaners."

HACERLE UN NÚMERO OCHO (A ALGUIEN), *Car., idiom.* To set someone up, to frame. *Ramón es inocente, pero la policía lo arrestó porque le hicieron un número ocho.* "Ramon is innocent, but the police arrested him because someone set him up."

HACERSE CALACA, *L.Am./N, idiom.* To die. *La abuelita de Marcelino se hizo calaca ayer.* "Marcelino's grandmother kicked the bucket yesterday."

HACERSE EL GIL, *L.Am./S, idiom.* To play dumb, to play the fool, to act stupid. *No te hagas el gil conmigo. ¡Dime la verdad!* "Don't play dumb with me. Tell me the truth!"

HACERSE EL LOCO, *L.Am./S, Spain, idiom.* To act ignorant or distracted. *Tú te haces el loco, pero nosotros sabemos que robaste el banco.* "You act dumb, but we know that you robbed the bank."

HACERSE EL MAJE, *L.Am./N, idiom.* To play dumb. *¡No te hagas el maje, yo sé que ayer saliste con Juana!* "Don't play dumb; I know that yesterday you went out with Juana!"

HACERSE EL SUECO, *Car., idiom.* To play dumb. *A fulano le gusta hacerse el sueco y no comprometerse.* "Paco likes to play dumb and not commit himself."

HACERSE LA MAJUANA, *Car., idiom.* To masturbate. *Lo encontraron haciéndose la majuana en el baño.* "They found him beating his meat in the bathroom."

HACERSE LA PICHA UN LÍO, *Spain, idiom.* To get into a mess, to get tangled up in something. *Juan no quería nada de drogas, pero por un amigo se hizo la picha un* *lío.* "Juan didn't want anything to do with drugs, but for a friend he got himself into a mess."

HACERSE LA ROSCA, *Car., idiom.* To masturbate, to jack off, to beat one's meat. *El tipo llamaba al teléfono sexual para hacerse la rosca.* "The guy called the sex phone and beat his meat."

HACERSE PATO, *L.Am./N, idiom.* To play dumb. *Cuando le pido un favor a Enrique, se hace pato.* "When I ask Enrique for a favor, he plays dumb."

HACERSE PICHÍ, *L.Am./S, idiom.* To urinate, to pee. *Apúrate, abre la puerta del baño que me hago pichí.* "Hurry up, open up the bathroom door; I want to pee."

HACERSE UN DESPOJO, *Car., idiom.* To dispel evil. *Con toda esta mala suerte, vas a tener que ir a casa del santero para que te haga un despojo.* "With all that bad luck, you should go to a voodoo priest to do an exorcism."

HACERSE UNA ALEMANITA, *Spain, idiom.* To masturbate, to jack off. (Lit. To do a little German girl; play on *a la manita,* "by the little hand.") *Le vieron en la lavandería haciéndose una alemanita.* "They saw him doing a little hand job in the laundry."

HACHA, *Spain, n., crim.* Ace, someone outstanding. (Lit. Ax.) *Oye, hacha, enséñame a hacer ese truco con la navaja.* "Ace, hey, show me that trick with the knife." **See also ESTAR HACHA, SER HACHA PARA ALGO**

HAMBRE, *L.Am./S, n.* Anger. (Lit. Hunger.) *El profe me agarró y ahora me tiene un hambre enorme.* "The teacher caught me, and now he is really pissed at me."

HASTA ATRÁS, *L.Am./N, idiom.* Very drunk or high. *Cuando vi a Gustavo en la fiesta, se notaba que iba hasta atrás.* "When I saw Gustavo at the party, you could tell he was three sheets to the wind."

HASTA EL GORRO, *L.Am./N, idiom.* Very drunk. *Mis primos se pusieron hasta el gorro con puro pulque.* "My cousins got blasted on pulque alone."

HASTA EL PERNO, *L.Am./S, n.* Sick person. *El pobrecito está en las últimas, lo dejé hasta el perno.* "The poor dude is in real bad shape; he's sick as a dog."

HASTA LA MADRE, 1. *Spain, idiom.* Fed up. *Ya me tienes hasta la madre con tus críticas.* "You have me fed up with your criticism." **2.** *L.Am./N, idiom.* Very drunk. *David andaba hasta la madre en el baile.* "David was plastered at the dance."

HASTA LA TAZA, *Car., idiom.* Fed up, full, completely. *Tu mal genio me tiene hasta la taza.* "Your bad temper got me totally fed up."

HAY QUE JODERSE, *Spain, idiom.* To put up with a difficult situation. *¿Qué vas a hacer ahora que te quitaron el piso? Nada, hay que joderse.* "What are you going to do now that they took your apartment? Nothing, just put the fuck up with it."

HEAVY, *L.Am./S, adj.* Unpleasant, mean. (From English "heavy.") *Ese tipo es muy heavy, amigo.* "That guy's a mean dude, my friend."

HECHO GARRAS, *L.Am./N, idiom.* In bad shape. *¿Qué te pasó mano, que estás hecho garras?* "What's the matter bro, that you are in such a bad shape?"

HELADA, *U.S., n.* Beer. (Lit. Cold.) *Vamos a tomar unas heladas después del trabajo.* "Let's have a couple of cool ones after work."

HEMBRA, *L.Am./C, n.* Sweetheart, girlfriend, girl. (Lit. Female.) *¡Qué contento va Ricardo con la nueva hembra!* "How happy Ricardo is with his new girl!"

HEMBRIMACHO, *Car., n.* Lesbian, hermaphrodite. *La hermana del dueño del bar es un hembrimacho.* "The sister of the bar owner is a dyke."

HEMBRONA, *Car., n.* Attractive young woman. *¡Qué hembrona es la nueva profesora de inglés!* "What a babe the new English professor is!"

HERMANOCRACIA, *Spain, n.* Nepotism. *Armando favorece a su hermano en el trabajo. Así es la hermanocia.*

"Armando favors his brother at work. That's nepotism for you."

HERRAMIENTA, *Spain, n.* Penis. (Lit. Tool.) *Ciérrate la braugeta o vas a perder la herramienta.* "Close your fly or you'll lose your tool."

HIERBA, *L.Am., Spain, n., drugs.* Marijuana. (Lit. Grass.) *Cuando entramos en el piso había olor a hierba.* "When we entered the apartment, there was a smell of grass."

HIERRO, 1. *Spain, n., crim.* Pistol, sawed-off shotgun. (Lit. Iron.) *Al verle al Chungo sacar el hierro el policía le pegó un tiro en la frente.* "When he saw the hoodlum pull out the rod, the cop shot him in the forehead." **2.** *Spain, n., crim.* Jimmy, crowbar. *El ladrón consiguió entrar usando un hierro.* "The thief was able to get in using a jimmy."

HIERROS, *Car., pl. n.* Journeyman's tools. (Lit. Irons.) *Se le olvidaron los hierros y no pudo hacer el trabajo.* "He forgot his tools and couldn't do the job."

HIGH, *L.Am./C, n.* The upper class. (From English "high.") *Rosalinda se cree que es de la high.* "Rosalinda thinks she's from the upper class."

HIGO, *Spain, n.* Vagina, pussy. (Lit. Fig.) *Deja de jugar con el higo, Juanita.* "Stop playing with your pussy, Juanita."

HIJO DE PUTA, *L.Am., n.* Son of a bitch. (Lit. Son of a whore.) *El hijo de puta ese me pegó otra vez.* "The son of a bitch hit me again."

¡HÍJOLE!, *L.Am./N, interj.* Boy! Boy oh boy! *¡Híjole! ¿Cómo no se dieron cuenta tus papás?* "Boy! How come your parents didn't notice?"

HIJOPUTA, *Spain, n.* Son of a bitch. *No quiero nada que ver con ese hijoputa.* "I don't want anything to do with that son of a bitch."

HIJOPUTADA, *Spain, n.* Dirty trick, rotten move. *¡Qué hijoputada me has hecho hijo mío! ¿Por qué les dijiste que estaba aquí?* "You did me rotten, son! Why did you tell them that I was here?"

HIJOPUTESCO, *Spain, adj.* Mean, dirty, rotten. *El tratamiento que le dio a Pedro fue realmente hijoputesco.* "The way he treated Pedro was really low-down."

HINCAR EL PICO, *Spain, idiom.* To die. *El caballo de Antonio hincó el pico ayer.* "Antonio's horse bit the dust yesterday."

HINCARLA, 1. *Spain, idiom.* To work. (Lit. To kneel.) *Esta semana la voy a hincar bien para terminar este proyecto.* "This week I am going to hit it hard to end this project." **2.** *Spain, idiom.* To die. *El padre de Lázaro la hincó anoche.* "Lazaro's father passed away last night."

HINCHA, *Spain, n., sports.* Dedicated fan. *Fernando es hincha empedernido del Sevilla.* "Fernando is a hard-core Seville fan."

HINCHADA, *Spain, n., sports.* Group of dedicated fans. *Llevaron a una hinchada del Sevilla a Madrid para el partido.* "They took a bunch of Seville fans to Madrid for the game."

HINCHAPELOTAS, *L.Am./S, idiom.* Bothersome, annoying person. *Nadie quiere a Juan por ser tan hinchapelotas.* "Nobody likes Juan because he is a ball buster."

HINCHAR LAS BOLAS/PELOTAS, *L.Am./S, idiom.* To bother, to annoy. *Ya viene otra vez Sergio a hincharme las bolas.* "Here comes Serge again to bust my balls."

HINCHÁRSELE LOS COJONES A ALGUIEN, *Spain, idiom.* To lose one's patience, to get fed up. *Paco, se me están hinchando los cojones. Deja de molestarme.* "Paco, you're busting my balls. Stop fucking around."

HISTORIA, *Spain, n., crim.* Subject, business, racket. (Lit. History.) *Bueno, cuéntame, ¿cuál es tu historia?* "Okay, tell me, what's your game?"

HOCICO, 1. *Spain, n.* Lips. (Lit. Muzzle.) *Rosario le pegó un beso en el hocico.* "Rosario slapped a kiss right on his snout." **2.** *Spain, n.* Nose. *No metas el hocico en mis asuntos. ¿Te enteras?* "Don't stick your nose into my business, do you understand?"

HOMBRE DE PAJA, *L.Am./N, idiom.* Straw man. *Usaron un hombre de paja para comprar la casa.* "They used a straw man to buy the house."

¡HÓRALE!, *U.S., idiom.* Right! That's it! *¡Hórale! Tienes razón compadre.* "That's it! You're right, pal."

HORAS DE VUELO, *L.Am., Spain, idiom.* Experience. *López tiene muchas horas de vuelo en cuestiones de la bolsa.* "Lopez has logged a lot of hours on stock market questions."

HORRIPILO, *L.Am./S, adj.* Ugly. *Este tipo está más feo que el hambre, es un horripilo.* "That guy is uglier than hunger. He is horrible."

HORROR, *Spain, n.* (*Used as adv.*). Much, many, a lot. (Lit. Horror.) *Me gustó esa novela un horror.* "I liked that novel a whole lot."

HORTERA, *Spain, adj.* Tacky, vulgar, tasteless. *La mujer del médico es muy hortera. Habla a gritos.* "The doctor's wife is real tacky. She yells when she talks."

HOSPI, *L.Am./C, n.* Hospital. *Me llevaron al hospi cuando me caí, pero no me pasaba nada.* "They took me to the hospital when I fell, but nothing was wrong with me."

¡HOSTI!, *Spain, interj.* Hell! Damn! (Euphemism for "¡Hostia!") *¡Hosti! Perdí mi libro.* "Shoot! I lost my book."

HOSTIA, 1. *Spain, n.* Punch, violent blow or crash. *Si me dices esto otra vez te voy a pegar una hostia.* "If you say that to me again, I am going to beat the shit out of you." **2.** *Spain, n.* State of mind. *¡Qué mala hostia tienes hoy, Pepe!* "What a bad attitude you have today, Pepe!" **3.** *Spain, n.* Thing, whatchamacallit. *Estoy intentando arreglar esta hostia pero no me sale.* "I am trying to fix this fucker but am not having any results."

HOSTIAZO, *Spain, n.* Punch. *El cojo le pegó un hostiazo con la muleta.* "The lame guy gave him a hell of a whack with the crutch."

HOTEL, *Spain, n., crim.* Jail. (Lit. Hotel.) *Le mandaron al hotel por veinte años. Había matado a su socio.* "They sent him to the hotel with bars for twenty years. He had killed his partner."

HOYO See HACER HOYOS DONDE HAY TIEZAS

HUACHO, *L.Am./N, n.* Soldier. *Hay huachos cuidando la carretera.* "There are GIs guarding the roads."

HUARACHE, *L.Am./N, n.* Sandal. *Me compré unos huaraches con suela de llanta.* "I bought some sandals with soles made from tires."

HUAYCO, *L.Am./S, n.* Vomit. *Se mandó un huayco de la patada.* "He got vomit all over the place."

HUESO, *Car., n.* Job given as political reward. (Lit. Bone.) *Por hacer campaña política se ganó un hueso muy bueno.* "For doing the political campaign, he won a good political appointment."

HUESO COLORADO, *L.Am./N, idiom.* Expression of legitimacy, through and through. *Cuando salió de la universidad ya era hueso colorado del partido.* "When he got out of the university, he was already an accredited party member."

HUESO SABROSO, *U.S., idiom.* Funny bone. *¡Uy! Me di un golpe al hueso sabroso y todavía tengo hormigueo.* "Boy, I hit my funny bone and I still feel tingling."

HUESUDA, *L.Am./S, idiom.* Death. (Lit. Bony.) *Yo no le tengo miedo a la huesuda.* "I'm not afraid of the Grim Reaper."

HUEVÁ See HUEVADA

HUEVADA, 1. *L.Am./S, Spain, n.* Screwup, dumb trick. *Yo sé que hice una huevada pero no sabía que iba a ser tan grave.* "I know that I screwed up, but I didn't know that it was so serious." **2.** *Spain, n.* Testicles. *El otro jugador le pegó una patada en la huevada.* "The other player gave him a kick in the balls."

HUEVAMEN, *Spain, n.* Testicles. *¡Vaya huevamen que*

tiene ese toro! "What a pair of balls that bull has!"

HUEVAZOS, *Spain, pl. n.* Large testicles. *Uno tiene que tener huevazos para enfrentar esa clase de situación.* "You've got to have a lot of balls in that type of situation."

HUEVERA, 1. *Spain, n.* Both testicles. *En una película que ·vi, el protagonista agarró la huevera de uno para amenazarlo.* "In a movie I saw, the main character grabbed another guy's balls to threaten him." **2.** *Spain, n., sports.* Genital protector. *Hoy muchos jugadores llevan hueveras para protegerse.* "Nowadays many players wear jockstraps to protect themselves."

HUEVO, *Spain, n.* Testicle. (Lit. Egg.) *Doctor, me duele el huevo izquierdo. ¿Cree Ud. que tengo una hernia?* "Doctor, my left nut is hurting me. Do you think I have a hernia?"

HUEVÓN, NA, 1. *L.Am./S, adj. or n.* Idiot, fool, stupid. *¿Sos huevón o te haces? ¿Cómo pudiste hacer ésto?* "Are you an idiot or are you just pretending? How could you do such a thing?" **2.** *Spain, adj. or n.* Goof-off. *Es muy huevón el esposo de Paty, nunca trabaja.* "Patty's husband is a real goof-off; he never works." **3.** *L.Am., Spain, adj. or n.* Stupid, used affectionately among friends. *Oye huevón, ¿qué te parece si vamos al cine esta noche?* "Hey stupid, how about going to a movie tonight?"

HUEVOS, *L.Am./N, n.* Testicles. (Lit. Eggs.) *A Gil le dieron una patada en los huevos.* "They gave Gil a kick in the balls."

HUEVUDO, DA, *Spain, adj.* Fantastic, wonderful, super cool. *Anoche fuimos a un lugar muy huevudo.* "Last night we went to a real cool place."

HUILA, *L.Am./N, n.* Prostitute. *Cuando quedó viuda, se metió de huila.* "When she was widowed, she became a hooker."

HUIRIHUIRI, *U.S., n.* Gossip. *Rosi, cuéntame el huirihuiri de tu cuñada.* "Rosie, tell me the gossip about your sister-in-law."

HUIRLOCHA, *U.S., n.* Old car, jalopy. *Mi huirlocha es tan fiel que no la voy a vender nunca.* "My jalopy is so faithful that I'll never sell it."

HUIRO, *L.Am./S, n.* Joint. *Yerba maldita, amor de mi vida, pásame el huiro compadre.* "Damn grass, love of my life! Pass me the joint, buddy."

HULE, 1. *Spain, n.* Fight, struggle. (Lit. Rubber.) *Hoy hubo hule en la oficina. González y Rodríguez se liaron a golpes.* "Today there was a brawl at the office. Gonzalez and Rodriguez hit each other." **2.** *U.S., n.* Condom, rubber. *Dicen que están dando hules a los jóvenes en la escuela para protegerlos del SIDA.* "They say they are giving out rubbers to people at school to protect them from AIDS."

HÚMEDA, *Spain, n.* Tongue. (Lit. Wet one.) *Los pelados se están haciendo agujeros hasta en la húmeda.* "The skinheads are even piercing holes in their tongues."

HUYÓN, NA, *Car., n.* Coward. *Yo soy muy huyón cuando se trata de insectos. No los tolero.* "I am real chicken when it comes to insects. I can't stand them."

ÍDEM DE LIENZO, *Spain, idiom.* I agree, ditto. *"Yo creo que la prensa se pasa a veces." "¡Ídem de lienzo!"* " 'I believe that the press goes too far sometimes.' 'Right on!' "

IGUALA, *Car., n.* Payoff, bribe. *El primer trabajo que tenía era llevar la iguala a los políticos del barrio.* "The first job I had was to take the payoffs to the neighborhood politicians."

IGUALADO, DA, 1. *L.Am./N, adj.* Disrespectful. *Álvaro no les cae bien a mis papás porque es muy igualado.* "My parents don't like Alvaro because he is very disrespectful." **2.** *Car., U.S., n.* Social climber. *La mujer de Alonzo es una igualada.* "Alonso's wife is a social climber."

IMPERMEABLE, *Spain, n.* Condom. (Lit. Raincoat.) *Ahora anuncian impermeables hasta en la tele.* "Now they even advertise rubbers on TV."

IMPORTAR UN CARAJO, *L.Am., Spain, idiom.* To not care, to not give a fuck. *Me importa un carajo lo que dices. ¡Aquí mando yo!* "I don't give a fuck what you say. I am the boss here!"

IMPORTAR UN CUERNO See IMPORTAR UN CARAJO

IMPORTAR UN PEPINO See IMPORTAR UN CARAJO

IMPORTAR UN PITO See **IMPORTAR UN CARAJO**

IMPORTAR UN RÁBANO See **IMPORTAR UN CARAJO**

IMPORTAR UNA MIERDA See **IMPORTAR UN CARAJO**

IMPUESTO, TA, *L.Am./N, adj.* Accustomed. (Lit. Imposed.) *Yo ya estoy impuesto al calor porque viví muchos años en la costa.* "I am already accustomed to the heat because I lived for many years on the coast."

INCHURBIDO, DA, *Car., adj.* Stupid, annoying. *Ese idiota enchurbido ya va a empezar con sus chistes pesados.* "That annoying asshole is gonna start up with his stupid jokes."

INCURSIONAR, *L.Am./S, v.* To kiss passionately, to neck heavily. (Lit. To raid.) *Amalia y Rodrigo pasaron toda la película incursionando.* "Amalia and Rodrigo necked during the entire movie."

INDIO, *L.Am./S, adj. or n.* Person of poor taste, hick, yokel. (Lit. Indian.) *El tipo que está saliendo con Julia es un indio.* "The guy that is going out with Julia is a yokel."

INFANTICIDA, *Spain, n.* Cradle robber. (Lit. Infanticide.) *Manolo, eres un infanticida, ¿por qué no sales con mujeres de tu edad?* "Manolo, you're a cradle robber. Why don't you go out with women your own age?"

INFARTO (DE) *Spain, idiom.* Surprising, shocking. *Las noticias eran de infarto. El avión cayó en medio de la ciudad.* "It is drop-dead news. The plane crashed in the middle of the city."

INFLAPOLLAS, 1. *Spain, n.* Cockteaser. *Esa chica es una inflapollas, muchos besos, mucho toqueteo y nada más.* "That girl is a cockteaser, a lot of kisses, a lot of petting, and nothing more." **2.** *Spain, n.* Idiot, jerk. *Ese funcionario es un inflapollas. No se puede tratar con él.* "That clerk is a jackass. You can't deal with him."

INFLAR, *L.Am./N, v.* To drink. (Lit. To inflate.) *No me* *gustan las fiestas, es puro inflar.* "I don't like parties; it's all drinking."

INGENEBRIO, *L.Am./N, n.* Construction engineer. (Combination of "ingeniero" [engineer] and "ebrio" [drunk].) *Dile al ingenebrio que no te están pagando.* "Tell the dizzy engineer that they are not paying you."

INGLESADO, DA, *U.S., adj.* Anglo-like. *Lucía tiene aspecto inglesado.* "Lucia has an Anglo look."

¡INGUIASU!, *L.Am./N, interj.* Damn! Hell! *¡Inguiasu! Cómo corren los taxistas.* "Damn! The speed of those taxi drivers!"

INSPECTOR DE AZOTEAS, *L.Am./N, idiom.* Tall person. *Jaime creció tanto que quedó para inspector de azoteas.* "Jaime grew so much he's able to inspect rooftops."

INTONADO, DA, *U.S., adj.* With it, tuned-in. *Tú estás bien intonado con lo que pasa en tu barrio, ¿verdad?* "You are tuned-in to what's going on in your neighborhood, right?"

INVERTIDA, *Car., n.* Lesbian. (Lit. Inverted.) *Eduardo cree que su nueva jefa es invertida.* "Eduardo believes that his new boss is a dyke."

IR A CAMÓN, *Car., idiom.* To go on foot. *Fuimos a la fiesta a camón.* "We went to the party on foot."

IR AL TACO, *L.Am./N, idiom.* To eat. *Ya tengo hambre, vámonos al taco.* "I am hungry; let's go put on the feedbag."

IR AL VAMPIRO, *Spain, idiom.* To sell blood to the blood bank. *"¿Cómo vas a sacar el dinero?" "Me voy al vampiro para venderle un litro de sangre."* " 'How are you going to get money?' 'I'll go to the Dracula Bank to sell a liter of blood.' "

IR CIEGO, 1. *Spain, idiom.* Blind drunk. *Bebí tanto anoche que iba ciego a casa.* "I had so much last night that I went home blind drunk." **2.** *Spain, idiom.* Drugged. *Cuando lo arrestaron iba ciego de la cocaína.* "When they arrested him, he was blind high on coke." **3.** *Spain, idiom.* To be furious. *Ojo con papá, va ciego por culpa tuya.* "Look out for Pop; he's blind with anger because of you."

IR DE BONITO, *Spain, idiom, mil.* To dress in uniform. *El sargento va de bonito.* "The sergeant is all decked out."

IR DE BUREO, *Spain, idiom.* To go partying. *Fuimos de bureo anoche y bailamos sin parar.* "We went partying last night and did nonstop dancing."

IR DE CRÁNEO, *Spain, idiom.* To be under pressure. *Con todo el trabajo que tengo me voy de cráneo.* "With all the work I have, I'm going to blow up."

IR DE CULO, *Spain, idiom.* To be overwhelmed by work, problems, etc. *Alfredo va de culo con todas las deudas que tiene.* "Alfredo is falling on his ass from all of his debts."

IR DE PRINGAO, *Spain, idiom.* To be a sucker, to be deceived. *Si tus padres no tienen cuidado van a ir de pringao con ese vendedor.* "If your parents aren't careful, they'll be duped by that salesman."

IR DE PUTAS, *Spain, idiom.* To go out looking for prostitutes. *Cuando estaba en la mili íbamos de putas.* "When I was in the service, we went whoring."

IRSE DE PARRANDA, *L.Am., idiom.* To go out partying. *Daniel se va de parranda todos los viernes por la noche.* "Daniel goes out on the town every Friday night."

IRSE DE PINTA, *L.Am./N, idiom.* To play hooky, to cut classes. *Cuando éramos niños nos íbamos de pinta para ir de pesca.* "When we were kids we would play hooky to go fishing."

ISMAEL, *Spain, n.* Email. *Te enviaré el trabajo por Ismael esta tarde.* "I will send you the job by email this afternoon.

IZQUIERDISTA, *U.S., adj. or n.* Left-handed person. (Lit. Leftist.) *Mi hijo salió izquierdista como su padre.* "My son turned out left-handed like his father."

JABALÍ, *Car., n.* Reactionary. (Lit. Boar.) *La facultad de filosofía está llena de jabalíes.* "The School of Philosophy is full of reactionaries."

JABONERO, RA, *Car., adj.* Flatterer, soft-soaper, brownnoser. *Mónica consiguió esa posición por jabonera.* "Monica got that position by being a brownnose."

JACAL, *L.Am./N, n.* Hut. *Vivían en un jacal en las afueras del pueblo.* "They lived in a shack outside of town."

JACHA, *L.Am./C, n.* Face. *¡Qué jacha más triste tiene Ramón!* "What a sad face Ramón has!"

JAINO, NA, *U.S., n.* Boyfriend, girlfriend. *El jaino de mi prima es gabacho.* "My cousin's boyfriend is a foreigner."

JAIPO, *U.S., n., drugs.* Hypodermic needle (From English "hypo.") *Están repartiendo jaipos para los adictos.* "They are giving out hypos for the addicts."

JALAÍTA, *Car., n.* Drag on a marijuana joint. *Entré en el cuarto de mi hijo y le pillé tomando una jalaíta.* "I entered my son's room and caught him taking a drag on a joint."

¡JÁLALE!, *U.S., interj.* Hurry up! Get a move on! *¡Jálale! Nos quedan quince minutos para llegar al cine.* "Hurry up! We've got fifteen minutes to get to the movies."

JALAR, 1. *L.Am./C, v.* To be sweethearts. (Lit. To pull.) *Tere y Gustavo jalan tres años ya.* "Tere and Gustavo have been going together for three years already." **2.** *L.Am./S, v.* To take drugs. *Esa gente está jalándolos hasta la chicharra.* "Those people are smoking them down to the bud."

JALAR PAREJO, *L.Am./N, idiom.* To pull together, to be equals. *Todos tenemos que ayudar, hay que jalar parejo.* "We all have to help each other; we must pull together."

JALARSE, *U.S., prnl. v.* To masturbate, to jack off. *Mi hermano siempre está en el baño jalándose.* "My brother is always in the bathroom jacking off."

¿JALAS O TE PANDEAS?, *L.Am./N, idiom.* Are you with me or against me? *Yo sí lo voy a intentar. ¿Jalas o te pandeas?* "Yes I am going to attempt it. Are you with me or against me?"

JALE, 1. *L.Am./S, n.* Attraction. *Tengo un jale increíble por ese flaco narizón.* "I have a huge attraction for that big-nosed dude." **2.** *L.Am./N, n.* Job, work, employment, occupation. *Pancho se consiguió jale de panadero.* "Pancho got a job as a baker."

JALEO, *Car., n.* Argument. *Todas las conversaciones de política terminan en jaleo.* "All the conversations about politics end up in an argument."

JAMA, *L.Am./N, n.* Food. *No hay jama en la nevera.* "There's no food in the icebox."

JAMAR, *L.Am./N, v.* To eat. *Vamos a jamar ahora.* "Let's eat now."

JAMÓN, *Car., n.* Trouble, difficulty. (Lit. Ham.) *Este jamón en que me metí no me deja dormir.* "This trouble I got myself in won't let me sleep."

JAMONA, 1. *Car., adj. or n.* Old maid. *La jamona que atiende la panadería siempre está contenta.* "The old maid who waits on you at the bakery is always happy." **2.** *L.Am./S, n.* Fat woman. *¡Esa jamona te tiene ganas!* "That fatty has the hots for you!"

JAMONERO, *Car., n.* Feeler, fondler. *Pepe es un tremendo jamonero, al menor descuido trata de manosearte.* "Pepe is a real feeler. If you're not careful he'll try to feel you up."

JANGAO, GÁ, *Car., adj. or n.* Drug addict. *Ese hombre que se sienta en la esquina es un jangao.* "That man sitting on the corner is a drug addict."

JARABE DE PICO, *L.Am./N, idiom.* Long speech. *El diputado es puro jarabe de pico.* "The representative is long-winded."

JARDÍN, *Car., n.* In baseball, the playing fields. (Lit. Garden.) *Jiménez pegó un flay al jardín derecho.* "Jiménez hit a fly into right field."

JARIA, *U.S., n.* Hunger. *¡Cuánta jaria me da ver a la gente comer tacos!* "I get so hungry watching people eat tacos!"

JARINA, *Car., n.* Light drizzle. *Está cayendo una jarina, mejor lleva tu paraguas.* "A little mist is falling, better take your umbrella."

JARINDONGA, *Car., n.* Policewoman. *Hay cada vez más jerindongas patrullando las calles.* "There are more and more policewomen patrolling the streets."

JARTERA, 1. *L.Am./S, n.* Laziness, bother, drag. *Me da jartera preparar mis presentaciones.* "It's a drag to prepare my presentations." **2.** *L.Am./S, n.* Unpleasant or boring thing. *Es una jartera ir a las clausuras de año escolástico.* "It's a pain in the neck to go to the end-of-school ceremonies."

JARTO, TA, *L.Am./S, adj.* Fed up, worn out. (From Spanish "harto.") *Tantas visitas los fines de semana me tienen jarta.* "So much company on weekends got me worn out."

JATANA, *U.S., n.* Guitar. *¿Trajiste tu jatana? Queremos oírte tocar.* "Did you bring your guitar? We want to hear you play."

JATEAR, *L.Am./S, v.* To sleep. *Alfredo está jateando hasta estas horas por la tranca de anoche.* "Alfredo is sleeping in late due to last night's drinking bout."

JATO, *L.Am./S, n.* Home, house. *Pintar el jato de Miguel resultó una pesadilla.* "Painting Miguel's house turned out to be a nightmare."

JAULA, 1. *Car., n.* Police lockup. (Lit. Cage.) *Dos oficiales lo metieron en la jaula.* "Two officers put him in the lockup." **2.** *Car., n.* Paddy wagon. *La jaula que pasó iba llena de presos.* "The paddy wagon that went by was full of prisoners."

JEBA, *L.Am., n.* Girlfriend. *La jeba de Beto es un bomboncito.* "Beto's girlfriend is a cutie."

JEBO, 1. *Car., n.* Handsome young man. *Estoy enamorada del jebo de enfrente.* "I am in love with the hunk across the way." **2.** *Car., n.* Sweetheart, beau. *Mi jebo me trata como a una reina.* "My beau treats me like a queen."

JEDIONDO, *Car., n.* Dominican peso. *Ya me gasté muchos jediondos apostando. Es hora de parar.* "I spent too many pesos betting; it's time to stop."

JEFA, *Car., n.* Domineering wife. *Mi jefa no me permite ir con mis amigos al bar.* "My boss doesn't let me go out with my pals to the bar."

JEFA DE RELACIONES PÚBLICAS, *L.Am./N, idiom.* Madam. *Si te lo quieres llevar, tienes que hablar con la jefa de relaciones públicas.* "If you want to take it with you, you have to talk to the madam of the house."

JEFE, FA, *L.Am./N, n.* Father or mother. *Si no llego temprano a la casa, mi jefe me va a matar.* "If I don't get home early, my dad is going to kill me."

JETA, *L.Am./S, n.* Thick lips. *Pepe se golpeó en la boca; ahora tiene tremenda jeta.* "Pepe got hit in the mouth; now he has big lips."

JETÓN, ONA, 1. *L.Am./N, adj.* Asleep. *Estaba bien jetón cuando sonó el reloj despertador.* "I was sound asleep when the alarm clock went off." **2.** *L.Am./S, adj.* Person with a big face, affectionate name, stupid. *¡Ven acá jetón, dame un abrazo!* "Come over here you big face; give me a hug!"

JEVA, *L.Am./S, n.* Woman, girl, girlfriend. *Ahora voy a bailar con mi jeva.* "Now I'm going to dance with my squeeze."

JEVO, *Car., n.* Young fellow, boy, boyfriend. *Los jevos prefieren esa música tan ruidosa.* "The kids love that noisy music."

JÍBARO, RA, *Car., adj. or n.* Hick, hillbilly. (Lit. Jivaro Indian.) *Ese jíbaro es muy mal educado.* "That hick is real rude."

JIJO DE LA JIJURRIA, *L.Am./N, idiom.* Euphemism for "son of a bitch." *Si Iván te hizo eso, entonces es un jijo de la jijurria.* "If Ivan did that, then he is a son of a gun."

JINCHO, CHA, *L.Am./S, adj.* Drunk. *José está jincho, así no puede manejar.* "Jose is wiped out, so he can't drive."

JINETE, TA, *Car., adj. or n.* Person of ill repute. (Lit. Jockey, rider.) *No te metas con ese jinete porque te puede hacer daño.* "Don't get involved with that lowlife because he can hurt you."

JINETEAR ALAZÁN, *L.Am./N, idiom.* To menstruate. *Por el mal humor, creo que la señora está jineteando alazán.* "Because of her bad mood I believe that the lady is on the rag."

JINETEAR EL DINERO, *L.Am./N, idiom.* To profit by delaying payment. *En lugar de pagarte de inmediato, Omar siempre te jinetea el dinero.* "Instead of paying you at once, Omar is always delaying to make an extra buck."

JINETERA, *Car., n.* Prostitute. (Lit. Female rider.) *En el muelle hay jineteras jóvenes y baratas.* "There are young and cheap whores at the pier."

JINGUETAZO, *Car., n.* Punch. *El jinguetazo que me pegó me mandó al piso.* "That whack he gave me sent me to the floor."

JODA LOCA (LA), *L.Am./S, idiom.* Lot of fun, a blast. *El carnaval fué la joda loca.* "The carnival was a blast."

JODER, 1. *L.Am./N, Spain, v.* To fuck. *Lo único que quiere hacer ese animal es joder y comer.* "The only thing that animal wants to do is fuck and eat. **2.** *L.Am./S, v.* To bother. (Lit. To fuck.) *No jodas más Félix, me estás cansando.* "Stop being a pest Felix; you're bothering me too much already." **3.** *L.Am., Spain, v.* To damage. *El mecánico me jodió el auto.* "The mechanic fucked up my car."

JODIDO, DA, 1. *Spain, n.* Bad, mean person. *No quiero nada que ver con ese jodido.* "I don't want anything to do with that fucker." **2.** *L.Am., adj.* Finicky. *Fernando es tan jodido que se demora horas en decidir qué ponerse.* "Fernando is so finicky that he takes hours to decide what to wear." **3.** *L.Am., adj.* Difficult. *El examen estuvo jodido, no sé si lo voy a pasar.* "The test was a mother; I don't know if I am going to pass it." **4.** *L.Am., adj.* Untrustworthy. *Ese tipo es un jodido, cúidate de él.* "That guy is a sleazy fucker; look out for him." **5.** *L.Am./S, n.* Unlucky. *Julio es un pobre jodido, perdió el trabajo, la mujer y todo.* "Juan is a poor fuckup; he lost his job, his wife, everything."

JODÓN, NA, 1. *L.Am./N, adj.* Sharp, capable. *Gregorio es muy jodón para jugar billar.* "Gregorio is real sharp at billiards." **2.** *L.Am./S, adj.* Annoying. *No me aguanto a tu hermano porque es muy jodón.* "I can't stand your brother because he is a pain in the ass."

JOLA, *U.S., n.* Money. *Préstame un poco de jola porque no tengo nada.* "Lend me a little gelt because I don't have any."

JONDO, DA, *Car., adj.* Deep. (From Spanish "hondo.") *Cuidado, que más adelante hay un hoyo jondo.* "Be careful, there is a deep hole further on."

JOROBAR, *L.Am./N, v.* To bother, to bug. *El hermanito de Héctor llora sólo para jorobar.* "Hector's little brother cries just to bug you."

JOSLA, *U.S., adj.* Fantastic, neat, cool. *Tienes un traje muy josla.* "You've got a real cool suit."

JOTO, *L.Am./N, n.* Pejorative for homosexual, fag. *A esa cantina van puros jotos.* "Just fags go to that bar."

JOVATO, TA, *L.Am./S, n.* Old person. *A mi vecino, el jovato, no lo viene a visitar nadie.* "My neighbor, the old fella, never gets any visitors."

JUANITA, *L.Am./N, n.* Marijuana, Mary Jane, pot, grass, weed. *Yo no le entro a las drogas, ni siquiera a la Juanita.* "I don't go for drugs, not even pot."

JUDÍA ERRANTE, *L.Am./N, n.* Streetwalker. (Lit. Wandering Jewess.) *A Penélope le gustó la vida de judía errante.* "Penelope liked the life of a streetwalker."

JUDIAR, *L.Am./S, v.* To annoy, to bother. *Los niños de mi vecino siempre me están judiando.* "My neighbor's kids are always annoying me."

¡JUE'PUCHA!, *L.Am./C, interj.* Interjection expressing surprise, admiration, disgust. *¡Jue'pucha! Perdí mis llaves.* "Damn! I lost my keys."

JUGADORA, *L.Am./S, n.* Loose girl. (Lit. Player.) *Raquel resultó una jugadora con todos los muchachos del barrio.* "Raquel ended up being a playgirl with all the guys from the neighborhood."

JUGAR DE VIVO, VIVA, *L.Am./C, idiom.* To be a know-it-all. *Jorge quería jugar de vivo pero lo cogieron en la estafa.* "Jorge thought he knew the score, but they caught him in the swindle."

JUILONA, *L.Am./N, n.* Loose woman. *La esposa de Enrique le salió muy juilona.* "Enrique's wife turned out to be a very loose woman."

JULEPE, 1. *Car., n.* Trouble. *Rosa siempre anda metida en julepes con la suegra.* "Rosa is always in trouble with her mother-in-law." **2.** *L.Am./S, n.* Sudden fear, panic. *Vi al maleante con un cuchillo y me dio un julepe bárbaro.* "I saw the thug with a knife, and I got the scare of my life."

JULEPERO, RA, *Car., n.* Troublemaker. *Pedro es un julepero y siempre anda peleando.* "Pedro is a troublemaker and is always fighting."

JULIA, *L.Am./N, n.* Police car or van. *Llegó la julia y cargaron con todos.* "The paddy wagon arrived and loaded them all up."

JUMA, *L.Am./C, n.* Drinking bout. *Antonio agarró la juma anoche.* "Antonio tied one on last night."

JUMEAR, *L.Am./N, v.* To stink. *¡Báñate, que te jumean los pies!* "Take a bath, your feet stink!"

JÚNIOR, 1. *L.Am./S, n.* Janitor or super. (Lit. Junior.) *Alguien derramó algo en el piso, llame al júnior.* "Somebody spilled something on the floor; call the super." **2.** *L.Am./N, n.* Person who lives off his or her parents. *Es un júnior que nunca ha tenido que trabajar.* "He's a daddy's boy who has never had to work."

JURUNGAR, *L.Am./S, v.* To search, to pat down, to frisk. *Me jurungaron cuando visité el penal.* "They frisked me when I visited the prison."

JUSTICIA, *U.S., n., crim.* Police. (Lit. Justice.) *Aquí viene la justicia.* "Here comes the fuzz."

¡LA PAPA!, *U.S., interj.* Great! Cool! Awesome! *"¿Qué te parece si vamos a Cancún?" "¡La papa!"* " 'What do you think if we go to Cancun?' 'Cool!' "

¡LA PESTE!, *L.Am./C, interj.* Expression of disgust or disappointment. *¡La peste! Dejé el regalo de Soledad en casa.* "Shoot! I left Soledad's present at home."

¡LA PUCHA!, *L.Am./C, interj.* Expression of disgust or disappointment. *¡La pucha! ¿Por qué no me dijo Ud. que la reparación me iba a costar tanto?* "Darn it! Why didn't you tell me that the repair was going to cost so much?"

¡LA PUÑA!, *L.Am./C, interj.* Expression of disgust or disappointment. *¡Ay, la puña! Dejé mi billetera en casa.* "Oh, damn it! I left my wallet at home."

LABURO, *L.Am./S, n.* Job, work. *No puedo salir esta noche porque tengo mucho laburo.* "I can't go out tonight because I've got a lot of work."

LADILLA, *L.Am./S, n.* Bothersome person. (Lit. Crab louse.) *¡Qué ladilla es Jorge!* "What a pest Jorge is!"

LADRILLAR, *L.Am./S, v.* To bother someone, to bug. *Pepe siempre me está ladrillando.* "Pepe is always bugging me."

LADRILLO, *L.Am./S, n.* A bore. (Lit. Brick.) *La película resultó ser un ladrillo.* "The movie turned out to be a drag."

LAGARTO, *L.Am./S, n.* Person trying to get something for nothing. (Lit. Lizard.) *Ese diputado es un lagarto, se metió en política para beneficiarse.* "That representive is a shark; he got into politics to help himself."

LÁGUER, *Car., n.* Lager beer. *Ven a tomarte un láguer conmigo.* "Come and have a beer with me."

LAJA, *Car., adj. or n.* Cheapskate, tightwad. *Mi novio es tan laja que no me invita ni a un café.* "My boyfriend is so tight that he doesn't even take me for a cup of coffee."

LAMBISCÓN, ONA *L.Am./N, adj. or n.* Kiss-ass, kissass. *Agustín es muy lambiscón con el profesor.* "Agustine is real kiss-ass with the professor."

LAMBÓN, NA, *Car., adj. or n.* Moocher. *No seas tan lambón. Hoy tienes que pagar por lo tuyo.* "Don't be a moocher. Today you are going to pay for your own."

LAMPAO, PÁ, *Car., adj.* Unemployed. *Julio lleva meses lampao y ni se preocupa.* "Julio has been out of work for months and he couldn't care less."

LANA, *L.Am./N, n.* Money. (Lit. Wool.) *Págame el boleto, no tengo lana.* "Pay my ticket; I don't have any dough."

LANCE, *L.Am./C, n.* Affair, fling. *Mauro tiene un lance con una chica del trabajo.* "Mauro is having a fling with a girl from work."

LANZADO, *L.Am./S, adj.* Daring. (Lit. Thrown.) *Juan se fue solo para la selva, es muy lanzado.* "Juan went to the jungle alone; he's ballsy."

LAPA, *L.Am., n.,* Clinging vine. *Lola es una lapa, siempre agarrada al brazo del novio.* "Lola is a clinging vine, always holding onto her boyfriend's arm."

LAPO, *Spain, n.* Phlegm, lunger, oyster. *El tío le escupió un lapo en la cara a Álvaro.* "The guy spit an oyster in Alvaro's face."

LAVADO, *L.Am./C, adj.* Broke. (Lit. Washed out.) *Después de comprarte el regalo quedé lavado.* "After buying your present, I'm broke."

LAVAR EL COCO, *L.Am./N, idiom.* To convince, to brainwash. *Matilde le estaba lavando el coco a su papá para que la dejara ir a la fiesta.* "Matilde was trying to brainwash her father into letting her go to the party."

LE RONCA LA MADRE DE LOS TOMATES, *Car., idiom.* Expression of surprise, wonder, amazement. *Me vende la talla equivocada y se pone brava porque le reclamo por el error. ¡Le ronca la madre de los tomates!* "He sells me the wrong size and then he gets angry when I complain. What gall!"

LECHERO, 1. *L.Am., n.* Lucky person. (Lit. Milkman.) *Él es un lechero, siempre se saca todos los premios gordos.* "He is a lucky fella; he always wins the big prizes." **2.** *Car., adj.* Well-off. *Ramiro está lechero desde que trabaja con esa empresa.* "Ramiro is doing okay since he's been working with that company." **3.** *Car., adj.* Tight, cheap. *Mi papá es tan lechero que no me compra ni regalo de Navidad.* "My father is so tight that he doesn't even buy me a Christmas present."

LECHUGA, *Car., n.* Dollar bill, greenback. (Lit. Lettuce.) *El hombre llevaba un maletín lleno de lechugas.* "The man was carrying a little suitcase full of lettuce."

LECUMBERRI HILTON HOTEL, *L.Am./N, n.* Mexican prison, penitentiary. *Al ladrón le dieron cinco años en el Lecumberri Hilton Hotel.* "They gave the thief five years in the Gray-Bar Hilton."

LEERLE LA CARTILLA A ALGUIEN, *L.Am., Spain, idiom.* To reprimand, to warn. *Antes de que empezara el curso escolar, le leí la cartilla sobre la conducta en la escuela.* "Before starting the school year, I warned him about conduct at school."

LELO, *L.Am., Spain, n.* Fool, idiot, dummy. *Arnulfo es muy lelo, se cree todo lo que le dicen.* "Arnulfo is a real idiot; he believes anything they tell him."

LENGÜETAZO, *Car., n.* Gossip. *Esa revista sólo publica lengüetazos.* "That magazine only publishes gossip."

LENGÜILARGO, GA, *Car., n.* Dirty mouth. *Ojalá deje de* *hablar ese lengüilargo, me tiene cansada.* "I hope that foul mouth stops talking; I am tired of it."

LENTEJUDO, *L.Am./N, n.* Four-eyes. *¿Se te hace guapo el lentejudo que está allí?* "Does four-eyes over there seem handsome to you?"

LENTODOS, *U.S., n.* Eyeglasses. *No veo nada. Dejé mis lentodos en casa.* "I don't see anything. I left my glasses at home."

LEONERA, *L.Am./N, n.* Bachelor pad. (Lit. Lion's cage.) *Entre Víctor y Pablo, pusieron una leonera.* "Victor and Pablo set up a bachelor pad together."

LEPERADA, *L.Am./N, n.* Stupid, ignorant, vulgar comment. *Lo único que sabe decir Jorge son puras leperadas.* "The only thing Jorge talks about is bullshit."

LÉPERO, *L.Am./N, n.* Vulgar person. *René es un lépero, no sabe comportarse.* "Rene is a boor; he doesn't know how to act."

LIAR LOS BÁRTULOS, *Spain, idiom.* To die. *El padre de Gustavo arregló todos sus asuntos y entonces lio los bártulos.* "Gustavo's father arranged his matters and then packed it in."

LIBRAR EL COCO, *Car., idiom.* To escape danger. *Pudimos librar el coco antes de que el tornado alcanzara la casa.* "We were able to escape before the tornado reached the house."

LICAR, *L.Am./N, v.* To look, to keep one's eyes peeled. *Yo estaba licando por si venía el profesor.* "I was keeping an eye out in case the professor came."

LIJA, *Car., adj. or n.* Intelligent, sharp person. (Lit. Sandpaper.) *Quisiera ser tan lija como mi padre.* "I wish I were as sharp as my dad."

LILO, LA, *L.Am./N, n.* Homosexual. *No me gusta ir a ese lugar, van puras lilas.* "I don't like that place; only fags go there."

LIMPIAR, *Car., v.* To kill. (Lit. To clean.) *Al coronel lo* *quieren limpiar los mafiosos.* "The mafiosi want to kill the colonel."

LIMPIO, PIA *U.S., L.Am., adj.* Broke. (Lit. Clean.) *No me pidas más plata porque estoy limpio.* "Don't ask me for more money because I am broke."

LIRA, *U.S., L.Am./N, n.* Guitar. (Lit. Lyre.) *Manuel va a llevar su lira al paseo de la escuela.* "Manuel is going to take his guitar on the school trip."

L.J., *L.Am./S, idiom.* Euphemism for Spanish "los juimos" ("We're leaving."). *Nosotros L.J. (elejota). Ya es tarde.* "We're leaving. It's late."

LLAMAR A CONTAR, *Car., idiom.* To reprimand. *Nena andaba regando chismes sobre Marta y ésta la llamó a contar.* "Nena was gossiping about Marta and Marta called her on it."

LLANTA, *U.S., n.* Fat midriff, spare tire. (Lit. Inner tube.) *Alberto, ¿cuándo vas a perder esa llanta?* "Albert, when are you going to lose that spare tire?"

LLANTAS, *L.Am., pl. n.* Love handles. (Lit. Inner tubes.) *Tengo que hacer ejercicio para rebajar estas llantas.* "I've got to do exercise to melt these blobs."

LLAPA See ÑAPA

LLAVE, *L.Am./S, n.* Close friend. (Lit. Key.) *José, quiero presentarte a mi llave Mario.* "Jose, I want to introduce you to my best buddy Mario."

LLEGAR ALTAMENTE, *L.Am./S, idiom.* To not care. *Me llega altamente, me tiene hasta la coronilla, ya me cansó.* "I don't care anymore, I've had it up to here, and I'm tired of it."

LLEVAR LOS PANTALONES, *L.Am., idiom.* To be in charge, to wear the pants. *Mi padre siempre ha llevado los pantalones en mi casa.* "My father has always worn the pants in my house."

LLEVARSE AL CATRE, *Spain, idiom.* To seduce someone. *Manolo se llevó la nueva empleada al catre.* "Manolo took the new employee to bed."

LLORAR A MOCO TENDIDO, *L.Am./S, idiom.* To cry one's eyes out. *Cuando murió mi perro lloré a moco tendido.* "When my dog died, I cried my eyes out."

LLORONA, *L.Am./N, n.* Female ghost. *Dicen que por aquí espanta la llorona.* "They say this place is haunted by the crying lady."

LLOVER EN LA MILPITA, *L.Am./N, idiom.* Run of bad luck. *Hoy me despidieron. Parece que no deja de llover en mi milpita.* "Today they fired me. It seems that it is always raining on my parade."

LLUEVA, TRUENE O RELAMPAGUEE, *Car., idiom.* No matter what, come hell or high water. *Estaré allí llueva, truene o relampaguee.* "I'll be there rain or shine."

LOBO, BA, *L.Am./S, adj.* Ugly, tacky. (Lit. Wolf.) *¿Viste el vestido tan lobo que se puso Liliana para la fiesta?* "Did you see the trashy dress Liliana wore for the party?"

LOCA, 1. *L.Am./N, adj.* Prostitute, woman of various men. *Esa mujer es una loca, ni me la presentes.* "That woman is a hooker; don't introduce her to me." **2.** *L.Am./S, n.* Male homosexual, fag. *Mira qué apretados llevan los pantalones esas locas.* "Look how tight those fags wear their pants."

LOCO, *L.Am./S, n.* One thousand soles (Peruvian currency). (Lit. Crazy.) *Si te consigues un loco nos vamos de parranda.* "If you get a thousand bucks, we will go party."

LOLA, *L.Am./S, n.* Prepubescent girl. (From Nabokov's *Lolita.*) *A esa lola ya se le asoman las tetas.* "That girl is beginning to grow tits."

LOLAS, *L.Am./N, pl. n.* Woman's breasts, tits, jugs, gozangas. *Siempre se pone ese vestidito para mostrar las lolas.* "She always wears that dress to show her boobies."

LOMPA, *L.Am./S, n.* Pants. *No seas ridículo y sácate esa lompa.* "Don't be ridiculous and go change those pants."

LOQUERO, *L.Am./S, n.* Psychiatrist. *No es para tanto, ella no necesita que la lleven al loquero.* "It's not such a big deal; she doesn't really need to go to the shrink."

LORCHO, *L.Am./S, n.* Indigenous person. *Cientos de lorchos llegan diariamente a la capital.* "Hundreds of natives arrive daily in the capital."

LORENZO, *L.Am./N, adj.* Naive, stupid. *Yo le dije a Chuy que estaba Lorenzo si creía que yo lo iba a seguir.* "I told Chuy that he was stupid if he thought I was going to follow him."

LORO, RA, 1. *L.Am./S, n.* Talker. (Lit. Parrot.) *Se metió un par de tragos y le dio la lora.* "He had a couple of drinks and let his tongue loose." **2.** *L.Am./S, n.* Booger. *Ese niño tiene loros verdes y amarillos.* "That kid has green and yellow boogers."

LÚA, *Car., n.* Guardian angel. *El lúa de Miguel lo salvó de morir en el accidente.* "Miguel's guardian angel saved him from death in the accident."

LUCA, *L.Am./S, n.* Thousand. *Me van a pagar cuarenta lucas por ese trabajito.* "They are going to pay me 40 grand for that little job."

LUCRECIA See LUCA

LUEGO LUEGO, *L.Am./N, adv.* Right away, immediately. *Y luego luego llegó la policía.* "And right away the police arrived."

LUEGUITO, *L.Am., adv.* Right away. *"¿Y cuándo llega Álvaro?" "Lueguito."* " 'And when does Alvaro arrive?' 'Right away.' "

LUNADA, *L.Am./N, n.* Beach party. *Todos los muchachos se juntaron para hacer una lunada frente al hotel.* "All the guys got together to have a beach party in front of the hotel."

LUQUEAR, *L.Am./S, v.* To look. *Dale una luqueadita a mi carro, que no se lo vayan a robar.* "Keep an eye on my car so it doesn't get stolen."

LUZ, *L.Am./N, n.* Money. (Lit. Light.) *Préstame una luz, que no traigo.* "Lend me some bread; I don't have any on me."

M

MABI, *Car., n.* Refreshing drink. *Por favor, sírvele unos mabis a mis amigos.* "Please, serve some refreshments to my friends."

MACANA, 1. *Car., adj.* Big and solid. *Ese árbol es una macana; nadie lo puede tumbar.* "That tree sure is strong; nobody can knock it down." **2.** *L.Am./S, n.* Something of little value. *¿Y esta macana es todo lo que él te regaló?* "And this piece of crap is all that he gave you?"

MACANO, NA, 1. *U.S., adj.* Cheap, ordinary, crappy. *¡Qué ropa más macana venden en esa tienda!* "What crappy clothing they sell at that store." **2.** *L.Am./S, n.* Something annoying. *Esta reunión es una macana. Nadie sabe por qué estamos aquí.* "This meeting is a piece of crap. Nobody knows why are we here."

MACANUDO, DA, *L.Am., adj.* Euphemism for "cojonudo," great, super, cool. *La nueva moto de Carlos es macanuda.* "Carlos's new cycle is cool."

MACETA, *L.Am./N, n.* Human head. (Lit. Flower pot.) *Estaba oscuro y me pegué en la maceta con la puerta.* "It was dark and I hit my noggin on the door."

MACHACADOR, DORA, *Car., adj.* Person who repeats frequently. *Me has contado lo mismo tres veces, qué machacador eres.* "You told me the same thing three times; what a repeater you are!"

MACHAQUEO, *Car., n.* Insistence. *Tu machaqueo me*

tiene loco, te dije que todavía no me quiero casar. "Harping on the same thing is driving me crazy; I told you I still don't want to get married."

MACHERA (LA), *L.Am./S, adj.* Good, excellent. *El computador que tiene Clara es la machera. Yo quiero uno así.* "The computer that Clara has is the coolest. I want one like that."

MACHERO, RA, *Car., adj. or n.* Joker. *María es tan machaquera que siempre nos hace reír.* "Maria is such a joker that she always makes us laugh."

MACHETE, *L.Am./S, adj.* Interesting. (Lit. Machete.) *Esa novela es bien machete.* "That novel is real cool."

MACHETERO, 1. *L.Am./N, n.* Loader. *Iban dos macheteros arriba del camión cargado con azúcar.* "There were two loaders up on the sugar truck." **2.** *L.Am./N, n.* Student who crams. *Oswaldo se saca puros dieces, pero es muy machetero.* "Oswaldo gets nothing but As, but he is a real crammer."

MACHITO, TA, *L.Am./C, adj. or n.* Blonde. *La novia de Carlos es machita.* "Carlos's girlfriend is blonde."

MACHO, *L.Am./S, adj.* Very strong or severe. (Lit. Male.) *Está haciendo un frío macho, ponte el saco.* "It's damn cold; put on a jacket."

MACHOTE, *L.Am./N, n.* Blank form. *A Domitila le dieron un machote para hacer la solicitud.* "They gave Domitila the boilerplate so she could apply."

MACHUCAR, *L.Am./N, v.* To run over. *Al regresar de la escuela, por poco y me machuca un coche.* "Going back to school, a car almost ran me over."

MACUECO, CA, *U.S., adj.* Left-handed. *Mi nieto es macueco como yo.* "My grandson is left-handed like me."

MADERA, *U.S., n.* Flattery. (Lit. Wood.) *Nancy cree que con madera va a adelantar.* "Nancy believes she will get ahead with flattery." **See also DAR MADERA**

MADRAZO, *L.Am./N, n.* Severe blow, hit, strike. *Oscar se* *enojó tanto que le dio un madrazo al otro.* "Oscar got so angry that he gave the other guy a mother of a punch."

MADRE, 1. *L.Am., n.* Nothing, a screw up, a mess. (Lit. Mother.) *Casi no quedó nada, dejaron la madre.* "There was hardly anything remaining; what they left was a mess." **2.** *L.Am./S., adj.* Very intense or strong. *Tengo un dolor de muela madre.* "I've got a mother of a toothache."

MADREADOR, *L.Am./N, n.* Bouncer, goon. *El hermano mayor de Ezequiel trabaja de madreador en una disco.* "Ezequiel's older brother works as a bouncer at a disco."

MADRECITA, *L.Am./N, n.* Anything of little importance. *Y pensar que con esa madrecita se puede detonar una bomba.* "And to think that that little mother could set off a bomb."

MADRINA, *L.Am./N, n.* Madam. (Lit. Godmother.) *A Rodrigo le gustaba más la madrina que sus chicas.* "Rodrigo liked the madam more than he liked her girls."

MADRINOLA, *L.Am./N, n.* Thingamajig, whachamacallit. *¿Cómo se llama esta madrinola?* "What do you call this thingamajig?"

MAE See MAJE, 1.

MAFUFO, FA, *L.Am./N, adj.* Strange. *No me gusta como se viste Carlos, se ve muy mafufo.* "I don't like the way Carlos dresses; he looks real strange."

MAICERO, RA, *L.Am./C, n.* Hick, country bumpkin. *El nuevo estudiante es muy maicero.* "The new student is a real hick."

MAJA See TIRAR MAJA

MAJADERO, RA, *L.Am./N, adj.* Vulgar, crass. *Ramón es un majadero que no tiene educación.* "Ramon is rude and without manners."

MAJAR, *L.Am./C, v.* To smash, to bruise. *Se majó el pie en la puerta.* "He smashed his foot in the door."

MAJE, 1. *L.Am./C, n.* Term used to greet men and women.

¡Oye maje! ¿Quieres venir conmigo al baile? "Hey, baby! Do you want to go to the dance with me?" **2.** *L.Am./N, adj.* Gullible. *Lupe es tan maje, cree todo lo que le dicen.* "Lupe is so gullible he believes everything they tell him." **See also HACERSE EL MAJE**

MAL LLEVADO, *L.Am./S, idiom.* Angry, nasty. *Pedro es mal llevado y nadie lo soporta.* "Pedro is nasty and nobody can stand him."

MALA PATA, *L.Am./S, idiom.* Bad luck. *¡Qué mala pata! Sólo por un número no me saqué la loto.* "What bad luck! I missed the lotto by one number."

MALACARA, *Car., adj. or n.* Scarface. *El mecánico que arregló mi carro es un malacara.* "The mechanic who fixed my car is a scarface."

MALANDRÍN, *L.Am./N, n.* Criminal, hood, crook. *No vayas a esa zona de noche, hay mucho malandrín.* "Don't go into that area at night; there are a lot of hoodlums."

MALAPAGA, *Car., n.* Deadbeat. *Yo te dije que no le prestaras dinero, él sigue siendo un tremendo malapaga.* "I told you not to lend him any money; he'll keep on being a terrible deadbeat."

MALBARATADOR, DORA, *Car., n.* Spendthrift. *Mi esposa es tan malbaratadora que se gastó todos nuestros ahorros.* "My wife is such a spendthrift that she spent all our savings."

MALDITO, TA, *U.S., adj.* Superior, hot. (Lit. Accursed.) *Daniel no es tan maldito como él cree.* "Daniel is not such hot stuff as he thinks."

MALETEAR, *L.Am./S, v.* To break down. *Perdone mi tardanza. Se me maleteó el auto y tuve que llamar un taxi.* "Sorry I'm late. My car went on the bum and I had to call a taxi."

MALEVO, VA, *L.Am./S, n.* Bum. *Este sitio se volvió peligroso, está lleno de malevos.* "This place has turned dangerous; it's full of bums."

MALILLO, LLA, *L.Am./N, adj.* Ill. *Ofelia se sentía malilla* *y tuvo que ir a su casa.* "Ophelia felt a bit sick and had to go home."

MALINCHISTA, *L.Am./N, n.* Mexican who prefers things from abroad. *Memo es tan malinchista que hasta los calzones los trae de los Estados Unidos.* "Memo is such a lover of foreign things that he even imports his underwear from the United States."

MALOGRADO, DA, *L.Am./S, n.* Drug addict. *Ese malogrado no tiene futuro si no deja las drogas.* "That druggie doesn't have a future if he doesn't quit drugs."

MALOJA, *Car., n.* Marijuana. *Mateo es adicto a la maloja.* "Mateo is addicted to grass."

MALOTE, *Car., n.* Troublemaker. *Pablo en un malote y por eso no lo invitan a ninguna parte.* "Pablo is a smartass and that's why they don't invite him anywhere."

MAMACITA, *L.Am./S, n.* Attractive woman. (Lit. Mommy.) *Me levanté una mamacita camino a la playa.* "I picked up a really good-looking chick on the way to the beach."

MAMADA, 1. *L.Am./N, n.* Fellatio, blow job. *Le preguntó a la prostituta cuánto cobraba por una mamada.* "He asked the prostitute how much she charged for a blow job." **2.** *L.Am./N, n.* Excuse. *Cuando le pedí trabajo a Walterio, me salió con puras mamadas.* "When I asked Walterio for a job, he just gave me excuses."

MAMADO, DA, 1. *L.Am./S, adj.* Drunk. *Dejamos a Julio en casa. Estaba bien mamado.* "We left Julio at his house. He was real stoned." **2.** *L.Am./S, adj.* Tired. *Después de hacer los aeróbicos me quedé mamada.* "After doing aerobics, I was wiped out."

MAMAR, *L.Am./C, v.* To fail a course. *Pepe teme que le van a mamar en sociología.* "Pepe is afraid they are going to flunk him in sociology."

MAMAR GALLO, *L.Am./S, idiom.* To bother, to annoy. *¡Niño, deja de mamar gallo! No me puedo concentrar.* "Boy, stop being a pain! I can't concentrate."

MAMELUCO, 1. *L.Am./S, n.* Overalls. *En esa escuela todos los niños chicos usan mamelucos.* "In that school all the small kids wear overalls." **2.** *L.Am./N, n.* One-piece baby's pajamas. *A Simón le ponían mameluco hasta los ocho años de edad.* "Simon was given one-piece pajamas until he was eight years of age."

MAMERA, *L.Am./S, n.* Something unpleasant, boring. *Esta ópera es una mamera, yo me voy antes de que termine.* "This opera is a drag. I believe I'm going to leave before it's over."

MAMITA, *L.Am./S, n.* Pretty woman. (Lit. Mommy.) *Oye, mamita, tu perfume me enloquece.* "Hey, baby, your perfume is driving me crazy."

MAMÓN, 1. *L.Am./N, n.* Affected, wimpish, sissy. *Los muchachos grandes no dejan a Adrián juntarse con ellos porque es muy mamón.* "The big kids don't let Adrian get together with them because he is a sissy." **2. MAMÓN, NA,** *L.Am./S, adj.* Bothersome, annoying. *El ruido del niño practicando la trompeta es muy mamón.* "The noise of the boy practicing the trumpet is a pain in the butt."

MAMÚA, *L.Am./S, n.* Drunkenness, drunken state. *Tu hermano tenía una mamúa encima anoche, ¿verdad?* "Your brother had a jag on last night, right?"

MAÑA, *L.Am., n.* Trick. *Esta puerta tiene su maña para abrirse.* "There is a trick to opening this door."

MANCAR, *L.Am./S, v.* To make a mistake. *Ya manqué, copié todas las preguntas al revés.* "I screwed up; I copied the questions backwards."

MANCHA, *L.Am./S, n.* Group of friends. (Lit. Spot.) *¿Dónde está toda la mancha? Parece que se los tragó la tierra.* "Where's the crowd? Looks like the ground just swallowed them."

MANCORNA, *L.Am./N, Car., n.* Partner, sidekick. *Voy a ir a Europa con mi mancorna.* "I am going to Europe with my sidekick."

MANDIL, *L.Am./N, n.* Henpecked man. *Arturo es muy*

mandil, siempre está en su casa a las ocho. "Arturo is really under the thumb; he has to be at home at eight o'clock."

MANEJADOR, *U.S., n.* Manager. (From English "manager.") *El manejador de la bodega es mi amigo.* "The warehouse manager is my friend."

MANGA, 1. *L.Am./N, n.* Beautiful woman, fox. (Lit. Sleeve.) *Quiero volver a mi rancho con una manga a mi lado.* "I want to return to the ranch with a good-looking babe at my side." **2.** *L.Am./N, n.* Bunch. *Hay una manga de chicas en ese club.* "There is a bunch of girls at that club." **3.** *L.Am./N, n.* Condom, rubber. *La mujer de Pedro encontró una manga en su billetera.* "Pedro's wife found a rubber in his wallet." **4.** *U.S., adj.* Attractive, sharp-looking. *Tu hermana es muy manga.* "Your sister is a looker."

MANGANTE, *Spain, n.* Thief. *Anoche arrestaron a dos mangantes cerca de mi casa.* "Last night they arrested two thieves close to my home."

MANGAR, 1. *L.Am./S, v.* To ask for something, to hit up. *Mi nieto Antonio me mangó guita para el cine.* "My grandson Antonio hit me up for movie money." **2.** *Spain, v.* To steal. *Cuidado con esos muchachos, porque mangan todo lo que pueden.* "Be careful of those boys, because they steal anything they can."

MANGAZA, *U.S., n.* Shapely girl. *Esa chica es una mangaza.* "That girl is a monument."

MANGO, 1. *L.Am./N, n.* Handsome man, hunk. (Lit. Mango.) *Maribel está saliendo con un mango.* "Maribel is going out with a hunk." **2.** *L.Am./S, n.* Peso. *Che, ¿me podés prestar mil mangos?* "Hey, can you lend me a thousand?" **3.** *L.Am./S, n.* Sol (Peruvian currency). *¿Me prestas dos mangos por favor?* "May I borrow two bucks, please?" **4.** *L.Am./N, n.* Good-looker, knockout. *En ese banco todas las cajeras son unos mangos.* "All the cashiers in that bank are knockouts."

MANGUEAR, *L.Am./S, v.* To obtain something for free.

Con su sonrisa Mercedes manguea todo lo que quiere. "With her smile, Mercedes gets anything she wants."

MANGUERO, RA, *L.Am./S, adj.* Person always asking for, or borrowing, things. *Mi vecina es una manguera, es la última vez que le regalo azúcar.* "My neighbor is a moocher; it's the last time I give her sugar."

MANÍ, *Car., n.* Money. (Lit. Peanut.) *No tengo maní para pagar el arriendo.* "I don't have the cash to pay the rent."

MANILARGO, GA, *L.Am., n.* Moocher. *Te advierto que el manilargo de Julio no va a pagar por nada.* "I warned you that that moocher Julio isn't going to pay for anything."

MANITO, *L.Am./N, n.* Friend, pal, bro. (Lit. Little hand.) *Oye manito, vamos a tomar unas cervezas.* "Listen bro, let's have a few beers."

MANO, *L.Am./N, n.* Brother, friend, pal, buddy. (Lit. Hand.) *Oye, mano, ¿me regalas un cigarro?* "Hey bro, how about giving me a cigarette?" **2.** *Spain, n.* Handy person. *Pedro es una mano, sabe arreglar todo.* "Pedro is a handyman; he knows how to fix everything."

MANO NEGRA, *L.Am./N, n.* Something wrong, something fishy. *Pienso que hay una mano negra en todo esto.* "I think there is something fishy in all of this."

MANO ROTA, *L.Am./N, idiom.* Spendthrift. *Nunca podrás ahorrar ni un sol, por ser tan mano rota.* "You will never be able to save a penny being such a big spender."

MANOLARGA, *Car., adj.* Fond of corporal punishment. *No seas tan manolarga, que los niños te van a coger miedo.* "Don't be so quick with your hand, or the kids will be afraid of you."

MANOPLA, 1. *L.Am./N, n.* Hand. *Andrés le agarró la manopla para no caerse.* "Andres grabbed his hand to keep from falling." **2.** *L.Am./S, n.* Blackjack. *Le pegó con una manopla y le voló los dientes.* "He hit him with a blackjack and broke all his teeth."

MAÑOSO, *L.Am./N, n.* Annoying person. *Rubén es muy*

mañoso, siempre se sale con la suya. "Ruben is a real pain in the neck; he always gets his way."

MANOTAS, *L.Am./N, n.* Thief, crook. *Dejé mi pluma, llegó Manotas y ya no está.* "I left my pen when Mr. Longhand came, and now it's not there anymore."

MANOTEADOR, *L.Am./N, n. crim.* Purse snatcher. *Todos salieron corriendo detrás del manoteador.* "Everyone ran after the purse snatcher."

MANOTEO, *L.Am./N, n., crim.* Theft. *Esa familia vive del manoteo.* "That family lives by stealing."

MANTECA, 1. *Car., n.* Drug. *Me opongo al consumo de manteca.* "I am against drug use." **2.** *L.Am./S, n.* Pretty young woman. *La secretaria de mi jefe es una manteca.* "My boss's secretary is a babe."

MANYAR, *L.Am./S, v.* To look. *Estuve manyando a ese tipo que parecía medio raro.* "I was checking out this dude who looked a bit strange."

MARACA, *U.S., n.* Dollar bill. *Pagan muchas maracas en esa fábrica.* "They pay a lot of bucks at that factory."

MARCAR, *L.Am./S, v.* To kiss. (Lit. To mark.) *Hoy los jóvenes marcan en pleno público, antes era mal mirado.* "Nowadays young people kiss in public, whereas in the past it was frowned upon."

MARCHAMO, *L.Am./C, n.* Vehicle tax sticker. *El policía me puso un parte porque no tenía el marchamo.* "The cop gave me a ticket because I didn't have the tax sticker."

MARÍA, 1. *L.Am./C, n.* Taxi meter. *Ese taxista tiene la maría estropeada y cobra lo que quiere.* "That taxi driver has a broken meter and he's charging what he wants." **2.** *Spain, n.* Marijuana. *Los hombres llevaban 100 kilos de María en su camión.* "The men had 100 kilos of Mary Jane in their truck."

MARIACHI, *L.Am./N, adj.* Incapable, unskilled. (Lit. Mariachi.) *El plomero me salió bien mariachi. Todavía tengo fugas.* "The plumber turned out to be a botcher—I still have leaks."

MARICA, 1. *Spain, n.* Effeminate male. *Juan tiene gestos de marica.* "Juan has the gestures of a fairy." **2.** *L.Am., Spain, n.* Homosexual. *Había un grupo de maricas en la feria. Tenían mucho talento para el baile.* "There was a group of fairies at the fair. They were very skilled at dancing."

MARICADA, *L.Am./S, n.* Stupidity. *Hizo la maricada de perder mi pasaje.* "He did the stupid thing of losing my ticket."

MARICÓN, 1. *L.Am., Spain, n.* Homosexual, fag. *Dicen que muchos maricones frecuentan ese bar.* "They say that a lot of fags frequent that bar." **2.** *L.Am., Spain, n.* Effeminate male. *Mira al maricón ese, camina igual que una mujer.* "Look at that fairy; he walks just like a woman. **3.** *L.Am., Spain, n.* Wimp. *Es muy maricón Tirso, siempre le llora a su esposa.* "Tirso is a real wimp. He is always whining to his wife."

MARICONA, *L.Am., Spain, n.* Lesbian. *Sospechan que esa muchacha es maricona.* "They suspect that that girl is a lezzie.

MARIGUANO, NA, *Car., adj. or n.* Marijuana user or dealer. *Estoy segura de que ese amigo tuyo es un mariguano.* "I am sure that that friend of yours is a pothead."

MARIMACHO, CHA, *L.Am./N, n.* Lesbian. *Josefa es tan marimacha que hasta tiene voz de hombre.* "Josefa is such a butch; she even has the voice of a man."

MARIMBA, *L.Am./S, n.* Marijuana. *Empezó a fumar marimba desde que se juntó con esos muchachos.* "He began to smoke pot when he got together with those boys."

MARIPOSILLA, *L.Am./N, n.* Prostitute. *Está bonita la muchacha, lástima que es mariposilla.* "The girl is pretty; what a shame she is a hooker."

MARIPOSÓN, *L.Am./N, n.* Effeminate. *Por su forma de caminar, se nota que es mariposón el muchacho.* "By his way of walking, you can tell the fellow is a fairy."

MARISCAL DE CAMPO, *L.Am./N, n.* Quarterback. *En el*

fútbol americano el mariscal de campo es elemento crucial. "In American football, the quarterback is a critical element."

MARMAJA, *L.Am./N, n.* Money. *Había mucha marmaja en la mesa de póquer.* "There was a lot of money on the poker table."

MARRO, *L.Am./N, n.* Cheapskate, tightwad. *A César todos lo conocen por marro.* "Everybody knows Cesar as a tightwad."

MARTILLAR, *L.Am./S, v.* To borrow, to pester for things. (Lit. To hammer.) *¡Deja de martillarme, Juan!* "Stop pestering me, Juan!"

MARTILLO, *L.Am./S, n.* Person who is always borrowing or asking for things, a moocher, a freeloader. (Lit. Hammer.) *Luisa es muy martillo.* "Luisa's a real freeloader."

MÁS PAPISTA QUE EL PAPA, *L.Am., idiom.* Holier-than-thou. *Siempre predicando, eres más papista que el papa.* "Always preaching, what a holier-than-thou person you are!"

MATABURROS, *U.S., n.* Dictionary. *El americano va a todas partes con su mataburros.* "Americans go everywhere with a dictionary."

MATADERO, *L.Am., n.* Automobile graveyard. (Lit. Slaughterhouse.) *Mi pobre carrito pronto va a terminar en el matadero.* "My poor little car will end up soon in the junkyard."

MATADURA, *Car., n.* Debt. *Tengo que pagar esta matadura antes del fin de mes.* "I've got to pay this debt before the end of the month."

MATAPERRO, *L.Am./S, n.* Misbehaving child. *El sobrino de Tomás es un mataperro.* "Thomas's nephew is a pain."

MATASANOS, *L.Am./N, n.* Physician, surgeon. *La mamá de Hilda fue al matasanos.* "Hilda's mom went to the quack."

MATEO, *L.Am./S, n.* Person who studies excessively, bookworm. *Jorge era el mateo de nuestra promoción.* "Jorge was the bookworm of our class."

MATRACA, 1. *L.Am./N, n. crim.* Machine gun. (Lit. Rattle.) *La policía encontró tres matracas y diez pistolas en la casa.* "The police found three machine guns and ten pistols at the house." **2.** *L.Am./N, n.* Old car, jalopy. *La matraca de Eduardo ya no anda.* "Eduardo's jalopy doesn't run anymore." **3.** *L.Am./S, n.* Bribe. *Si le das una pequeña matraca te deja entrar.* "If you give him a little something, he'll let you in."

MATRAQUEAR, *L.Am./S, v.* To bribe. *Si me para el oficial, lo voy a tratar de matraquear.* "If the officer stops me, I'll try to grease his palm."

MATRICÚLATE, *L.Am./S, idiom.* Hurry up! *Matricúlate rápido con la dolorosa.* "Hurry up with the check."

MAYATE, 1. *L.Am./N, n.* Effeminate homosexual. *Pasó el mayate y todos los muchachos empezaron a silbar.* "The fairy went by and all the fellas began to whistle." **2.** *L.Am./N, n.* Pejorative term for a black person used in Mexico and the United States. *El amigo de Luis es mayate de los Estados Unidos.* "Luis's friend is a black from the States."

MAYATIVO, VA, *L.Am./N, adj.* Loud. *El novio de Estela traía una camisa muy mayativa.* "Estela's boyfriend was wearing a very loud shirt."

MEAR AGUA BENDITA, *Spain, idiom.* Very religious or sanctimonious person. (Lit. To pee holy water.) *Isabel es tan religiosa que tiene que mear agua bendita.* "Isabel is so pious she must pee holy water."

MEAR FUERA DEL TARRO, *L.Am./N, idiom.* To be wrong, to be off base. *Oye mano, estás meando fuera del tarro. No soy yo quien le dijo.* "Listen bro, you're way off base. It wasn't me who told him."

MECATE, *L.Am./N, adj.* Rough, unpolished. *El novio de Juanita es bien mecate pero buena gente.* "Juanita's boyfriend is rough around the edges, but not a bad sort."

MECHADERA, *L.Am./S, n.* Fight. *Hubo una tremenda mechadera en el estadio anoche.* "There was a big fight in the stadium last night."

MECO, *L.Am./N, adj.* Crude, uncivilized. *¡Qué meco es el nuevo administrador!* "What an animal the new administrator is!"

MEDIA (LA), *L.Am./S, idiom.* Big. *Hoy tuve la media tarea en el trabajo.* "Today I had the big assignment at work."

MEDIA GAMBA, *Spain, idiom.* Fifty pesetas. *Eso me costó media gamba.* "That cost me half a hundred."

MEDIA NARANJA, *L.Am./S, idiom.* One's wife, significant other, better half. *Antes de darte la respuesta tengo que consultar con mi media naranja.* "Before giving you the answer, I have to check with my better half."

MEDIA TEJA, *L.Am./C, n.* Fifty-colon note. *Sólo tenía media teja en el bolsillo cuando lo encontraron.* "He only had a 50-colon note in his pocket when they found him."

MEJICLE, *U.S., n.* Mexico. *¡Oye carnal! ¿Vamos para Mejicle?* "Listen bro! Shall we go to Mexico?"

MELÓN, *Spain, n.* Head. (Lit. Melon.) *El calor me hizo doler el melón.* "The heat gave me a headache."

MELONES, *L.Am., Spain, pl. n.* Woman's breasts. (Lit. Melons.) *Nadie tiene melones como los de María.* "Nobody has melons like Mary."

MENSACA, *Spain, n.* Messenger. *Dile al mensaca que lleve estos documentos al banco.* "Tell the messenger to take these documents to the bank."

MENSO, SA, *U.S., adj. or n.* Ignorant, stupid person. *¿Tu hermano dejó la escuela? ¡Qué menso!* "Your brother quit school? What a fool!"

MENUDO, *L.Am./C, n.* Small change. *Le tuve que dar un billete grande porque no tenía menudo.* "I had to give a large bill because I didn't have small change."

MEÓDROMO, *Spain, n.* Urinal. *Necesito usar el meódromo.* "I need to use the pisser."

MERA, *L.Am./C, n.* Luck. *¡Qué mera! El camión se paró a unos centímetros de mí.* "What luck! The truck stopped just inches from me."

MERCO, *L.Am./S, n.* Food. *¿Está listo el merco mamá?* "Is the food ready, Mom?"

MERENGAR, *Spain, v.* To annoy, to bother. *No me empieces a merengar porque te pego.* "Don't start bugging me or I will hit you."

MERLUZA, *Spain, n.* Drunkenness. (Lit. Hake.) *La merluza de anoche fue la peor de mi vida.* "Last night's binge was the worst of my life."

MERLUZO, ZA, *Spain, adj.* Stupid, silly. *El merluzo de tu novio siempre cuenta malos chistes.* "That silly boyfriend of yours is always telling bad jokes."

MERO, *U.S., adj.* The very one. *Ese es el mero bato de quién te dije.* "That guy is the very dude I told you about."

MERO MERO, *U.S., n.* The big boss, the chief. *Mi hijo es el mero mero de la oficina.* "My son is top dog at the office."

METEPATAS, *Spain, n.* Person who always does or says the wrong thing. *Ojalá Pilar no hable porque es una metepatas.* "God willing Pilar won't talk, because she sticks her foot in her mouth."

METER CABALLO, *U.S., idiom.* To criticize someone, to bad-mouth, to be on someone's back, to be on someone's case. *Hermano, siempre estás metiendo caballo a tu hijo y eso no está bien.* "Brother, you are always on your son's back, and that's not right."

METER COMBO, *L.Am./S, idiom.* To hit someone. *Percy le metió un combo a Pepe por nada.* "Percy whacked Pepe for the hell of it."

METER EL CHOCLO, *L.Am./N, idiom.* To stick one's foot in it. *Ya metiste el choclo. No has debido decirle lo de la fiesta.* "Now you stuck your foot in it. You shouldn't have told him about the party."

METER EL SESO, *Spain, idiom.* To think. *Tengo que meter el seso para tomar una decisión.* "I have to put my thinking cap on to decide."

METER LA HABANA EN GUANABACOA, *Car., idiom.* To jam something in where it doesn't fit. *Cada vez que vas a comprarte zapatos, quieres meter La Habana en Guanabacoa.* "Every time you want to buy shoes you want to squeeze a gallon of water in a thimble."

METER LA PATA, *L.Am./S, v.* To do or to say something wrong. *Metí la pata cuando critiqué a Pepe frente a su mamá.* "I screwed up when I criticized Pepe in front of his mother."

METER LA UÑA, *L.Am./N, idiom, crim.* To rob, to steal. *Despidieron a Pepe por meter la uña en la caja.* "They fired Pepe for sticking his fingers in the cash register."

METER LOMO, *L.Am./S, idiom.* To work hard, to put forth an effort, to plug away. *Dicen que metiendo lomo se logra el éxito.* "They say that plugging away is the road to success."

METERSE A, *L.Am., idiom.* To become something. *Mi hijo se quiere meter a sacerdote.* "My son wants to become a priest."

METERSE EN CAMISA DE ONCE VARAS, *L.Am., idiom.* To get in over one's head. *Óscar se metió en camisa de once varas. Eso le pasa por meterse a hacer un trabajo del que no sabe nada.* "Oscar got in over his head. That's what happens when you try to do a job you know nothing about."

METÉRSELE, *L.Am./S, prnl. v.* To get a particular idea or thought. *A Bety se le metió que el jefe la odia.* "Bety got it into her head that the boss hates her."

METETE, *L.Am./S, n.* Busybody, meddler. *Este es un metete que en todo quiere intervenir.* "This guy is such a meddler, he wants to participate in everything."

METIDO, DA, *L.Am., adj.* Meddlesome. *No preguntes*

tanto, no seas metida. "Don't ask so much; don't be so nosy."

MICA, *L.Am./S, n.* Shirt. *¡Oye, cumpa, esa mica vio mejores días.* "Hey buddy, your shirt is too worn-out."

MICHICATO, *L.Am./S, n.* Tightwad. *No le gusta gastar nunca, es un michicato.* "He doesn't like to spend anything. He is a cheapskate."

MICROBIO, *Spain, n.* Small child. (Lit. Microbe.) *Todas las mamás van a traer a sus microbios.* "All the mothers are going to bring their small fry."

MIEDITIS AGUDITIS, *L.Am., idiom.* Very fearful. *Tengo mieditis aguditis porque mañana es mi operación.* "I am scared to death because tomorrow is my operation."

¡MIÉRCOLES!, *L.Am./S, interj.* Euphemism for "mierda" (shit). *¡Miércoles! ¡Quemé todo el documento!* "Shoot! I deleted the whole document."

MIERDA, 1. *L.Am./S, adj. or n.* Bad or mean person. *Mi jefe es una mierda, me hace trabajar horas extras y no me paga.* "My boss is a shit; he makes me work overtime and never pays me." **2.** *Spain, L.Am., n.* Filth, shit, crap. *La casa de los drogatos estaba llena de mierda.* "The drug house was full of shit." **3.** *Spain, L.Am., n.* Something of poor quality. *Este televisor nunca funciona bien, es una mierda.* "This TV never works right; it's a piece of shit."

MIERDOSO, SA, *L.Am./S, Spain, adj. or n.* Despicable. *Clara está aburrida porque el jefe es un mierdoso.* "Clara is bored because she's got a shitty boss."

MIGRA, *U.S., n.* Immigration and Naturalization Service, immigration agent. *La migra llevó a mi compadre para deportarlo.* "Immigration took my buddy away to deport him."

MILICO, *L.Am./S, n., mil.* Soldier. *Gustavo, el primo de Paco, es milico.* "Gustavo, Paco's cousin, is a G.I."

MILLONETIS, *Spain, adj.* Rich, wealthy. *Los padres de mi esposo son millonetis.* "My husband's parents are in the clover."

MINA, *L.Am./S, n.* Woman. (Lit. Mine.) *Vamos a la playa a mirar las minas.* "Let's go to the beach to dig the babes."

MINGO, A, *Car., n.* Best friend. *El mingo de Daniel vive a tres cuadras de mi casa.* "Daniel's best buddy lives three blocks from my house."

MINÓN, *L.Am./S, adj. or n.* Beautiful woman. *Me voy a casar con una minón.* "I am going to marry a fox."

MIRÓN, NA, *L.Am., n.* Ogler. *No seas tan mirón, Juan, respétame un poco.* "Don't be such an ogler, Juan; have a little respect for me."

MISHIADURA, *L.Am./S, n.* Poverty. *Ya no aguanto vivir en esta mishiadura.* "I can't stand living in this misery."

MISIO, *L.Am./S, adj.* Poor. *Él nunca tiene dinero, siempre está misio.* "He never has money. He is always broke."

MITRA, *L.Am./S, n.* Head. (Lit. Miter.) *Se cayó del segundo piso y se rompió la mitra.* "He fell from the second floor and broke his head."

MOCHAR, *U.S., v.* To mooch. *Pepe siempre me está mochando cigarros.* "Pepe is always mooching cigars from me."

MOCHILA, *Spain, n.* Hunchback. (Lit. Backpack.) *Si sigues caminando así, te vas a volver mochila.* "If you keep walking like that, you'll become a hunchback."

MOCHO, CHA, *L.Am., adj.* One-armed. *El detective estaba buscando un hombre mocho.* "The detective was looking for a one-armed man."

MOCO, 1. *Spain, n.* Exaggeration. (Lit. Mucus.) *Esa historia tiene que ser un moco.* "That story has to be an exaggeration." **2.** *L.Am./S, idiom.* A little money. *Gano un moco después de la escuela.* "I make a few bucks after school."

MOCOSO, SA, *L.Am./S, n.* Child. *Estos mocosos no se cansan de fregar la paciencia.* "These kids won't stop bugging."

MOGOLLÓN, *Spain, n.* Large amount. *Tengo un mogollón*

de trabajo increíble. "I've got an unbelievable pile of work."

MOJADO, DA, *L.Am./N, n.* Wetback. (Lit. Wet.) *Le arrestaron al otro lado por ser mojado.* "They arrested him on the other side for being a wetback."

MOJAR EL BIZCOCHO, *Spain, idiom.* For a male to have sex. *He pasado un mes sin mojar el bizcocho.* "I've gone a month without dipping my stick."

MOJONERO, RA, *L.Am./S, n.* Teller of tall tales. *No puedes creerle a Marisa porque es muy mojonera.* "You can't believe Marisa because she's full of bull."

MOJOSO, *Car., n.* Dominican peso. *¿Cuántos mojosos pagaste por tu casa nueva?* "How many pesos did you pay for your new house?"

MOLESTAR, *L.Am./S, v.* To court, to woo. (Lit. To bother.) *Un muchacho está molestando a Paty desde hace un mes.* "That boy has been wooing Patty for a month now."

MOLLEJÚO, JÚA, *L.Am./S, adj.* Full to the rim, overflowing, complete. *No te exagero, me pusieron un plato mollejúo de camarones.* "I'm not exaggerating, they served me a plate overflowing with shrimp."

MOLÓN, NA, *Spain, adj.* Pretty, attractive. *La vecina nueva está molona. Tengo que conocerla.* "The new neighbor is a fox. I've got to meet her."

MONA, *L.Am./S, Spain, n.* Drunkenness. (Lit. Female monkey.) *Es la segunda mona de esta semana, no tomes más.* "It's the second spree you had this week. Don't drink anymore."

MOÑA, 1. *Spain, n.* Drunkenness. *El sábado agarré una moña horrible.* "Saturday I got into a huge drunk." **2.** *Spain, n.* Effeminate, homosexual. *El andar de Ricardo es como de moña.* "Ricardo's walk is like a fairy's."

MONDONGUERO, RA, *Car., n.* Vulgar or crass individual. *Esa mujer es una mondonguera, no la invites más.* "That woman is a gross-out. Don't invite her anymore."

MONGA, *L.Am./S, adj.* Silly (girl). *La pobre era tan monga que cayó redondita en la trampa.* "The poor woman was so dippy she fell right into the trap."

MONO, 1. *L.Am./S, n.* Foul-mouthed, unkempt person. (Lit. Monkey.) *El primo de Lola es un mono.* "Lola's cousin is a scuzzo." **2. MONO, NA,** *L.Am./S, n. or adj.* Blonde, light-skinned. *Los hijos de Rogelio son monos porque la madre es sueca.* "Rogelio's children are towheads because their mother is Swedish." **3.** *Spain, n.* Uniformed police officer, cop. *Algo pasó allá porque hay muchos monos al frente.* "Something happened there because there are a lot of cops out in front."

MONSE, *L.Am./S, adj.* Slow, dense. *¿No te das cuenta que tú le gustas a ella? No seas monse.* "Don't you see that she likes you? Don't be so dense."

MONTADO, *L.Am./C, n.* One who takes advantage of others, freeloader. (Lit. Mounted.) *Guido es un montado. Le invité por un fin de semana y se quedó un mes.* "Guido is a freeloader; I invited him for a weekend and he stayed a month."

MONTAJE, *L.Am., n.* Farce, scam, setup. (Lit. Montage.) *Todo ese negocio es un montaje.* "All that business is a setup."

MONTAR, *L.Am./C, v.* To take advantage of someone. (Lit. To mount.) *Víctor es uno que va montando siempre.* "Victor is one who always goes around freeloading."

MONTAR CEREBRO, *Car., idiom.* To fantasize. *No te rinde en el trabajo porque te lo pasas montando cerebro.* "You don't perform on the job because you spend your time daydreaming."

MONTARSE UNA HISTORIA, *Spain, idiom.* To invent a story. *Tuve que montarme una historia para poder faltar al trabajo.* "I had to make up a story to miss work."

MONTÁRSELA, *L.Am./S, prnl. v.* To insistently bother another with something. *Se la monté a Enrique por la bobada que dijo el otro día.* "I kept on bugging Enrique about the stupid thing he said the other day."

MONUMENTO, *L.Am., n.* Beautiful woman. (Lit. Monument.) *La modelo de ese comercial es un monumento.* "The model in that commercial is a goddess."

MORA, *U.S., n., crim.* Juvenile detention center. *Julio sale de la mora mañana.* "Julio gets out of juvenile tomorrow."

MORALLA, *L.Am./N, n.* Small change. *¿Tienes moralla para el teléfono?* "Do you have change for the telephone?"

MORDIDA, *L.Am./N, n., crim.* Bribe. (Lit. Bite.) *Hoy en día no te piden tanta mordida como antes.* "Nowadays they don't ask you for a bribe as much as they used to."

MORFAR, *L.Am./S, v.* To eat. *Mi tía nos invitó a morfar a su casa mañana.* "My aunt invited us to chow down at her house tomorrow."

MORFI, *L.Am./S, n.* Food. *Paremos aquí para comprar morfi.* "Let's stop here to buy some chow."

MORLACO, *L.Am./N, n.* Money, cash. *Tuve que darle todo el morlaco que tenía.* "I had to give him all the money I had."

MOROCHO, CHA, 1. *L.Am./S, adj.* Dark-haired. *La mujer de Néstor es una morocha muy alta.* "Nestor's wife is a tall brunette." **2.** *L.Am./N, adj. or n.* Black person. *Mi papá no quiere a mi novio por ser morocho.* "My father doesn't like my boyfriend because he is black."

MORRA, *L.Am./S, n.* Leg. *Me duele la morra.* "My leg hurts."

MORREO, *Spain, n.* Passionate kissing. *Cuando entré estaban en pleno morreo.* "When I went in they were sucking face."

MORRIÑA, *Car., n.* Jealous rage. *A mi novio le dio la morriña cuando me vio bailando con otro.* "My boyfriend went into a rage when he saw me dancing with another."

MORROCOTUDO, DA, 1. *L.Am., adj.* Impressive. *El dis-*

curso del presidente fué morrocotudo. "The president's speech was something else." **2.** *L.Am./N, adj.* Big, strong. *Para este trabajo se necesita un tipo morrocotudo.* "For this job you need to be a big strong guy." **3.** *L.Am./N, adj.* Great, fantastic. *Ese concierto fue morrocotudo.* "That concert was fantastic."

MOSAICO, *L.Am./S, n.* Waiter, waitress. *Pídele la cuenta al mosaico.* "Ask the waiter for the check."

MOSCA, 1. *Car., n.* Annoyance. (Lit. Fly.) *Esa música tuya es una mosca, no la resisto.* "That music of yours is a pain; I can't stand it." **2.** *L.Am./N, n.* Moocher, sponger. *No seas mosca Ramón. Te dije que no tengo dinero.* "Don't be a sponger, Ramon; I told you I don't have any money." **3.** *L.Am./S, n.* Fast person. *Liliana es super mosca, a ella no se le escapa ninguno.* "Lillian is super fast; nothing gets by her." **4.** *L.Am., adj.* Angry. *Se puso mosca por lo que le dije.* "He got pissed at what I said." **5.** *L.Am./N, n.* Money. *No tengo mosca para comprarte el regalo.* "I don't have the dough to buy you the gift."

MOSCA MUERTA, *L.Am./S, idiom.* One who appears to be innocent or naive. *No te hagas la mosca muerta. Tú sabes muy bien lo que hiciste.* "Don't play the innocent with me. You know very well what you did."

MOSQUEARSE, *L.Am., prnl. v.* To get angry. *Mi esposo se mosqueó cuando salí sin avisarle.* "My husband got teed off when I left without telling him."

¡MOSTRO!, *L.Am./S, interj.* Expression of joy. *¡Mostro que pudiste venir a la fiesta!* "Great that you could come to the party!"

MOTE, *L.Am./S, n.* Accent. *Este gringo tiene un tremendo mote.* "This Anglo has a thick accent."

MOTIVITO, *Car., n.* Party, get-together. *Vamos a celebrar tu cumpleaños con un motivito.* "Let's celebrate your birthday with a little get-together."

MOTOLA, *L.Am./S, n.* Head. *Me duele mucho la motola.* "My noggin hurts a lot."

MOTOSEAR, *L.Am./S, v.* To take a nap. *No hables fuerte, que Paco está motoseando.* "Don't talk so loud. Paco is cutting Zs."

MOTOSO, *L.Am./S, n.* Short nap. *Estoy cansadísima, voy a echarme un motoso.* "I am really tired; I am going to take a little siesta."

MOVER EL BIGOTE, *Spain, idiom.* To eat, to chow down. *Vamos a casa de mi hermana a mover el bigote.* "Let's go to my sister's to chow down."

MOVIDA, 1. *L.Am., n.* Action. (Lit. Move.) *Esa película tuvo mucha movida.* "That movie had plenty of action." **2.** *L.Am., n.* Situation. *¿Cómo va la movida?* "What's doing?" **3.** *L.Am., n.* Shady business. *Me propuso una movida y le dije que no.* "He proposed a shady deal to me and I said no."

MUCHACHA, *L.Am., Spain, n.* Maid. (Lit. Young woman.) *Hoy no vino la muchacha a planchar.* "Today the maid didn't come to iron."

MUCHITANGA, *Car., n.* Crowd. *La muchitanga en el concierto era tal que no pudimos entrar.* "The crowd at the concert was such that we couldn't go in."

MUEBLE, *L.Am./N, n.* Vehicle. (Lit. Furniture.) *Mi mueble no arrancó esta mañana.* "My car didn't start this morning."

MUERTO, *L.Am./S, n.* A bad debt. (Lit. Dead.) *Tengo un muerto que no voy a poder pagar.* "I've got a bad debt that I am not going to be able to pay."

MUFOSO, SA, *L.Am./S, adj.* Annoyed or upset. *Claudia vive mufosa sin razón.* "Claudia is always annoyed without reason."

MUJER DE LA VIDA, *L.Am., Spain, idiom.* Prostitute. *Todas las de esa familia son mujeres de la vida.* "All the women in that family are ladies of the night."

MULA, 1. *L.Am./S, adj.* Fake, false. (Lit. Male.) *Los Levis que lleva Antonio son mulas.* "The Levi's Antonio is wearing are fakes." **2.** *L.Am./S., n.* Money. *Lo siento, no* *tenemos suficiente mula para ir a Miami de vacaciones.* "I'm sorry, we don't have enough green to go to Miami on vacation." **3.** *L.Am./S., n.* Head. *Le pegaron durísimo en la mula y perdió el conocimiento.* "They hit him hard on the noodle and he lost consciousness."

MULLAR, *Spain, v.* To kill. *Descubrieron que la mafia quiere mullar al ministro.* "They discovered that the Mafia wanted to bump the minister off."

MULO, *U.S., n.* Money. *No tengo mulo ni para una cerveza.* "I don't even have money for a beer."

N

NALGAMEN, *Spain, n.* Buttocks. *Mariela tiene un nalgamen de muerte.* "Mariela has an ass to die for."

ÑAME, *L.Am./S, n.* Foot. *Me duelen los ñames.* "My dogs are hurting."

ÑANGO, *L.Am./N, adj.* Skinny, weak. *Estás muy ñango, Fernando.* "You're real skinny, Fernando."

ÑAPA, *L.Am./S, n.* Extra. *El panadero me dio tres panes de ñapa.* "The baker gave me three extra loaves."

NARCO, *Car., n.* Undercover drug agent. *El narco descubrió la operación de los mafiosos.* "The narc discovered the Mafia operation."

NARIZOTAS, *L.Am., adj.* Big-nosed. *Fíjate en el novio de Mary, es un narizotas.* "Mary's boyfriend is a big-nosed guy."

NATA, *Car., adj.* Excellent. (Lit. Cream.) *El libro que acabé de leer es una nata.* "The book that I just read is a winner."

NAVE, *L.Am./C, n.* Car. (Lit. Ship.) *Tengo la nave en el taller.* "I've got my wheels at the shop."

NEGREAR, *L.Am./S, v.* To exclude, to ignore. *Negrearon a Julio al no invitarlo a la fiesta.* "They put Julio on the black list when they didn't invite him to the party."

NERDO, *L.Am./C, n.* Nerd. (From English "nerd.") *Hay un grupo de nerdos en mi clase.* "There's a group of nerds in my class."

ÑERO, *L.Am./S, n.* Homeless person, bum. *Me da pesar cuando veo a los ñeros andando para un lado y otro.* "I feel so bad when I see the homeless walking back and forth."

NI BORRACHO, *L.Am., idiom.* No way. *No veré esa película ni borracho.* "There's no way that I'll go see that movie."

NI CAGANDO See NI BORRACHO

¡NI DE VAINAS!, *L.Am./S, idiom.* Emphatically no. No way! *¡Ni de vainas voy a dejarte usar el auto esta noche!* "There's no way I'm going to let you use the car tonight!"

NI FOLLA, *Spain, idiom.* Nothing, not a fucking thing. *No hay ni folla que tomar en esta casa.* "There isn't a fucking thing to drink in this house."

NI MU, *L.Am., idiom.* Absolutely nothing. *El pobre Santiago no sabe ni mu.* "Poor Santiago doesn't know crap."

NICA, *L.Am./C, n.* Nicaraguan. *El novio de Nerina es nica.* "Nerina's boyfriend is a Nicaraguan."

NICHE, *L.Am./S, adj.* Tasteless, unsophisticated. *¿Por qué llevas esa camisa niche?* "What are you wearing that hick shirt for?"

NICLE, *U.S., n.* Nickel, five-cent coin. (From English "nickel.") *No tengo ni un nicle.* "I don't even have a nickel."

NIEVE, *L.Am./N, n.* Ice cream. (Lit. Snow.) *Vamos a tomar una copa de nieve.* "Let's have a dish of ice cream."

NIGUA, *Car., adj.* Short (person). *Todos los hombres de mi familia son niguas.* "All the men in my family are shorties."

NIÑAS, *L.Am./S, pl. n.* Loose women. (Lit. Girls.) *No camines tan tarde por la Avenida Arequipa porque te pueden confundir con una de las niñas.* "Don't walk so late down Arequipa Avenue because you might be mistaken for one of the streetwalkers."

NIÑO, ÑA DE PAPÁ, *L.Am., Spain, idiom.* Daddy's boy/girl. *María siempre ha sido una niña de papá.* "Maria has always been a daddy's girl."

¡ÑO!, *Car., n.* Euphemism for "coño," as "shoot" is a euphemism for "shit" in English. *¡Ño! ¡Qué martillazo me di en el dedo!* "Shoot! What a blow I got on my finger!"

NO COMERSE NI UNA ROSCA, *L.Am., idiom.* Unable to make it with anyone. *Tengo mala suerte con las mujeres, no me como ni una rosca.* "I have bad luck with women; I can't make it with anybody."

NO DAR UN GOLPE, *Car., idiom.* To be lazy, to be a bum. *Pedro no da un golpe, sólo quiere dormir y ver televisión.* "Pedro doesn't do a lick. He just wants to sleep and watch television."

NO EMBETUNAR LOS ZAPATOS (A ALGUIEN), *L.Am./C, idiom.* To be inferior. *Mateo no le embetuna los zapatos a Don Julio.* "Mateo isn't worthy of even shining Don Julio's shoes."

NO ESTOY NI AHÍ, *L.Am./S, idiom.* I couldn't care less. *"¿Sabes que le dieron tu trabajo a Clara?" "No estoy ni ahí."* " 'Did you know that they gave your job to Clara?' 'I couldn't care less.' "

NO HABER MAS CÁSCARAS, *Spain, idiom.* There is no alternative, no solution. *Estamos entre la espada y la pared, no hay más cáscaras.* "We are between a rock and a hard place; there is no other way."

NO TENER MALOS BIGOTES, *L.Am./N, idiom.* Euphemism for beautiful woman. *No tiene malos bigotes la nueva doctora.* "The new doctor isn't bad looking."

NO TENER PELOS EN LA LENGUA, *L.Am., Spain, idiom.* To say what one thinks, to talk straight. *Isabel dice las verdades con todas sus letras. No tiene pelos en la lengua.* "Isabel talks straight. She says what she thinks."

NO TRAGAR (A ALGUIEN), *L.Am., Spain, idiom.* To dislike someone, to not be able to stand someone. *María dice que su mamá no me traga porque soy feo.* "Maria says that her mother can't stand me because I am ugly."

NO VALER NI UN CARAJO, *L.Am., idiom.* Not worth a damn. *Tu opinión no vale ni un carajo.* "You're opinion isn't worth dick."

NO VALER UN CACAHUATE, *U.S., idiom.* To not be worth a damn. *Esa casa no vale un cacahuate.* "That house isn't worth a damn."

ÑONGO, *Car., n.* Jerk, stupid. *Nena no se da cuenta de que su hijo es un ñongo.* "Nena doesn't realize that her son is a jerk."

¡NONINES!, *Car., interj.* No! *¡Nonines! No te puedo comprar eso ahora.* "No! I can't buy you that now."

ÑOÑO, ÑA, 1. *L.Am./N, adj.* Old-fashioned, passé. *Esa muchacha es muy ñoña.* "That girl is very old-fashioned." **2.** *Car., adj.* Spoiled. *El niñito de los Ramírez en un ñoño.* "The Ramirez's little boy is a spoiled brat."

NOQUEAR, *L.Am., v.* To knock out. (From English "knock out.") *Tengo ganas de noquear a ese estúpido.* "I feel like KOing that idiot."

ÑORSA, *L.Am./S, n.* Lady. *Esa ñorsa es la madre de mi mejor amigo.* "That lady is my best friend's mother."

NOS BÉLMONT See NOS VIDRIOS

NOS VIDRIOS, *L.Am./S, idiom.* (Play on Spanish "nos vemos.") Good-bye. *Nos vidrios mañana.* "See you tomorrow."

NOTA, *L.Am./S, adj., youth.* Excellent, great, cool. (Lit. Note.) *Los zapatos nuevos que compré son una nota.* "The new shoes I bought are so cool."

NOVELERO, RA, *L.Am./S, n.* Gossip. *Ese Pancho es un novelero de primera.* "Pancho is a first-class gossip."

OCLAYOS, *L.Am./N, pl. n.* Eyes, peepers. *No sé qué tiene en los oclayos que debe usar lentes.* "I don't know what's wrong with his eyes, but he has to use glasses."

OCOTERO, *L.Am./N, n.* Troublemaker. *El hermano de Armando es muy ocotero.* "Armando's brother is a real troublemaker."

OJAL, *L.Am., n.* Anus, asshole. (Lit. Buttonhole.) *Me tengo que meter el supositorio por el ojal.* "I've got to stick the suppository you know where."

OJEROSO, *L.Am./N, n.* Coward. *No seas ojeroso Lorenzo, ese perro no te hace nada.* "Don't be a chicken, Lorenzo, that dog won't do anything to you."

OJETE, 1. *Spain, n.,* Anus, asshole. *¡Si no le gusta, métaselo por el ojete!* "If you don't like it, stick it up your ass!" **2.** *L.Am./N, n.* Mean, terrible person. *Gabriel es un ojete, no quiso dejarme jugar con su balón.* "Gabriel is a meany, he didn't want me to play with his ball."

OJO A LA FUNERALA, *Spain, idiom.* Black eye. *El esposo le puso un ojo a la funerala.* "Her husband gave her a shiner."

OJO AL CRISTO, *L.Am./C, idiom.* Look out! *¡Ojo al Cristo! Hay peligro en esa zona.* "Look out! There is danger in that area."

OJOS, *L.Am./N, pl. n.* Money. *No puedo ir a la tienda* *porque sin ojos no llego lejos.* "I can't go to the store because without cash I won't go far."

OLER A RAYOS, *L.Am., idiom.* To stink. *Este baño huele a rayos.* "This bathroom stinks!"

OLERSE ALGO, *L.Am., v.* To suspect. *No le dijimos a Ernesto que íbamos, para que no fuera a olerse lo de la fiesta.* "We didn't tell Ernesto we were going so that he wouldn't get a whiff about the party."

OLLA, *L.Am./S, n.* Place where drugs are sold. (Lit. Pot.) *Esa olla atrae a todos los drogados.* "That drug spot attracts all the druggies."

¡OLVÍDAME!, *L.Am., interj.* Leave me alone! *¡Olvídame! Ya no quiero verte más.* "Leave me alone! I don't want to see you anymore."

ONCES, *L.Am./S., n.* Tea or coffee and cookies in late afternoon. *Te invito a tomar onces mañana.* "Come to tea."

ONDA, 1. *L.Am./N, n.* Situation. *Yo no agarraba la onda.* "I wasn't getting it." **2.** *L.Am./S, idiom.* Something good or bad, good vibes or bad vibes. *¡Qué buena onda es la nueva película de Spielberg!* "Spielberg's new movie is bump'n!"

¡ÓRALE!, 1. *L.Am./N, interj.* Now! *"¡Órale, no empujen!"—gritó Paco cuando subió al metro.* " 'Now, no pushing!' yelled Paco when he got on the subway." **2.** *L.Am./N, interj.* Agreed! Understood! *"¿Entonces, vamos al baile?"—preguntó Manuel. "¡Órale!"—contestó Jaime.* " 'So, are we going to the dance?' asked Manuel. 'Okay!' answered Jaime."

ORÉGANO, *L.Am./N, n.* Marijuana, Mary Jane, pot, grass, weed. (Lit. Oregano.) *Alejandro fuma cigarros de orégano.* "Alejandro smokes oregano cigarettes."

OREJA, *L.Am./N, n.* Eavesdropper. (Lit. Ear.) *No hables fuerte porque mi tía es una oreja.* "Don't talk so loud—my aunt is very nosy."

ORTO, *L.Am./S, n.* Ass. *Me provoca agarrarte el orto a* *patadas por grosero.* "I feel like kicking you in the ass for being so rude."

OTORRINO, *L.Am., adj. or n.* Otorhinolaryngologist. *Tengo que ir al otorrino porque casi no oigo.* "I've got to go to the otorhino because I can barely hear."

OVEJUNO, NA, *Car., adj.* Having a big head of hair. *Quisiera ser ovejuna como tú, ya casi estoy calva.* "I would like to have a head of hair like you; I am almost bald."

PA' SEGUIDA, *Car., idiom.* Right away. *Voy a tener esto listo pa' seguida.* "I am going to have this ready in a jiffy."

PACA, *L.Am./C, n.* Police. *¿Dónde está la paca cuando se necesita?* "Where are the fuzz when you need them?"

PACHANGA, *L.Am./N, n.* Party. *Fuimos a la pachanga después de la boda.* "We went out partying after the wedding."

PACHANGUERO, RA, 1. *Spain, adj.* Vulgar, in bad taste. *Ese comentario que hiciste fue realmente pachanguero.* "That comment you made was really in poor taste." **2.** *L.Am., adj.* Party animal. *Ricardo es muy pachanguero. Siempre llega a las 3:00 de la mañana.* "Ricardo is a party guy. He is always getting home at 3 A.M."

PACHARACA, *L.Am./S, n.* Loose girl. *No te juntes con esa tipa, es una pacharaca.* "Don't be too friendly with her; she is a very loose girl."

PACHICHI, 1. *L.Am./N, adj.* Old (person). *Mi abuelo está muy pachichi.* "My grandfather is getting on in years." **2.** *L.Am./N, adj.* Old, wrinkled. *Las naranjas ya estaban viejas y pachichis.* "The oranges were old and wrinkled."

PACHO, *L.Am./C, n.* Funny situation. *La caída de Marcela en el altar fue todo un pacho.* "Marcella's fall at the altar was a riot."

PACHOCHA, *L.Am./N, n.* Money, cash, moolah. *Roberto dejó a su novia porque ella no tenía pachocha.* "Roberto left his girlfriend because she didn't have any moolah."

PACHUCO, 1. *L.Am./C, n.* Bum, scuzzo. *El hermano de Julia es un pachuco, no hace nada, ni trabaja ni estudia.* "Julia's brother is a bum. He doesn't do anything; he neither works nor studies." **2.** *L.Am./N, adj.* Flashy. *José llegó al baile con un traje muy pachuco.* "Jose showed up at the dance with a real flashy suit."

PACO, 1. *L.Am./S, n.* Police, cops. *¿Qué pasa con tantos pacos por aquí?* "What's shaking with so much fuzz around here?" **2.** *L.Am./S, n.* Package. *Francisco regresa a su casa todos los días con un paco sospechoso.* "Francisco goes back to his house with a suspicious pack every day."

PADRE, *L.Am./N, adj.* Good, cool, fun. (Lit. Father.) *Me llegó la revista y está bien padre.* "I got the magazine and it's great."

PADREJÓN, *Car., n.* Menstrual cramp. *La aspirina me alivia los padrejones.* "Aspirin relieves my cramps."

PADROTE, 1. *L.Am./N, n.* Pimp. *El delincuente también era el padrote de la prostituta.* "The hoodlum was also the prostitute's pimp." **2.** *L.Am./N, adj.* Excellent, neat, cool. *¿Viste cómo pintaron el coche de Alex? Quedó bien padrote.* "Did you see how they painted Alex's car? It turned out real cool."

PAGANINI, *L.Am./S, n.* Pejorative term for he or she who pays. *Invitemos a Daniel, necesitamos un paganini.* "Let's invite Daniel; we need a sugar daddy."

PAGAR EL PATO, *L.Am., idiom.* To take responsibility for something. *Yo siempre pago el pato por todos tus errores.* "I always pay the piper for all your mistakes."

PAGAR LAS CONTRIBUCIONES, *L.Am./N, idiom.* To defecate, to shit. *Me gusta leer mientras pago las contribuciones.* "I like to read while I make a deposit."

¡PAILAS!, *L.Am./S, interj.* Interjection employed when one makes a mistake. *¡Pailas! Le pregunté a la señora por su marido sin pensar que murió recién.* "Damn! I asked the lady about her husband without thinking that he died recently."

PAISA, *L.Am./N, n.* Fellow countryman. *Quiero presentarte a mi paisa César.* "I want to introduce you to my countryman Cesar."

PAISANO, *L.Am./N, n.* Spaniard. *El dueño de esa tiendecita es un paisano.* "The owner of that little store is a Spaniard."

PAJA, *L.Am., n.* Small talk, trivialities, bull. (Lit. Straw.) *Sarita sólo habla paja.* "Sarita just talks about petty things."

PAJAREADO, DA, *L.Am./S, adj.* Confused. *Las clases de álgebra tienen a Carlos bien pajareado.* "The algebra lessons got Carlos all messed up."

PÁJARO, *L.Am., n.* Penis. (Lit. Bird.) *Ese viejo anda mostrándole el pájaro a todas en la calle.* "That old guy is walking around showing his birdie to everybody in the street."

PÁJARO NALGÓN, *L.Am./N, n.* Useless person. *Luis es puro pájaro nalgón, habla mucho pero no sabe hacer nada.* "Luis is pure bull; he talks a lot but he doesn't know how to do anything."

PAJARÓN, NA, *L.Am./S, adj.* Negligent, careless, unattentive. *Adolfo es un pajarón empedernido.* "Adolfo is a confirmed scatterbrain."

PÁJAROS FRUTEROS, *L.Am./S, idiom.* Street children. *Caminar por las calles de Miraflores es casi imposible, está plagado de pájaros fruteros.* "Walking through the streets of Miraflores is almost impossible; it's full of street kids."

PAJAROTA, *Car., adj. or n.* Vulgar woman. *Debiera darte vergüenza esa pajarota con que andas.* "You should be ashamed of that pig you are going out with."

PAJARRACO, CA, *Car., n.* Ill-mannered person. *Ese pa-*

jarraco no sabe comportarse en ninguna parte. "That turkey doesn't know how to behave anywhere."

PAJERO, RA, 1. *L.Am./S, adj. or n.* Masturbator. *Ese es tan pajero que ni trata de salir con mujeres.* "That guy jerks off so much he doesn't even try to go out with women." **2.** *L.Am./N, adj.* Lazy. *Isidro es muy pajero, no le gusta trabajar.* "Isidro is real lazy; he doesn't like to work." **3.** *Spain, n.* Person who mixes the truth with lies. *No le creas a Raúl porque es un pajero.* "Don't believe Raul because he puts a lot of bull in what he says."

¡PALABRA!, *L.Am., interj.* Expression of agreement, consent. (Lit. Word.) *¡Palabra! Te prometo que voy contigo.* "Right! I promise to go with you."

PALABRA DOMINGUERA, *Car., idiom.* Ten-dollar word. *Aquí no digas esa palabra dominguera.* "Don't say that ten-dollar word here."

¡PALABRAS!, *Car., interj.* Expression of disbelief. (Lit. Words.) *¡Palabras! No te lo puedo creer.* "No way! I can't believe you."

PALABRO, *Spain, n.* Bad word. *De su boca sólo saltan palabros.* "Only dirty words spew out of his mouth."

PALABRÓN, *L.Am., n.* Obscene or vulgar word. *Esos palabrones no los puedes decir en mi casa.* "You can't say those dirty words in my house."

PALANCA, *L.Am., n.* Influence, clout, pull. (Lit. Lever.) *Felipe reprobó el examen de admisión pero entró con palancas.* "Felipe failed the entrance exam, but he got in with the right connections."

PALANQUEAR, *L.Am., v.* To use one's influence. *Tienes que palanquear para que te den el puesto en esa empresa.* "You've got to use your influence so that they'll give you the position at that company."

PALERO, *L.Am./S, n.* Liar. *Mi vecino resultó ser un palero.* "My neighbor turned out to be quite a liar."

PALETA, *L.Am., n.* Lollipop. *Yo pedí una paleta de fresa.* "I asked for a strawberry lollipop."

PALIACATE, *L.Am./N, n.* Brightly colored handkerchief. *Como hacía mucho sol, me amarré un paliacate.* "Since it was very sunny, I put a colorful handkerchief on."

PÁLIDA, *L.Am./S, n.* Negative comment. (Lit. Pale.) *Maruja es muy pesimista. Si dice algo es una pálida.* "Maruja is very pessimistic. If she says anything it's always a negative comment." **2.** *L.Am./S, n.* Mountain sickness. *A los extranjeros que andan por las montañas siempre les da la pálida.* "The foreigners who walk in the mountains always get mountain sickness."

PALILLO, *L.Am., n.* Very thin person. (Lit. Stick.) *Diana casi no come y ya está como un palillo.* "Diana hardly eats and now she is like a beanpole."

PALIZA, *L.Am., n.* Beating. *La paliza que le dieron a mi hermano fue cruel.* "The beating they gave my brother was bad."

PALO, 1. *L.Am./S, n.* Million. (Lit. Stick.) *Quisiera sacarme unos palos en la lotería.* "I'd like to hit a couple of million in the lottery." **2.** *L.Am., n.* Penis. *Quisiera cortarle el palo a ese violador.* "I would like to cut that rapist's dick off." **3.** *L.Am., adj.* Boring, dull. *La famosa obra de teatro resultó ser un palo.* "The famous theatrical work turned out to be a drag." **4.** *L.Am./S, n.* Drink. *Vamos a echarnos un palo en el bar de la esquina.* "Let's have a drink at the bar on the corner." **See also ECHAR UN PALO, SER UN PALO**

PALOMA, *Car., n.* Pretty young woman. (Lit. Dove.) *No hago más que pensar en la paloma que conocí ayer.* "I don't do anything but think of the doll I met yesterday."

PALOMA BLANCA, *L.Am./N, n.* Innocent person. *Los rateros querían fingir que eran unas palomas blancas.* "The hoodlums wanted to pretend they were nice guys."

PALTAS, *L.Am./S, pl. n.* Problems. (Lit. Avocados.) *Ya no te hagas más paltas y dile la verdad.* "Don't cause yourself more problems and just tell him the truth."

PAMPLÓN, NA, *Car., adj. or n.* Fat person. *Con la edad me* *he vuelto pamplón.* "With age I've gotten fat."

PANA, *L.Am., n.* Friend. *Esta noche voy a ver a mi pana Ricardo.* "Tonight I am going to see my pal, Ricardo."

PANCHO, *L.Am./S, n.* Hot dog. *Me gustan los panchos con mucha mostaza y cebolla.* "I like hot dogs with a lot of mustard and onions."

PANCHÓLARES, *L.Am./N, pl. n.* Pesos. *Con tantas devaluaciones, nuestros panchólares sólo sirven de papel higiénico.* "With so many devaluations our pesos are good only as toilet paper."

PANDA, *Car., n.* Trick. *Germán se la pasa haciéndole pandas a la gente.* "Herman goes overboard pulling tricks on people."

PANDERO, *Spain, n.* Butt, ass. *Mira como mueve Stella el pandero cuando baila.* "Look how Stella moves her bootie when she dances."

PANGAR, *L.Am./S, v.* To dent a car. *Mi hijo me pangó el coche anoche, pero lo va a pagar él.* "My son dented my car last night, but he's going to pay for it."

PANOCHA, *L.Am./N, n.* Vagina, pussy. *Ando con Olivia para ver si me da panocha.* "I am hanging out with Olivia to see if she gives me a little pussy."

PANTERA, *L.Am./N, n.* Brave person, hero. (Lit. Panther.) *El señor que rescató a mi hermana es muy pantera.* "The man who rescued my sister is a hero."

PANZA DE AGUA, *L.Am./S, idiom.* Big belly. *El tío Julio es un panza de agua pero no deja de tomar cerveza.* "Uncle Julio has a beer gut but he won't stop drinking beer."

PANZONA, *L.Am./N, n.* Pregnant woman. *La esposa del vecino ya anda panzona.* "The neighbor's wife already has a belly."

PANZONEAR, *L.Am./N, v.* To get pregnant. *A la hija de mi compadre ya la panzonearon.* "Now they've knocked up my buddy's daughter."

PAPA, 1. *L.Am., n.* Nothing. (Lit. Potato.) *Laura no sabe ni papa de historia patria.* "Laura doesn't know diddly-squat about national history." **2.** *L.Am., n.* Lie. *Cuando su mamá le llamó, Tere le echó puras papas.* "When her mother called her, Terry threw some lies at her." **3.** *L.Am./N, n.* Soft job. *¡Qué buena papa tienes compay!* "What a soft job you have, pal."

PAPA ENTERRADA, *L.Am./N, idiom.* Stupid, slow. *No me gusta jugar al básquet, soy una papa enterrada.* "I don't like to play basketball; I am a real schmo."

PAPALOTE, 1. *L.Am./N, n.* Kite. *Los niños volaban papalotes en el parque.* "The kids were flying kites in the park." **2.** *Car., n.* Windmill. *El papalote bombeaba del pozo.* The windmill pumped water from the well."

PAPAR MOSCAS, *L.Am./N, idiom.* To be distracted. *Perdón, no te escuché, estaba papando moscas.* "Excuse me, I didn't hear you; I was daydreaming."

PAPAZOTE, *L.Am./N, adj. or n.* Handsome man. *A mí me gusta el novio de Irma, está bien papazote.* "I like Irma's boyfriend; he is a neat guy."

PAPEAR, *L.Am./S, v.* To eat. *A Roberto le gusta papear todo el tiempo y se está poniendo gordo.* "Roberto likes to eat all the time. He is getting fat."

PAPELETA, *Car., n.* Difficulty. *Tranquila, que esta papeleta pasará pronto.* "Take it easy; this problem will go away soon."

PAPIRO, *L.Am./N, n.* Paper money. (Lit. Papyrus.) *No pude comprar la camisa porque no traía papiros.* "Couldn't buy the shirt because I didn't have the bills."

PAPITO, *L.Am./N, adj. or n.* Handsome man. (Lit. Daddy.) *Eugenia me dijo que la entrevistó un papito.* "Eugenia told me she was interviewed by a hunk."

PAPUCHI, *L.Am., n.* Daddy. *Esta bicicleta me la regaló mi papuchi.* "My daddy gave me this bicycle."

PAPUCHO, CHA, *L.Am., adj.* Good-looking. *Quiero salir con el hermano de Graciela, está bien papucho.* "I want to go out with Graciela's brother; he is real cute."

PAQUETE, 1. *L.Am., n.* Male genitals. (Lit. Package.) *El actor salió mostrando todo el paquete en su nueva película.* "The actor came out showing it all in his new movie." **2.** *Spain, adj.* Inept, clumsy, incompetent. *Jairo perdió el trabajo por ser tan paquete.* "Jairo lost a job for being so clumsy." **3.** *L.Am./N, n.* Matter, business. *Ya no pude con el paquete y le pedí ayuda a mi jefe.* "I couldn't handle the matter and I asked my boss for help."

PAQUETERO, *Car., adj.* Liar. *Pepe es tremendo paquetero, se pasó toda la fiesta diciendo mentiras.* "Pepe is a terrible liar; he spent the whole party telling lies."

PARA NADA, *L.Am./N, idiom.* No, no way. *Cuando le preguntaron a Carla si le gustaba Daniel, dijo "para nada."* "When they asked Carla if she liked Daniel, she said, 'no way.' "

PARACAIDISTA, 1. *L.Am., n.* Party crasher. (Lit. Parachutist.) *La fiesta de Marisa fue arruinada cuando llegaron unos paracaidistas.* "Marisa's party was ruined when some party crashers arrived." **2.** *L.Am./S, n.* Unexpected visitor. *Apúrate que en cualquier momento llega un paracaidista.* "Hurry up! We could get a visitor at any time." **3.** *L.Am./N, n.* Squatter. *Amanecieron más de cien familias de paracaidistas dentro del predio.* "More than a hundred families appeared on the property this morning."

PARACHOQUES, *L.Am., pl. n.* Woman's breasts. (Lit. Bumpers.) *Marcela tiene muy buenos parachoques.* "Marcella has some nice bumpers."

PARADO, DA, 1. *L.Am./N, adj.* Hard, erect. (Lit. Standing.) *Nando la traía parada cuando salió del cabaret.* "Nando had a hard-on when he left the cabaret." **2.** *L.Am., adj.* Connected, in good with. *Tito consiguió trabajo porque está bien parado con el diputado.* "Tito got work because he was well-connected with the representative."

PARAGUAS, *Spain, n.* Condom. (Lit. Umbrella.) *El uso del paraguas ayuda a prevenir el SIDA.* "Using a rubber helps to prevent AIDS."

PARAGÜERO, *Car., n.* Sunday driver. (Lit. Umbrella stand.) *Daniel maneja muy mal porque siempre ha sido un paragüero.* "Daniel drives terribly because he's always been a Sunday driver."

PARAR BOLAS, 1. *L.Am./S, idiom.* To pay attention. *Párale bolas a tu hermana cuando te aconseje.* "Pay attention to your sister when she gives you advice." **2.** *L.Am./S, idiom.* To court. *Me parece que Carlos le está parando bolas a mi prima.* "I think Carlos is going after my cousin."

PARAR LA OREJA, *L.Am., idiom.* To pay attention. *Para la oreja para no tener que repetirte las instrucciones.* "Pay attention so that I don't have to repeat the instructions."

PARAR LOS TACOS (A ALGUIEN), *L.Am./N, idiom.* To scold, to chew out. *El jefe le paró los tacos a Manuel por no haber cumplido el trabajo a tiempo.* "The boss read Manuel the riot act for not having finished the job on time."

PARCA, 1. *L.Am./S, idiom.* Death. *La parca persigue a esa familia.* "The Grim Reaper follows that family." **2.** *L.Am./S, n.* Police officer, patrol car. *No hagas nada malo porque te va a llevar la parca.* "Don't do anything bad because the police car will take you away."

PARCHE, 1. *L.Am./S, n.* Group of friends, gang of pals. (Lit. Patch.) *Jesús y Bartolomé se fueron con el parche a la playa.* "Jesus and Bartholomew went with the gang to the beach." **2.** *L.Am./S, adj.* Paid up, even. *Ya te pagué, ahora estamos parches.* "I already paid you; now we are even." **3.** *L.Am./S, n.* Bad temper. *Amaneció con el parche y no se le puede ni hablar.* "He woke up upset and you can't even talk to him." **4.** L.Am./S, n. Oddball. *Santiago fue el parche en la fiesta de aniversario de mis papás.* "Santiago was the oddball at my parent's anniversary party."

PARCHUDO, DA, *L.Am./S, adj.* Moody, upset. *¿Por qué*

estás tan parchudo hoy? "Why are you so moody today?"

PARECER ÁRBOL DE NAVIDAD, *L.Am./N, idiom.* To be overdressed. *Úrsula parecía árbol de Navidad cuando fue a la fiesta.* "Ursula looked like a Christmas tree when she went to the party."

PAREJERO, RA, *Car., adj. or n.* Vain, conceited. *Se cree muy bonita la parejera.* "That stuck-up fool thinks she is very pretty."

PARGO, 1. *Car., n.* Prostitute's customer. (Lit. Porgy.) *Carlos es un pargo, todos los fines de semana va donde esas mujeres.* "Carlos is a john. Every weekend he goes to those women." **2. PARGO, GA,** *L.Am./S, n.* Person who makes affected gestures. *Ese intérprete es un pargo.* "That interpreter is a real arm-waver."

PARIGUAYO, YA, *Car., adj. or n.* Wallflower. *La pariguaya de Rosario siempre se queda ahí sentada.* "Wallflower Rosario always just sits there."

PARIR CHAYOTES, *L.Am./N, idiom.* To bust one's ass. *Yo me puse a parir chayotes cuando tuve que entregar el trabajo.* "I began to bust my ass to deliver the job."

PARNA, *L.Am./N, n.* Friend, pal, buddy. *Daniel es mi parna. Somos compañeros desde la niñez.* "Daniel is my pal. We've been buddies since childhood."

PARO, 1. *L.Am./N, n.* Excuse, favor. *Pepe se volvió puros paros cuando le pidieron ir a la tienda.* "Pepe had nothing but excuses when they asked him to go to the store." **2.** *L.Am./S, n.* Workers' strike. *Mañana es el paro de los profesores.* "The teachers' strike is tomorrow."

PARQUEADO, DA, *L.Am./S, adj.* Watched. (Lit. Parked.) *Valentino está parqueado desde que giró varios cheques sin fondo.* "Valentino is being watched since he wrote several rubber checks."

PARRANDA, *L.Am., n.* Party. *¡La parranda de anoche estuvo como cañón!* "Last night's party was a blast!" **See also IRSE DE PARRANDA**

PARRANDEAR, *L.Am./S, v.* To party. *No seas perezoso,*

ven a parrandear con nosotros. "Don't be lazy; come party with us."

PARRANDERO, RA, *L.Am., adj.* Party person. *Cuca es muy parrandera, no sale de la disco.* "Cuca is a real party girl—she never leaves the disco."

PARSERO, *L.Am./S, n.* Close friend. *Federico es el parsero de nuestro hijo.* "Federico is our son's close friend."

PARTIR EL TURRÓN, *L.Am./N, idiom.* To begin using the informal address "tú." *Vamos partiendo el turrón, ¿te parece?* "Let's get on a first-name basis, what do you say?"

PARTIR LA BOCA, *L.Am., idiom.* To punch in the mouth. *Si vuelves a decir eso, te parto la boca.* "If you say that again, I'll bust your mouth."

PARTIR LA CARA, *L.Am., idiom.* To punch in the face. *A Mario le partieron la cara por no respetar a Gabriela.* "They socked Mario in the face for being disrespectful to Gabriela."

PARTIRSE LA MADRE, *L.Am./N, idiom.* To viciously beat each other. *Si no me dejas en paz, nos vamos a partir la madre.* "If you don't leave me alone, we'll get into a scrape."

¡PASA!, *L.Am./S, interj.* Leave! Get out! *¡Pasa, pasa compadrito y deja de fastidiarme la paciencia!* "Get out of here dude, and quit bothering me!"

PASA DE PELUCHE, *L.Am./N, idiom.* Fantastic, great, cool, bitchin', bump'n. *No, mano, el BMW ese se pasa de peluche.* "No, bro, that BMW is bitchin'."

PASAO, SA, *Car., adj.* Forward, pushy. *No te dejes convencer por Lucas, es un pasao.* "Don't let Lucas persuade you; he's pushy."

PASAR, 1. *L.Am./S, v.* To like somebody. (Lit. To pass.) *No paso a ese empleado tan antipático.* "I can't stand that nasty employee." **2.** *L.Am./N, v.* To like something. *A mí me pasa un montón el fútbol.* "I dig football a lot."

PASAR A LA BÁSCULA, *L.Am./N, idiom.* Search, frisk. *Cuando entramos a la disco nos pasaron a la báscula.* "When we entered the disco, they frisked us."

PASAR DE LANZA, *L.Am./N, idiom.* To exaggerate, to make fun of. *Rafael se pasa de lanza con sus bromas pesadas.* "Rafael goes too far with his bad jokes."

PASAR EL TUFO, *L.Am./S, idiom.* To let someone know. *Pásale el tufo a Francisco que la pelea de Tyson es el viernes.* "Tell Francisco that the Tyson fight is on Friday."

PASAR EL YARA, *L.Am./S, idiom.* To warn. *Pásale el yara a Carlos que si no me paga mañana, le quitaré el carro.* "Warn Carlos that if he doesn't pay me by tomorrow, I'll take the car back."

PASAR LA BROCHA, *L.Am./C, idiom.* To curry favor, to play up to someone. *Luisa siempre está pasándole la brocha al jefe.* "Luisa is always playing up to the boss."

PASAR LA CERCA, *Car., idiom.* To go too far. *Pablo no sabe parar y siempre pasa la cerca.* "Pablo doesn't know when to stop and he always goes too far."

PASAR LA LENGUA, *Car., idiom.* To flatter. *Pasando la lengua no vas a lograr conquistarme.* "Flattery will get you nowhere."

PASAR LA NENA, *Car., idiom.* To smuggle drugs through customs. *Adela se gana la vida pasando la nena a los Estados Unidos.* "Adela makes her living by smuggling drugs into the United States."

PASAR PIOLA, *L.Am./S, idiom.* To gain approval or acceptance, to pass muster. *Apenas pasé piola en la inspección de esta mañana.* "I barely passed this morning's inspection."

PASAR RASPANDO, *L.Am./S, idiom.* To barely pass anything. *Claudia pasó inglés raspando.* "Claudia passed English by the skin of her teeth."

PASARELA, *L.Am./S, idiom.* Passing the ball during a soccer game. *No te guardes, pasarela para Kempes.* "Don't hold back. Pass it to Kempes."

PASARLA DE TODOS LOS COLORES, *Spain, idiom.* To go through difficult times. *Desde que me divorcié la estoy pasando de todos los colores.* "Since my divorce, I am going through a lot."

PASARSE, 1. *L.Am., prnl. v.* To go beyond normal behavior. *Ya te pasaste con esos comentarios.* "You went too far with those comments." **2.** *L.Am./S, prnl. v.* To exaggerate. *Está bien que estés enferma pero ya no te pases.* "I understand that you are sick but don't overdo it."

PASÁRSELE LAS CUCHARADAS, *L.Am./N, idiom.* To get drunk. *Mi mamá tuvo que manejar porque a mi papá se le pasaron las cucharadas.* "My mother had to drive because my father was plastered."

PASEO, *L.Am., n.* Something easy, a cinch. (Lit. Stroll.) *Álgebra para mí es un paseo.* "For me, algebra is a cinch."

PASERO, RA, *Car., n.* Liar. *Desde chiquita Marina ha sido una pasera y ya nadie le cree.* "Since she was little, Marina has been a liar and now nobody believes her."

PASMA, *Spain, n.* Police. *¿Ya llamaste a la pasma?* "Did you call the police already?"

PASMAO, MÁ, *Car., adj.* Confused, stunned. *Me quedé pasmá cuando me contaron que iba a tener gemelos.* "I was stunned when they told me I was going to have twins."

PASME, *Car., n.* Disappointment. *Mi matrimonio ha sido un pasme desde el comienzo.* "My marriage has been a downer since the beginning."

PASOTA, *Car., adj.* Old-fashioned. *Mi mamá es tan pasota que no quiere aprender a usar la computadora.* "My mom is so old-fashioned that she doesn't want to learn to use the computer."

PASTA, *Spain, n.* Money. (Lit. Paste.) *Tendré que pedirle pasta prestada a Miguel.* "I'll have to borrow some money from Miguel."

PASTEL, *Spain, adj.* Bad, fake. (Lit. Pastry.) *El diamante* *de tu abuelita es un pastel.* "Your grandmother's diamond is a fake."

PASTELERO, *L.Am./S, n.* Handler of basic cocaine paste. (Lit. Pastry cook.) *Esa cuadra donde mi primo vivía tiene un nuevo pastelero.* "The block where my cousin lived has a new coke cook."

¡PASU-MACHU!, *L.Am./S, interj.* Wow! *¡Pasu-machu! Esta comida está bien picante.* "Wow! This food is very spicy."

PATA, 1. *L.Am./S, n.* Friend. (Lit. Animal leg.) *Mi pata José y yo fuimos de parranda.* "My buddy Jose and I went partying." **2.** *Car., n.* Lesbian. (Lit. Duck.) *Mi compañera de trabajo es pata y se viste como hombre.* "My coworker is a lesbian and dresses like a man." **3.** *L.Am., n.* Foot. (Lit. Animal leg.) *Me pisó la pata cuando venía en el metro.* "He stepped on my foot when I was on the subway."

PATA DE PERRO, *L.Am./S, idiom.* Wanderer. *Samuel es pata de perro, siempre anda de viaje.* "Samuel is a rambler who's always traveling."

PATADA, 1. *L.Am., adj. or n.* Terrible, unpleasant. (Lit. Kick.) *Las cosas que escribió Nacho en su diario son la patada.* "The things Nacho wrote in his diary are terrible." **2.** *L.Am./N, n.* Unpleasant smell, stink. *Cuando abrí la puerta me dio una patada de marijuana.* "When I opened the door I got a jolt of weed smoke."

PATATÚS, *L.Am./S, n.* Attack of nerves. *Me va a dar el patatús cuando suba al avión.* "I'm going to get butterflies in my stomach when I get on the plane."

PATERO, RA, *L.Am./S, adj. or n.* Sycophant, bootlicker, ass-kisser. *Sólo por ser un patero lo ascendieron de puesto.* "He got promoted just for being an ass-kisser."

PATILLANO, *Car., adj.* Flat-footed. *Aun si eres patillano vas a tener que prestar el servicio militar.* "Even if you are flat-footed, you'll have to do military service."

PATINAR, 1. *L.Am./N, v.* To be indifferent, to not care. (Lit.

To skate.) *Tu vida privada me patina.* "Your private life doesn't concern me." **2.** *Car., v.* To make mistakes. *Si vuelves a patinar vas a perder este trabajo.* "If you slip up again you are going to lose this job." **3.** *Car., v.* To say the wrong thing. *Patiné cuando estaba hablando con Lilia y se ofendió.* "I slipped up when I was talking to Lillie and she got offended." **4.** *Car., v.* To stutter. *Habla despacio, a ver si dejas de patinar.* "Speak slowly to see if you stop stuttering."

PATINAR EL EMBRAGUE, *Spain, idiom.* To be crazy. *A Rogelio parece que le patina el embrague.* "Rogelio seems to be slipping upstairs."

PATINAZO, *Car., n.* Big blunder. *Ese patinazo tuyo en la entrevista te va a costar el puesto.* "That blunder of yours at the interview will keep you from getting the job."

PATO, 1. *L.Am./N, n.* Bedpan. (Lit. Duck.) *Cuando trabajaba en el hospital me tenían limpiando patos.* "When I worked at the hospital, they had me cleaning bedpans." **2.** *L.Am., n.* Homosexual. *Entramos y enseguida nos dimos cuenta que era fiesta de patos.* "We came in and right away realized it was a party for gays. **3.** *L.Am./S, n.* Party crasher. *Jorge siempre entra de pato a todas las fiestas.* "Jorge always crashes all the parties."

PAVADA, *L.Am./S, pl. n.* Silliness, foolishness, nonsense. *Deja de decirme pavadas.* "Cut out the foolishness."

PAVO, 1. *Spain, n.* Guy, dude. (Lit. Turkey.) *Me gusta el pavo que se sienta junto a mí en clase.* "I like the dude that sits next to me in class." **2.** *Car., n.* Naive boy. *Mi hijo no sabe aún de esas cosas, es un pavo.* "My son doesn't know about those things yet; he is a naive boy." **3. PAVO, VA,** *L.Am./S, n.* Fool. *Adela es una pava.* "Adela is a scatterbrain."

PEA, *L.Am., n.* Drunkenness. *La pea de Armando fue una vergüenza en la fiesta.* "Armando's drunkenness was an embarrassment at the party."

PECHONALIDAD, *L.Am., n.* Big boobs. *Liliana, me gusta* *mucho tu pechonalidad.* "Liliana, I dig your boobies very much."

PECHUGAS, *L.Am., pl. n.* Woman's breasts, boobs. *En la playa gozamos admirando las pechugas.* "At the beach, we enjoyed ogling boobs."

PECHUGONA, *L.Am., adj.* Big-breasted woman. *Tengo que encontrar un vestido que me disimule lo pechugona.* "I've got to find a dress that won't show my big boobs so much."

PÉCORA, *L.Am./S, n.* Foot odor. *¡Con esas pécoras, matas a cualquiera!* "With those smelly feet you could kill someone!"

PEDA, *L.Am./N, n.* Drinking bout. *Cuando me botó mi novia me puse una peda de pura decepción.* "When my girlfriend broke up with me, I got plastered out of pure grief."

PEDALIAR, *L.Am./N, v.* To walk, to go on foot. *No traíamos dinero para el autobús y tuvimos que pedaliar.* "We didn't have money for the bus, so we had to hoof it."

PEDINCHE, *L.Am./N, adj. or n.* Moocher. *No me gusta parar en los semáforos con tanto niño pedinche.* "I don't like to stop at the lights with so many mooching kids."

PEDIR LA ENTRADA, *L.Am./C, idiom.* To ask permission to visit a girlfriend. *Daniel pidió la entrada y el padre de Jimena dijo que no.* "Daniel asked permission to visit Jimena and her father said no."

PEDIR TAIN, *L.Am./N, idiom.* To ask for time out. (From English "time.") *Nos estaban dando una goliza tan bárbara que pedimos tain.* "They were getting so many goals against us that we asked for time."

PEDO, *L.Am./N, adj.* Drunk. (Lit. Fart.) *Ando pedo porque vengo de la boda de un amigo.* "I'm soused because I'm coming back from a friend's wedding."

PEGA, *L.Am./S, n.* Job. *José encontró una pega nueva.* "Jose found a new job."

PEGAJOSO, *L.Am./S, adj.* Annoying. (Lit. Sticky.) *No seas pegajoso, ¡déjame tranquilo!* "Don't be annoying; leave me alone!"

PEGAR CON TUBO, *L.Am./N, idiom.* To succeed, to make it. *La música extranjera está pegando con tubo.* "Foreign music is really making it."

PEGAR EL DIENTE, *Car., idiom.* To eat, to chow down. *Termina de pegar el diente que nos tenemos que ir.* "Finish eating, we have to go."

PEGARLE A ALGO, *L.Am./S, Spain, idiom.* To have talent. *Desde pequeño le he pegado a la pintura.* "Since I was small I've had talent for painting."

PEGÁRSELE EL ARROZ, *Spain, idiom.* To unwittingly become pregnant. *La primera noche se le pegó el arroz.* "She was knocked up the first night."

PEGOSTE, *L.Am./N, n.* Pest. *El hermanito de Melita es un pegoste terrible.* "Melita's brother is a terrible pest."

PELA, *L.Am./S, n.* Beating. *Papá, nunca se me olvidará la pela que me diste.* "Pop, I'll never forget the spanking you gave me."

PELADEZ, *L.Am./N, n.* Stupidity, stupid thing, nonsense. *No me gusta que cuenten chistes colorados porque dicen puras peladeces.* "I don't like it when they tell dirty jokes because everything they say is nonsense."

PELADO, DA, 1. *L.Am., adj. or n.* Bald. *David se quedó pelado a los treinta.* "David went bald at thirty." **2.** *L.Am., adj.* Without money, broke. *No le hagas caso a ese tipo, es un pobre pelado.* "Don't pay any attention to that guy; he is always broke." **3.** *L.Am./N, adj. or n.* Vulgar person. *No me gusta juntarme con el primo de Corina porque es un pelado.* "I don't like to get together with Corina's cousin 'cause he's a scuzzo." **4.** *L.Am./S, n.* Child or adolescent. *Ese pelado se la pasa siempre en la calle.* "That kid is always on the street."

PELAGATOS, *L.Am./S, adj. or n.* Poor person. *Le hizo creer que tenía dinero, pero era un pelagatos.* "He made her believe that he had money, but he was totally broke."

PELAMACHOS, *Car., adj. or n.* Woman who fleeces men, a golddigger. *Ruth es una pelamachos y por eso vive tan bien.* "Ruth is a golddigger and that's why she lives so well."

PELAO, LÁ, *Car., n.* Wise guy or gal, smartass. *Ese pelao siempre cree que tiene la última palabra.* "That wiseass always believes he has the last word."

PELAR, 1. *L.Am./S, v.* To speak poorly of someone, to criticize. (Lit. To skin.) *Los empleados pelaban a José por su manera de trabajar.* "The employees disparaged Jose because of his way of working." **2.** *L.Am./N, v.* To pay attention. *Si tu novio te pide ir a la cama, no le vayas a pelar.* "If your boyfriend asks you to go to bed with him, don't pay any attention."

PELAR EL CABLE, *L.Am./S, idiom.* To have inappropriate attitudes or to make ridiculous comments. *A esa mujer se le pela el cable, dice que deben cerrar los periódicos.* "That woman has her wires crossed; she says they should close the newspapers."

PELAR EL DIENTE, *L.Am./S, idiom.* To smile. *¡Todos a pelar el diente para la foto!* "Everybody, smile for the picture!"

PELAR GALLO, *L.Am./N, idiom.* To take off, to escape, to run away. *Apenas se veía venir la patrulla y todos pelaron gallo.* "Although you could barely see the patrol car coming, everybody hit the road."

PELAR LA PAVA, 1. *Car., v.* To be alone romancing one's sweetheart. *Pelar la pava a la luz de la luna contigo es como un sueño.* "Romancing you in the moonlight is like a dream." **2.** *Car., v.* To be goofing around. *Ponte serio, deja de pelar la pava.* "Get serious; stop goofing around."

¡PELE EL OJO!, *L.Am./C, idiom, interj.* Keep your eyes peeled! *¡Pele el ojo! Hay un hoyo delante.* "Eyes open! There's a hole ahead."

PELELE, *L.Am./C, n.* Ne'er-do-well, bum, dropout. *Mi sobrino es un pelele, pero mi hermana lo tolera y lo mantiene.* "My nephew is a bum, but my sister tolerates him and supports him."

PELI, *L.Am., n.* Movie. *La peli que arrendamos ayer estuvo buenísima.* "The movie we rented yesterday was terrific."

PELICULERO, RA, 1. *L.Am./S, n.* Braggart. *Jaime es bien peliculero delante de las chicas.* "Jaime is a real show-off in front of the girls." **2.** *L.Am., n.* Storyteller. *Javier es un peliculero muy divertido.* "Javier is a very funny storyteller."

PELIENTO, TA, *L.Am./S, adj. or n.* Lowlife. *No hay más que pelientos en esa parte de la ciudad.* "There's nothing but lowlifes in that part of the city."

PELLEJO, 1. *Spain, n.* Lowlife individual. (Lit. Hide.) *El funcionario de esa oficina es un pellejo que trata mal a todo el mundo.* The official at that office is a lowlife who mistreats everybody. **2.** *Spain, n.* Womanizer. *Álvaro es un pellejo, quiere conquistar a todas las mujeres.* Alvaro is a lech; he wants to seduce all women. **3.** *L.Am., n.* Skin. *Elías no pensó más que en salvarse el pellejo cuando nos detuvo la policía.* "Elias just thought about saving his own skin when the police detained us."

PELO See DEJARLO A UNO EN PELO, SER DEL MISMO PELO, VENIR UNA COSA AL PELO

PELÓN, 1. *L.Am./C, n.* Party, celebration. (Lit. Baldy.) *Cuando me gradué me dieron un pelón.* "When I graduated, they gave me a blast." **2.** *L.Am./N, adj. or n.* Baldy. *"¡Apaguen ese foco!" gritaron cuando entró el pelón.* " 'Turn off that light!' they yelled when the baldy walked in." **3.** *L.Am., adj.* Difficult. *Está pelón pasar de año si no estudias.* "It's tough to pass the year if you don't study."

PELONA, *L.Am., n.* Death. (Lit. Baldy.) *Me enfermé y la pelona estuvo a punto de llevarme.* "I got sick and the Grim Reaper almost carried me off."

PELOTA, 1. *L.Am./S, n.* Importance. *Olvidémonos de ese* *asunto. No tiene pelota.* "Let's forget this matter. It's not worth it." **2.** *L.Am./S., n.* Idiot. *Ese muchacho es un pelota, no te merece.* "That fella is a jerk; he doesn't deserve you." **See also HACER LA PELOTA**

PELOTERO, RA, *Car., adj.* Sycophant, flatterer, brown-noser. *No aguanto más a esa pelotera porque sólo quiere estar bien con los jefes.* "I can't stand that bootlicker anymore; all she wants is to be OK with the bosses."

PELOTILLA, *Car., n.* Argument among spouses. *Todos los días tenemos una pelotilla, algo anda mal aquí.* "Everyday we have a spat; something is wrong here."

PELOTUDO, DA, 1. *Car., adj. or n.* Lazy, lazy person. *Ese pelotudo no ayuda para nada en la casa.* "That lazybones doesn't help out at all around the house." **2.** *L.Am./S, adj. or n.* Useless individual, dopey, stupid. *¡Nunca haces nada bien, pelotudo!* "You never do anything right, you jerk!"

PELUSA, 1. *L.Am./N, n.* Rabble, riffraff. (Lit. Lint.) *A mí me gusta juntarme con pura gente bien, no con la pelusa.* "I like to get together with the good people and not the riffraff." **2.** *L.Am./S, n.* Poor child. *Esos pelusas viven bajo el puente.* "Those homeless kids live under the bridge."

PENCA, 1. *Spain, n.* Leg. *Jugando fútbol me dieron una patada en la penca.* "Playing soccer, they kicked me in the gam." **2.** *L.Am./S, n.* Penis. *¡José tiene una penca de medio metro!"* Jose has a dick that's one foot long!"

PENDANGO, GA, *Car., n.* Jerk, wimp. *Todos los novios que se consigue Marcela son unos pendangos.* "All the boyfriends that Marcela gets are a bunch of wimps."

PENDEJADA, *L.Am., n.* Stupidity. *Las pendejadas que dices me tienen aburrida.* "The bullshit you talk is boring me to death."

PENDEJEAR, 1. *L.Am., v.* To screw up, to fuck up. *No me cae bien Genaro, siempre anda pendejeando a todo el mundo.* "I don't like Genaro; he's always screwing everybody up." **2.** *L.Am./S, v.* To do stupid things. *Deja de pendejear, que pareces cretino.* "Stop doing dumb things; you seem retarded."

PENDEJISMO, *L.Am./N, n.* Screwup, fuckup. *Yo le expliqué al supervisor que lo de Ramón era mero pendejismo.* "I explained to the supervisor that the thing about Ramon was just a screwup."

PENDEJO, JA, 1. *L.Am., adj.* Clumsy, incapable. *Mi amigo americano es zurdo y parece pendejo para escribir.* "My American friend is left-handed and looks retarded when he writes." **2.** *L.Am., adj.* Stupid, slow. *Ezequiel es un pendejo si cree que le voy a regalar mi bicicleta.* "Ezequiel is a fool if he thinks I'll give him my bicycle." **3.** *L.Am./S, adj.* Childish, immature. *Son pesados esos pendejos, quién dijera que son adultos.* "Those dumb jerks are a pain; who would have said that they are adults."

PENI, *L.Am./N, n.* Penitentiary, prison. *Marcos estuvo cinco años en la peni.* "Marcos was in the pen for five years."

PENSADORA, *L.Am./S, n.* Head. (Lit. Think.) *Usa la pensadora, Beatriz, o te meterás en problemas.* "Use your head, Beatriz, or you will get in trouble."

PENÚLTIMA, *L.Am., n.* The last drink of the evening. (Lit. Penultimate.) *Tómese la penúltima antes de irse.* "Have one for the road before you leave."

PEOR ES NADA, 1. *L.Am/N, idiom.* Expression referring to one's romantic interest. *Le dije a Marcela que aquí estaba su peor es nada.* "I told Marcella that her sweetie was here." **2.** *L.Am./S, idiom.* Wife. *Mi peor es nada quemó la comida.* "My good-for-nothing burned the food."

PEPA, *L.Am./S, n.* Face. *A Javier lo patearon en la pepa en el bar.* "Javier was kicked in the face at the bar." **See also TOCARLE A UNO LA SIN PEPA, SOLTAR LA PEPA**

PEPENADOR, *L.Am./N, n.* Scavenger. *Gabriel tiene un tío que se gana la vida de pepenador.* "Gabriel has an uncle who makes a living as a trashman."

PEPÓN, *L.Am./S, adj. or n.* Good looks. *María tiene un primo bien pepón.* "Maria has a very good-looking cousin."

¡PERA!, *L.Am./N, interj.* Wait! (Lit. Pear.) *"¡Pera, pera!" dijo el niño, "que yo voy primero."* " 'Wait, wait!' the boy said, 'I'm going first.' "

PERCANTA, *L.Am./S, n.* Woman. *En estos tiempos hasta las percantas quieren meterse en política.* "These days even the gals want to get into politics."

PERCHA, 1. *L.Am., n.* Good figure, nice shape. (Lit. Clothes rack.) *Qué percha la de la esposa de Alejo.* "Alejo's wife has a great figure." **2.** *L.Am., n.* Sunday suit. *Me voy a poner la percha para ir a comer con mis suegros.* "I'm going to put on my Sunday best to go eat with my in-laws."

PERDER EL CULO, *Spain, idiom.* To give up everything for someone or something. *Perdí el culo por tí y así me pagas.* "I lost everything over you and that's how you repay me."

PERDERSE, *L.Am., prnl. v.* To get out. (Lit. To get lost.) *Perdámonos antes de que llegue la policía.* "Let's scram before the police get here."

PERICA, 1. *L.Am./S, n., drugs.* Cocaine. *La perica está fregando a muchas familias aquí y allá.* "The white stuff is screwing up families everywhere." **2.** *Spain, n.* Young woman. *A mí me gustan las pericas inteligentes.* "I dig smart chicks." **See also ¡VAYA A LA PERICA!**

PERIQUITO, TA, *Car., n., drugs.* Cocaine. (Lit. Parakeet.) *Afortunadamente Hugo ya no es adicto al periquito.* "Fortunately, Hugo is no longer addicted to coke."

PERNO, NA, *L.Am./S, adj.* Stupid, incompetent. (Lit. Bolt.) *El mecánico en ese garaje es un perno, no confíes en él.* "The mechanic at that garage is useless; don't count on him."

PERRA, 1. *L.Am./C, adj. or n.* Bitch, woman of various men. (Lit. Bitch.) *Esa mujer es una perra. Tiene un hom-*

bre diferente todos los días. "That woman is a bitch. She has a different man every day." **2.** *L.Am./S, pl. n.* Foot odor. *¡Qué perras! Anda, lávate los pies.* "What a smell! Go wash your feet."

PERRETA, *L.Am./S, n.* Fit. *Le dio una perreta de los mil demonios.* "She threw a fit."

PERRO, *L.Am./C, adj. or n.* Unfaithful man. (Lit. Dog.) *El marido de Lupe es un perro.* "Lupe's husband is a cheating dog." **2.** *L.Am./S, adj. or n.* Mean, despicable person. *Ese hombre es un perro, hace sufrir a todo el mundo.* "That man is a cur; he makes everybody suffer."

PESADO, DA, *L.Am./N, adj.* Dull, boring, annoying. (Lit. Heavy.) *El primo de Jorge es un pesado, nunca nos deja en paz.* "Jorge's cousin is a pain; he never leaves us alone."

PESCADO, *L.Am./S, n.* Woman. (Lit. Fish.) *En la fiesta de esta noche habrá muy buenos pescados.* "There will be good-looking women at the party tonight."

PESCAR EN LAS MORAS, *U.S., idiom.* To catch red-handed. *Le pescaron en las moras vendiendo juana.* "They caught the dude red-handed selling pot."

PESETA, *U.S., n.* Twenty-five-cent piece, quarter. (Lit. Peseta.) *Préstame una peseta para el teléfono.* "Lend me a quarter for the telephone."

PESETERO, RA, *Spain, n.* Materialistic person, somebody interested in money. *Sólo te interesa el dinero, eres una pesetera.* "You're only interested in money; you are a money-grubber."

PESO, *U.S., n.* Dollar. (Lit. Peso.) *Sólo pagan seis pesos la hora en esa fábrica.* "They only pay six bucks an hour at that factory."

PESO MIERDA, *Spain, idiom.* Flyweight. *Vamos a ver la pelea de peso mierda.* "Let's watch the flyweights fight."

PESTE, *L.Am., adj. or n.* Bad person or thing. (Lit. Pox.) *Pedro, eres la peste. Me prometiste el trabajo para hoy.* "Pedro, you are the worst. You promised the job for today."

PESTE A GRAJO, *Car., idiom.* Body odor. *Si no te bañas, vas a coger tremenda peste a grajo.* "If you don't bathe, you are going to have terrible B.O."

PESTOSOS, *Spain, pl. n.* Socks. *No me quito los zapatos porque tengo los pestosos rotos.* "I don't take off my shoes because I've got holes in my smelly socks."

PETACA, 1. *Car., adj. or n.* Loafer. *Alberto es una petaca que nunca trabaja.* "Alberto is a loafer who never works." **2.** *L.Am./N, n.* Buttock, cheek. *Cuando me senté en el autobús alcancé lugar para una sola petaca.* "When I sat down on the bus there was only enough room for one cheek."

PETACONA, *L.Am./N, adj. or n.* Full-figured woman, big-butted woman. *La esposa del carnicero está bien petacona, no tiene ni en qué sentarse.* "The butcher's wife is a big-butted woman; she doesn't even have a place to sit on."

PETANCO, *Car., n.* Bum. *Al frente de la iglesia se paran todos los petancos a pedir limosna.* "All the bums stand in front of the church to beg."

PETARDO, *Spain, n., drugs.* Joint. (Lit. Firecracker.) *Querían que me fumara un petardo y dije que no.* "They wanted me to smoke a joint and I said no."

PETATE See PETANCO

PETATEARSE, *L.Am./N, prnl. v.* To die. *Eso del dengue es muy serio, hasta hay quien se petatea de eso.* "The thing about dengue fever is that it is very serious; people even die from it."

PETISO, SA See PETIZO

PETIZO, ZA, *L.Am./S, adj.* Short. *Miguel se ve muy chistoso junto a la petiza de su novia.* "Miguel looks funny next to his tiny girlfriend."

PEZUÑA, *Spain, n.* Foot. (Lit. Hoof.) *Marta me pisó la pezuña cuando estábamos bailando.* "Martha stepped on my hoof when we were dancing."

PIANISTA, *L.Am./S, n., crim.* Skilled pickpocket. *Tu amigo Alfredo resultó ser un pianista, me robó la cartera y ni cuenta me di.* "Your friend Alfredo turned out to be a very skilled pickpocket—he stole my wallet and I didn't even notice."

PIANO, PIANO, *L.Am./N, idiom.* Calm down, cool it. *Piano, piano, Marcos, estás muy nervioso.* "Calm down Marcos; you are very edgy."

PIANTADO, DA, *L.Am./S, adj.* Crazy. *Pobre Pablo, quedó piantado desde que la mujer lo dejó.* "Poor Pablo, he has been crazy since his wife left him."

PIAR, *Spain, v.* To talk too much. (Lit. To chirp.) *Me reuní con mis amigas y pasamos cuatro horas piando.* "I got together with my friends and we spent four hours gabbing."

PIBE, 1. *L.Am./S, n.* Boy. *Dile al pibe que es hora de hacer la tarea.* "Tell the kid it is time to do his homework." **2. PIBE, BA,** *L.Am./S, adj. or n.* Young person, kid. *Todos los pibes del décimo grado van a ir a la excursión.* "All the tenth-grade kids are going on an excursion."

PICADA, *Car., n., crim.* Petty theft. *Por una miserable picada terminamos en la cárcel.* "For a miserable little theft, we end up in jail."

PICADO, DA, 1. *L.Am./C, adj.* Tipsy. *Pepe baila más cuando está picado que cuando no bebe.* "Pepe dances more when he's tipsy than when he doesn't drink." **2.** *L.Am., adj.* Jealous. *Efraim se pone bien picado cuando ve a la novia hablar con otro.* "Efraim gets green with jealousy when he sees his girl talking to another guy."

PICAR, *Spain, v., crim.* To kill. (Lit. To puncture.) *Anoche trataron de picarme en ese callejón.* "Last night they tried to bump me off in that alleyway."

PICAR PIEDRA, *L.Am./N, idiom.* To campaign for office. (Lit. To break stone.) *El candidato viajaba a todas partes picando piedra para darse a conocer.* "The candidate campaigned all over to get exposure."

PICARSE, 1. *Car., prnl. v.* To get a little drunk. *Me tomé dos copas de vino y me piqué.* "I had two glasses of wine and got tipsy." **2.** *L.Am., prnl. v.* To get upset. *Se picó cuando la muchacha se rio de él.* "He got upset when the girl laughed at him."

PICHA, *Spain, n.* Penis. *Una mujer le cortó la picha al marido.* "A woman cut off her husband's dick."

PICHICATO, TA, *L.Am./N, adj. or n.* Cheap, tightwad, cheapskate. *Su papá es tan pichicato que les cuenta los refrescos que se toman en casa.* "His father is such a cheapskate that he counts the sodas they drink at home."

PICHIRRE, *L.Am./S, adj.* Cheap, tight. *Mi padre es muy pichirre y no quiere comprar nada bueno.* "My father is very tight and never wants to buy anything good."

PICHO, CHA, 1. *L.Am./S, adj.* Rotten. *Esa banana está picha, tírala a la basura.* "That banana is yucky; throw it in the trash." **2.** *L.Am./S, adj.* Worthless, false. *Los Jiménez descubrieron que su Picasso es picho.* "The Jimenezes discovered that their Picasso is fake."

PICHÓN, 1. *Car., adj. or n.* Handsome young man, hunk. (Lit. Young pigeon.) *Ese pichón está perfecto para mi hija.* "That hunk is perfect for my daughter." **2.** *Car., n.* Cigarette butt. *No tires los pichones al piso.* "Don't throw butts on the floor." **3.** *L.Am./N, n.* Easy rival, pushover. *A mí me agarraron de pichón cuando les dije que no sabía jugar.* "They took me for a pushover when I told them I didn't know how to play." **4. PICHÓN, NA,** *L.Am., n.* Novice. *Soy una pichona de cocinera, sé tres recetas.* "I am a novice at cooking. I know three recipes."

PICHONA, *Car., adj. or n.* Pretty young woman. (Lit. Young pigeon.) *Paco me presentó a una pichona lindísima.* "Paco introduced me to a beautiful chick."

PICHULA, *L.Am./S, n.* Penis, dick. *El perrito chihuahua de Pancho tiene la pichula tan grande que se cree gran danés.* "Pancho's little chihuahua has such a big dick that he thinks he is a Great Dane."

PICO See PICHULA

PICO O MONA, *L.Am./N, idiom.* Heads or tails. *Vamos a jugar para ver quien va a limpiar el carro. Qué quieres, ¿pico o mona?* "Let's play to see who is going to clean the car. What do you want, heads or tails?"

PICOTA, *Spain, n.* Nose. (Lit. Top, point.) *Adela se cayó de la bici y se partió la picota.* "Adela fell off the bike and broke her snoz."

PICOTEADO, DA, *L.Am./N, adj.* Pockmarked. *Ignacio quedó todo picoteado de la cara después del acné.* "Ignacio's face was all pockmarked from acne."

PICÚ, CÚA, *Car., adj. or n.* Person of bad character, lowlife. *No quiero tener nada que ver con ese picú.* "I don't want to have anything to do with that rotten bum."

PICUDO, DA, 1. *L.Am./N, adj.* Knowledgeable, sharp. *Si quieres comprar en esa tienda, ve a Paco, él es el picudo de allí.* "If you want to buy in that store, go see Paco; he is the guy in the know there." **2.** *L.Am./N, adj.* Skilled or good at something. *Juan es muy picudo en ajedrez.* Juan is very good at chess. **3.** *L.Am./N, adj.* Difficult, complicated, tricky. *Esa maniobra es bien picuda.* That maneuver is very tricky.

PIEDRA, 1. *L.Am./S, adj.* Good-looking. (Lit. Stone.) *Mi amigo Chito es tan piedra que tiene a las chicas esperando en cola.* "My friend Chito is such a good-looker that he has many girls waiting in line." **2.** *L.Am./S, n.* Anger. *Me dio tanta piedra cuando se me dañó el televisor que lo cogí a patadas.* "I got so angry when my TV broke down that I started kicking it."

PIEDRAS, *L.Am./S, pl. n.* Lies, untruths, fibs. *Lo único que sabes hablar son piedras.* "You only know how to tell lies."

PIEL, *Spain, n.* Wallet. (Lit. Skin.) *Ayer en el centro me robaron la piel.* "They stole my wallet downtown yesterday."

PIERNÓDROMO, *L.Am./S, n.* Nightclub. *Me gustaría ir a* *bailar esta noche a un piernódromo de salsa.* "I would like to go dancing to a salsa nightclub tonight."

PIFIA, *L.Am./S, n.* Mistake, error, goof. *Ese trabajo tiene muchas pifias, Ud. tiene que corregirlas.* "That job had a lot of goofs; you have to correct them."

PIFIARLA, *L.Am., v.* To make a mistake. *No le cuentes a nadie que la volví a pifiar.* "Don't tell anyone I made the same boo-boo again."

PILA, *L.Am./S, n.* Large amount, quantity. (Lit. Pile.) *Tengo una pila de trabajo y no sé por donde empezar.* "I've got a pile of work and I don't know where to begin."

¡PILAS!, *L.Am./S, interj.* Warning. *¡Pilas! ¡Que se cae!* "Look out! It's going to fall!"

PÍLDORA, *L.Am./S, n.* Oral contraceptive. (Lit. Pill.) *Si hubieras tomado la píldora, no estarías embarazada.* "If you had taken the pill, you wouldn't be pregnant."

PILLADO, 1. *Spain, n.* Bad situation. *No sé cómo salir de este pillado.* "I don't know how to get out of this mess." **2. PILLADO, DA,** *L.Am., adj.* Caught. *¡Estás pillado, devuelve lo que te robaste!* "You're caught; return what you stole!"

PILLAR, 1. *L.Am., v.* To catch. *El papá de Mary nos pilló besándonos.* "Mary's father caught us kissing." **2.** *Spain, v., crim.* To rob, to steal. *Carmen se pilló unas flores en el almacén.* "Carmen pinched some flowers at the department store."

PILÓN, *L.Am./N, n.* Sales incentive, gift. *¡Mira, compré el estéreo y me regalaron un CD de pilón!* "Look, I bought the stereo and they gave me a CD as a bonus!"

PILTRAFA, *L.Am., adj. or n.* Crude, vulgar person. *Esa piltrafa tiene prohibida la entrada a mi casa.* "That trash isn't allowed in my house."

PIÑA, 1. *L.Am./S, n.* Accident. (Lit. Pineapple.) *Claudia tuvo una piña terrible viniendo por la autopista.* "Claudia had a terrible accident coming down the highway." **2.** *L.Am./S, n.* Blow. *En la pelea le dieron tantas piñas* *que terminó en el hospital.* "He got so many blows in the fight that he wound up in the hospital."

PINCEL, *L.Am./S, n.* Knife. (Lit. Brush.) *Al pobre Julián lo agarraron con pincel sólo para robarle la cartera.* "Poor Julian was attacked with a knife just to get his wallet stolen."

PINCHA, *Car., n.* Job, gig. *¿Qué tal te va en tu nueva pincha?* "How's the new job going?"

PINCHAR, *L.Am./S, v.* To stab with a knife. (Lit. To prick.) *Como no quise entregarles mi reloj, los ladrones me pincharon.* "Since I didn't want to give them my watch, the thieves stabbed me."

PINCHAZO, *L.Am./S, n.* Knife cut or stab. (Lit. Prick.) *A Andrea la mataron a pinchazos.* "They stabbed Andrea to death."

PINCHE, 1. *L.Am./S, adj.* No good, bad, damned. *Él le regaló un reloj de oro y ella le correspondió con un pinche pisacorbata.* "He gave her a gold watch and she matched the gift with a stinking tie tack." **2.** *L.Am./C, adj.* Cheap, tight. *Jaime es tan pinche que siempre quiere leer el periódico de los demás.* "Jaime is so tight he always wants to read somebody else's newspaper." **3.** *L.Am./N, adj.* Damn, fucking. *El jefe de Olivia es un pinche viejo verde.* "Olivia's boss is a fucking dirty old man."

PINCHO, *L.Am./N, n.* Shish kebab. *En ese restaurante venden unos pinchos riquísimos.* "At that restaurant they sell delicious shish kebabs."

PINGA, *L.Am./N, n., drugs.* Drug, pill. *Yo vi a César vendiendo pingas en la escuela.* "I saw Cesar selling pills in school."

PINGO, 1. *L.Am./N, n.* Mischievous child. *Ese pingo me desinfló los neumáticos.* "That rotten kid let the air out of my tires." **2.** *L.Am./N, n., drugs.* Drug addict. *Benjamín se hizo pingo con las Valium que le robaba a su mamá.* "Benjamin became an addict on the Valium he stole from his mother." **3.** *L.Am./S, n.* Horse. *Perdí* *todo lo que tenía en un pingo.* "I lost everything I had on a horse."

PINGÜINO, *L.Am./S, n.* Nun. (Lit. Penguin.) *Cinco pingüinos están tomando el curso conmigo.* "Five nuns are taking the course with me."

PIÑOS, *Spain, pl. n.* Teeth. *Si no los cepillas se te van a dañar los piños.* "If you don't brush, you're going to hurt your pearly whites."

PIÑOSO, *L.Am./S, adj.* Unfortunate. *Juan es muy piñoso porque siempre le chocan su auto.* "Juan is very unlucky because his car always gets hit."

PINTA, 1. *L.Am./C, n.* Strange-looking person. *No te metas con ese pinta, no le tengo confianza.* "Leave that weirdo alone; I am not sure about him." **2.** *L.Am./S, n.* Appearance. *La novia de Leopoldo tiene una pinta horrible.* "Leopoldo's girlfriend looks horrible." **3.** *L.Am./S, n., crim.* Criminal, hood. *Arrestaron a dos pintas por robar mi auto.* "They arrested two hoods for stealing my car." **See also IRSE DE PINTA**

PÍNTELA COMO QUIERA, *L.Am./S, idiom.* If you don't like it, do as you please. *Píntela como quiera, yo cumplí con contarle lo que pasó.* "Do whatever you like; I did my part by telling you what happened."

PINTO, TA, *Car., adj.* Freckled. *La niña de Lucía es pinta y pelirroja.* "Lucia's girl is redheaded and freckled."

PIOJO, JA, *Car., n.* Child, rugrat. (Lit. Louse.) *Los piojos son felices en el nuevo parque.* "The rugrats are happy in the new park."

PIOJOSA, *L.Am./S, n.* Head. (Lit. Lousy.) *Usa la piojosa antes de meter la pata.* "Use your head before you get in trouble."

PIOLA, *L.Am./S, adj.* Talented, handy. *Tu hijo es piola para la mecánica.* "Your son is good at mechanics."

PIOLADA, *L.Am./S, n.* Something done with talent. *El concierto que dieron los muchachos anoche fue una piolada.* "The concert the boys gave last night was a knockout."

PIPA, *L.Am./N, n.* Tank truck. (Lit. Pipe.) *Cuando se descompuso la bomba, nos tuvieron que llevar agua en pipas.* "When the pump broke down, they had to bring us water in tank trucks."

PIPÍ, 1. *L.Am., n.* Child's penis. *A mi nene le hicieron la circuncisión y le duele mucho el pipí.* "They circumcised my little boy and now his little doohickey hurts." **2.** *L.Am., Spain, n.* Urine, pee. *Concha tuvo que hacer pipí y mi mamá la llevó al baño.* "Concha had to pee and my mother took her to the bathroom."

PIPÓN, NA, *L.Am./S, adj. or n.* Big belly. *Mi compadre Ricky se está poniendo muy pipón por tomar muchas heladas.* "My pal Ricky is getting a big belly from drinking too many cold ones."

PIQUEO, *L.Am./S, n.* Appetizer. *En el restaurante de mi hermano Luis sirven los mejores piqueos de la ciudad.* "In my brother Luis's restaurant they serve the best appetizers in the city."

PIQUININI, NA, *Car., n.* Small child. *Todas mis amigas van a venir mañana con sus piquininis.* "All my girlfriends are coming tomorrow with their tots."

PIRADO, DA, *L.Am./N, adj.* Crazy. *Cada día dice más insensateces, creo que está pirado.* "Every day he talks more nonsense. I think he is off his rocker."

PIRARSE, 1. *L.Am./N, prnl. v.* To go crazy. *Santiago se piró por completo y lo van a internar.* "Santiago went completely nuts and they have to hospitalize him." **2.** *Car., prnl. v.* To take off, to leave. *Si no te gusta la fiesta, te piras y ya está.* "If you don't like the party, take a hike."

PIRATA, *L.Am., n., crim.* Borderline crook, person of dubious activities. (Lit. Pirate.) *Ese tipo es un pirata y va a terminar en la cárcel.* "That guy is a crook and he is going to wind up in jail."

PIRINOLA, *L.Am./N, n.* Penis. *Beto está tan chiquito que le tienes que ayudar a sacar la pirinola.* "Beto is so small that you have to help him pull out his weenie."

PIROBO, BA, *L.Am./S, adj., youth.* Preppy. *Esos pirobos no saben lo que es la vida. Tienen de todo y no les falta nada.* "Those preppies don't know what life is. They have everthing and lack nothing."

PIRUJA, *L.Am./N, n.* Prostitute. *Se me acercó una piruja que parecía niña de lo joven que estaba.* "The hooker who approached me was so young that she looked like a little girl."

PIRULÍ, *Spain, n.* Child's penis. *Le estoy enseñando a mi bebé a que no juegue con su pirulí.* "I am teaching my baby not to play with his dickey."

PIRULO, *L.Am./S, n.* Chain used as a weapon. *No te olvides de tu pirulo cuando regreses al viejo barrio.* "Don't forget your chain when you go back to the old neighborhood."

PISHAR, *L.Am./S, v.* To pee. (From Italian "pischar.") *Si no encuentro un baño, me voy a pishar aquí mismo.* "If I don't find a bathroom, I am going to take a leak right here."

PISOS, *L.Am./S, pl. n.* Shoes. (Lit. Floors.) *Mira cómo tienes los pisos de gastados.* "Look how worn out your shoes are."

PISTEAR, *L.Am./N, v.* To drink. *Armando siempre se va a pistear con los amigos después del trabajo.* "Armando always goes out to bend elbows with his buddies after work."

PISTO, *L.Am./N, n.* Alcoholic drink. *Raúl nada más se tomó un pisto de ron en la fiesta.* "Raul just had a shot of rum at the party."

PITACHA, *L.Am./S, adj. or n.* Short and fat woman. *Tu amiga Rina es una pitacha.* "Your friend Rina is short and fat."

PITAR, *L.Am./S, v.* To referee a game. *Ese partido lo va a pitar un colombiano.* "A Colombian is going to ref that game."

PITEADERA, *L.Am./S, n.* Protest. *Los presos comenzaron* *la piteadera cuando no les sirvieron desayuno.* "The prisoners started a protest when they were not served breakfast."

PITO, 1. *L.Am./S, n., drugs.* Marijuana joint. (Lit. Whistle.) *Vimos a los muchachos fumando un pito en el garaje.* "We saw the boys smoking a joint in the garage." **2.** *L.Am., n.* Penis. *Juan vive obsesionado con el tamaño de su pito.* "Juan is obsessed with the size of his cock." **3.** *L.Am./S, n.* Woman who remains a virgin. *Juan dice que su novia llegará pito a la luna de miel.* "Juan says that his fiancée will still be a virgin for their honeymoon."

PITOPAUSIA, *Spain, n.* Male menopause. *El mal genio de mi papá seguro se debe a la pitopausia.* "My father's bad temper is surely due to dickapause."

PITRI MITRI, *L.Am./S, idiom.* Expression of approval. *Flaquita, te pasaste, tu auto está de la pitri mitri.* "Far-out baby! Your car is awesome."

PITUCO, CA, *L.Am./S, adj.* Arrogant, pedantic. *Ese pituco se cree la divina pomada.* "That stuck-up fool thinks he is hot stuff."

PITUFO, FA, *L.Am./S, adj. or n.* Short person. (Lit. Smurf.) *Todas en mi familia somos pitufas pero bonitas.* "In my family, we are all shorties but pretties."

PITUTO, *L.Am./S, n.* Recommendation, influence. *Gerardo tenía muchos pitutos y así le dieron la beca.* "Gerardo had a lot of recommendations, so they gave him the scholarship."

PIYAMA DE TRIPLAY, *L.Am./N, n.* Coffin. *Fuimos al velorio para ver la piyama de triplay que le compraron a Juan.* "We went to the wake to see the coffin they bought Juan."

PIZELI, *L.Am./S, adj.* Submissive. *Tu amigo pizeli hace todo lo que su mujer le dice.* "Your wimpy friend does everything his wife says."

PLANCHA, *L.Am./S, n.* Social blunder. (Lit. Iron.) *¡Qué* *plancha! No sabía qué tenedor usar.* "What a stumble! I didn't know which fork to use."

PLANCHAR, 1. *L.Am./S, v.* To commit a social blunder. (Lit. To iron.) *José planchó fuerte cuando se le salió un pedo.* "Jose really screwed up when he let loose a fart." **2.** *L.Am./S, v.* To remain seated at a party, to be a wall-flower. *Nadie la sacó a bailar y se quedó planchando.* "Nobody asked her to dance and she remained a wall-flower."

PLANCHAR LA OREJA, *Spain, idiom.* To sleep. *Esta noche me voy a planchar la oreja temprano.* "Tonight I am going to hit the sack early."

PLANCITO, *L.Am./S, n.* To get lucky. (Lit. Little plan.) *Creo que voy a tener un plancito esta noche.* "I think I'll get lucky tonight."

PLANETERA, *L.Am./S, n.* Slut. *Yo creo que Sofía es una planetera.* "I think Sofia is a slut."

PLANTE, *Car., n.* Lover, suitor. *Dicen que la esposa de Rodrigo tiene un plante secreto.* "They say that Rodrigo's wife has a secret lover."

PLASMA, *Car., adj.* Incompetent. *El hombre que vino a arreglar la lavadora es un plasma.* "The man who came to fix the washer is a lummox."

PLASTA, 1. *L.Am., adj.* Boring, mean. *Ese amigo tuyo es una plasta, no lo traigas más.* "That friend of yours is a bummer; don't bring him anymore." **2.** *L.Am./S, n.* Annoying person. *Esa amiga de mi mamá es una plasta, la detesto.* "That friend of my mother's is a pain in the ass. I can't stand her."

PLÁSTICO, *L.Am., Spain, n.* Credit card. (Lit. Plastic.) *Voy a pagar los muebles con plástico.* "I am going to pay for the furniture with plastic."

PLATA, *L.Am./S, n.* Money. (Lit. Silver.) *La falta de plata me tiene muy preocupado.* "The lack of cash has got me worried."

PLATANAZO, ZA, *L.Am./S, adj. or n.* Very tall individual.

Julián es un platanazo, está bueno para jugar baloncesto. "Julian is a very tall guy; he will be good for basketball."

PLATERO, RA, *L.Am./C, adj. or n.* Person who likes to make money. (Lit. Silversmith.) *Paco es un platero, no le importa lo que tiene que hacer para enriquecerse.* "Paco is a moneymaker; he doesn't care what he has to do to get rich."

PLATUDO, DA, *L.Am., adj.* Wealthy. *El cuñado de Rodrigo es muy platudo pero no le ayuda en nada.* "Rodrigo's brother-in-law is made of money, but he doesn't help him at all."

PLAYO, *L.Am./C, n.* Homosexual. *El hijo de la programadora es un playo.* "The programmer's son is a fairy."

PLEANGOCHA, *L.Am., adj. or n.* Vulgar, low-class. *Lola es muy pleangocha en su forma de hablar.* "Lola is very salty in her way of talking."

PLEBE, 1. *L.Am./N, n.* People, populace. (Lit. Plebs.) *Toda la plebe fue a ver el concierto de Julio Iglesias.* "Everybody went to see Julio Iglesias's concert." **2.** *L.Am./S, n.* Person of low taste and low class. *Dile a tu amigo que no me interesa salir con él porque es muy plebe.* "Tell your friend that I am not interested in going out with him because he is a yokel."

PLEITISTA, *L.Am./S, n.* Attorney or legal defender. *Tu pleitista es bien gritón. Ojalá que gane el caso.* "Your attorney is very loud. I hope he wins the case."

PLOMO, *L.Am./S, n.* Bus passenger who is just in for the ride. (Lit. Lead.) *En el autobús de Lima/Callao siempre viajan muchos plomos.* "In the Lima/Callao bus there are many passengers who ride aimlessly."

PLOMOS, *L.Am./S, pl. n.* Lungs. *Deja de fumar, que te daña los plomos.* "Quit smoking; it is messing up your lungs."

PLOMOS QUEMADOS, *L.Am./S, idiom.* Damaged lungs. *No me hizo caso y ahora tiene los plomos quemados.* "He didn't listen to me and now his lungs are messed up."

PLUMA, 1. *L.Am./N, n.* Fart. (Lit. Feather.) *Miguel se echó una pluma dentro del elevador.* "Miguel cut a fart in the elevator." **2.** *L.Am./S, n.* Sharp pocket knife. *Qué buena pluma te regaló tu papá, pero ten cuidado.* "That's a nice knife your dad gave you, but be careful."

PLUMA BLANCA, *L.Am./N, n.* Big boss, top man or woman. *Pedí hablar con el pluma blanca.* "I asked to talk to the big boss."

POCA LUZ, *L.Am./N, n.* Person who uses glasses. *A Carlos le decían "el poca luz" porque usaba lentes.* "They called Carlos 'shady' because he used glasses."

POCA MADRE, *L.Am./N, adj. or n.* Jerk. *¡Qué poca madre aquél, venir a cobrarle a la viuda en el velorio!* "What a jerk that guy is, to try to collect from the widow at the wake."

POCHISMO, *L.Am./N, n.* Use of hispanized English words or expressions by some American Hispanics, usually on the border. *La palabra "troca" es un pochismo.* "The word 'troca' is a Tex-Mex expression."

POCHO, 1. *L.Am./N, n.* Mixture of English and Spanish spoken on the border. *Fernando habla muy pocho porque nació en Los Ángeles.* "Fernando speaks a lot of Spanglish because he was born in Los Angeles." **2.** *L.Am., adj. or n.* U.S. citizen of Hispanic blood. *Lorenzo se pasa por mexicano pero es pocho, nacido en Texas.* "Lorenzo passes for a Mexican but he is a Latino born in Texas."

POCHOLO, LA, *Spain, adj.* Handsome, pretty, nice. *Qué hijos tan pocholos tienes.* "You have some cool kids."

POLA, *L.Am./S, n.* Beer. *Voy a salir esta noche con mis amigos a tomarme unas polas.* "I'll go out tonight with my friends and have some suds."

POLADA, *L.Am./C, n.* Something done in poor taste. *Alberto hizo una polada en el restaurante cuando eructó.* "Alberto was gross at the restaurant when he belched."

POLI, *L.Am., Spain, n.* Police. *La poli llegó justo a tiempo.* "The cops arrived just in time."

POLICÍA ACOSTADO, *L.Am./S, n.* Speed bump. *Pusieron policías acostados por toda la cuadra para evitar accidentes.* "They put speed bumps along the whole block to avoid accidents."

POLILLA, *L.Am./S, n.* Hooker. (Lit. Moth.) *La calle Del Río está llena de polillas.* "Del Rio Street is full of hookers."

POLIZONTE, *L.Am./S, n.* Police officer. *El polizonte se llevó a Fercho en la patrulla.* "The cop took Fercho off in the patrol car."

POLLA, *Spain, n.* Penis. (Lit. Chick.) *Una polla dura no tiene conciencia.* "A hard dick has no conscience."

POLLERO, *L.Am./N, n.* People smuggler. (Lit. Chicken dealer.) *Norma tuvo que pagarle 300 dólares al pollero para pasar la frontera.* "Norma had to pay $300 to the smuggler to get her across the border."

POLLO, 1. *L.Am./S, n.* Phlegmy spit. (Lit. Chicken.) *Lo castigaron por estarse tirando pollos todo el tiempo.* "He was grounded because he was spitting oysters all the time." **2. POLLO, LLA,** *L.Am./S., adj. or n.* Young person. *Germán se casó con una polla.* "German married a young thing."

POLO, LA, *L.Am./C, adj. or n.* Hick, yokel. *El primo de Roberto es un polo, no lo quiero en mi casa.* "Robert's cousin is a hick. I don't want him at my house."

POLOLO, LA, *L.Am./S, n.* Boyfriend, girlfriend. *"¿Dónde está Julia?" "Se fue con el pololo."* " 'Where is Julia?' 'She went with her boyfriend.' "

POLVO, *L.Am./S, n.* Sexual intercourse. (Lit. Dust.) *Llevo como dos semanas sin echar un polvo.* "It's been about two weeks since I've had a piece of ass."

POMADA, *Spain, n.* High society. (Lit. Pomade.) *Quiero casarme con un hombre de la pomada.* "I want to marry a man from high society."

POMO, 1. *L.Am./S, n.* Nothing. (Lit. Pome.) *Sonia dice que está a dieta y no quiere comer un pomo.* "Sonia says she is on a diet and doesn't want to eat a thing." **2.** *L.Am./N, n.* Drink. *A Ricardo le gusta juntarse con los amigos a tomarse sus pomos.* "Ricardo likes to get together with his buddies and have a few drinks."

POMPA, *L.Am./N, n.* Buttocks. (Bubble.) *Tuvieron un concurso en la disco para ver quién tenía las pompas más sexis.* "They had a contest at the disco to see who had the sexiest butt."

POMPIS, *Spain, n.* Buttocks, behind, butt. *El pompis de Ángela es como de concurso.* "Angela's butt is right out of a beauty contest."

PONCHADO, DA, *L.Am./N, adj.* Putting on bulk. *Lalo se puso bien ponchado desde que empezó a ir al gimnasio.* "Lalo got beefier since he started going to the gym."

PONCHAR, *L.Am./N, v.* To have a flat tire. *Por suerte iba lento cuando se ponchó la rueda.* "Fortunately, I was going slow when the tire got flat."

PONCHAR TARJETA, *L.Am./N, idiom.* To check in. *Antes de ir con los amigos tuve que ponchar tarjeta con mi novia.* "Before going out with my friends, I had to check in with my girlfriend."

PONER A CIEN, 1. *L.Am./S, idiom.* To sexually arouse someone. *Con tus caricias me pones a cien.* "Your caresses get me going." **2.** *L.Am./S, idiom.* To get very angry. *Mi mamá se puso a cien cuando rompí su florero preferido.* "My mother went through the roof when I broke her favorite flower vase."

PONER COMO CAMOTE, *L.Am./N, idiom.* To put down. *Mi papá me puso como camote cuando lo mandó llamar el profesor.* "My father put me down when he was called by the professor."

PONER EL DEDO, *L.Am./N, idiom, crim.* To accuse, to squeal on. *Detuvieron al ladrón después de que su amigo le puso el dedo.* "They apprehended the thief after his friend fingered him."

PONER LOS CUERNOS, *L.Am./S, v.* To cheat on one's

spouse or significant other. (Lit. To put the horns on someone.) *Gloria le está poniendo los cuernos al marido y él ni cuenta se da.* "Gloria is cheating on her husband and he doesn't even notice."

PONER UN CUATRO, *L.Am./N, idiom.* To set a trap. *Le pusieron un cuatro para hacerlo confesar.* "They set a trap to make him confess."

PONERLE LA TAPA AL POMO, *Car., idiom.* To go too far, to be the straw that broke the camel's back. *Y para ponerle la tapa al pomo, se me cayó el refresco encima del vestido.* "And to make matters worse, the soda got splashed on my dress."

PONERSE AL BRINCO, *L.Am./N, idiom.* To get jumpy, to attack. *Hernán se puso al brinco cuando vio a David con su novia.* "Hernan attacked David when he saw him with his girlfriend."

PONERSE CHANGO, *L.Am./N, idiom.* To get sharp, to bone up. *Hay que ponerse chango para que no te roben en el mercado.* "You've got to be wide awake so that they don't steal from you at the market."

PONERSE CHIVA, *L.Am./C, idiom.* To get angry. *Mi padre se puso chiva conmigo cuando llegué tarde.* "My father got pissed off with me when I got home late."

PONERSE CIEGO, *Spain, idiom.* To get blind drunk. *Óscar se puso ciego tomando tequila anoche.* "Oscar got blind drunk drinking tequila last night."

PONERSE COMO UNA MOTO, *Spain, idiom.* To become very active under the influence of alcohol or drugs. *Cada vez que te emborrachas te pones como una moto.* "Every time we get drunk, you get revved up like a motorcycle."

PONERSE CON ALGO, *Car., idiom.* To contribute something. *Dile a tu amigo que si va con nosotros tiene que ponerse con algo.* "Tell your friend that if he's coming with us he should pitch in with something."

PONERSE LAS BOTAS, *L.Am./S, idiom.* To enjoy something to full satisfaction. *Me pondré las botas cuando vaya al viaje.* "I will have a ball when I go on the trip."

PONERSE LAS PILAS, 1. *L.Am./C, idiom.* To pay attention, to listen up. (Lit. To put the batteries in.) *Cuando ponen algo del espacio en la tele mi hijo se pone las pilas.* "When they put something about space on TV, my son gets turned on." **2.** *L.Am./C, idiom.* To be in a hurry. *Ponte las pilas muchacha si quieres llegar a tiempo.* "Get a move on, girl, if you want to arrive on time." **3.** *L.Am./S, idiom.* To be alert for an unexpected situation. *Oye, compadrito, ponte las pilas antes de que te serruchen el piso.* "Hey man, you better get right on it before they get ahead of you."

PONERSE NEGRO, GRA, *L.Am./S, idiom.* To get angry. *Cecilia se puso negra cuando le estrellaron el carro.* "Cecilia blew her top when they crashed her car."

PONÉRSELE, *L.Am./S, prnl. v.* To imagine. *Se me puso que no te gustaría mi corte de pelo.* "I got the idea that you didn't like my haircut."

PONJA, *L.Am./S, adj.* Japanese. *En el Perú hay una colonia ponja muy grande.* "In Peru there is a big Japanese colony."

PONQUÉ, *L.Am./S, n.* Cake. *El ponqué de cumpleaños que le hice a Daniel quedó riquísimo.* "The birthday cake I baked for Daniel was delicious."

PONTE BONITO, *L.Am./S, idiom.* You better behave. *Ponte bonito Jaimito o te vas a la cama sin cenar.* "You better behave, Jaimito, or you will go to bed without dinner."

POPÓ, *L.Am., n.* Excrement, crap, shit. *Luisa tuvo que levantarse en la noche para hacer popó.* "Luisa had to get up at night to do poo."

POPOFF, *L.Am./N, adj.* Elegant, ritzy. *Mari estás muy popoff con ese vestido.* "Mari, you are real ritzy in that dress."

POPOTE, *L.Am./N, n.* Drinking straw. *No me gusta tomar refresco sin popote en los restaurantes.* "I don't like to have sodas without a straw in restaurants."

POR ANGAS O POR MANGAS, *L.Am./N, idiom.* One way or another. *Bueno, por angas o por mangas, me voy para España el mes que viene.* "Well, one way or another I am going to Spain next month."

POR LA MACETA, *Car., idiom.* Very well, great. *Fui a visitar a mi familia en el pueblo y todos están por la maceta.* "I went to visit my family in the village and they were all in good shape."

POR LO BAJO, 1. *L.Am./S, idiom.* Clandestinely. *La policía le tomó a Carlos varias fotos por lo bajo.* "The police took several pictures of Carlos on the sly." **2.** *L.Am./S, idiom.* At least. *Te tocarán cien pesos por lo bajo.* "You'll get at least a hundred bucks."

¡POR LOS COJONES!, *Spain, interj.* Expression of negation or rejection. *¡Por los cojones! Yo no quiero hablar con él.* "Balls! I don't want to talk with him."

POR PIOCHA, *L.Am./N, idiom.* Each, per person. *Pagamos la cuenta del restaurante y salió a cien pesos por piocha.* "We paid the bill at the restaurant and it turned out to be a hundred pesos per person."

POR SI LAS MOSCAS, *L.Am./S, idiom.* Just in case. *Voy a llevar la sombrilla por si las moscas.* "I am going to take an umbrella just in case."

PORFA, *L.Am., idiom.* Please. (Contraction of "por favor.") *Porfa José, dime cuando me vas a pagar.* "Puleeze Jose, tell me when you are going to pay me."

PORFIRIO, *L.Am./S, adj.* Stubborn. *No seas porfirio, éste no es el camino correcto.* "Don't be stubborn; this is not the right way."

PORONGOS, *L.Am./S, pl. n.* Big breasts, boobs, gozongas. *Oye Daniel, chequea los porongos de Lolita.* "Hey, Daniel, check out Lolita's gozongas."

PORQUERÍA, *L.Am., n.* Useless, worthless person. *Despidieron al entrenador porque era una porquería.* "They fired the trainer because he was a worthless shit."

PORTACACA, *L.Am./S, n.* Big buttocks, big butt. *Con ese tremendo portacaca va a tener que usar dos sillas para sentarse.* "With that tremendous butt he'll have to use two chairs to sit down."

PORTUGUÉS, *L.Am./S, n.* Movie moocher. (Lit. Portuguese.) *Tengo que llevar al portugués de mi primo al cine.* "I have to take my movie-mooching cousin to the movies."

POSTA, *L.Am./S, n.* Truth. *Le dije la posta. Estaba enfermo y no tomé el examen.* "I told you the truth. I didn't take the test because I was sick."

POTO, *L.Am./S, n.* Ass. *Los niños de hoy quieren aprender a manejar antes de saber limpiarse el poto.* "Today's kids want to learn to drive before they can wipe their butt."

POTRERO, RA, *Spain, adj.* Lucky. (Lit. Herdsman for colts.) *El potrero de Miguel se ganó la lotería.* "That lucky son of a gun, Miguel, won the lottery."

POZOS, *L.Am./S, pl. n., youth.* Pants pockets. (Lit. Wells.) *Los pantalones de la juventud de hoy tienen tremendos pozos.* "These days young people's pants have enormous pockets."

PRECIOSO, *L.Am./S, n., crim.* Prisoner. (Lit. Precious.) *Mi compadre César está de precioso por estafar al Sr. Gómez.* "My buddy Cesar is a jailbird for having swindled Mr. Gómez."

PRENDER EL FOCO, *L.Am./N, idiom.* To have an idea. *Se me prendió el foco tan pronto vi el problema.* "I got an idea as soon as I saw the problem."

PRENDIDO, DA, 1. *L.Am., adj.* Turned on. *Yo iba tan prendido que ni sé quién empezó la pelea.* "I was so excited, I don't even know who started the fight." **2.** *L.Am., adj.* Great, cool. *Te va a gustar el conjunto nuevo, su música está prendidísima.* "You're gonna like the new group; their music is really cool." **3.** *L.Am./S, adj.* Drunk. *Después de dos cervezas ya está prendido.* "After two beers he's already drunk."

PREPO, *L.Am./S, adv.* Obligatorily. (From Spanish "prepotencia.") *Juan pidió perdón de prepo.* "Juan asked for forgiveness because he had to."

PRIMÍPARO, RA, *L.Am./S, adj. or n., youth.* Freshman. *Los primíparos tienen todos caras de bebés.* "All the freshmen have baby faces."

PRINCESA, *Spain, n.* Young male homosexual. (Lit. Princess.) *El vecino es maricón y vive con su princesa.* "The neighbor is a fag and he lives with his princess."

PRINGA PIE, *L.Am./C, idiom.* Diarrhea. *No pude salir en todo el fin de semana porque tenía pringa pie.* "I couldn't go out all weekend because I had the runs."

PRINGAR, 1. *Spain, v.* To work hard. *Tuve que pringar todo el día.* "I had to bust my balls all day long." **2.** *Spain, v.* To die. *Dicen que mi abuelo ya casi se va a pringar.* "My grandfather is about to give up the ghost." **3.** *Spain, v.* To fail. *Lo he intentado muchas veces y siempre pringo.* "I've tried it many times but I've always screwed up."

PROFE, *L.Am./S, n.* Professor. *El profe de matemáticas es muy inteligente.* "The math prof is very intelligent."

PRÓFUGA DEL METATE, *L.Am./N, n.* Topless dancer. *Aunque fingía ser de la alta, sabíamos que era prófuga del metate.* "Even though she pretended to be high class, we knew she was a topless dancer."

PROPIO, PIA, *L.Am./S, adj.* Great, excellent, cool, hot. *Tu nuevo vestido es bien propio.* "Your new dress is real hot."

PROSTI, *L.Am./N, n.* Prostitute. *Ha de ser buena muchacha la novia de Iván, pero se viste como prosti.* "Ivan's girlfriend must be a nice girl, but she dresses like a hooker."

PROVOCAR, *L.Am./N, v.* To feel like, to fancy. (Lit. To provoke.) *"¿Qué te provoca tomar?" "Pues me provoca un vinito rojo".* " 'What do you feel like drinking?' 'I've got a yen for a little red wine.' "

¡PUCHA!, 1. *L.Am./S, interj.* Shucks! Shoot! Shit! *¡Pucha!*

¡Dejé mi libro en casa! "Shoot! I left my book at home."

PUCHACHAS, *L.Am./N, pl. n.* Prostitutes. *Se acercaron unas puchachas a nuestra mesa para que las invitáramos a una copa.* "Some hookers came to our table to get drinks from us."

PUCHEAR, *L.Am./S, v.* To smoke. *Ya le dije que deje de puchear, que le va a hacer daño.* "I told him to quit smoking, that it was going to harm him."

PUCHERO, *L.Am., n.* Pout. *Mi hijo hace pucheros cuando no lo complacen.* "My son pouts when they don't please him."

PUCHO, 1. *L.Am./S, n.* Cigarette. *Oye, dame un pucho.* "Hey, give me a smoke." **2.** *L.Am., n.* Cigarette butt. *Ese señor se fuma hasta los puchos.* "That man even smokes the butts."

PUCHO POR PUCHO, *L.Am./S, idiom.* Little by little. *Con dieta y ejercicio bajarás de peso pucho por pucho.* "With diet and exercise, you will lose weight little by little."

PUDRIRSE, 1. *L.Am./S, prnl. v.* To get bored. (Lit. To rot oneself.) *No quiero ir a esa fiesta pues sé que me voy a pudrir.* "I don't want to go to that party because I know I am going to get bored stiff." **2.** *L.Am./S, prnl. v.* To get angry. *¿Se pudrió tu novia porque no la llamaste en su cumpleaños?* "Did your girlfriend hit the roof when you didn't call her on her birthday?"

PUENTEAR, *L.Am./S, v.* To discriminate. *El amigo de Francisco dice que lo puentearon por el color de su piel.* "Francisco's friend says that they discriminated against him for the color of his skin."

PUERCADA, *Spain, n.* Dirty trick. *No le puedo perdonar la puercada que me hizo.* "I can't forget the rotten trick he pulled on me."

PUJO, JA, *Car., n.* Unpleasant person. *No invites a Fabio porque todos opinan que es un pujo.* "Don't invite Fabio because everybody thinks that he is a jerk."

PULENTO, *L.Am./S, adj.* Useful. *El limón es pulento para adelgazar.* "Lemon is good for losing weight."

PULGUERO, *Spain, n.* Bed. *Ceci se la ha pasado todo el día en el pulguero.* "Ceci has spent the whole day in bed."

PULIR HEBILLAS, *L.Am./S, idiom.* To dance very close. (Lit. To polish belt buckles.) *A mí me encanta pulir hebillas.* "I dig tight dancing."

PULLA, *Car., n.* Insult, gibe. *¡No permito que me tires una pulla más!* "I won't allow you to give me another quip!"

PULMÓN, *L.Am./N, n.* Effeminate homosexual. (Lit. Lung.) *Mario no me cae bien porque es pulmón.* "I don't like Mario because he is a fag."

PULPO, *Spain, n.* Pain in the neck. (Lit. Octopus.) *No resisto su manera de ser, es un pulpo.* "I can't stand the way he is; he is a pain in the neck."

PULSEAR, *L.Am./S, v.* To test. *Eduardo está pulseando a su novia para asegurarse de que no está interesada en su dinero.* "Eduardo is checking out his girlfriend to make sure she's not after his money."

PULSERAS, *L.Am./S, pl. n., crim.* Handcuffs. (Lit. Bracelets.) *Le pusieron las pulseras y lo llevaron a la cárcel.* "They put the bracelets on him and carried him to jail."

PUÑETA, 1. *L.Am./C, adv.* A lot, much, a whole lot. *Me gusta ese vestido en puñeta.* "I like that dress a bunch." **2.** *Spain, adj.* Unpleasant (person or thing). *El tráfico en esta ciudad es una puñeta.* "Traffic in this city is a bitch."

PUÑETERO, RA, 1. *Spain, n.* Jackass, tool. *No se puede contar con un puñetero como Santiago.* "You can't count on a jackass like Santiago." **2.** *Spain, adj. or n.* Abusive, mean, or vulgar person. *Ten cuidado con ese puñetero, traicionaría a su propia madre.* "Be careful of that bastard; he would betray his own mother." **3.** *Spain, adj.* Difficult, complicated. *Aprender un nuevo programa de computación es puñetero.* "To learn a new computer program is a bitch."

PUNGUISTA, *L.Am./S, n., crim.* Pickpocket. *El punguista tenía mi billetera en su bolsillo.* "The pickpocket had my wallet in his pocket."

PUÑO, *L.Am./C, adv.* A bunch, a lot. (Lit. Fist.) *Anita tenía un puño de interés en ver Madrid.* "Anita wanted to see Madrid a lot."

PUNTA, *L.Am./S, n.* Knife. (Lit. Tip.) *Lo expulsaron del colegio por llevar una punta.* "They expelled him from school for carrying a shiv."

PUPA, *Car., n.* Sore, wound. *Esta pupa está como infectada, ve al médico.* "This sore looks infected; go to the doctor."

PURA BOCA, *L.Am./S, idiom.* Talker. *Ese Félix es pura boca, sólo hace la mitad de lo que dice.* "That Felix is just a mouth; he only does half of what he says."

¡PURA VIDA!, *L.Am./C, interj.* Expression of pleasure or satisfaction. *"¿Cómo te encuentras en tu nuevo matrimonio?" "¡Pura vida!"* " 'How are you doing in your new marriage?' 'Copacetic!' "

PURO, RA, *Car., n.* Father, mother. (Lit. Pure.) *A mi pura le debo la vida, así que con mucho cariño le doy lo que ella quiera.* "I owe my life to my mom, so, with a lot of affection, I give her what she wants."

PUSCO, *Spain, n.* Revolver. *Cuando sacó el pusco, todos se quedaron quietos.* "When he pulled out the rod, everybody went quiet."

PUTA, *L.Am., adj. or n.* Prostitute, woman of various men. *Raquel tiene fama de puta en el pueblo.* "Raquel has a reputation in town of being a whore."

PUTAMADRAL, *L.Am./N, n.* Crowd. *Hubo un putamadral de gente en el estadio hoy.* "There was a crowd at the stadium today."

PUTEO, *L.Am./S, n.* Prostitution. *Esa mujer se dedica al puteo.* "That woman is in the whoring business."

PUTILLA, *L.Am./S, n.* Aspiring prostitute, wannabe hooker. *De la manera que se porta yo diría que es putilla.* "From the way she acts, I would say she's a wannabe hooker."

¿QUÉ ACELGA?, *L.Am./S, idiom.* What's happenin'? *Hola Marta, ¿qué acelga?* "Hi Martha, what's cookin'?"

¡QUÉ BAÑAZO!, *L.Am./C, interj.* How embarrassing! How ridiculous! *¡Qué bañazo! Perdió la carrera contra un principiante.* "How embarrassing! He lost the race to a greenhorn."

¡QUÉ CARAJO!, *L.Am./S, interj.* Damn! Hell! *¡Qué carajo! Ya se nos hizo tarde.* "Damn! The time got away from us."

¿QUÉ JAIS?, *L.Am./N, idiom.* Greeting. *"¿Qué jais?" Preguntó Sebastián cuando me vio en la escuela.* " 'What's happening?' said Sebastian when he saw me at school."

¡QUÉ NOTA!, *L.Am./S, interj., youth.* Expression of joy or accomplishment. *¡Qué nota! Por fin me dieron el puesto que tanto deseaba.* "Wow! I finally got the job I wanted so much."

¡QUÉ ONDA!, *L.Am./S, interj.* Expression of shock. *¡Qué onda, cuñao! ¿Cuándo saliste de la cana?* "Holy shit! When did you get out of jail?"

¡QUÉ ONDA? *L.Am., idiom.* Greeting and inquiry. *¿Qué onda? Te va a dejar ir tu mamá al paseo?* "What's going on? Is your mom letting you go on the trip?"

¡QUÉ PAJA!, *L.Am./S, interj.* Expression of agreement. *¡Qué paja! Vienes con nosotros de parranda.* "How nice! You're going to party with us."

¡QUÉ PIÑA!, *L.Am./S, interj.* Expression of bad luck. *¡Qué piña! Por más que trata y trata nunca le sale nada bien.* "Tough luck! He keeps trying again and again but nothing works out."

QUEBRADA, *L.Am./N, n.* Opportunity, chance, break. *Dame una quebrada de pasar a hablar con el director.* "Give me a chance to talk to the director."

QUEBRAR, *L.Am./N, v., crim.* To kill, to murder. (Lit. To break.) *Y al que no le parezca, ahorita me lo quiebro.* "And whoever doesn't like it, gets it here and now."

QUEBRAR LA MUÑECA, *L.Am., idiom.* To be effeminate. *Mi peluquero quiebra la muñeca.* "My hairdresser is limp-wristed."

QUEDADA, *L.Am./N, n.* Old maid. (Lit. Left out.) *La tía Paulina ya es una quedada.* "Aunt Paulina is an old maid already."

QUEDADO, DA, *L.Am./S, adj.* Timid. (Lit. Left out.) *Él no saluda porque es un poquito quedado.* "He doesn't say hello because he's a bit shy."

QUEDAR COCHINO, *L.Am./S, idiom.* To look bad, to be embarrassed. *Me hiciste quedar cochino. ¿Por qué le dijiste que no estaba enfermo?* "You made me look bad. Why did you tell him that I wasn't sick?"

QUEDAR COMO UN PÁJARO, *Spain, idiom.* To die peacefully. *Lo encontraron muerto en su cama, quedó como un pájaro.* "They found him dead in his bed; he died in his sleep."

QUEDARLE TRES AFEITÁS, *Car., idiom.* To be close to death. *Julio está tan mal que yo creo que le quedan tres afeitás.* "Julio is so sick, I believe he is at death's door."

QUEDARSE BIZCO, *L.Am./S, idiom.* To be stunned, to be astonished. *Me quedé bizco al ver semejante cosa.* "I was floored to see such a thing."

QUEDARSE EN EL CHASÍS, *L.Am./S, idiom.* Dramatic weight loss. *Después de esa enfermedad Humberto quedó en el chasís.* "After that illness, Humberto wasted down to skin and bones."

QUEDARSE FRÍO, *L.Am./S, idiom.* To die. *Al pobre señor le dio un infarto y quedó frío.* "The poor man had a heart attack and bought the farm."

QUEDARSE PIOLA, *L.Am./S, idiom.* Don't worry, don't get upset, keep calm. *Quédate piola, linda, que yo le explico a tu papá lo que pasó.* "Cool it honey, I'll explain what happened to your father."

QUEJICA, *Spain, n.* Whiner. *Todo te molesta, eres un quejica.* "Everything bothers you; you're a whiner."

QUELITE, *L.Am./N, n.* Live-in lover, common-law wife, kept woman. *El diputado llegó a la fiesta con su quelite.* "The representative showed up at the party with his mistress."

QUEMACOCOS, *L.Am./N, n.* Sunroof. *Arnoldo mandó ponerle quemacocos al coche nuevo.* "Arnoldo had a sunroof installed in his new car."

QUEMADO, DA, 1. *Spain, adj.* Emotionally exhausted. (Lit. Burned.) *Tantas penas me han dejado quemada.* "So much suffering burned me out." **2.** *L.Am./S, adj.* Bad luck. *Ando quemado. Ayer perdí mi trabajo y hoy me rompí la nariz.* "I'm under a cloud; yesterday I lost my job and today I broke my nose."

QUEMAR, *L.Am./S, v., crim.* To shoot. (Lit. To burn.) *El ladrón se puso nervioso y comenzó a quemar a todo el mundo.* "The thief got nervous and began to shoot everyone."

QUEMARSE LAS CEJAS, *L.Am./S, idiom.* To study hard. *Pepito va a llegar muy lejos, pues desde chiquito le gusta quemarse las cejas.* "Pepito will go far; since he was a boy he liked to crack the books."

QUERINDONGA, *Spain, n.* Lover, mistress. *Dicen que el esposo de Juana tiene una querindonga en el pueblo.* "They say that Juana's husband has a playmate in town."

QUESO, *L.Am./S, n.* Foot odor. (Lit. Cheese.) *Por lo menos anda y lávate los pies antes de irte a la cama, ¡qué* *queso!* "At least go and wash your feet before going to bed. Such a smell!"

QUÍA, *L.Am./S, n.* Name used to avoid naming someone, you-know-who. *El quía dejo una nota en el escritorio del jefe esta mañana.* "You-know-who left a note on the boss's desk this morning."

QUILLARSE, *Car., prnl. v.* To get angry or annoyed. *Si lo sigues molestando así, se va a quillar.* "If you keep bothering him like that, he is going to lose his temper."

QUILOMBO, *L.Am./S, n.* Disturbance, fuss, commotion. *Los estudiantes armaron un quilombo cuando la policía paró la manifestación.* "The students raised hell when the police stopped the demonstration."

QUINA, *L.Am./S, n.* Five hundred soles (Peruvian currency.) *¡Qué mala suerte! Se me cayó una quina del bolsillo.* "What bad luck! A five-hundred-sol bill fell out of my pocket."

QUINCEARSE, *L.Am./S, prnl. v.* To make a mistake. *Estudió historia y el examen era de geografía, ¡se quinceó!* "He studied history and the test was on geography. He screwed up!"

QUINE, *L.Am./S, n.* Bruise. *¡Si me sigues fastidiando te voy a meter un quine!* "If you keep bugging me, I'm going to make you black and blue!"

QUISQUILLOSO, SA, *L.Am., adj.* Finicky, picky (person). *Cada día te vuelves más quisquilloso, nada te gusta.* "Every day you are getting pickier. You don't like anything."

QUITARSE, 1. *L.Am./C, prnl. v.* To take back one's word. (Lit. To remove oneself.) *Una vez dicho un insulto es muy difícil quitarse después.* "Once an insult is said, it is difficult to take it back." **2.** *L.Am./S, prnl. v.* To leave. *Se quitó temprano de la fiesta diciendo que tenía que trabajar al día siguiente.* "He left the party early, saying he had to work the next day."

¡QUIUBO!, *L.Am./S, idiom.* Greeting. *¡Quiubo!* "What's up, dude!"

RACA, *L.Am./S, adj.* Stingy. *La comida en este restaurante está bien raca.* "They're stingy with the food in this restaurant."

RACUACHI, *L.Am./S, adj.* Ridiculous, bizarre. *Eustaquio se viste tan racuachi que todos se ríen de él.* "Eustaquio's clothes are so bizarre; everybody laughs at him."

RADIOBEMBA, *Car., n.* Gossip, grapevine. *De esa noticia me enteré por radiobemba.* "I heard that piece of news through the grapevine."

RADIO-JETA, *L.Am./S, n., crim.* Informer. *Cuidado con lo que dices delante de radio-jeta, es peligroso.* "Be careful with what you say in front of that stool pigeon; he's dangerous."

RAFLE, *Car., adj., crim.* Thief. *Ese tipo es un rafle, llama a la policía.* "That guy is a crook; call the police."

RAJA, 1. *L.Am./S, n.* Ass, butt. *¿No me vas a prestar la radio? Entonces, ¡métetela en la raja!* "You won't lend me the radio? Then stick it up your ass!" **2.** *L.Am./S, n.* Luck. *Te catearon en química, ¡qué mala raja!* "You flunked chemistry; what bad luck!"

RAJAR, 1. *L.Am./S, v.* To criticize. (Lit. To split.) *Si vas a empezar a rajar a mi amigo, mejor me voy.* "If you are going to start putting my friend down, I'd better leave." **2.** *Spain, v., crim.* To harm, to kill. *No te metas en problemas con esos tipos, que te van a rajar.* "Don't get into

385

it with those guys or they'll take care of you." **3.** *L.Am./S, v.* To fail. *Rajaron a Jimena en matemáticas.* "They failed Jimena in math." **4.** *L.Am./S, v.* To take off running. *No le dije nada y de pronto sale rajando.* "I didn't say anything to him but all of a sudden he took off running."

RAJARSE, 1. *L.Am./S., prnl. v.* To fail a subject. (Lit. To split oneself.) *Me rajé en matemáticas otra vez.* "I flunked math again." **2.** *L.Am./S, prnl. v.* To take off, to go away, to leave. *Mariela se rajó antes de que se acabara la conferencia.* "Mariela hit the road as soon as the conference was over." **3.** *L.Am./S, prnl. v.* To treat somebody. *Me rajé con Juan y Pablo y pagué el almuerzo.* "I treated Juan and Pablo to lunch."

RAJÓN, 1. *L.Am./N, adj. or n.* Person who goes back on his or her word. *El patrón nos prometió un aumento y ahora se pone rajón.* "The boss promised us a raise and now he is going back on his word." **2.** *L.Am./N, n.* Quitter. *Jaime, si dejas la universidad te conocerán como rajón.* "Jaime, if you leave the University, you will be known as a quitter." **3. RAJÓN, NA,** *L.Am./C, adj. or n.* Conceited, braggart, show-off. *Adela es una rajona, siempre hablando de su abolengo.* "Adela is very snooty, always talking about her ancestry."

RANCHO, *L.Am./S, n.* Army food, chow. (Lit. Ranch.) *A Danny le gusta el servicio pero se queja del rancho.* "Danny likes the service but he complains about the chow."

RAPONERO, RA, *L.Am./S, adj. or n., crim.* Thief. *La poli encontró al raponero escondido debajo del puente.* "The police found the crook hiding under the bridge."

RARO, *L.Am., adj.* Effeminate. (Lit. Strange.) *Creo que el amigo de Martín es raro.* "I believe that Martin's friend is a bit limp-wristed."

RASCABUCHADOR, *Car., n.* Voyeur, Peeping Tom. *Ten cuidado con las ventanas, dicen que anda un rascabuchador por el barrio.* "Careful with the windows, they say there is a Peeping Tom running around the neighborhood."

RASCADO, DA, *L.Am./S, adj.* Drunk. (Lit. Scratched.) *Felipe no puede manejar porque está rascado.* "Felipe can't drive because he is wasted."

RASCAR, 1. *L.Am./S, v.* To get drunk. (Lit. To scratch.) *Si tomas más cerveza te vas a rascar.* "If you drink more beer, you're going to get plastered." **2.** *Car., v.* To spank. *Me van a rascar por haber insultado a mi hermana.* "I'm going to get spanked for insulting my sister."

RASCARSE LA BARRIGA, *L.Am., idiom.* To do nothing. *Me pasé todo el sábado rascándome la barriga.* "I spent all day Saturday sitting around scratching my belly."

RASPAR CANILLAS, *L.Am./S, idiom.* To dance. (Lit. To scrape shins.) *Salgamos a raspar canillas el sábado.* "Let's go out and cut a rug on Saturday."

RATA, *L.Am./C, adj. or n., crim.* Thief. (Lit. Rat.) *Los dueños de esa tienda son unas ratas con esos precios.* "The owners of that store are ripoff artists with those prices."

RATI, *L.Am./S, n.* Plainclothes policeman, detective. *Los ratis vinieron ayer buscándote.* "The fuzz came looking for you yesterday."

RATÓN, 1. *L.Am./N, n.* Hangover. (Lit. Mouse.) *César va a tener un ratón cuando se despierte.* "Cesar is going to have a big head when he wakes up." **2.** *Car., n.* Bad person. *El director es un ratón, ojalá lo trasladen a otra ciudad.* "The director is vermin; God willing, they'll transfer him to another city."

RAYA, 1. *Car., n.* Dominican peso. (Lit. Scratch, line.) *Me robaron cien rayas del escritorio.* "They swiped a hundred bucks from my desk." **2.** *L.Am./S, n.* Peruvian secret police. *¡Yara, yara! Acabamos de manyar un raya por los alrededores.* "Watch out, watch out! We've just seen an undercover cop around here." **See also DÍA DE RAYA**

RAYADO, DA, 1. *L.Am./S, adj.* Crazy. (Lit. Scratched.) *Clara se casó con un rayado.* "Clara married a crazy guy." **2.** *L.Am./S, adj.* Drugged. *José anda rayado desde los quince.* "Jose's been high since he was fifteen."

RAYAR, 1. *L.Am./C, v.* To pass a car. (Lit. To cross out.) *Nos rayaron a una velocidad tremenda.* "They passed us at a tremendous speed." **2.** *L.Am./C, v.* To fail a subject. *Me rayaron en historia.* "They failed me in history."

RAYAR EL DISCO, *L.Am./N, idiom.* To repeat oneself. *A mi padre le gusta rayar el disco.* "My father likes to repeat himself."

RAYARSE, 1. *L.Am./S, prnl. v.* To go crazy. (Lit. To get scratched.) *Dicen que Luisa se rayó al perder el novio.* "They say that Luisa went nuts on losing her boyfriend." **2.** *L.Am./S, prnl. v.* To get high. *Se rayó y se cayó de la moto.* "He got high and fell off the motorcycle."

RAZA, 1. *L.Am./S, n.* Nerve. (Lit. Race.) *Le presté mi libro de matemáticas y ahora dice que es suyo, ¡qué raza!* "I lent him my math book and now he says that it's his. What nerve!" **2.** *L.Am./N, n.* Hispanic, Mexican-American. *Había mucha raza en la fiesta.* "There were many Hispanics at the party."

REBOTARSE, *L.Am./S, prnl. v.* To get annoyed. (Lit. To bounce oneself.) *Me estoy rebotando con tanto ruido.* "I am getting uptight with so much noise."

REBOTE, *L.Am./S, n.* Annoyance. (Lit. Bounce.) *El rock metálico es un rebote para mí.* "As far as I am concerned, heavy metal is a pain in the ass."

RECETA, *Car., n.* Traffic ticket. (Lit. Prescription.) *Es la tercera receta que me gano por manejar muy rápido.* "It is the third ticket I get for speeding."

RECHÓNFIL, *L.Am./S, adj.* Obese. *Estás muy rechónfil, ¿cuándo te pones a dieta?* "You're real chubby; when are you going on a diet?"

REDUCIDOR, *L.Am./S, n., crim.* Seller of stolen goods, fence. (Lit. Reducer.) *A mi amigo Oscar lo metieron a la cárcel por reducidor.* "They put my friend Oscar in jail for being a fence."

REFERÍ, *L.Am./S, n.* Traffic police. (From English "referee.") *El referí me dijo que cruzara a pesar de haber luz roja.* "The traffic cop told me to pass in spite of the red light."

REFILAR, *L.Am./S, v.* To bribe. *Me han dicho que con refilar al policía se acaba la multa.* "I was told that paying the cop puts an end to the fine."

REGALÓN, NA, 1. *L.Am./S, adj.* Spoiled, pampered. *Mi hermano menor es el regalón de la familia.* "My youngest brother is the spoiled one in the family." **2.** *Car., adj.* Youngest. *Andrés es el regalón de la familia.* "Andres is the youngest of the family."

REGLAR, *L.Am., v.* To menstruate. *No puedo ir a la piscina porque estoy reglando.* "I can't go to the pool because I'm having my period."

RELAJO, *L.Am./S, n.* Disorder. *El tráfico es un relajo porque nadie obedece las reglas.* "Traffic is a mess because no one obeys the rules."

RELAMÍO, MÍA, *Car., adj.* Nervy, cheeky. *A ese relamío no le importa ofender con sus comentarios.* "That impertinent fellow doesn't care about offending with his comments."

RELOJEAR, *L.Am./S, v.* To look out of the corner of one's eye. *El vecino se lo pasa relojeándome cuando salgo a tomar el sol.* "My neighbor spies on me out of the corner of his eye when I go out sunbathing."

REMACHAR, *L.Am./S, v.* To kill, to eliminate someone, to bump off. (Lit. To rivet.) *¿Quiere Ud. que remache a alguien de la competencia?* "Do you want me to bump off someone from the competition?"

REMANDINGO, *Car., n.* Disorder, mess. *Llegué a mi casa y me encontré un tremendo remandingo.* "I arrived home and found a terrible mess."

REMATADO, DA, *L.Am./S, adj.* Crazy. *El rematado de Genaro salió corriendo desnudo por las calles.* "That crazy Genaro went running nude through the streets."

REMOLINO, *L.Am./S, n.* Mix-up. (Lit. Whirlpool.) *Cada vez que habla el jefe, se arma un remolino en el trabajo.* "Whenever the boss talks, things get all mixed up at work."

REPASAR, *L.Am./S, v.* To prowl, to case. *Hay un tipo que he visto repasando tu barrio, ten cuidado.* "There is a guy I've seen casing your neighborhood; be careful."

REPETIPUA, *L.Am./S, n.* Repeat, seconds. *La comida fue buena pero no suficiente. Pidamos un repetipua.* "The meal was good but not enough. Let's ask for seconds."

REPOLLO, *L.Am./S, n.* Big hairdo. (Lit. Cabbage.) *En la fiesta había unas viejas con repollos estrafalarios.* "There were some old crows at the party with outlandish hairdos."

REQUINTAR, *L.Am./S, v.* To protest. *Esos estudiantes siempre están requintando. No se conforman con nada.* "Those students are always bitching. They're never satisfied with anything."

RESACA, *Spain, L.Am., n.* Hangover. (Lit. Undertow.) *Si sigues tomando te quejarás mañana de la resaca.* "If you keep on drinking, you'll complain of a hangover tomorrow."

RESBALAR, 1. *L.Am./S, v.* To be unconcerned, to be indifferent. (Lit. To slip.) *Me resbala que mi suegro no me quiera.* "It doesn't bother me in the least that my father-in-law doesn't love me." **2.** *L.Am./S, v.* To fall in disgrace. *La pobre Teresita se resbaló a los quince años y ahora el resbalón mismo cumple quince.* "Poor Teresita had her slip at fifteen and now the slip himself has turned fifteen."

RESPETABLE, *L.Am./S, n.* Audience. (Lit. Respectable.) *Mis éxitos como cantante se los debo al respetable.* "I owe my success as a singer to my audience."

RESTAURANTE, *L.Am./S, n.* Nursing woman's breasts. (Lit. Restaurant.) *Cúbrete bien el restaurante cuando alimentes al bebé.* "Cover the milk store when you feed the baby."

RETABLO, *Spain, n.* Elderly person. (Lit. Altarpiece.) *Todos los miembros de mi familia son retablos ahora.* "All the members of my family are senior citizens now."

RETACO, CA, *L.Am./S, adj. or n.* Short, shorty. *Ese retaco se cree lo máximo, ya, bájalo de la nube.* "That shorty thinks he is the greatest. Wake him up from his dream."

RETAGUARDIA, *L.Am./S, n.* Behind, butt, ass. (Lit. Rear guard.) *En el bus un hombre me agarró la retaguardia.* "A man grabbed my rear on the bus."

RETOBAR, *L.Am./S, v.* To not follow orders. *El problema que tenía Juan en el servicio militar era que siempre estaba retobando.* "The problem Juan had in the service was that he never followed orders."

RETRATAR, *L.Am./S, v.* To give a beaver shot. (Lit. To photograph.) *Ana se levantó la falda y nos retrató a todos.* "Ana lifted her skirt and gave everybody a beaver shot."

RETRÓGRADO, DA, *L.Am., adj.* Old-fashioned. (Lit. Retrogressive.) *Mis papás son unos retrógrados y no me dejan salir de noche.* "My parents are reactionaries who won't let me go out at night."

REVOLCÓN, *L.Am./S, n.* Affair. (Lit. Tumble.) *Él ha tenido tres revolcones desde que se casó.* "He's had three affairs since he got married."

RICA, *L.Am./S, adj.* Shapely, having a good figure. (Lit. Tasty.) *La recepcionista que contraté está rica.* "The receptionist I hired is luscious."

RIPIO, *L.Am./S, n.* Coin. (Lit. Riprap.) *No me pidas dinero prestado porque no tengo un ripio.* "Don't ask me for a loan because I don't have a cent."

ROCA, *L.Am./S, n.* Car. (Lit. Rock.) *La roca que le regalaron por su graduación es bonito.* "The car they gave him for his graduation is pretty."

ROCO, *L.Am./C, adj.* Old. *Mi padre está muy roco pero sigue trabajando.* "My father is very old but he keeps on working."

ROCOTÓ, *L.Am./S, n.* Communist. *Desde que Carlitos ingresó a la universidad se volvió rocotó.* "Since Carlos went to the university, he turned Red."

RODANTE, *Spain, n.* Car. (Lit. Rolling.) *A mi rodante le están fallando los frenos.* "The brakes are going on my chariot."

ROJO, *L.Am./C, n.* One-thousand-colon note. (Lit. Red.) *Vi que tienes un puño de rojos en tu billetera.* "I saw that you have a bunch of red bills in your wallet."

ROLLISTA, *Spain, n.* Storyteller, bullshitter. *Eres un rollista y no te creo nada.* "You're a bullshitter and I don't believe you at all."

ROLLO, *L.Am./S, n.* Story. *El rollo que me contó Lola fue una exageración.* "The story Lola told me was an exaggeration."

ROMPERLA, *L.Am./S, idiom, youth.* To be great, super, the most. (Lit. To break it.) *El cuadro último que pintó Jorge la rompe.* "The last painting Jorge painted is the most."

ROMPERSE EL CRÁNEO, *L.Am./S, idiom.* To think a lot. *Me he roto el cráneo tratando de entender esta ecuación.* "I busted my head trying to understand that equation."

ROÑA, *Spain, n.* Cheapskate. *Ricardo es una roña y siempre termino yo pagando.* "Ricardo is a cheapskate and I always wind up paying." **See also HACER ROÑA**

ROÑOSO, SA, *L.Am./S, adj. or n.* Dirty. *Ese tipo es un roñoso y no lo quiero como novio de mi hija.* "That guy is a scuzzo and I don't want him as a boyfriend for my daughter."

ROSCA, *Car., n.* Fatty waistline, spare tire, love handles. (Lit. Doughnut.) *Tengo que hacer ejercicio para rebajar estas roscas.* "I have to exercise to get rid of these love handles."

ROSCO, *Spain, n.* Zero, failing grade. *Me pusieron un rosco en español por no hacer la tarea.* "I got a zero in Spanish for not doing the homework."

ROSCÓN, *L.Am./S, adj. or n.* Homosexual. *Me contaron que el gerente es roscón.* "I was told that the manager is a fag."

ROTO, TA, 1. *L.Am./S, n.* Crude, gross individual, lout. (Lit. Broken.) *No aguanto a ese roto de tu marido.* "I can't stand your lout of a husband." **2.** *L.Am./S, n.* Member of the lower class. *Ya se alzaron los rotos.* "The rabble is up in arms again."

RUBIA, *L.Am./C, n.* Beer. (Lit. Blonde.) *Pedro, échame una rubia bien fría.* "Pedro, give me a cold blonde one."

RULETEAR, *L.Am./N, v.* To drive a cab. *Juan lleva tiempo ruleteando.* "Juan has been driving a cab for quite some time."

RULETERA, *L.Am./N, n.* Streetwalker, hooker. *Encontraron a una ruletera muerta en la calle.* "They found a hooker dead on the street."

RULETERO, *L.Am./N, n.* Cabdriver. *El ruletero quería cobrarme el doble.* "The cabbie wanted to charge me double."

RUMBIAR, *L.Am./S, v.* To party. *Todos los muchachos se fueron a rumbiar después de la comida.* "All the fellows went partying after dinner."

RUPIA, *Spain, n.* Peseta. (Lit. Ruppee.) *Me gané cinco mil rupias en una rifa.* "I won five thousand peas in a raffle."

RUTERO, RA, *Car., adj. or n.* Party animal, club-hopper. *Esta zona de la ciudad es visitada por todos los ruteros.* "That area of the city is visited by all the bar-hoppers."

¡SABE CUÁNDO!, *L.Am./C, idiom.* Emphatically no. Never! *"¿Va Ud. a jubilarse en la capital?" "¡Sabe cuándo!"* " 'Are you going to retire in the capital?' 'No way!' "

SABER A RAYOS, *L.Am./S, idiom.* To taste terrible. *Esa fruta que compraste sabe a rayos.* "The fruit that you bought tastes like shit."

SACABULLAS, *L.Am./N, n.* Bouncer. *Tonio es el sacabullas en un club de destape.* "Antonio is the bouncer at a strip club."

SACAMUELAS, *L.Am./S, n.* Dentist. *Jairo es el sacamuelas del pueblo.* "Jairo is the town tooth puller."

SACAR DE QUICIO, *L.Am., idiom.* To drive crazy. *Tu falta de educación me saca de quicio.* "Your lack of manners is driving me nuts."

SACAR EL CUERO, *L.Am./S, idiom.* To criticize. *Después de que Paty se fue, las amigas se quedaron sacándole el cuero.* "After Patty left, her friends stayed to gossip about her."

SACAR LA LECHE, *L.Am./S, idiom.* To exhaust. *En este trabajo me están sacando la leche.* "In this job, they are wringing the last drop out of me."

SACAR LA VUELTA, 1. *L.Am./N, idiom.* To be unfaithful. *Ella es una bandida, siempre le saca la vuelta a su* *marido.* "She's a whore; she is always cheating on her husband." **2.** *L.Am./S, idiom.* To procrastinate. *Primero sacó a vuelta a limpiar la bañera y ahora a lavar las ollas.* "First he put off cleaning the bathtub and now he's postponing washing the pots."

SACAR SAL, *L.Am./C, idiom.* Unlucky. *Siempre saco sal en la lotería, no sé por qué juego.* "I'm never lucky in the lottery; I don't know why I play."

SACAR UN OJO DE LA CARA, *L.Am./N, idiom.* To charge very much. *Me sacaron un ojo de la cara por este par de zapatos.* "They got an arm and a leg from me for this pair of shoes."

SACAR UNA ROJA, *L.Am., idiom.* To fail a subject. *Saqué una roja en inglés.* "I flunked English."

SACO, *L.Am./S, n., crim.* Jail. (Lit. Sac.) *El padre de Francisco lleva dos años en el saco.* "Francisco's father has been in the pen for two years."

SACO DE PULGAS, *Car., idiom.* Nervous, antsy person. (Lit. Fleabag.) *Cálmate, que estás como un saco de pulgas.* "Calm down; you're as nervous as a jumping flea."

¡SACÚDETE!, *L.Am./S, interj.* Get out of here! (Lit. Shake yourself.) *¡Deja de molestarme y sacúdete de aquí!* "Quit bothering me and get out of here!"

SAFACÓN, *L.Am., n.* Trash can. *Todo lo que encuentra el bebé lo echa en el safacón.* "Everything the baby finds, he throws in the trash can."

SALADO, DA, 1. *Spain, adj.* Funny, lively. (Lit. Salty.) *El novio de mi sobrina es un chico salado.* "My niece's boyfriend is a lively fellow." **2.** *L.Am., adj.* Unlucky. *Lolita es muy salada en el amor. La dejan todos los novios.* "Lolita is very unlucky at love. All her boyfriends leave her."

SALAME, *L.Am./S, adj. or n.* Stupid, fool. (Lit. Salami.) *Siempre que ves a Clara te portas como un salame.* "Every time you see Clara, you act like a jerk."

SALAO, LÁ, *Spain, adj.* Lively, funny. (From Spanish "salado.") *Es increíble que a su edad siga siendo tan salao.* "It is unbelievable that at his age he's still so lively."

SALIR COMO BOLA POR TRONERA, *Car., idiom.* To leave, to take off. *Cuando vio lo que había hecho, salió como bola por tronera.* "When he saw what he had done, he took off like a bat out of hell."

SALIR PITANDO, *L.Am., idiom.* To depart suddenly. *Ceci salió pitando antes de acabarse el concierto.* "Ceci left like a flash before the concert was over."

SALÍRSELE EL SESO POR LA BOCA, *Spain, idiom.* To talk nonsense. *Cada vez que Carlos habla se le sale el seso por la boca.* "Every time Carlos talks, crap runs out of his mouth."

SALSERO, RA, *L.Am., n.* Fan of salsa music and dance. *Mis amigos son unos salseros muy alegres.* "My friends are very happy salsa fans."

SALTACHARCOS, *L.Am./S, adj. or n.* High-water pants. *El niño creció y ahora todos sus pantalones son saltacharcos.* "The boy grew and now all his pants are high-waters."

SAMPADO, *L.Am./S, adj.* Drunk. *Estaba tan sampado que ni se acordaba donde estaba su casa.* "He was so drunk he could not remember where his house was."

SAMPÓN, NA, *L.Am./S, adj. or n.* Unpleasant person. *Este es un sampón, siempre está donde no lo invitan.* "He is a pest; he always shows up where he is not invited."

SANGRILIVIANO, NA, *Car., adj.* Nice (person). *Quiero mucho a mi suegra, es muy sangriliviana.* "I really love my mother-in-law; she's a sweetheart."

¡SAPE!, *L.Am./S, interj.* Expression used to scare off a cat. *¡Sape, gato cochino!* "Shoo! Bad cat!"

SAPO, PA, 1. *L.Am./S, adj.* Gossipy. (Lit. Toad.) *La sapa de Rosario siempre tiene algo nuevo que contarnos.* "Tattle-tale Rosario always has something new to tell us."

2. *L.Am./S, adj.* Curious. *¡Qué sapo eres! De todo te quieres enterar.* "How nosy you are; you want to find out about everything."

SARDINO, NA, 1. *L.Am./S, adj. or n.* Teenager. *Juanjo pensaba abrir un club para sardinos.* "Juanjo wanted to open a club for teenagers." **2.** *L.Am./S, adj. or n.* Inexperienced person, beginner, tenderfoot, greenhorn. *No voy a volar con Julio. Como piloto es un sardino.* "I'm not going to fly with Julio. He's a greenhorn pilot."

SARGENTO, TA, *L.Am., adj. or n.* Bossy woman. (Lit. Sergeant.) *Mi abuela siempre fue una sargenta y todos la respetaban.* "My grandmother always was a sergeant and everybody respected her."

SATEAR, *Car., v.* To flirt. *Esa muchacha no se cansó de satear durante toda la fiesta.* "That girl didn't get tired of flirting during the whole party."

SECRETA, *Spain, n.* Plainclothes police. (Lit. Secret.) *Parece que ese asunto lo investigará la secreta.* "It seems that matter will be investigated by the plainclothes boys."

SEGUNDO FRENTE, *L.Am./S, n.* Lover, mistress. *El director está visitando su segundo frente.* "The director is visiting his other woman."

SELE, *L.Am./C, adj.* Immature, green. *El hijo de Juan es todavía muy sele para ese trabajo.* "Juan's son is still wet behind the ears for that job."

SEÑORITA, *L.Am., n.* Teacher. (Lit. Miss.) *La señorita me felicitó por mis buenas calificaciones.* "The teacher gave me a pat on the back for my good grades."

¡SEPA MOYA!, *L.Am./S, interj.* Who knows! *"¿Cuándo vas a terminar ese trabajo?" "¡Sepa Moya!"* " 'When are you going to finish that job?' 'Who knows!' "

SER CAGAÍTO, A, *Car., idiom.* To be just like. *Ese niño es cagaíto a su padre.* "That boy is the spitting image of his father."

SER COMO EL ARROZ BLANCO, *Car., idiom.* To be

everywhere. *Lo veo en todas partes, es como el arroz blanco.* "I see him everywhere; he is like coal in Newcastle."

SER COMO MOSCA DE PESEBRE, *Car., idiom.* To be abrasive. *El odioso de Mario es como mosca de pesebre.* "That bastard Mario is like a horsefly."

SER CORNETA, *Car., idiom.* To be a cuckold. *Cuida a tu mujer o si no vas a ser un corneta.* "Take care of your wife or be a cuckold."

SER CULO DE BOTELLA, *Car., idiom.* To be a fake gem. *Las esmeraldas que vende ese hombre son culo de botella.* "The emeralds that guy sells are made from soda bottles."

SER CULO Y MIERDA, *Spain, idiom.* Two people who are totally alike. *María y el esposo son culo y mierda.* "Maria and her husband are like two peas in a pod."

SER DE LA ACERA DE ENFRENTE, *Spain, idiom.* To be homosexual. *Mi cuñado confesó que es de la acera de enfrente.* "My brother-in-law confessed that he is on the other team."

SER DE LA OTRA BANDA, *L.Am., Spain, idiom.* To be homosexual. *En mi familia nadie es de la otra banda.* "No one in my family is on the other team."

SER DEL AÑO DE LA NANA, *Car., idiom.* To be very old. *Esas costumbres son del año de la nana.* "Those customs are as old as the pyramids."

SER DEL AÑO LA PERA, *Spain, idiom.* To be very old. *Sole, esos zapatos son del año la pera.* "Sole, those shoes are as old as my grandmother."

SER DEL MISMO PELO, *L.Am./N, idiom.* To be of the same group or class, birds of a feather. *Ramón y Samuel son del mismo pelo.* "Ramon and Samuel are birds of a feather."

SER DEL OTRO BANDO See **SER DE LA OTRA BANDA**

SER EL QUE BATE EL COBRE, *Car., idiom.* To be in charge. *Pedro siempre quiere ser el que bate el cobre.* "Peter always wants to be top dog."

SER EL QUE PICA EL BACALAO, *Car., idiom.* To be the one who decides. *Mi hermano mayor es el que pica el bacalao.* "My older brother is the one who calls the shots."

SER GENTE DE LA ORILLA, *Car., idiom.* To be crass, crude, vulgar, uncouth. *No nos gustan los nuevos vecinos porque son gente de la orilla.* "We don't like the new neighbors because they are rough people."

SER HACHA PARA ALGO, *L.Am., idiom.* To be skilled at something. *Mi padre era muy hacha para la música.* "My father was very good at music."

SER LARGO DE UÑAS, *L.Am./N, idiom.* To have light fingers. *No le deje solo a ese muchacho porque es muy largo de uñas.* "Don't leave that fellow alone because he is light-fingered."

SER MÁS BRUTO QUE MANDADO HACER, *L.Am./S, idiom.* To be very stupid. *La empleada de mi mamá es más bruta que mandada hacer.* "My mother's employee is dumber than a door."

SER MÁS BUENO QUE PAN DE ROSCA, *L.Am./N, idiom.* To be very good. *Agustín es más bueno que pan de rosca.* "Agustin is as good as gold."

SER MÁS DE CAMPO QUE LAS AMAPOLAS, *Spain, idiom.* To be an authentic hick. (Lit. To be more country than poppies.) *¡Qué cateto eres! ¡Eres más de campo que las amapolas!* "What a hick you are! You're more country than the Grand Ole Opry!"

SER MÁS DESGRACIADO QUE EL PUPAS, *Spain, idiom.* To have hard luck. *El pobre de mi cuñado es más desgraciado que el pupas.* "My poor brother-in-law is as unlucky as Kilroy."

SER MÁS FEO QUE CARRACUCA, *Spain, idiom.* To be very ugly. *La nueva esposa de Guillermo es más* *fea que carracuca.* "Guillermo's new wife is uglier than sin."

SER MÁS LENTO QUE EL CABALLO DEL MALO, *Spain, idiom.* Very slow. (Lit. To be slower than the outlaw's horse.) *Sonia llega tarde porque es más lenta que el caballo del malo.* "Sonia arrives late because she is slower than an outlaw's horse."

SER MÁS PESADO QUE UN MAL MATRIMONIO, *L.Am./S, idiom.* To be difficult to put up with. *Tu amigo es más pesado que un mal matrimonio.* "Your friend is nastier than a bad marriage."

SER MÁS VIEJO QUE MATUSALÉN, *Car., idiom.* To be very old. *No sé qué edad tiene, pero es más viejo que Matusalén.* "I don't know how old she is, but she is as old as Methuselah."

SER PÁJAROS DE LA MISMA PLUMA, *Car., idiom.* To be alike. *Con razón Lalo es tu amigo, ustedes son pájaros de la misma pluma.* "Of course Lalo is your friend; you are birds of a feather."

SER PEOR QUE LA MAYA, *Car., idiom.* To be bad, to be perverse. *Esa mujer es peor que la maya, maltrata a toda su familia.* "That woman is horrible; she mistreats her entire family."

SER PEOR QUE SAN CIRIACO, *Car., idiom.* To be a bad person. *Ese malvado es peor que San Ciriaco.* "That bastard is worse than Judas."

SER PEOR QUE UN PUJO DE COCO, *Car., idiom.* To be a bad person. *Lo odio, es peor que un pujo de coco.* "I hate him; he is worse than bad."

SER UN CABEZA HUECA, *L.Am./S, idiom.* To be very stupid. *No aprendes nada, eres un cabeza hueca.* "You don't learn anything. You're an airhead."

SER UN CARNE, *Car., idiom.* To be stupid. *Si te dejas engañar así es porque eres un carne.* "If you let yourself be fooled like that, it's because you are stupid."

SER UN HIJO DE LA GRAN YEGUA, *Spain, idiom.* To

be a son of a bitch. (Euphemism for "hijo de la gran puta.") *Lo odio, es un hijo de la gran yegua.* "I hate him; he is a son of a gun."

SER UN HUEVO TIBIO, *Spain, idiom.* To be slow. *¡Muévete, pareces huevo tibio!* "Get a move on! You're worse than a turtle."

SER UN PEDAZO DE PAN, *L.Am., Spain, idiom.* To be a good person. *Sergio es buenísima persona, es un pedazo de pan.* "Sergio is a very good person; he is as good as gold."

SER UNA CASA SOLA, *Car., idiom.* To be selfish, to be a loner. *A Armando no le gusta compartir con nadie, es una casa sola.* "Armando doesn't like to share with anybody; he is a loner."

SER UNA PETACA, *L.Am., idiom.* To be lazy, to be negligent. *Todos los empleados de este banco son unas petacas.* "All the employees at that bank are a bunch of dopes."

SER UNA PLUMA, *Car., idiom.* To be a great dancer. *Me fascina bailar con Santiago porque es una pluma.* "I love dancing with Santiago because he's light as a feather on his feet."

SER UÑA Y CARNE, *Spain, idiom.* To be inseparable. *José y Alvaro son uña y carne, los vemos juntos en todas partes.* José and Alvaro are bosom buddies; we see them together everywhere.

SER UÑA Y MUGRE, *L.Am./S, idiom.* To be inseparable. *Claudia y su mejor amiga son uña y mugre.* "Claudia and her best friend are like two peas in a pod."

SERVICIO, *L.Am., n.* Restroom. (Lit. Service.) *Por favor, muéstreme dónde queda el servicio.* "Please, show me where the restroom is."

SERVILLETA, *L.Am./S, n.* Maid. (Lit. Napkin.) *Y aunque tú no lo creas, el tarado se enredó con la servilleta.* "Although you would not believe it, this idiot got involved with the maid."

SIETE, *L.Am., n.* Right-angle tear in clothing. (Lit. Seven.)

Mi mujer dice que siempre me estoy haciendo sietes en mis sacos. "My wife says that I am always ripping sevens in my jackets."

SIFRINO, NA, *L.Am./S, adj. or n.* Snob. *Maruja es una sifrina.* "Maruja is a snob."

SINHUESO, *L.Am./S, n.* Tongue. (Lit. Boneless.) *Inés no para de mover la sinhueso, lleva tres horas hablando.* "Ines doesn't stop wagging her tongue; she's been talking for three hours."

SINIQUITATE, *Car., adj.* Stupid. *Ese siniquitate no va a durar mucho en el trabajo.* "That idiot isn't going to last long at the job."

SIRLAR, *Spain, v., crim.* To rob with a jackknife. *Un par de maleantes me sirlaron anoche.* "A couple of bandits held me up with a knife last night."

SIRLERO, RA, *Spain, adj. or n., crim.* One who robs with a knife. *El policía atrapó al sirlero que me robó.* "The police got the knife-wielding thief who robbed me."

SOBADO, DA, 1. *L.Am./S, adj.* In bad shape. *Mi pobre perrito está sobado, no va a durar mucho.* "My poor doggie isn't doing well; he won't last long." **2.** *L.Am./S, n.* Deceptive character. *Ese tipo es un sobado y nos engañó a todos.* "That guy is a trickster and lied to all of us."

SOBAR, *L.Am./S, v.* To bother, to annoy with nonsense. *No la sobes más, que ya está de mal genio.* "Don't bug her anymore; she is already in a bad mood."

SOBAR EL BALÓN, *Spain, idiom.* To hog the ball. *Cuidado con Jiménez, le gusta sobar el balón.* "Careful with Jimenez, he likes to keep the ball for himself."

SOBÓN, NA, *L.Am./S, adj. or n.* A pain in the neck. *Gustavo se ha vuelto muy sobón, ya no lo soporto.* "Gustavo has become a real pain in the ass; I can't stand him."

SOBRE, *L.Am./S, n.* Bed. (Lit. Envelope.) *Estoy muy cansado, me voy a meter en el sobre.* "I am real tired. I'll hit the sack."

SOCADO, DA, 1. *L.Am./C, adj.* Drunk. *José estaba bien socado en la fiesta de Julio.* "Jose was very drunk at Julio's party." **2.** *L.Am./C, adj.* Tight. *Estos zapatos nuevos me quedan socados.* "These new shoes are tight on me."

SOCRATITO, TA, *Car., n.* Know-it-all. *No intentes contradecir a Rosario porque ya sabes que es una socratita.* "Don't try to contradict Rosario because you know she is a know-it-all."

SODA, *L.Am./C, n.* Modest restaurant. (Lit. Soda.) *Comimos anoche en una soda.* "Last night we ate at a little hole in the wall."

SOGÁN, *L.Am./S, n.* Fear. *Me dio un sogán terrible cuando vi la araña junto a mi cama.* "I got scared out of my pants when I saw the spider next to my bed."

SOLATA, *Spain, adj. or n.* Loner. *Dora es una solata y no tiene amigos.* "Dora is a loner who doesn't have friends."

SOLTAR EL PAQUETE, *Spain, idiom.* To give birth. *Creo que me llegó la hora de soltar el paquete.* "I believe it's time for me to let loose of this baby."

SOLTAR LA PEPA, *L.Am./N, idiom.* To let loose of one's money. *Mi hijo nunca quiere soltar la pepa. Es muy tacaño.* "My son never lets go of his money. He is a real cheapskate."

SOMBRA, *L.Am./S, idiom.* Prison. *Vas a terminar en la sombra si sigues robando.* "You're going to end up in the clink if you keep robbing."

SONRISA DE CHOCLO, *L.Am./S, idiom.* Fake smile. *No me fío de ese tipo, siempre anda con sonrisa de choclo.* "I don't trust that guy; he's always got a fake smile on his face."

SOPA DE SESOS, *Car., idiom.* Intellectual or deep conversation. *Las sopas de sesos que tengo contigo son muy interesantes.* "Those deep conversations that I have with you are very interesting."

SOPLADO, DA, *L.Am./C, adv.* Very fast. (Lit. Blown.) *Rodolfo vino soplado para casa cuando le dieron el mensaje.* "Rodolfo came barreling home when they gave him the message."

SOPLAPOLLAS, *Spain, n.* Stupid, silly, dumb person. *Ese soplapollas ni siquiera ha podido aprender a manejar.* "That stupid jerk couldn't even learn to drive."

SOPLAR, 1. *Spain, v.* To drink. (Lit. To blow.) *Tengo ganas de soplarme una cerveza bien fría.* "I feel like whistling down a good cold beer." **2.** *Spain, v.* To steal. *Ese estafador me sopló todos mis ahorros.* "That swindler ripped me off of all my savings." **3.** *L.Am./S, v.* To cheat by giving answers away during a test. *Pasé el examen porque Julián me sopló todas las respuestas.* "I passed the test because Julian told me all the answers." **4.** *L.Am., v.* To have sex, to get it on. *Una pareja estaba soplando en el parque.* "A couple was getting it on in the park."

SOPONCIO, *L.Am./S, n.* Attack of nerves. *Me va a dar un soponcio si compruebo que el engaño es verdad.* "I am going to have an attack if I find that his deception is true."

¡SOQUE!, *L.Am./C, interj.* Hurry up! *¡Soque! Nos están esperando.* "Step on it! They are waiting for us."

SOROCHE, *L.Am./S, n.* Mountain sickness. *Al primo de Juan le dio el soroche durante la excursión en las montañas.* "Juan's cousin got mountain sickness during the excursion."

SOROCO, CA, *L.Am./S, adj. or n.* Stupid, dumb. *Armando es un soroco. No aprende de la experiencia.* "Armando is a dunce. He doesn't learn from experience."

SUAVE, *L.Am./N, n. youth.* Fantastic, cool. (Lit. Soft.) *¡Vóytelas! Ese es el carro más suave que jamás he visto.* "Awesome! That's the coolest car I have ever seen."

¡SUAVE!, *L.Am./C, interj.* Wait! *¡Suave! Ahora voy, sólo necesito un momento.* "Hold on! I'm coming, just a sec."

SUBMARINO, *Car., n.* Undercover officer. (Lit. Submarine.) *Me asignaron como submarino para investigar el asesinato.* "They sent me as an undercover agent to investigate the murder case."

SUBTE, 1. *L.Am./S, n.* Subway. *Si te vas en el subte llegarás más rápido.* "If you take the subway, you'll get there faster." **2.** *L.Am./S, n.* Underground railroad, newspaper, etc. *Vamos a publicar un subte político.* "We are going to publish an underground political newspaper."

SUDACA, *Spain, adj. or n.* South American. *La cantidad de sudacas en esta universidad ha aumentado mucho.* "The number of American Southies at this university has increased a lot."

SUDAR LA GOTA GORDA, 1. *L.Am./S, idiom.* To work hard. *A José le toca sudar la gota gorda para mantener a su familia.* "Jose has to work his butt off to support his family." **2.** *Car., idiom.* To be very worried about something. *Estoy sudando la gota gorda por el examen de mañana.* "I'm sweating bullets about the test tomorrow."

SUDAR TINTA, *L.Am./S, idiom.* To put forth great effort. *Para ganar tienes que sudar tinta en los próximos entrenamientos.* "To win you have to sweat blood at the next training sessions."

SUPER, *L.Am./S, adv.* Adverb used to intensify any adjective. (Lit. Super.) *Estoy súper entusiasmada con el viaje a Italia.* "I am superexcited about the trip to Italy."

SURNAR, *Car., v.* To sleep. *Me pasé la mañana surnando, estaba cansadísima.* "I snored the whole morning; I was dead tired."

TABAS, *L.Am./S, n.* Shoes. *Oye, ya cambia de tabas, ésas ya están con hoyos.* "Hey, go change those shoes; they already have holes in them."

TABLA, *L.Am./S, adj. or n.* Flat-chested woman. (Lit. Plank.) *Los hombres no me miran porque soy una tabla.* "Men don't look at me because I am flat as a board."

TABO, *L.Am./C, n., crim.* Jail. *Los hermanos Gómez están en el tabo.* "The Gomez brothers are in the slammer."

TACHERO, *L.Am./S, n.* Taxi driver. *El tachero me llamó a decirme que olvidé mi billetera en su taxi.* "The cabby called to tell me that I left my wallet in his cab."

TACHO, *L.Am./S, n.* Taxi. *Viajar en tacho se volvió un lujo; es carísimo.* "To travel by cab has become a luxury; it is very expensive."

TACO See PÁRALE LOS TACOS A ALGUIEN, HACER O HACERSE TACO, ECHARSE UN TACO DE OJO

TAITA, *L.Am./S, n.* Father. *El taita de mi novia es profesor de filosofía.* "My girlfriend's pop is a philosophy professor."

TALEGO, *Spain, n., crim.* Jail. (Lit. Sac.) *Lo metieron en el talego por asesinar a un hombre.* "They put him in the can for murdering a man."

TALLA, *L.Am./S, n.* Amusing remark, wisecrack. *Armando* *dijo una talla hiriente a Graciela.* "Armando made a nasty wisecrack to Graciela."

TANDA, 1. *L.Am./C, n.* Schedule. *El teatro tiene una tanda de cuatro funciones.* "The theater has a four-show program." **2.** *L.Am., n.* Drinking bout, binge. *Los amigos y yo estuvimos en una tanda de cuatro horas.* "My friends and I were on a four-hour binge." **3.** *L.Am./S, n.* Beating. *José me dio una tanda por manosear a su hermana.* "Jose gave me a hiding after I touched his sister."

TARAMBANA, *L.Am./S, n.* Clumsy, slow person. *La nueva secretaria es una tarambana, ¿quién la recomendó?* "The new secretary is a dud. Who recommended her?"

TARRO, 1. *L.Am./N, n.* Luck. *Qué tarro el de Ignacio, conquistó a la más bonita.* "Ignacio is so lucky, he caught the prettiest one." **2.** *Spain, n.* Head. *Tanto calor me hace doler el tarro.* "So much heat gives me a headache."

TARTALA, *L.Am./S, adj. or n.* Jalopy. *¡Cómprate un carro nuevo! Yo no me monto más en esa tartala.* "Buy yourself a new car! I am not getting into that bag of nuts anymore."

TARTAMUDA, *Spain, n.* Machine gun. (Lit. Stutterer.) *Todos los escoltas llevaban tartamudas en las manos.* "All the escorts were carrying burp guns in their hands."

TATA, *L.Am., n.* Parent, father or mother. *Los tatas de Juanito son maestros.* "Juanito's parents are teachers."

¿TATO?, *Car., idiom.* Is everything OK? (From "¿Está todo bien?") *Sé que tu esposa tuvo bebé. ¿Tato?* "I know your wife had a baby. Is everything OK?"

TAZA, *L.Am./S, n.* Toilet bowl. (Lit. Cup.) *Mi niño echó mi anillo a la taza del baño.* "My boy threw my ring into the toilet bowl."

¡TE CONOZCO BACALAO AUNQUE VENGAS DISFRAZAO!, *Car., idiom.* I know you, I'm on to you. *A mí no me puedes engañar. Te conozco bacalao aunque vengas disfrazao!* "You can't fool me; I am on to you!"

¡TE CONOZCO MOSCA!, *L.Am./S, idiom.* Expression of

mistrust. *No lo niegues. ¡Yo te conozco mosca!* "Don't deny it. I know you too well!"

TECA, *L.Am./S, n.* Money. *¿Cuánta teca te queda después de la parranda?* "How much money do you have left after painting the town?"

TECLA, *L.Am./S, n.* Old woman. *Pobre teclita, está sola en este mundo.* "Poor old lady, she is alone in this world."

TEJA, 1. *L.Am./C, n.* One-hundred-colon note. (Lit. Roof tile.) *Tuve que prestarle una teja a Abelardo.* "I had to lend Abelardo a hundred spot." **2.** *Car., n.* Hair. *Péinate la teja porque así luces muy mal.* "Comb your hair because right now you look terrible."

TEJADO, *Spain, n.* Head. (Lit. Roof.) *Mi abuelita anda mal del tejado.* "My grandmother is not too well upstairs."

TELE, *L.Am./S, n.* Television. *Pusieron el discurso del presidente en la tele.* "They showed the President's speech on TV."

TEMPLADO, 1. *L.Am./S, adj.* In love. *El flaquito esta muy templado con Rosa.* "The skinny guy is very much in love with Rose." **2. TEMPLADO, DA,** *L.Am./N, adj.* Strict. *La mamá de Adriana es muy templada y no le abre si llega después de las doce.* "Adriana's mom is very strict and doesn't let her in if she comes home after midnight."

TENAZ, *L.Am./S, adj.* Large, big, enormous. (Lit. Tenacious.) *Tengo un hambre tenaz.* "I am so hungry I could eat a horse."

TENER BARRIGA, *Spain, idiom.* To be pregnant. *Patricia tiene barriga y está feliz.* "Patricia is getting a belly and she is happy."

TENER BUEN LOMO, *L.Am./N, idiom.* To be good-looking. *La nueva secretaria tiene buen lomo.* "The new secretary is good-looking."

TENER CARA, 1. *L.Am./S, idiom.* To be cheeky enough to do something. *¿Después de lo que hizo todavía tiene cara de llamarme?* "After what you did, you have the gall to call me?" **2.** *L.Am./S, idiom.* To seem, to appear. *La co-*

mida tiene cara de estar deliciosa. "The food looks delicious."

TENER CARA DE ALPARGATA VIEJA, *Spain, idiom.* To have an old wrinkled face. *Tiene cara de alpargata vieja.* "He has the face of an old shoe."

TENER COJONES, *Spain, idiom.* To be brave, to have balls. *Álvaro tiene cojones. Cazó un tigre en África.* "Alvaro has got balls. He hunted a tiger in Africa."

TENER CORAZÓN DE ALAMBRE DE PÚAS, *Car., idiom.* To be hard-hearted. *Nada te conmueve, tienes corazón de alambre de púas.* "Nothing moves you. You have a barbed-wire heart."

TENER CULO, *Spain, idiom.* To be afraid. *Mi hermana tiene culo y no quiere ir al dentista.* "My sister is afraid and doesn't want to go to the dentist."

TENER EL CORAZÓN EN LA BOCA, 1. *L.Am./S, idiom.* To be afraid or worried. *A mi hijo lo mandaron a la guerra y me quedé con el corazón en la boca.* "They sent my son off to war and I stayed behind with my heart in my throat." **2.** *Car., idiom.* To be out of breath. *He caminado horas tratando de encontrarte y ahora tengo el corazón en la boca.* "I walked for hours trying to find you and now I'm out of breath."

TENER FRITO A ALGUIEN, *L.Am./S, idiom.* To try one's patience. *Mi suegra me tiene frito con tanta preguntadera.* "My mother-in-law has me at the end of my rope with so many questions."

TENER GOMA, *L.Am./S, idiom.* To be crazy about, to be excited. *Ignacio tiene mucha goma con el fútbol, va a todos los partidos.* "Ignacio is a real soccer fan; he goes to all the games."

TENER GUAYABITOS EN LA AZOTEA, *Car., idiom.* To be crazy. *Pepe tiene guayabitos en la azotea, no se le puede hacer mucho caso.* "Pepe has bats in his belfry."

TENER GÜECHO, *L.Am./C, idiom.* To be gullible, to be born yesterday. *Pepita tiene güecho, compra todo lo que* *le ofrecen.* "Pepita is a sucker; she buys anything they offer her."

TENER HÍGADOS, *Spain, idiom.* To be bold, cheeky, cynical. *¿Tienes hígados para hacer semejante comentario delante de mis padres?* "You've got the gall to make such a comment in front of my parents?"

TENER HUEVOS DE AVIÓN, *L.Am./S, idiom.* To want to do too much. *Armando tiene huevos de avión, quiere abarcar todo.* "Armando goes overboard; he takes on too much."

TENER LECHE, *Spain, idiom.* To be lucky. *Definitivamente tienes leche, siempre ganas.* "You sure are a lucky dog. You always win."

TENER MALA LECHE, *Spain, idiom.* To be mean. *Pobre María, su esposo siempre tiene mala leche.* "Poor Maria, her husband is always in a mean mood."

TENER MALA PATA, *L.Am., idiom.* To have bad luck. *Claudia tiene tan mala pata que ya le han robado el carro dos veces.* "Claudia has such bad luck that they have stolen her car twice."

TENER MANO IZQUIERDA, *Car., idiom.* To be diplomatic. *Pepe sabe como manejar situaciones difíciles porque siempre ha tenido mucha mano izquierda.* "Gustavo knows how to handle difficult situations because he's always been diplomatic."

TENER MENOS CARNE QUE EL PUCHERO DE UNA GITANA, *Spain, idiom.* To be very thin. *Ella tiene menos carne que el puchero de una gitana.* "She's got less meat on her than you'd find in a gypsy's stew."

TENER MUCHO COCO, *L.Am./S, idiom.* To be very intelligent. *David tiene mucho coco, aprende rapidísimo.* "David's got a good head; he learns fast."

TENER PATILLA, *Spain, idiom.* To be bold, cheeky, cynical. *Tienes patilla, me insultas y luego quieres que te bese.* "You've got a nerve; you insult me and then you want me to kiss you."

TENER RIÑONES, *Spain, idiom.* To be brave, to have guts. *El se enfrenta a cualquier cosa. Tiene riñones.* "He confronts anything. He's got guts."

TENER UN AQUEL, 1. *Car., idiom.* To have a lover. *Dicen que Helena tiene un aquel por ahí escondido.* "They're saying that Helena has a hidden lover." **2.** *L.Am., idiom.* To have that certain something. *Me encanta esa muchacha. Es que tiene un aquel.* "I love that girl. She has that certain something."

TENER UN CHINO ATRÁS, *Car., idiom.* To have bad luck. *Todo me sale mal últimamente, creo que tengo un chino atrás.* "Lately everything has turned out bad for me. I must have a jinx."

TENER UN PICO DE ORO, *Car., idiom.* To be a smooth talker. *Me encanta oír hablar a Jorge, tiene un pico de oro.* "I love to hear Jorge talk; he is such a smooth talker."

TENERLE ROÑA A ALGUIEN, *Car., idiom.* To dislike someone. *Nena le tiene tremenda roña a Marta.* "Nena can't stand Martha."

TEPERETE, *L.Am./N, n.* One who abstains from alcohol, teetotaler. *El padre de Alonso es un teperete.* "Alonzo's father is a teetotaler."

TEPOCATE, *L.Am./N, n.* Kid. *Ese pobre tepocate no tiene ni padre ni madre.* "That poor kid doesn't have a father or mother."

TERRAZA See TEJADO

TETAZAS, *L.Am./S, pl. n.* Big breasts. *Nunca he visto tetazas como las de Dolores.* "I've never seen big boobs like Dolores's."

TETONA See TETUDA

TETUDA, *L.Am./S, adj.* Big-breasted woman. *Todas las mujeres de esa familia son tetudas.* "All the women in that family have big jugs."

TICO, CA, *L.Am./C, n.* Costa Rican. *Nosotros los ticos vivimos bien.* "We Ticos live well."

TIESO, SA, *L.Am./S, adj.* Dead. (Lit. Stiff.) *Cuando me levanté mi gatito estaba tieso.* "When I got up, my cat was stiff."

TIGRA, *L.Am./C, adj.* Boring. *El discurso del director fue bien tigra.* "The director's speech was a real drag."

TIGRE, *Car., n.* Womanizer. (Lit. Tiger.) *Fercho es un tigre y no le queda mujer sin conquistar.* "Fercho is a womanizer and there is no woman he hasn't seduced."

TIGRESA, *L.Am./S, n.* Predatory woman. (Lit. Tigress.) *Ten cuidado con Julieta porque tiene fama de tigresa.* "Be careful with Julieta because she's known as a vamp."

TIMBA, *L.Am./S, n.* Gambling den. *En esa timba si pierdes estás bien, pero si ganas, no sales.* "In that rathole, if you lose you are OK, but if you win you won't come out."

TIMBEAR, *L.Am./S, v.* To gamble. *El próximo fin de semana vamos todos a timbear al casino.* "Next weekend, let's go play at the casino."

TIMBIRICHE, *Car., n.* Humble home or business. *Mi timbiriche es chiquito, pero los clientes encuentran lo que necesitan.* "My little hole in the wall is tiny, but customers find what they want."

TINTERILLO, *L.Am./N, n.* Shyster. *A ese tinterillo sólo le interesa el dinero.* "That shyster only cares about money."

TINTO, 1. *L.Am./S, Spain, n.* Red wine. *Écheme un tinto con sifón, por favor.* "Pour me a red wine and seltzer, please." **2.** *L.Am./S, n.* Coffee. (Lit. Dyed, tinted.) *Tomo mi tinto todas las mañanas con un poco de pan.* "I have my black coffee every morning with a little bread." **3. TINTO, TA,** *U.S., adj. or n.* Black person. *Vino a verte tu amigo tinto.* "Your black friend came to see you."

TÍO, A, *Spain, n.* Guy, gal. (Lit. Uncle, aunt.) *Ese tío que viene ahí fue conmigo a la universidad.* "That guy approaching us went to the university with me."

TIRA, *L.Am./S, n.* Detective. *Los tiras están buscándonos, mejor será que nos hagamos humo.* "The plainclothes are looking for us; it would be best if we take off." **See also RATI**

TIRADA, *Car., n.* Swindle, deception. *Ese negocio tuyo me huele a tirada.* "That business of yours smells like a swindle."

TIRADO, DA, *L.Am./S, adj.* Easy. (Lit. Thrown.) *El examen de inglés estuvo tirado.* "The English test was a cinch."

TIRANTE, *U.S., adj.* Dead, stiff. (Lit. Stretched.) *Cuando lo encontraron estaba ya tirante.* "When they found him, he was already stiff."

TIRAR (CON ALGUIEN), *L.Am./S, v.* To have sexual intercourse. *Dicen que Ignacio está tirando con Rosa.* "They say Ignacio is humping Rosa."

TIRAR LA MANGA, *L.Am./S, idiom.* To beg, to mooch. *En cada esquina hay alguien tirando la manga.* "There is someone pulling your sleeve on every corner."

TIRAR LA TOALLA, *L.Am./S, idiom.* To give up, to quit. *No tires la toalla, todavía puedes lograrlo.* "Don't throw in the towel yet; you can still make it."

TIRAR LOS TRASTOS, *Spain, idiom.* To argue. *Mi papá y mi mamá se están tirando los trastos otra vez.* "My mom and dad are throwing things at each other."

TIRAR PANA, *L.Am./S, idiom.* To brag. *A Antonio le gusta tirar pana cada vez que su equipo gana.* "Antonio likes to brag every time his team wins."

TIRARSE (A ALGUIEN), *L.Am./S, idiom.* To have sex with someone, to get in someone's pants. *Quería tirarme a Sara pero me rechazó.* "I wanted to get into Sara's pants but she wouldn't let me."

TIRARSE LA PERA, *L.Am./S, idiom.* To play hooky. *Nos tiramos la pera y gozamos como chanchos.* "We skipped school and had lots of fun."

TIRARSE LAS HUEVAS, *L.Am./S, idiom.* To do nothing. *Se fue el jefe y todos nos tiramos las huevas.* "The boss left and nobody did anything anymore."

TIRARSE PLACAS, *Car., idiom.* To get x-rayed. *Debes tirarte unas placas para averiguar el motivo de esos dolores.* "You should get some X rays to find out the reason for these pains."

TIRÁRSELAS, *L.Am., prnl. v.* To put on airs. *Yolanda se las tira de tener antepasados famosos.* "Yolanda puts on airs for having famous ancestors."

TIRO, *L.Am., n.* Moment, second. (Lit. Shot.) *¡Espera! Estaré contigo al tiro.* "Hold on! I'll be with you in a sec."

TISA, *L.Am./S, adj.* Elegant. *Ese terno de color azul marino te queda tisa.* "That navy blue suit looks so good on you."

TIZNAR AL CARBONERO, *L.Am./N, idiom, crim.* To con a confidence man. *La verdad es que no se puede tiznar al carbonero.* "The truth is that you can't swindle a swindler."

TIZNARSE, *L.Am./N, prnl. v.* To get drunk. (Lit. To get stained with soot.) *Anoche nos tiznamos en la cantina de Sóstenes.* "Last night we got blasted at Sostenes's bar."

TLACO, *L.Am./N, n.* Coin, cash. *No tengo el tlaco para pagar la multa.* "I don't have the moola to pay the fine."

TLAPIOYA, *L.Am./N, n. crim.* Jail. *Metieron a mi hermano en la tlapioya.* "They put my brother in the clink."

TOCAR EL PIANO, *Spain, idiom.* To wash dishes. *En mi casa ella cocina y yo toco el piano.* "At my house she cooks and I do the dishes."

TOCAR LA CAMPANA, *Spain, idiom.* To masturbate. *El muchacho fue sorprendido tocando la campana.* "The boy was caught playing with himself."

TOCAR MADERA, *L.Am./S, idiom.* Knock on wood. *Hasta ahora el negocio ha funcionado bien, toco madera.* "Up till now the business has worked well, knock on wood."

TOCARLE A UNO LA SIN PEPA, *L.Am./N, idiom.* To be

lucky. *A mi me tocó la sin pepa cuando me dieron este trabajo.* "I had a stroke of luck when they gave me this job."

TOCHE, *L.Am./S, adj.* Stupid, silly. *Pepe anda toche. Le presté un CD y me devolvió un libro.* "Pepe got silly. I lent him a CD and he returned a book."

TOCO, *L.Am./S, adv.* Very much, a lot. *La comida italiana le gusta un toco a mi madre.* "My mother likes Italian food a whole bunch."

TOCÓN, *L.Am./S, n.* Feeler, groper. *No me gusta bailar con él porque es un tocón.* "I don't like to dance with him because he has fast fingers."

TOLETE, *Car., n.* Dominican peso. *Dile a tu hermano que me pague mis veinte toletes.* "Tell your brother to pay me my twenty bucks."

TOMAR CALDO DE MICO, *L.Am./S, idiom.* Strange, weird. *El hablador de Jorge debió haber tomado caldo de mico porque no ha dicho nada hoy.* "Jorge, the talker, must have swallowed something because he hasn't said a thing today."

TOMAR POR CULO, 1. *Spain, idiom.* To have anal sex. *Ese marica toma por culo.* "That fag takes it in the ass." **2.** *Spain, idiom.* Expression of rejection. *Cuando el tipo no me quiso pagar lo mandé a tomar por culo.* "When the guy didn't want to pay me, I told him to stick it up his ass."

¡TÓMATELAS!, *L.Am./S, interj.* Get out of here! *¡Tómatelas! No quiero verte más por aquí.* "Get out of here! I don't want to see you around here anymore."

TOMBO, 1. *L.Am./S, n.* Police. *La plaza estaba llena de tombos cuando explotó la bomba.* "The plaza was full of coppers when the bomb blew up." **2.** *L.Am./C, n.* Traffic cop. *Un tombo le puso un parte a Gustavo por mucha velocidad.* "A traffic cop gave Gustavo a ticket for speeding."

TONEL, *L.Am./S, n.* Obese person. (Lit. Barrel.) *En las va-*

caciones me puse como un tonel. "On vacation I swelled like a barrel."

TONO, *L.Am./S, n.* Party. (Lit. Tone.) *¡El tono salió excelente!* "The party was excellent!"

TOPO, *L.Am./S, n.* Spy who infiltrates an organization, mole. (Lit. Mole.) *Creemos que Diego es un topo de la CIA.* "We believe that Diego is a CIA mole."

TOPOCHO, CHA, *L.Am./S, adj. or n.* Fat person. *¿Cuánto está comiendo Pedro? No era topocho en el colegio.* "How much is Pedro eating? He wasn't a fat guy in school."

TOQUETEAR, *L.Am., Spain, v.* To feel up, to grope. *Deja de toquetearme enfrente de todos.* "Stop feeling me up in front of everybody."

TOREAR, *L.Am./S, v.* To provoke, to anger. (Lit. To bullfight.) *Eugenio siempre está toreando al padre, hasta que éste se harta.* "Eugenio is always getting his father's goat, until he gets fed up."

TORRE, *L.Am./S, n.* Head. (Lit. Tower.) *Ese muchacho no tiene nada en la torre.* "That fella doesn't have anything upstairs."

TORTILLERA, *L.Am., Spain, adj. or n.* Lesbian. *En esta academia hoy muchas tortilleras.* "There are a lot of dykes in that academy."

TOSTADO, DA, *Car., adj.* Disturbed, upset, crazed. (Lit. Toasted.) *Actúa rarísimo; está definitivamente tostado.* "He acts strange; he's definitely got toast for brains."

TOSTAO See TOSTADO

¡TO'TÁ!, *Car., interj.* Everything is fine! *¡To'tá! Gracias por preguntar.* "It's all good! Thanks for asking."

TOTACHA, *U.S., n.* Chicano slang. *Cuando hablamos totacha no nos entienden los blanquitos.* "When we speak Chicano, the honkeys don't understand us."

TOTACHAR, *U.S., v.* To speak in Chicano slang. *Los batos estaban totachando y los anglos no agarraban nada.*

"The dudes were speaking Chicano and the Anglos weren't catching anything."

TRABADO, DA, *L.Am./S, adj., drugs.* Drugged. (Lit. Jammed.) *Parece que Julio está trabado. Habla muy lento y no se le entiende mucho.* "Looks like Julio is stoned. He talks very slow and doesn't make much sense."

TRÁCALA, *U.S., n.* Debt. *No puedo hacer nada con toda la trácala que tengo.* "I can't do anything with all the debt I have."

TRACALADA, *L.Am./S, adj.* Much, many, a lot of, lotsa, scads. *Había una tracalada de gente en el concierto.* "There were lotsa people at the concert."

TRACALERO, *U.S., n.* Debtor, person who is always in debt. *Mi cuñado es muy tracalero, le debe a todo el mundo.* "My brother-in-law is a royal debtor. He owes everybody."

TRAER GENTE EN LA AZOTEA, *L.Am./C, idiom.* To be crazy. *Daniel trae gente en la azotea, se pasó toda la tarde hablando solo.* "Daniel is loony upstairs; he spent the whole afternoon talking to himself."

TRAFERO, *L.Am./S, n.* Con artist. *El hijo resultó más trafero que el padre.* "He turned out a better con artist than his father."

TRÁFICO, *Car., n.* Traffic cop. (Lit. Traffic.) *El tráfico me paró por haberme pasado el semáforo en rojo.* "The traffic cop stopped me because I went through a red light."

TRAGADO, DA, *L.Am./S, adj.* To be in love. (Lit. Swallowed.) *Llevo un año tragado de ti y ahora te lo confieso.* "I have been nuts about you for a year and now I confess it to you."

TRAGO, *L.Am., Spain, n.* Alcoholic drink. (Lit. Drink.) *Invité a los muchachos a tomarse unos tragos.* "I invited the fellas to have a few drinks."

TRAGÓN, NA, *L.Am./C, adj. or n.* Bookworm. (Lit. Swallower.) *El hermano de Lupita es un tragón, siempre está* *en la biblioteca.* "Lupita's brother is a nerd; he's always in the library."

TRAÍDO, *L.Am./C, n.* Partner, lover, mistress. (Lit. Brought.) *El señor González tiene un traído muy joven.* "Mr. Gonzalez has a very young boyfriend."

TRAILA, *U.S., n.* Trailer. *Los narcos encontraron la hierba en una traila.* "The narcs found the grass in a trailer."

TRAJE DE LUCES, *L.Am./S, n.* Elegant dress or suit. *José se puso el traje de luces para la entrevista.* "Jose put on his Sunday best for the interview."

TRAMO, *L.Am./C, n.* Improvised sales stand. (Lit. Section, span.) *El viejito montó un tramo en la esquina y vende toda clase de chucherías.* "The old man set up a stand on the corner and is selling all types of trinkets."

TRAMOYA, *L.Am./S, n.* Swindle, ripoff. *Esos nuevos productos para rejuvenecer son una tramoya.* "These new rejuvenation products are a ripoff."

TRANCA, 1. *L.Am./S, n.* Binge. (Lit. Cudgel, club.) *La tranca de anoche fue la peor de mi vida.* "Last night's binge was the worst of my life." **2.** *L.Am./S, adj.* Difficult. *El examen de entrada a la universidad fue tranquísimo.* "The admission test for the university was really tough."

TRANQUI, *L.Am./S, adj.* Calm. *Tranqui mami, que no me pasará nada.* "Chill out Mom, nothing will happen to me."

TRANSAR, 1. *L.Am./S, v.* To have sex. *Hugo y Dora seguro que van a transar después de salir del bar.* "Hugo and Dora are sure to go to bed after they leave the bar." **2.** *L.Am./S, v.* To give in. *Quería un carro más costoso, pero tuve que transarme por éste.* "I wanted a more expensive car, but had to give in and get this one."

TRAPICHEO, *L.Am./N, v.* To have an affair. *Elías tenía un trapicheo con la mujer del alcalde.* "Elias had an affair with the mayor's wife."

TRASNOCHAR, *L.Am., v.* To stay up all night. *Hoy me voy* *a trasnochar estudiando geometría.* "I'll spend all night studying geometry."

TRASTIENDA, *Spain, n.* Behind, butt, ass. (Lit. Back room.) *Tiene la trastienda tan grande que no cabe en la silla.* "She's got such a big behind it doesn't fit in the chair."

TREMENDA MAMI, *Car., idiom.* Pretty woman. *La esposa de mi abogado es una tremenda mami.* "My lawyer's wife is a great-looking babe."

TRINCAR, 1. *Spain, v., crim.* To kill. *Me soñé que un asesino me quería trincar.* "I dreamed that a killer wanted to do me in." **2.** *Spain, v., crim.* To nab, to arrest. *La poli te va a trincar si no dejas de robar.* "The cops are going to nab you if you don't stop robbing."

TRIPA, *L.Am./S, idiom.* Very good, excellent. (Lit. Gut.) *Estos dibujos están tripas.* "These drawings are really cool!"

TRIPEAR, *L.Am./S, v.* To have fun. *Vamos a tripear a Caracas.* "Let's go chillin' to Caracas."

TRIPEO, *L.Am./S, n.* Fun. *Eso es un tripeo.* "That's a mad-wicked time."

TRIPERO, RA, *Spain, adj.* Gluttonous. *Estás así de gordo por ser tan tripero.* "You're so fat because you are so piggy."

TRISITO, *L.Am./S, adv.* A little bit. *¿Me puedes dar un trisito de tu helado?* "Can you give me a little bit of your ice cream?"

TROCA, *U.S., n.* Truck. (From English "truck.") *Nos trajeron aquí en una troca.* "They brought us here in a truck."

TROLA, *L.Am./S, adj. or n.* Lesbian. *Rosa casi se muere cuando le contaron que su hija es una trola.* "Rosa almost died when they told her that her daughter is a dyke."

TROLE, *U.S., adj.* Crazy. *Ese chavo es bien trole.* "That kid is real crazy."

TROLO, *L.Am./S, adj. or n.* Effeminate. *El peluquero de la esquina es un trolo.* "The hairstylist on the corner is a fairy."

TROMPA, *U.S., n.* Mouth. (Lit. Snout, trunk.) *José, ciérrate la trompa.* "Jose, shut your trap."

TROMPEAR, *L.Am., v.* To beat someone in the face. *José se puso celoso y trompeó al que me miraba tanto.* "Jose got jealous and smacked the guy looking at me."

TROMPETA, *Spain, adj.* Drunk. (Lit. Trumpet.) *Nancy está trompeta otra vez.* "Nancy is buzzed again."

TRONADO, DA, *L.Am./S, adj.* Crazy. (Lit. Thundered.) *No le pongas atención, está tronado.* "Don't pay attention to him; he is nuts."

TRONCHARSE, *L.Am./S, prnl. v.* To crack up laughing. *El chiste que me contaste me hizo tronchar.* "That joke you told me cracked me up."

TRONCHO, *L.Am./S, n., drugs.* Cigarette rolled with marijuana or other drug. *Estoy angustiado cuñao, pásame un tronchito.* "I am depressed buddy; pass me a joint."

TROZO DE PAN, *Spain, idiom.* Very nice, friendly. *Afortunadamente mi suegra es un trozo de pan.* "Fortunately, my mother-in-law is a sweetie."

TRUCHO, CHA, 1. *L.Am./S, n.* Liar. *Cuidado con ese muchacho, es un trucho, no se puede fiar de lo que dice.* "Be careful with that fellow; he's a liar—you can't trust what he says." **2.** *L.Am./S, adj.* False, fake. *Esa esmeralda que me regaló Paco resultó ser trucha.* "That emerald Paco gave me turned out to be a fake."

TUBO, 1. *Spain, n.* Telephone. (Lit. Tube.) *¡Necesito el tubo, cuelga ya!* "I need the horn; hang up already!" **2.** *L.Am./S, n., crim.* Jail. *Roberto está en el tubo por pegarle a la mujer.* "Robert is in the clink for beating his wife." **3.** *Spain, adj.* Bad, dull, boring. *El libro que me recomendaste es un tubo.* "The book you recommended sucks."

TUCÁN, *L.Am./C, n.* Five-thousand-colon note. *Conque no* *tenías dinero, entonces, ¿qué haces con este tucán?* "So you don't have any money? Then what are you doing with this five grand?"

TUCO, *Car., n.* Money. *Se me acabó el tuco por tanto apostar.* "I'm out of money from betting so much."

TUFO, *L.Am., n.* Bad odor. *Tienes un tufo a cerveza insoportable.* "You stink of beer."

TUMBABURROS See MATABURROS

TUMBAR, 1. *L.Am./N, v., crim.* To kill. (Lit. To knock down.) *Tumbaron al policía cuando intentó detenerlos.* "They bumped off the cop when he tried to detain them." **2.** *L.Am./N, v.* To fail a test. *Voy a tumbar el examen porque no estudié.* "I am going to flunk the test because I didn't study." **3.** *Car., v., crim.* To dismiss criminal charges. *Tumbaron los cargos contra mi hijo.* "They threw out the charges against my son." **4.** *L.Am./S, v.* To trick, to defraud. *Nos querían tumbar a todos con esas joyas falsas.* "They wanted to rip us off with all those false jewels."

TUNDA, *L.Am./S, n.* Beating. *El papá de tu novia descubrió que dejaste embarazada a su hija. ¡Prepárate para la tunda!* "Your girlfriend's father discovered that you got his daughter pregnant. Get ready for a beating!"

TURNO, *L.Am./C, n.* Fiesta, fair. (Lit. Turn.) *Anoche fuimos al turno de Heredia.* "Last night we went to the Heredia fair."

U, *L.Am., n.* University. *El año que viene voy a la U.* "Next year I'm going to college."

¡UN CUERNO!, *Spain, interj.* Expression of rejection, refusal, disagreement. *¡Un cuerno! No lo voy a hacer así.* "Shit! I am not going to do it like that."

¡ÚJULE!, *L.Am./N, interj.* Holy cow! *¡Újule! ¿Cómo hiciste ese truco?* "Holy cow! How did you do that trick?"

UN TIRITO, *L.Am./S, n.* A little bit. *Me faltó un tirito para estrellarme con ese árbol.* "I just missed crashing into that tree."

UNA FRÍA, *Car., n.* A cold beer. *Voy a tomarme una fría para refrescarme.* "I am going to have a cold one to refresh myself."

UNA PÁLIDA, *L.Am./S, adj.* Boring or tedious. *Ese documental es una pálida.* "That documentary is dullsville."

UNA TORTA, 1. *L.Am./S, n.* Blow, collision. *El avión se dio una torta contra el mar y nadie se salvó.* "The aircraft smacked into the sea and everyone died." **2.** *L.Am./C, n.* Slap, smack. *Mamá entró y me pegó una torta en la cabeza.* "Mom came in and gave me a smack on the head."

UÓN, *L.Am./S, n.* Greeting used among male friends. (From Spanish "huevón.") *¿Qué pasa, uón?* "What's up, bro?"

¡UPE!, *L.Am./C, interj.* Expression used when knocking at door. *"¡Upe!" "¿Quién llama?" "El cobrador."* " 'Knock, knock!' 'Who's there?' 'The collector.' "

UVA, *Spain, adj. or n.* Bad-tempered, mean-spirited person. (Lit. Grape.) *No seas tan uva, cálmate.* "Don't be such a meanie; calm down."

VACA, 1. *L.Am./S, n.* Pooling of resources, money. (Lit. Cow.) *Hicimos una vaca para comprarle un boleto a Luisa.* "We made a kitty to buy a ticket for Luisa." **2.** *L.Am., n.* Fat person. *No comas tanto que te vas a volver una vaca.* "Don't eat so much or you will turn into a cow." **3.** *L.Am./S, n.* Bad person. *Ese vaca mató a tres gatitos. Algún día matará a una persona.* "That bum killed three kittens. Someday he will kill a person."

VACILAR, *L.Am./S, v.* To joke, to ridicule. (Lit. To hesitate.) *No empieces a vacilar porque Pilar se molesta.* "Don't start kidding around because Pilar gets upset."

VAINA, 1. *L.Am./S, idiom.* Problem. *¡Qué vaina! Se me rompió el vibrador.* "What a bitch! I broke the vibrator." **2.** *L.Am./S, n.* Thing. *Carga tantas vainas en el bolsillo que no le cabe ni una moneda más.* "He puts so much stuff in his pocket that there is no room for one more coin."

¡VALE!, *L.Am., Spain, interj.* OK, alright! *¿Vamos al centro? ¡Vale, vámonos!* "Shall we go downtown? OK, let's go!"

VALER HUEVO, *L.Am./S., idiom.* To not care. *Me vale huevo lo que opine tu papá de mí.* "I don't give a shit what your father thinks of me."

VALER UN PIMIENTO, *Spain, idiom.* To be worthless.

La opinión de ese hombre vale un pimiento. "That man's opinion isn't worth a nickel."

VARAS, *L.Am./C, pl. n.* Excuses, pretexts. (Lit. Sticks.) *Javier siempre viene con varas para no trabajar.* "Javier always comes up with excuses for not working."

VARO, *L.Am./N, n.* One peso. *Este CD me costó ciento cincuenta varos.* "This CD cost me 150 pesos."

¿VAS A SEGUIR?, *L.Am./S, idiom.* Expression used when someone keeps harping on the same thing. *¿Vas a seguir Roberto?* "Are you going to keep it up, Roberto?"

VATO, *L.Am./N, n.* Person, man. *Ese vato me quedó a deber una lana.* "That dude owes me some bread."

VEJIGO, *L.Am., n.* Kid. *Javier se casó hace seis años y ya tiene tres vejigos.* "Javier got married six years ago and now he has three brats."

VELÁRSELA, *L.Am./S, prnl. v.* To pester. *Se la veló con eso de que tiene que adelgazar.* "He played her the broken record about having to lose weight."

VENDERLE EL CAJETÍN, *Car., idiom.* To leave, to take off. *Jaime ve que no está enamorado de la novia y quiere venderle el cajetín.* "Jaime sees that he is not in love with his girlfriend and he wants to split as soon as possible."

VENIR UNA COSA AL PELO, *L.Am./N, idiom.* To be just right. *Este regalo me viene al pelo.* "This present is just what the doctor ordered."

VER LA PATA A LA PERICA, *Car., idiom.* To know one's intentions. *No me engañes que ya le vi la pata a la perica.* "Don't fool me; I wasn't born yesterday."

VERDE, 1. *L.Am./S, adj.* Vulgar, nasty. (Lit. Green.) *Detesto los chistes verdes.* "I hate dirty jokes." **2.** *L.Am./C, adj.* Very studious. *Jaime no quiere salir, es muy verde y quiere estudiar.* "Jaime doesn't want to go out; he's a real nerd and wants to study." **See also VIEJO VERDE**

VERDURA, *L.Am./S, n.* Truth. (Lit. Vegetable.) *Es la verdura, mamá.* "It's the truth, Mom."

VERGA, *L.Am./S interj.* Expression of surprise or disappointment. Damn! (Lit. Penis.) *¡A la verga, no me dieron la beca!* "Damn, they didn't give me the scholarship!"

VERLA FEA, *L.Am./C, idiom.* To be going through difficulties. *La familia Ruiz la está viendo fea desde que Julio perdió el trabajo.* "The Ruiz family has fallen on hard times since Julio lost his job."

VERRACO, CA, *L.Am./S, adj. or n., youth.* Wonderful, great person. *Qué hermano tan verraco tiene Graciela.* "What a cool brother Graciela has."

VERRAQUERA, *L.Am./S, adj., youth.* Very good, great. *El partido de fútbol fue una verraquera.* "That soccer game was a blast."

¡VETE A HACER PUÑETAS!, *Spain, interj.* Get the hell out of here! *¡Vete a hacer puñetas! No te quiero volver a ver.* "Get the hell out of here! I don't want to see you again."

¡VETE A LA MIERDA!, *L.Am., Spain, interj.* Go to hell! *¡Si no me quieres, vete a la mierda!* "If you don't like me, go to hell!"

¡VETE A LA PERICA!, *L.Am./N, interj.* Go to hell! *Pues si no quieres pagarme ¡vete a la perica!* "Well, if you don't want to pay me, go to hell!"

¡VETE AL CUERNO!, *Spain, interj.* Expression of rejection. *¡Vete al cuerno! No me insistas más.* "Buzz off! Don't insist anymore."

¡VETE AL SIPOTE!, *Car., interj.* Go to hell! *¡Vete al sipote! Estoy cansada de ti.* "Go to hell! I am tired of you."

¡VETE P'AL CARAJO!, *L.Am./S, interj.* Go to hell! *¡Te odio, vete p'al carajo!* "I hate you, go to hell!"

VIANDAS, *Car., pl. n.* Fruits and vegetables. (Lit. Food.) *No anda bien del estómago y el médico le recetó viandas.* "She's got a stomach problem and the doctor prescribed fruits and vegetables."

VIDRIOS, *L.Am., pl. n.* Glasses. *Se me rompieron los vidrios jugando fútbol.* "I broke my glasses playing football."

VIDÚ, *L.Am./S, n.* Life. *¿Dónde has estado perdido? ¿Qué es de la vidú?* "Where have you been? How's life?"

VIEJA, *L.Am./S., n.* Woman. (Lit. Old woman.) *Esa vieja sí que está buena.* "That broad is fine."

VIEJO, JA, *L.Am./S, n.* Father/Mother. (Lit. Old person.) *Le tengo que pedir permiso a mi vieja para poder ir a bailar contigo.* "I have to ask permission of my mom to go to the dance with you."

VIEJO VERDE, *L.Am./S, n.* Dirty old man. *El profe es un viejo verde, le gusta sobar a todas las muchachas.* "The teacher is a dirty old man who likes to paw the girls."

VINO, 1. *L.Am./C, n.* Gossip. (Lit. Wine.) *He oído un vino acerca de la Sra. López.* "I've heard a choice bit about Mrs. Lopez." **2. VINO, NA,** *L.Am./C, adj.* Gossipy. *La chica esa es muy vina.* "That girl is a real blabbermouth."

VINO CAÑERÍA, *Spain, idiom.* Glass of tap water. *Échame un vaso de ese vino cañería.* "Pour me a glass of that tap wine."

VÍSERAS, *U.S., n.* Sunglasses. (Lit. Visors.) *Era un cuate que llevaba víseras.* "It was a Mexican wearing shades."

VIVIR COMO UN CURA, *L.Am./S, idiom.* To live well. *Alejo se fue para la ciudad y vive como un cura.* "Alejo moved to the city and lives like a king."

VIVIR DEL CUENTO, *Spain, idiom.* To make a living without working. *Carolina está viviendo del cuento desde hace años.* "Carolina has been living on air for years."

VIVO, VA, 1. *L.Am., adj.* Alert, sharp. *Me sorprende lo vivo que es tu bebé.* "I am surprised to see how alert your baby is." **2.** *L.Am./S, n.* Tricky person. *Toño es un vivo que estafa a todos.* "Toño is a con artist who tricks everybody."

VOLADO, DA, 1. *L.Am./S, adj.* Scatterbrained, inconsiderate. *Andrés es tan volado que jamás llega a tiempo.* "Andres is so empty-headed he never arrives on time. **2.** *L.Am./S, adj., drugs.* High on drugs. *Cuando lo agarraron, el muchacho estaba volado.* "When they grabbed him, the fella was high as a kite."

VOLANDO CANALETE, *L.Am./C, idiom.* On foot. *Mi auto se estropeó y tuve que ir volando canalete para el trabajo.* "My car broke down and I had to hoof it to work."

VOLAR, *L.Am./S, v., drugs.* To be high on drugs. (Lit. To fly.) *Toño está volando, quién sabe qué fumó.* "Toño is high; who knows what he smoked."

VOLAR LA BATA, *L.Am./S, idiom.* Excess, overboard, out of sight. *Mi padre tiene una hipertensión que le vuela la bata.* "My father's blood pressure is out of sight."

VOLATÍN, *L.Am./S, adj.* Slightly drunk, tipsy. *Estoy de volatín, bien picadito.* "I am slightly drunk, just a bit tipsy."

VOLTEADO, *L.Am./S, adj.* Gay. *A su papá le dio mucha rabia cuando descubrió que era volteado.* "His father started foaming at the mouth when he found out his son was gay."

VOLTEARSE LA ROSCA, *L.Am./C, idiom.* To become a homosexual. *Al marido de mi prima se le volteó la rosca y la dejó.* "My cousin's husband went over to the other team and left her."

¡VÓYTELAS!, *L.Am./N, interj.* Holy cow! Goodness gracious! *¡Vóytelas! ¿Cómo pudiste comprar un regalo tan caro?* "My goodness! How could you buy such an expensive gift?"

WIRCHO, *L.Am./S, adj.* Rude, coarse. *¡Qué wircho es el novio de Paula!* "Paula's boyfriend is a jerk!"

¿Y DE AHÍ?, *L.Am./C, idiom.* And? And then, what? *"Así que le dije que me iba." "¿Y de ahí?" "Pues, me fui."* " 'So I told him I was going.' 'And then what?' 'Well, then I just left.' "

¡YA CHOLE!, *L.Am./N, interj.* Give me a break! *¡Ya chole! Tú sabes que no puedo ir contigo.* "Give me a break! You know I can't go with you."

YA ESTÁ EL CAFÉ COLADO, *L.Am., idiom.* The deal is done, it's in the bag. *Después de la reunión yo pensaba que el café ya estaba colado.* "When I left the meeting, I thought that the deal was in the bag."

¡YARA!, *L.Am./S, interj.* Be careful! *¡Yara! ¡Se viene la tormenta!* "Watch out! The storm is coming."

YEYO, *L.Am./S, n.* Mountain sickness. *Cuando íbamos llegando a la cima del monte me dio un yeyo.* "When we were reaching the top of the mountain I got a little woozy."

YOGURCITO, *Spain, adj. or n.* Sweet young thing. *Te amo, yogurcito.* "I love you, cream puff."

YOGURÍN, *Spain, adj. or n.* Handsome young man. *¡Me conquistaré a ese yogurín!* "I'll get that hunk!"

YUNTA, *L.Am./S, n.* Good friend. (Lit. Yoke.) *Carlos es yunta de Emilio.* "Carlos is Emilio's good friend."

YUTA, *L.Am./S, n.* Police. *No olvides llamar a la yuta si ves algo sospechoso.* "Don't forget to call the coppers if you see something suspicious."

ZAFACOCA, *L.Am./N, n.* Argument, fight. *Anoche tuve una zafacoca con mi hermano.* "Last night I had a scrap with my brother."

ZAFADO, DA, *L.Am./N, adj.* Crazy, nuts. *Tu hermano está zafado si cree que mi hermana va a salir con él.* "Your brother is nuts if he thinks that my sister will go out with him."

ZAGA, *L.Am./S, n., sports.* Team's defense. *La zaga del equipo es buenísima.* "The team guard is terrific."

ZAGUERO, *L.Am./S, n., sports.* Defensive player. *Lucho es el mejor zaguero que conozco.* "Lucho is the best defensive player I know."

ZAPALLO, *L.Am./S, n.* Head. (Lit. Pumpkin.) *A zapallo grande, seso pequeñito.* "A big head but a small brain."

ZAPATERO, *L.Am./S, n., sports.* (Lit. Shoemaker.) Scoreless player. *Roldán se quedó zapatero en tres sets de tenis.* "Roldán was scoreless after three sets of tennis."

ZAPIOLA See ZAPALLO

ZARAGATE, *L.Am./N, n.* Rascal, hooligan. *El hijo de mi hermano es un zaragate, cualquier día se va a meter en un lío.* "My brother's son is a rascal, and he'll get in trouble any day now."

ZOPILOTE, *U.S., n., crim.* Police officer. *Mi tío es zopilote del municipio.* "My uncle is a cop at city hall."

ZORRA, 1. *L.Am./S, n.* Horse-drawn cart. (Lit. Fox.) *Una zorra se me atravesó y me hizo estrellar.* "A horse-drawn cart crossed in front of me and made me crash." **2.** *L.Am./C, n.* Loose woman, whore. *Dicen que Raquel es una zorra, ¿tendría yo suerte con ella?* "They say that Raquel is easy. Would I stand a chance with her?" **3.** *L.Am./S, n.* Vagina, pussy, beaver. *Los hombres van a ese club para ver las zorras de las bailarinas.* "Men go to that club to see the dancers' beavers."

ZORRO, RRA, *L.Am./C, adj. or n.* (Lit. Fox.) Astute, sharp, or wise person. *Natasha es una zorra para las inversiones.* "Natasha is sharp as a fox about investments."

ZUMBADO, DA, 1. *Spain, adj.* Overwhelmed. *Tadeo está como zumbado desde que su mujer murió.* "Tadeo is very weary since his wife died." **2.** *L.Am./S, adj.* Deceiving. *No seas zumbada, ese truco no te va a funcionar.* "Don't be tricky; that game of yours is not going to work."

ZUMBAR, 1. *L.Am./S, v.* To annoy, to joke. (Lit. To buzz.) *No me zumbes más, que me voy a poner bravo.* "Don't bug me anymore or I'll get angry." **2.** *Spain, v., crim.* To rob. *Me zumbaron el reloj cuando iba en el bus.* "They clipped my watch when I was on the bus."